The Alternative Handbook

'Alternative media' are media produced by the socially, culturally and politically excluded: they are always independently run and often community-focused, ranging from pirate radio to activist publications, from digital video experiments to radical work on the Web. *The Alternative Media Handbook* explores the many and diverse media forms that these non-mainstream media take.

The Alternative Media Handbook gives brief histories of alternative radio, video and film, press and activity on the Web, then offers an overview of global alternative media work through numerous case studies, before moving on to provide practical information about alternative media production and how to get involved in it.

The Alternative Media Handbook includes both theoretical and practical approaches and information, including sections on:

- successful fundraising
- podcasting
- blogging
- publishing
- pitching a project
- radio production
- culture jamming
- access to broadcasting.

Kate Coyer is an independent radio producer, media activist and post-doctoral research fellow with the Annenberg School for Communication at the University of Pennsylvania and Central European University in Budapest.

Tony Dowmunt has been involved in alternative video and television production since 1975 and is now course tutor on the MA in Screen Documentary at Goldsmiths, University of London.

Alan Fountain is currently Chief Executive of European Audiovisual Entrepreneurs (EAVE), a professional development programme for film and television producers. He was the first Commissioning Editor for Independent Film and TV at Channel Four, 1981–94.

Media Practice

Edited by James Curran, Goldsmiths, University of London

The *Media Practice* handbooks are comprehensive resource books for students of media and journalism, and for anyone planning a career as a media professional. Each handbook combines a clear introduction to understanding how the media work with practical information about the structure, processes and skills involved in working in today's media industries, providing not only a guide on 'how to do it' but also a critical reflection on contemporary media practice.

The Newspapers Handbook 4th edition

Richard Keeble

The Radio Handbook 2nd edition

Carole Fleming

The Advertising Handbook 2nd edition

Sean Brierley

The Television Handbook 3rd edition

Jonathan Bignell and Jeremy Orlebar

The Photography Handbook 2nd edition

Terence Wright

The Magazines Handbook 2nd edition

Jenny McKay

The Public Relations Handbook 3rd edition

Alison Theaker

The Cyberspace Handbook

Jason Whittaker

The Fashion Handbook

Tim Jackson and David Shaw

The New Media Handbook

Andrew Dewdney and Peter Ride

The Alternative Media Handbook

Kate Coyer, Tony Dowmunt and Alan Fountain

The Alternative Media Handbook

Kate Coyer, Tony Dowmunt
and Alan Fountain

Routledge
Taylor & Francis Group

LONDON AND NEW YORK

First published 2007
by Routledge
2 Park Square, Milton Park, Abingdon, Oxon OX14 4RN

Simultaneously published in the USA and Canada
by Routledge
270 Madison Ave, New York, NY 10016

Routledge is an imprint of the Taylor & Francis Group, an informa business

Typeset in Times and Helvetica by
The Running Head Limited, Cambridge, www.therunninghead.com
Printed and bound in Great Britain by
MPG Books Ltd, Bodmin, Cornwall

British Library Cataloguing in Publication Data
A catalogue record for this book is available from the British Library

Library of Congress Cataloging in Publication Data
Coyer, Kate.
The alternative media handbook / Kate Coyer, Tony Dowmunt, and Alan Fountain.
p. cm. (Media practice)
1. Alternative mass media. I. Dowmunt, Tony. II. Fountain, Alan. III. Title.
P96.A44C69 2007
302.23—dc22
2007027081

ISBN 10: 0–415–35966–X (hbk)
ISBN 10: 0–415–35965–1 (pbk)

ISBN 13: 978–0–415–35966–5 (hbk)
ISBN 13: 978–0–415–35965–8 (pbk)

Contents

Illustrations

Contributors

Jen Angel is a media activist currently living in the San Francisco Bay Area. Her main project is Aid & Abet Booking, www.aidandabet.org.

Chris Atton is Reader in Journalism at the School of Creative Industries, Napier University, Edinburgh, Scotland. He is a leading UK and international scholar in the study of alternative and community media and has published three books in this area: *Alternative Literature* (Gower 1996), *Alternative Media* (Sage 2002) and *An Alternative Internet* (Edinburgh University Press 2004).

Joe Biel is an author, filmmaker, designer, and multidisciplinary artist currently living in Bloomington, Indiana. His films include the award-winning *A Hundred Dollars and a T-Shirt: A Documentary about Zines in the Northwest, Martinis in the Bike Lane, Tennessee State Prison, Of Dice and Men,* and *Last Train Out of North America*. He founded Microcosm Publishing in 1996.

Simon Blanchard is a Senior Research Fellow in the Department of Media Production at the University of Lincoln.

Su Braden is an independent development communications researcher, and author of *Video for Development: A Casebook from Vietnam* with Than Thi Thien Huong (Stylus Publishing 1998), *Committing Photography* (Pluto Press 1983), and *Artists and People* (Routledge 1978).

Michael Chanan is a filmmaker, writer and Professor of Cultural Studies at the University of the West of England. His latest film is *Detroit: Ruin of a City*. Details at www.mchanan.dial.pipex.com

Gregor Claude is a lecturer at Goldsmiths, University of London. His research interests include cultural industries, the digital media and media theory, and intellectual property.

Kate Coyer is a post-doctoral research fellow with the Annenberg School for Communication, University of Pennsylvania and Central European University,

Budapest, and recently completed her PhD in Media and Communications at Goldsmiths College. She is an independent radio producer and media activist whose past publications include a chapter in *Global Activism, Global Media* by de Jong et al. (2005).

James Curran is Professor of Communications at Goldsmiths, University of London. He is the author or editor of 18 books about the mass media, including *Media and Power* (Routledge 2002), *Power without Responsibility* with Jean Seaton (Routledge 2003, 6th edition) and *Culture Wars* with Ivor Gaber and Julian Petley (Edinburgh University Press 2005).

James Deane is Head of Policy Development for BBC World Service Trust. He was formerly managing director of the Communication for Social Change Consortium, and a founding member and Executive Director of the Panos Institute.

Tony Dowmunt has practised, taught and written about alternative video and television for the last 30 years, and is currently the course tutor on the MA in Screen Documentary at Goldsmiths, University of London. His publications include *Video with Young People* (InterAction 1980, reissued by Cassell 1987) and *Channels of Resistance: Global Television and Local Empowerment* (British Film Institute 1993), which accompanied the TV series of the same name.

Andrew Dubber is Senior Lecturer in the Music Industries at UCE Birmingham, and author of the New Music Strategies website. He is a broadcaster, blogger, podcaster and founder of the New Zealand Society of Low Power FM Broadcasters.

Mark Dunford is Executive Director of Hi8us Projects Limited, a charity specialising in community-based collaborative production work and the lead partner in Inclusion Through Media (ITM), an Equal-funded development partnership operating in the UK and Europe. He also works as a consultant through DS Media Consulting.

Jacqui Ewart teaches journalism at Griffith University in Brisbane.

Natalie Fenton is a Senior Lecturer in the Department of Media and Communications at Goldsmiths, University of London. She teaches, researches and has published widely on media, civil society and the public sphere.

Susan Forde teaches journalism at Griffith University in Brisbane.

Alan Fountain has been involved in various aspects of media since the 1970s. He is currently Chief Executive of European Audiovisual Entrepreneurs (EAVE), a professional development programme for European film and television producers, Chair of the Hi8us Projects Board and Professor Emeritus, Middlesex University. He was one of the founding commissioning editors at Channel 4 Television 1981–94.

Kerrie Foxwell is a doctoral candidate and Senior Researcher at Griffith University in Brisbane.

David Garcia is a visual artist, writer, organiser and co-founder of the Next 5 Minutes festival of Tactical Media, and Professor of Design for Digital Cultures, University of Portsmouth and Hogeschool voor de Kunsten Utrecht.

Julia Guest is a documentary producer and director. She has been working as a photographer and filmmaker for the past ten years across the Middle East and in the UK, and in Iraq since 1998.

Adnan Hadzi has a strong interest in new forms of distribution and collaborative working systems, which led him to doing a PhD on 'collective documentaries' at Goldsmiths. As part of his practical research Deptford.TV was launched, an audio-visual documentation of the regeneration process of the Deptford area, south-east London.

Katie Haegele lives outside Philadelphia, where she works as a freelance journalist, reviewer and essayist. She makes the zines 'The La-La Theory', 'Word Math' and 'Breakdancing for the Pope', a poetry collection.

Magz Hall produces You Are Hear (www.youarehear.co.uk, audio available on www.totallyradio.com) and is chair of the South London Radio Arts Group. She is a radio lecturer at Canterbury Christ Church University and is currently researching a practice-based PhD at LCC London University of the Arts, looking at the role of new radio technology and radio arts practice.

Dorothy Kidd worked for many years in Canada as an alternative media activist, and now teaches Media Studies and participates in the movement for the democratisation of global media.

Julia Knight is Reader in Moving Image at the University of Sunderland, and has been leading an AHRC-funded research project into independent film and video distribution in the UK for the past three years.

Mirella von Lindenfels is the Managing Director of Communications Inc Limited, a consultancy which specialises in working with international NGOs. She has spent her career in the NGO sector including as Head of Media for Greenpeace and Director of Communications for Amnesty International, International HQ.

Martin Lucas (www.martinlucas.net) is a videomaker and media educator in New York. He was an early member of Paper Tiger Television and a producer of The Gulf Crisis TV Project, and currently teaches in the Film and Media Studies Department at Hunter College, City University of New York.

Manu Luksch was Artistic Director of Media Lab Munich before she founded the London-based interdisciplinary arts production company ambientTV.net.

Michael Meadows is Associate Professor and teaches journalism at Griffith University in Brisbane.

Graham Meikle is the author of *Interpreting News* (Palgrave 2008), *Future Active: Media Activism and the Internet* (Routledge 2002). He is Senior Lecturer in the Media Department at Macquarie University in Sydney.

Owen Mundy is an artist who uses a variety of media to examine issues of class and culture for all potential audiences. He has a BFA in photography from Indiana University (2002) and will complete an MFA in Visual Arts from the University of California, San Diego, in 2008. He is currently a Visiting Assistant Professor in Art at Florida State University in Tallahassee, FL.

Molefi Nolovu is a co-founder of Radio Rasa in Soweto, South Africa and a part of the Indymedia collective. He is currently studying Community Development, Media and Comparative Literature at the University of Kwa-Zulu Natal and is involved in an academic research institute called the Center for Civil Society.

Lennaart van Oldenborgh is a documentary filmmaker and media tactician living and working in London.

Charlotte Hill O'Neal, born 1951 in Kansas City, Kansas. She has lived in Africa since 1970 with her husband, Mzee Pete O'Neal. Mama Charlotte is a mother of two, an artist, writer, musician, film maker, long time community activist, and co-Director of the United African Alliance Community Center UAACC based in Imbaseni Village, outside Arusha, Tanzania.

Lilja Otto is a former editorial assistant at *Yes!* magazine.

Mukul Patel's networked installations, sound art and scores for dance and film draw on influences as diverse as OuLiPo and Indian classical music.

João Alexandre Peschanski works as a journalist at the Brazilian alternative weekly *Brasil de Fato*, which was founded by several social movements, such as the Landless Workers Movement (MST) and the Workers Central Union. He is currently finishing a Master's Programme in Political Science at the University of São Paulo.

Angela Phillips runs the Journalism MA at Goldsmiths College. She started working as a photographer and writer on the alternative press of the 1970s and subsequently for national newspapers and magazines. She blogs on Guardian Comment is Free.

Mandy Rose is Editor of New Media at BBC Wales. Her Department produces websites for Wales, employs emerging technologies to enhance BBC Wales and Network broadcast output, and innovates in participatory media. Mandy joined the BBC as a producer/director on *The Late Show* before setting up and co-producing the Video Nation project for BBC 2.

'Sam and Annie' are volunteers who have worked on Indymedia UK since its inception. They believe that in actively making media they are making their own protest, demonstrating with keyboards, cables and cameras, and that nothing compares to the baptism of fire that comes through getting involved with Indymedia during a major mobilisation. They write occasionally, representing no one save their anonymised selves. Their insistence on remaining nameless reflects the necessary caution exercised by many IMC volunteers to not abuse their position by becoming a known name, commentator, expert or 'voice of the movement'. They despise the type of media whore who just wants to work in alternative media to add points to their CV, or to make a name for themselves before catching that well paid corporate job.

Aaron Sarver is an independent audio producer and writer based in Chicago. His work has appeared in *In These Times*, *The Chicago Reader*, *Alternet.org*, and on *Free Speech Radio News*. For nearly three years he produced and co-hosted the radio programme, *Fire on the Prairie*, which featured interviews with progressive writers and activists, and is archived at fireontheprairie.com.

Sue Scheibler is Associate Professor in the School of Film and Television at Loyola Marymount University where she teaches film and television studies classes, including a very popular class in video game history, theory and aesthetics.

Salvatore Scifo is a PhD candidate and Visiting Lecturer at the Communication and Media Research Institute, University of Westminster, London.

Steph 99 is a bike-riding, tree-hugging, science-fetishising, turntable-loving Unix geek from Philadelphia. She feels strongly that some of the most interesting stuff in society happens in youth subculture.

Pete Tridish is one of the founders of pirate station, Radio Mutiny, 91.3 FM in Philadelphia. He is also a founder of the Prometheus Radio Project, an organisation that organises for low-power radio and provides free assistance to LPFM applicants. He actively participated in the FCC rule-making and the grassroots organising campaign that led up to the adoption of LPFM.

Foreword

James Curran

Most books in this *Media Practice* handbook series are primers: practical guides to how to communicate in different media sectors such as print journalism, radio, public relations and advertising. They also offer critical reflection and analysis, making books in this series different from the large number of skills manuals that have long been around.

This series has flourished primarily because it has responded to the changed requirements of the educational system. When the teaching of media production shifted from the imparting of skills in further education institutions to broad-based education at universities, more critical and analytical media practice books were needed than those readily available. Partly for this reason, most volumes in this series have become standard works, revised and updated in successive new editions.

This book marks a new departure in the series. It is a response not to changes in the educational system, but to the needs of society that universities are failing, for the most part, to meet. The teaching of journalism in Britain, and indeed in much of the world, has been shaped by the 'professional' values and doxa of American journalism schools. These teach the virtues of neutrality, factuality, dispassion, balance and accuracy, and lay down rules governing how stories should be reported. While media work outside journalism is not quite so heavily policed, it tends nonetheless to draw upon certain generic conventions that are strongly supported in the media industry and also in university teaching.

This tendency towards uniformity, to imparting the 'correct' way to do media practice, fails to take account of the differentiated nature of the media system. It discounts the possibilities and potentialities of new communications technology. Above all, it fails to register that different ways of doing media practice promote open and effective communication within society.

Thus the objectivity tradition of journalism contributes to the welfare of society in certain important ways (which is why right-wing calls for broadcasting impartiality rules to be rescinded in Europe, as they have been in the US, need to be resisted). The ideals of impartiality and balance act as a check on state and big-business control of the media, provide a rein on the prejudices of the affluent who staff the higher echelons of journalism, and also sustain audience access to differing viewpoints. But, in practice, the objectivity tradition can lead to decontextualised, uninformative reporting, and the privileging of the voices of the powerful and accredited.

Media pluralism is best secured when the objectivity tradition is accompanied by advocacy and interpretative and subjective styles of journalism. These alternative traditions of journalism enable divergent social groups to define and constitute themselves, facilitate internal strategic debate, and further the forceful transmission of their concerns and viewpoints to a wider public. The engaged media of working-class groups; the feminist movement; sexual minorities; ethnic minorities; peace, environmentalist and anti-global poverty groups; and others, have all extended the diversity of the media system, and enabled grassroots voices to be better heard. Journalism has several legitimate registers, which contribute in different ways to the functioning of democracy. For this reason, universities established first and foremost to serve society should teach different ways of doing journalism, rather than only one approved way.

The orientation of this book is inspirational rather than technical. It views grassroots expression as a state of mind, an orientation, and a sense of affiliation rather than a specific set of skills to acquire (though the need for skill is not discounted). It therefore describes what different groups have done through different media, in different contexts. For example, the McSpotlight website is an integral part of the campaign against McDonald's and what it represents, community radio stations in Africa have opened up new channels of democratic self-expression, notable feminist magazines have changed public attitudes, alternative television producers have experimented and broken new ground in aesthetic terms, ezines have facilitated the creation of a virtual community of users and enthusiasts, the free culture movement is fighting to maintain the openness of the Internet. These and many more examples, drawn from around the world, are documented here. They provide instances where groups have found a voice and gained an audience, facilitated by the emergence of new technologies of communication and the existence of like-minded people. After reading what these different groups have achieved, it will be difficult – hopefully – for some media studies students to resist putting their skills to work, and applying them in unorthodox ways that are currently untaught and unsanctioned. It is also hoped that some seasoned activists will find this book useful. If these two things prove to be the case, this maverick addition to the *Media Practice* handbook series will not have been in vain.

1 Introduction

Tony Dowmunt (with Kate Coyer)

In the past decade or so there has been a massive explosion of 'alternative media' activity. Facilitated by the spread of the Internet and other digital technologies, and accelerated by global protest movements, more people's lives than ever before have been touched by various forms of media resistance – as readers, audiences and producers. If you have blogged, vlogged, or moblogged; read a fanzine of a new band – online or in print; admired a piece of colourful graffiti on a grim urban wall or subway train; taken a picture on your mobile at a demonstration or street event and sent it to friends; been interviewed on a student radio station; or contributed to a student newspaper, then you have had an encounter of some kind with 'alternative media' as we are defining it in this book: media forms that are on a smaller scale, more accessible and participatory, and less constrained by bureaucracy or commercial interests than the mainstream media and often in some way in explicit opposition to them.

At the same time as alternative media have grown, mainstream media have become more and more globally pervasive and visible, driven primarily by the needs and pressures exerted by an ever-expanding, globally triumphant capitalist economy. These media are not primarily (or, in many cases, at all) concerned with social values, the sharing of information or communication as a public good. The primary goal of commercial media is to deliver audiences to the advertisers who fund them and make them profitable, and most non-commercial or publicly funded mainstream media are competing in the same market place, and as a consequence their social functions tend to be distorted by the same pressures: they still may provide an occasional home for 'alternative' programming, but increasingly rarely. These commercial pressures are continuing, and spreading right across the globe, but while they are certainly dominant, they are not monolithic, and they do not go unopposed. In particular, the increasing reach of the Internet and availability of digital media have fostered the growth of the alternative media counter-culture which this book explores.

Raymond Williams, over 30 years ago and right at the start of the recent history of 'alternative media', wrote with cautious optimism about the new media technologies he saw developing around him then:

There are contradictory factors, in the whole social development, which make it possible to use some or all of the new technology for purposes quite different from those of the existing social order: certainly locally and perhaps more generally. (Williams 1974: 136)

Alternative media activity, which exploits new technical developments for its own 'different purposes', is now prevalent at local, national and global levels, 'opening up cracks in the mass media monolith through which strange flowers grow' (Waltz 2005: vii). However, this exciting and messy explosion of new forms, new content and different modes of distribution poses a basic question.

Radical Software

The historic US video magazine Radical Software was started by Beryl Korot and Phyllis (Gershuny) Segura, and published by the Raindance Foundation (co-founder Ira Schneider) in the spring of 1970 – soon after low-cost portable video equipment became available to artists and other potential videomakers.

This is an extract from the first issue, a statement by Gene Youngblood:

The media must be liberated, must be removed from private ownership and commercial sponsorship, must be placed in the service of all humanity. We must make the media believable. We must assume conscious control over the videosphere. We must wrench the intermedia network free from the archaic and corrupt intelligence that now dominates it. GENE YOUNGBLOOD *The Videosphere*

Figure 1.1 Radical Software quote. Gene Youngblood, The Videosphere. All 11 issues of Radical Software are available on their website, designed by Davidson Gigliotti, at www.radicalsoftware.org

What exactly are 'alternative media'?

There are almost as many answers to this as there are people thinking and writing about it, coming up with competing labels and definitions. 'Alternative media' is probably the most common label, but some prefer 'radical' or 'independent' media, and others 'citizens'', 'tactical', 'activist' or 'autonomous' media. Then there are the allied concepts and practices of 'community' and 'participatory' media. None of these are empty phrases: they all express differing beliefs about the cultural and political function of this area of work, some of which we will try to untangle and explain in the following pages.

Partly as a result of the rise in alternative media activity over the last decade, the first few years of the twenty-first century have also seen a related growth in the amount of writing and theorising about the activity, and attempts to define it. We are going to review some of this work here, and, along the way, outline the provisional position of our own that we have been using in compiling this handbook.

Alternative . . . or radical?

Chris Atton uses the term 'alternative media' to mean 'a range of media projects, interventions and networks that work against, or seek to develop different forms of, the dominant, expected (and broadly accepted) ways of "doing" media' (2004: ix). This is a useful definition as it includes projects outside a narrow definition of 'media', and allows space for consideration of, for instance, broader activities such as the open-source and anti-copyright movements that are aligned with many alternative media projects. Atton believes that alternative media must encompass all cultural forms of independent production and should display the following characteristics (Atton 2002b: 27):

- radical content, be it political or cultural
- strong aesthetic form
- employ 'reproductive innovations/adaptations' (ibid) taking full advantage of the available and cutting-edge technology
- alternative means of distribution and anti-copyright ethos
- transformation of social roles and relations into collective organisations and de-professionalisation and
- transformation of communications processes – 'horizontal linkages' (ibid.).

It is rare that any one instance of alternative media activity will display all, or even most, of these characteristics, but the list does usefully address the double nature of the role of alternative media – to provide content (cultural or political) that differs from that in the dominant media, and to offer examples of alternate modes of production that are more democratic and participatory, organised horizontally rather than hierarchically. These functions are both 'counter-hegemonic', as Atton explains:

> We might consider the entire range of alternative and radical media as representing challenges to hegemony, whether on an explicit political platform, or employing the kinds of indirect challenges through experimentation and the transformation of existing roles, routines, emblems and signs that Hebdige (1979) locates at the heart of counter-hegemonic subcultural styles. (ibid.: 19)

The political nature of alternative media is often present irrespective of content, located in the mere act of producing. John Downing, in his case for the concept of 'radical media', which emphasises the emergence of media from political and social movements, states that 'alternative media is almost oxymoronic. Everything is, at some point, alternative to something else' (2001: ix). Radical media, for Downing, includes forms such as dance and graffiti, and is defined by its subversive relationship with mainstream power and authority.

Similarly Nick Couldry and James Curran define alternative media as 'media production that challenges, at least implicitly, actual concentrations of media power, whatever form those concentrations may take in different locations' (2003: 7). However, they state that, for their purposes,

> 'alternative media' remains the more flexible *comparative* term since it involves no judgements about the empowering effects of the media practices analyzed. What we bring together here may or may not be media practice that is politically radical or socially empowering; but in every case whether indirectly or directly, media power is part of what is at stake. (ibid.: 7; original emphasis)

Couldry has argued powerfully elsewhere that alternative media are in structural opposition to 'the place of media power' (Couldry 2000) which mainstream media occupy. The latter have carved out a 'ritual space' in modern societies and, by implication, the task of alternative media is that of contesting this space, of 'unravelling the myth of the centre' (Couldry 2003a: 37). In his view the myth that 'the media' have managed to sell us (very effectively) is that they occupy a central space in society that is somehow magically separated from us. So only a very few of us are 'in the media', most of us are outside it and the 'place of media power' excludes us, seemingly naturally, as of right.

A potential danger of this kind of polarised vision of the mainstream/alternative relationship is that it encourages us to see the two as wholly separate. To counter this Atton posits his 'hegemonic approach' which 'suggests a complexity of relations between radical and mainstream that previous binary models have been unable to identify' (Atton 2004: 10). This approach allows us to see the field as having distinctly movable internal boundaries, boundaries which are the products of specific societies at specific times. So, for instance, a media form which in one time or context could be seen as 'mainstream', in another could be defined as 'alternative'. Corinna Sturmer describes how the arrival of MTV in the Sweden of the 1980s – which up to that point had been dominated by sober public-service television – acted as a channel of youthful resistance to mainstream culture, and this 'explains the popularity of MTV: voluntary exile for bored Swedish youth' (Sturmer 1993: 58). The Arabic news station Al Jazeera is now one of a handful of global suppliers of TV news footage, and employs the internationally known presenter David Frost, so can hardly very easily be seen as 'alternative'. Yet, in the sense that its coverage provides a counter to the consistently Western bias in the portrayal of the Muslim world in the rest of the world's media, it does indeed provide an 'alternative' – and enough of one that apparently the US sought to silence it by bombing its Baghdad headquarters in the last Iraq war. The issue is one of power and hegemony: who, in what context, has the power to define a media agenda, and who (for instance Swedish youth or the entire Muslim world) are excluded in that context. Alternative media for us, in this book, are the media produced by the socially, culturally and politically excluded.

The 'complexity of relations between radical and mainstream' (Atton 2004: 10) has been significantly increased by the proliferation of digital media and the convergences offered by the Internet. We now live in a 'mediascape' in which, at least according to Google, we spend more time in the UK on the Net than we do watching TV. A recent, controversial survey conducted by Google found that the average Briton spends around 164 minutes online every day, compared with 148 minutes watching television (Johnson 2006). These changes have a qualitative, as well as quantitative, effect on media audiences. The more personalised distribution systems embodied in the Internet are, according to Chris Anderson, undermining the 'mass' media by turning us all into niche culture enthusiasts (Anderson 2006). We could also speculate that these changes are happening because the Web offers more participation – more power and involvement – to the user than TV does to its audiences, and that this demonstrates an increasing thirst for more alternative-style media, or at least a desire to 'write' as well as 'read', to make as well as receive, our own media. Another recent poll, for instance, showed that a third of 14–21-year-olds in the UK are producing their own content online, in blogs or on personal websites (Gibson 2005), or on sites like MySpace and YouTube. Of course this does not necessarily mean that this activity is radical or alternative in any way (MySpace is, after all, now owned by Rupert Murdoch and YouTube has been bought by Google), but it certainly reinforces the point that the Web complicates the simple alternative/mainstream binary and problematises the issue of what is or is not 'alternative'.

The concept of 'tactical media' began to question the alternative/mainstream binary, emerging as it did from the Internet and communications revolution of the 1990s.

Tactical media David Garcia

The term was originally coined to identify and describe a movement which occupies a 'no-man's land' on the borders of experimental media – art, journalism and political activism – a zone that was, in part, made possible by the mass availability of a powerful and flexible new generation of media tools. This constellation of tools and disciplines was also accompanied by a distinctive set of rejections: of the position of objectivity in journalism, of the discipline and instrumentalism of traditional political movements, and finally of the mythic baggage and atavistic personality cults of the art world. This organised 'negativity' together with a love of fast, ephemeral, improvised collaborations gave this culture its own distinctive spirit and style and helped to usher in new levels of unpredictability and volatility to both cultural politics and the wider media landscape.

The early phase of tactical media re-injected a new energy into the flagging project of 'cultural politics'. It fused the radical and pragmatic info politics of the hackers with well-established practice based on critiques of representation. The resulting tactical media was also part of (and arguably compromised by) the wider internet and communications revolution of the 1990s which, like the music of the 1960s, acted as a universal solvent not only breaking down disciplinary boundaries but also the boundaries separating long established political formations.

The subversive power some of us naively attributed to this new 'media politics' appeared to be borne out by the role that all forms of media seemed to have played in the collapse of the Soviet Empire. It seemed as though old-style armed insurrection had been superseded by digital dissent and media revolutions. It was as if the *Samizdat* spirit, extended and intensified by the proliferation of Do-it-yourself media, had rendered the centralised statist tyrannies of the Soviet Union untenable. Some of us allowed ourselves to believe that it would only be a matter of time before the same forces would challenge our own tired and tarnished oligarchies. This would be the era of the painless 'win–win' revolution in which change would occur simply through the hacker ethos of challenging the domains of forbidden knowledge, accompanied by a general belief that top-down power had lost its edge.

The original catalyst for the notion of 'tactical media' was the 'Next 5 Minutes', a series of international festivals, revolving around the fusion of art, politics and media. The festival was (and still is) organised irregularly, whenever the urgency is felt to bring a new edition together. There have been four N5M festivals since the first one in January 1993. In fact, the first edition of the N5M was not a conference of media in general but of what we called 'tactical television' (we broadened it to tactical media in later editions). Originally we introduced the term 'tactical' to escape the rigid dichotomy of commercial and national TV on the one

Figure 1.2 The 'Next 5 Minutes' logo

hand and the marginal independent TV on the other. It was about what we saw as a new kind of television in which TV makers of all kinds shared 'a social and cultural position with no fixed institutional or discursive relationship with the world of television. What they had were tactics; TV tactics depending on very specific circumstances in space and time' (Raimakers 1992). From this modest set of proposals we set out to bring together as many makers who were working on this basis as we could. Nothing, however, prepared us for the level of interest and excitement particularly from central and eastern Europe, where the optimism of those who felt they had played a key role in overthrowing the Russian empire was in continuous and visible counterpoint with the dubious role of media in fermenting the early phase of the war which was about to tear the former Yugoslavia apart.

Above and beyond regional issues the incredible excitement, attendance level, and mainstream media interest in the event made it clear that we had identified a much larger phenomenon than we had at first realized. This led us to a number of follow up events and the development of a theoretical lexicon, which remains influential to this day.

At the time of writing (2006) the landscape is quite different. For one thing the Internet – then in its infancy – is now the dominant communications paradigm, a fact which both universalizes the tactical whilst simultaneously showing its limits. One of the effects of this has been to semi-institutionalize the ideas of Tactical Media. Not all these changes are bad. There is far greater realism about the limits of what media activism alone can achieve, information may 'want to be free' but information alone will not free us. Alongside greater realism there are signs of a more ambitious sense of scale, a growing willingness to strategically globalise dissent and to relinquish some of the prime shibboleths of tactical media, particularly the cult of 'ephemerality'. In place of hit and run guerrilla activism, the direct opposite is now required, 'duration'. Those of us who continue to value Tactical Media's unique freedoms of mobility, speed and creativity must find ways of reconciling these practices with longer-term commitments and deeper engagements.

Citizens' media

'Citizens' media' is Clemencia Rodriguez's preferred term. She recounts a profound experience of hers from the 1980s, when she produced a video documentary on grassroots organisations in a rural area in the Colombian Andes. As she tells it, a group gathered around to view her raw footage, people never having seen themselves on camera, watching their own reflections and analysis of their lives and struggles. Rodriguez reflects at the start of her book,

> As I tried to conceptualize all these experiences, I found myself in a vacuum. I realized that the theoretical framework and concepts that we communication scholars have used to explore and understand alternative communication and media are in a different realm. Our theorizing uses categories too narrow to encompass the lived experiences of those involved with alternative media. (2001: 3)

She characterises these as

> rigid categories of power and binary conceptions of domination and subordination that elude the fluidity and complexity of alternative media as a social, political, and cultural phenomenon. It's like trying to capture the beauty of a dancer's movements with one photograph. (ibid.: 3–4)

In arguing for a shift from the language of alternative media to citizens' media, Rodriguez uses Chantal Mouffe's recasting of the concept of citizen and citizenship away from legal definitions that leave out migrants and undocumented people, towards a form of identification, 'a type of political identity: something to be constructed, not empirically given' (ibid.: 18–19). Citizenship in this light is thus not about voting and protesting and a rights-based system, but about expressing citizenship in a multiplicity of forms, such as a transformation of symbolic codes and traditional social relations and hierarchies (ibid.: 19–20). Rodriguez suggests that citizens' media

> implies first that a collectivity is *enacting* its citizenship by actively intervening and transforming the established mediascape; second, that these media are contesting social codes, legitimized identities, and institutionalized social relations; and third, that these community practices are empowering the community involved, to the point where these transformations and changes are possible. (ibid.: 20; original emphasis)

This focus on social processes leads her to a view of citizens' media as belonging to the ordinary, impermanent and transitory realm of the everyday:

> Power happens in the realm of the quotidian, and what makes citizens' media fascinating is how they stir power in kaleidoscopic movements which fade

soon after they emerge, like movements in a dance toward empowerment. (Ibid. 2001: 21)

'Activist' and 'autonomous' media

These are the two final labels we will examine here. Mitzi Waltz believes that it is 'important to understand that "alternative" and "activist" do not necessarily mean the same thing. Activist media, as the term implies, encourage readers to get actively involved in social change' (2005: 3). She does not assume this change need be progressive – 'alternative' in the sense of radical politically – and so activist media could 'advocate absolutely mainstream actions, such as voting for the politician of your choice or volunteering for charity' (ibid). 'Alternative' media, by implication, would not have such a cosy relationship with the mainstream.

Paradoxically, it is precisely an accusation of this kind of cosiness that champions of the 'autonomous' label make about 'alternative media'. *Autonomous Media* is the title of a recent book (Langlois and Dubois 2005) which proposes a crucial difference between 'alternative' and 'autonomous' media:

> A distinction is made between alternative media activists, those who work to reform mainstream media, and autonomous media activists, those who seek to bypass mainstream media by fostering new forms of participatory and democratic communication. (Uzelman 2005: 17)

In other words, the distinction is between reformist and revolutionary positions, the former leading to an accommodation with the status quo, the latter, in the view of the advocates of 'autonomous media', being a more reliable route to radical and structural transformation of the mediascape.

'By directly confronting the mainstream corporate media, or by taking direct action to bypass them altogether, media activists facilitate the spread of social movement rhizomes' (ibid. 2005: 17). Uzelman tells how his 'rhizome' metaphor comes from Deleuze and Guattari's use of the word 'to describe horizontally linked, non-hierarchical forms of social organisation, thought, communication' (ibid.: 27), and voices his concern that alternative media strategies may actually work against these forms of organisation and reinforce hierarchies 'by demanding change of powerful institutions', which could 'in some respects take for granted the legitimacy of these powerful institutions' (ibid.: 25).

Su Braden made an allied point to us in a note about her contribution to this book (see pp. 212–23), questioning the usefulness of the word 'alternative' itself, suggesting that it lends the mainstream an unwarranted legitimacy:

> I am only a little sad that we have to call these media 'alternative' – surely media is a word that comes from medium and means approximately 'tool' or 'material', and cannot therefore really be 'alternative' unless it is 'an alternative

use of' – even then, it seems to denote 'secondary' and so invites us to accept it as secondary. Surely it is time, now or never, to accept that we are representatives of a legitimate and even 'mainstream' use of media technology?

Certainly our conviction in writing this book is that there is nothing 'secondary' about 'alternative' media. Indeed, in that they provide resistance, opposition and counterexamples to tired and reactionary mainstream uses of media, they are of primary social, cultural and political importance. Nevertheless they remain, by definition, significantly less powerful and privileged than the mainstream, and for that reason we are happy to stick with the 'alternative' label – rather than 'autonomous'. Given the pervasiveness of mainstream media power in our societies, it is difficult to see how any absolute goal of 'autonomy' can be achieved, or should even be striven for, as Uzelman seems to acknowledge when he says 'Autonomous media strategies . . . are *relatively* [our emphasis] independent from corporate and government power' (Uzelman 2005: 23).

Our own view is that questions of power, its distribution and exclusions, are key, and that all alternative media work exists and flourishes in the various spaces of 'relative independence' from, and negotiation with, institutional power. In other words, like all cultural practices, it is embedded in the real social relations that surround it. It will already be clear that alternative media practices, more obviously than most other media, come out of the specific social, political and cultural circumstances they face. So, for instance, one of the major themes that will thread its way through this book is the interdependence of alternative media and social and political movements.

We do not want to suggest that alternative media are merely instrumental 'vehicles' for social movements. A lot of alternative media activities are almost 'social movements' in their own right (see Indymedia p. 78). However, what remains true is that alternative media and the movements that they engender and are engendered by are interdependent. They never exist on their own; it is always 'media plus organisation' (Stoney 2005).

'Media plus organisation . . .'

George Stoney, born in 1916, was an early advocate and pioneer of video as a tool for social change. He was the executive producer of the National Film Board of Canada's Challenge for Change/Société Nouvelle from 1966 to 1970, and in 1972 co-founded the Alternate Media Center with Red Burns at New York University, which trained the first generation of public-access producers/activists in the US (see p. 136 for a contemporary account). Since then he has produced and directed numerous social and educational works in video and film, and continues working to this day.

A recent project has been his work with an inmate drama group at Sing Sing prison with whom he made the film *Getting Out*, which has been widely used by post-incarceration groups. George wrote to these groups saying 'thanks for showing it, but the real point is for you to make your own tapes in your own communities – that's when it works, and this (my film) is showing you how it can be done' (Stoney 2005).

His view of alternative media work has remained consistent over the years of his involvement: 'Change doesn't happen just by the media. It's media plus, media plus organisation' (ibid.).

Figure 1.3 George Stoney (Photos: Tony Dowmunt)

As we have already said, our analysis hinges on our concept of power (economic, social, political and cultural) and of its uneven distribution between peoples throughout the world. Ownership and control of media, of the means to produce and disseminate information and meanings in society, for the most part still reflect and reproduce the other inequalities (economic, social and political) that exist both within and between the world's nation states. As long as these inequalities exist there will be alternative media activists motivated to challenge them.

However, this is not a picture of simple binaries: alternative versus mainstream, radical versus conservative, the powerful versus the powerless. Each instance of alternative media is embedded in a particular social and political context, so that what may be 'alternative' in one context is mainstream in another (as we saw in the case of Al Jazeera above). Also, each theory or definition of alternative media is at the same time a theory of political change. Each definition contains an analysis of what is wrong or unjust about the distribution of media power, and, at least by implication, makes propositions about how to make progressive change.

Finally, one of the curious facts that the debates outlined in the previous pages highlight, is the degree to which 'alternative media' has become a hot topic in academic and university circles. This has been very helpful to those of us involved in making these media in clarifying our thinking, and therefore improving and refining our practice. However, as authors of this book we are aware of a potential danger: if the discussion only circulates within universities and between academics, rather than in conversation with activists and practitioners, it remains sterile and unproductive. After all, 'The philosophers have only *interpreted* the world, in various ways; the point, however, is to *change* it' (Marx and Engels 1968). So what we are attempting in this handbook is a conversation between practice and theory, and back again, because we too believe that ultimately 'the answer lies in practice' (Couldry 2003b: 41).

This handbook

So, unsurprisingly, this book gets more 'practical' as it goes along. The first section – 'Where alternative media came from' – looks at the development of alternative practices that have arisen over the last 30 to 40 years in radio, film, video and television, the press and, finally, the Web.

The next and longest section – 'What's happening now' – includes a wide range of contemporary media projects, but is not exhaustive. The scale and scope of current work in alternative media are too wide to fit into one book, but we have tried to include indicative examples of both the variety of work that is happening and a sense of its geographical (global) spread. The section is based on case studies, for the most part written by people with some experience of what they are describing, as activists or academics. Because of the diversity that is a hallmark of alternative media, we believe strongly that for a book of this kind to be useful, it has to both come from, and reflect, many different voices and points of view. So our contributors (see pp. xiii–xvii) come from a variety of backgrounds and disciplines, and their contributions vary from short 'breakout' sections to longer essays, and from wide-ranging analytical pieces to closer accounts of particular practices.

The following section – 'Doing it yourself' – will be of the most immediate use to readers who are interested in becoming involved themselves in alternative media activity. It looks at ways of getting started in alternative media work, such as training and fundraising, but also features a range of practical contributions from activists across many different media, and points the way to a wide selection of other useful resources.

We hope that this handbook will serve as an introduction to the field, but also encourage the reader to go further than we have space to here. You can use the Bibliography at the back to locate any authored work referred to in the text which is followed by the author's name and date of publication in brackets (including some Web references). So, for instance, Couldry (2003a) refers to 'Couldry, N. (2003a) *Media Rituals: A Critical Approach*, London: Routledge' in the (alphabetically arranged) Bibliography. There are also a large number of relevant websites mentioned in the various sections of the book, all of them accessed by us in 2006–7.

We hope you will be able to use this handbook to learn more about alternative media, and, as importantly, to get involved in the work.

Part I
Where alternative media came from

2 Mysteries of the black box unbound

An alternative history of radio

Kate Coyer

> The history of broadcasting is that dynamics have always been driven by people outside the system.
>
> Lawrie Hallett, Ofcom

Introduction

Talk of the death of radio is premature.

This is an exciting time to be involved in what might otherwise feel like boring, 100-year-old technology – an analogue dinosaur in a new digital millennium. The FM airwaves are opening up to new, independent entrants for the first time in many years in some countries, and the first time ever in others (in Britain, as recently as 2003). What this means is that many more people have the chance to get involved in – or, with a group, start – their own licensed neighbourhood-based, FM radio stations. And I specify 'licensed' because from the earliest days of radio there have always been – and will always be – people broadcasting outside the system. But access to broadcasting should not just be for those – the so-called 'reckless' – in a position to risk harassment, fines and possible imprisonment by the government. Rather, governments should recognise the right of people to communicate using the public airwaves and provide opportunities for legal usage.

Pirate radio broadcasters have emerged – and continue to emerge – all over the world, in places that lack sufficient legal means for citizens to have access to the radio waves. They operate in opposition to government-controlled airwaves as a crucial means of providing information and news during times of civil war and unrest, and for some, just for fun, or 'because we can'. Governments have used pirate radio as a means of broadcasting clandestine information across otherwise closed borders. Even in an era of increasingly Internet-based radio listening, FM pirate radio stations continue to emerge as forms of resistance to the corporate domination of the airwaves, and as alternative media outlets in their own right, in large part because radio is an affordable technology, easy to operate, and accessible for listening audiences.

Not unlike the way that YouTube has taken amateur video to a new level, the history of radio is a history of amateur activity. Though we think of radio today as primarily a product of professional public service and commercial broadcasting systems, the reality is that much of the technology, impetus and early radio production came from people working outside the system – individuals who tinkered with home-made kits, engineers who spent weekends experimenting with the new wireless technology, enthusiasts starting their own stations. And though there is a tendency to write-off pirates as irresponsible projects of gang members or hackers, the failure of many media scholars, policy makers, and the general public to adequately account for the impact of pirate radio, is a disservice to an important site of the battle over media ownership and so-called 'citizen' access to the airwaves.

This chapter will offer a brief history of radio in Britain and the United States from an alternative perspective, one that focuses primarily on the role of amateurs, pirates and community broadcasters. This history is often left out of shorthand accounts, but there exists a parallel story of radio that runs alongside that of the BBC, Clear Channel and Capital Radio, and it is from these amateur engineers and radio activists that we have seen some of the most important advances in technology and policy. In chapter 8, we will examine community radio today, but the history begins with pirates.

The first radio pirates

'Radio pirates' (or 'microbroadcasters' as some activists prefer) are those who broadcast without a licence. Hind and Mosco (1985) argue the first radio pirates were actually the early inventors of the 1900s like Guglielmo Marconi and Reginald Fessindon, themselves unlicensed because, of course, there was no licence to be given out since the medium was only just being invented! The term 'pirate broadcaster' was initially used to describe amateurs who stepped on another hobbyist's signal, and was coined at a time when there was no government regulation of the airwaves. By 1922 Marconi had obtained the permission of the British government to broadcast, but was only allowed 15 minutes of airtime per week, which was hardly in keeping with the enthusiasm for the new technology. In the 1920s, it has been estimated, upwards of 250,000 people in Britain alone were involved in amateur radio in some fashion. And it was the amateurs who most vociferously opposed the state monopoly on radio, were instrumental in lobbying against a commercial system and created popular excitement around radio through home-made crystal radio sets.

These early days of radio were the open province of technologically savvy amateurs – not unlike how hackers and open-source advocates have been instrumental in developing new technologies. Virtually anyone with a transmitter and an interest in broadcasting had access to the airwaves. Radio columns and periodicals devoted to the amateur enthusiasts were launched. Fictional serials for young adults, such as *The Radio Girls* by Margaret Penrose captured the amateur adventurist Zeitgeist for youth: 'Every Man a Scientist – or, in the 1920 version, Every Boy an Engineer' (Walker 2001: 16).

However, the advent of broadcasting brought with it anxieties for other industries. This initial fear of competition from 'old' technologies towards the newest entrants is something we have seen throughout media history. During this early period of wireless, the patent system became a means of controlling ownership over the technology that made up radio transmitters and receivers – and quickly resulted in very few companies controlling the industry. As a result, amateurs were effectively locked out unless they collaborated with a corporation (such as RCA) because they lost access, literally, to crucial parts needed for experimentation. Some early patent laws provided protections for amateurs to utilise proprietary technology, but that did not last. The newspapers were against the burgeoning radio industry – they were scared of the competition and even the BBC was not allowed to set up its own news department for a few years after its creation. The theatre industry and the Musicians' Union were opposed to radio, fearing no one would go to live concerts in person if they could hear them on the radio, forcing serious limitations on the amount of records radio stations were allowed to play (called 'needle time'). In the United States news agencies stopped offering their services to stations when radio's popularity flourished, out of competitive fears, pushing the first networks (NBC and CBS) to create their own news departments.

The systems that evolved in Britain and the US were antithetical to each other, with the BBC emerging as a non-commercial public service broadcaster and America adopting a wholly market-driven commercial system. Despite their differing motivations, both were successful in knocking out the amateurs, or reducing their access to the airwaves to almost nil. However, alternatives emerged in the unlikeliest of places.

> Radio attracted – and continues to attract – all manner of people and interests. When her radio station was closed by then Secretary of Commerce Herbert Hoover in 1925, evangelist Aimee Semple McPherson sent him an angry telegram that read, 'Please order your minions of Satan to leave my station alone. You cannot expect the Almighty to abide by your wavelength nonsense. When I offer my prayers to Him I must fit into His wave reception. Open this station at once' (Hadden and Swann 1982: 188–9).

British pirates by sea

The BBC was brought to life in the 1920s as a public monopoly funded by a licence fee under John Reith's vision of public service broadcasting, a non-commercial service designed to educate, inform and enliven public discourse by providing quality content to the entirety of the nation. However, one of the shortcomings of Reith's vision of 'giving the people what they need rather than what they want' meant that certain forms of popular entertainment were excluded. Jazz, for example, was not in keeping with high-minded notions of public taste more keen on symphony orchestras. European-based stations broadcasting across the English Channel into Britain began to offer commercial alternatives from early on, Radio Normandie and Radio Luxembourg among them.

In the 1960s, a new breed of radio alternatives took to the airwaves. Though an independent television service (ITV) was established in 1954, the BBC remained the sole licensed radio broadcaster in Britain until the mid-1960s, yet they did not have much in the way of local broadcasting services and many felt they were again neglecting the popular music scene. In 1960s Britain, the heyday of the Beatles and the Rolling Stones, the BBC broadcast limited hours of pop music per week, by no means satisfying audience demand for new music. During this time, one of the most intriguing phenomena in European radio history was to occur: offshore pirate radio. Stations like Radio Caroline, Radio Invicta, Radio 390, Radio Scotland, Radio Essex and Radio London broadcast from re-tooled fishing boats anchored in the English Channel and the North Atlantic. They were the sound of a generation BBC radio had left behind. And because they broadcast from international waters, there were no national laws to stop them.

Many of these offshore pirates were immensely popular with British audiences. Within only months of going on air, Radio Caroline had drawn seven million listeners (Hind and Mosco, 1985). The phenomenon was not unique to Britain either. In 1965, European nations agreed to pass legislation in their respective countries to eliminate the offshore pirates. Thus in 1967, the British government passed the Marine etc. Broadcasting (Offences) Act that virtually eliminated the offshore stations by outlawing any person or company from doing business with an offshore station. Since national governments had no authority to regulate this activity in international waters, they passed laws to regulate the activity of their citizens. However, actions taken by some of the pirates helped bring about their eventual demise. Competitive behaviour among pirates that had resulted in a few public scandals (including a death), and the acceptance of political advertising by pirates (including anti-Labour adverts in retaliation for their lack of support for the pirates) did not endear them to the then Labour government. There was also the appointment of Postmaster General Tony Benn, who opposed commercial radio in any form, be it pirate or licensed (Lewis and Booth 1989).

Largely in response to the pirates' popularity, the BBC underwent major restructuring. Radio 1 was created as a popular music station in 1967 (legendary DJ John Peel, among its first hires, remained with the station until his death in

2004) as well as BBC local radio stations. And in 1973, the BBC's hold on the licensed radio airwaves ended with the creation of Independent Local Radio (ILR), the first commercial radio stations in Britain. While some of these early local commercial stations were community-run efforts, the economic value of the licence proved too great and most community-run, amateur stations eventually sold their licenses to for-profit, commercial enterprises.

During this period, some institutions did manage to gain access to the airwaves, albeit in limited form. In 1951, hospital radio was created for in-house broadcasting via cable lines. By the late 1980s, nearly 80% of all hospitals had some form of radio services, run as low-budget operations relying primarily on volunteers. Hospital radio has proved to be an underrated though significant space for unpaid training and experience in radio, with many radio producers getting their start in hospital radio. Likewise, student radio began to take hold around 1967 when some unlicensed experimental broadcasts took place. By 1972, the National Association of Student Broadcasters was created, thus establishing the beginnings of an organised network that would later help campaign for community and campus media.

It is important to mention these two institutional forms of local broadcasting because emerging out of them were people active both in producing community-based radio and, politically, in lobbying for a community media sector. These stations demonstrate how incremental and piecemeal the opening of the airwaves in Britain has been.

The rise of the land-based pirates

Black music radio

Pirate radio is a form of alternative media that defies narrow definitions focused on radical content and social movements. Some people wanted to build counter-institutions while others just wanted to play their music. The massive number of black music pirate stations emerging in the 1970s and 1980s were largely stations geared more around a love of music and frustration that black music was largely absent from Radio 1 and the local commercial stations. While the commercial activity surrounding some of the pirates and their propensity to sometimes interfere with licensed stations engenders disregard (often contempt) for the sector, there have always been a number of significant stations that defied expectations and had a lasting impact.

In the 1970s, pirate station Radio Invicta was at the forefront of bringing soul music to London radio. From 1974 to 1977, Invicta broadcast only on bank holidays, expanding from 12-hour broadcasts to 48 hours of live continuous broadcasting. By this time, Invicta had a strong fan base and up to ten people working as part of the organisation. Motivated by the BBC's unsuccessful attempt to broadcast a regular soul programme, they began broadcasting every Sunday night, organising bus trips to soul festivals for listeners. Eventually, the authorities caught up with them. In 1982–3, there were so many pirates broadcasting on Sundays (a day with typically the weakest mainstream radio fare), that British telecom authorities were out in force every Sunday cracking down on the unlicensed broadcasters.

Dread Broadcasting Corporation (DBC)
(excerpt from *Rebel Radio*, Hind and Mosco 1985: 97–8)

From Brixton or whether Tottenham you have fe tune in to this yah rebel station.

One station which did manage to keep going until late 1984 was the Dread Broadcasting Corporation. Soul fans had listened to Invicta since 1970, but fans of reggae had to wait until 1981 for their music, when the cleverly named DBC came on the air. DBC took the slogan 'Tune In If Yu Rankin', and had their base in London's Ladbroke Grove. On Sunday afternoons, after BBC Radio London's solitary and tepid reggae show, you could now tune in to the real thing – although reception on medium wave was somewhat patchy. The music played was more than enough to satisfy listeners, but the presentation was electric. Nothing like this had been heard on the radio before in London. Both music and presenters were Jamaican. Their presentation style is now familiar to many radio listeners but it was breath-taking when first introduced on the underground stations.

Watch Out, watch out, DBC is about
You could lick up the herb or drink up the stout
You should a hear the children them a jump and shout
Watch out watch out, DBC is about.

There was no mistaking where DBC's DJs were at. Papa Lepke had served his apprenticeship with a London sound system. And when colleague Papa Chuckie played a session, you knew it was for real. When they went on the air they brought with them conviction, passion and experience. DBC used special effects and equipment to enhance the music, and the DJs would toast their commentary over the top . . . DJ Miss P, who got her start on DBC in the 1980s, said, 'there's never been a station run like DBC. Our format allows us to play music that would otherwise never be heard publicly. We create movement within the industry'.

Early DBC broadcasts entailed putting prerecorded programmes onto tape, and then climbing up a 22-storey tower block to transmit them from the roof.

Each programme lasted an hour, after which there would be silence while the tape was changed. Despite all the setbacks associated with replacing equipment after a raid, and court cases, and the greater restrictions and penalties that were laid down by the Telecommunications Bill, which passed through Parliament in summer 1984, DBC responded by broadcasting live, 12 hours a day, seven days a week. An opinion poll recorded DBC as the 17th most popular radio station nationally. Listening figures were assessed to be as high as 100,000. Miss P: 'We know we're breaking the law . . . so we expect to get busted. We just have to turn a blind eye and get a new transmitter.' The station went off air just after Notting Hill Carnival in 1984.

> On a typical Friday evening we'd be in the lift of a tower block taking the equipment up. Our pockets were bulging with cassettes, and we'd have the aerial and cable plus transmitter and tape machine. The lifts were always full of people coming back with their shopping, and they knew what was going on, but never said anything. Once we arrived at the top, getting onto the roof was the next problem. Before we discovered master keys we had to climb up. All the time we were up there we had to keep a look out for caretakers, who would come and ask what we were doing if they heard a noise. Sometimes we'd get around them, sometimes not. Provided there were no raids or technical faults, we'd be on air for the next six or seven hours. (Hind and Mosco 1985: 99)

Broadcasting in this way minimised the risk for programmers who would never be at the site if and when the station were busted, and meant that if the station were raided, they would lose their transmitter and be fined, but they wouldn't lose a host of studio equipment.

Political pirates

There were, of course, a number of pirates who took to the air for political programming. Some stations made their mark using short, clever bursts of piracy:

> In July 1984, listeners in the north of Nottinghamshire who were tuned to their local commercial station Radio Trent were witnesses to a surprising and unusual example of radio piracy in Britain. After the standard musical fare building up to that day's particular on-the-hour time-check jingle, listeners were greeted not with the official ILR news bulletin, but with a rhetorical call to save the nation's minefields, to join the coal strike, and to think about the implications of the mining dispute gripping the country. (Hind and Mosco 1985: 40)

Dubbed Radio Arthur, these broadcasters were clearly not intending to run their own station, but instead used its pirate broadcasts as an act of civil disobedience

– they made requests on air for donations to the striking miners, and asked that donations be brought to the offices of Radio Trent (ibid.).

London Open Radio

Members of the Community Communications Group (COMCOM) formed London Open Radio (LOR) in 1980 to lobby government in support of community broadcasting in London. Our Radio sought to be an open access station, attracting a wide variety of progressive interests across London. Programming included Radio Solidarity, news, opinion and music from 'occupied' Poland, broadcast half in Polish; Women on the Waves, feminist radio featuring programmes on the Greenham Common Women's Peace camp and a demonstration by the English Collective of Prostitutes; *Gaywaves*, Britain's first gay radio programme; and The Message, radical politics from an anarchist bookstore in Brixton. The station was eventually shut down by government following their broadcast of an interview with the then-leader of Sinn Fein.

There were right wing pirates like Radio Enoch in the Midlands, broadcasting 'in the fight against socialist government and trade union interference!' And stations like Sheffield Peace Radio, set up to broadcast during the 1983 Campaign for Nuclear Disarmament (CND) conference. The station, originally intended to broadcast just for the weekend event, was buoyed with their success and continued broadcasting for another six months until stopped by authorities. There was a growing frustration within the peace movement that their cause was receiving scant attention in mainstream media – including the BBC and local commercial broadcasters. An organiser lamented: 'It is obviously very unfair when the only way the peace movement can get a hearing is on a pirate station' (ibid.: 56).

Women's radio

Short term, Restricted Service Licence (RSL) radio opened up the airwaves in 1991 for a number of groups – college stations, communities of interests, festivals, sporting events, etc. Thus, in the early 1990s there were also a number of women's radio stations on air, Bristol's Fem FM being the first. It is not coincidental that people with the least amount of economic power often rely on low tech, low cost, and more accessible forms of communication, even if illegal, because they are simply using the means they have at their disposal. And it is where their audiences are likely to be found.

Fem FM broadcast for eight days in 1992. At the time, women were underrepresented in both mainstream and community stations – only 22% of full-time paid staff in community radio across Europe were women (Mitchell citing Lewis 1994). There were women-run stations that followed, like Brazen Radio in London, Elle FM in Merseyside, and Venus FM in Bradford (still broadcasting in partnership with Bradford Community Radio). Each focused not only on feminist content, but on training women to produce and engineer their own radio programmes. Brazen Radio was only on air for weeks, but in the lead-up, trained over 500 women, many of whom participated in the broadcast. Each of the stations broadcast a mix of talk and music programming, with specialist shows including: *Bus Pass Possee* – older women; *The Big 'O'* – lesbians; *Sisters Against Symmetry* – women with disabilities; *Rang Tarang* – Asian women; *Sportstalk; Girlzone* – youth; *Visions of Black; Health and Self; Women in the Media*; community news; local training and job opportunities; and culture, arts and comedy programmes.

Galway Pirate Women

In Ireland, the year 1987 was when the first unlicensed local women's radio station went on air during a festival in Galway. The station, Women's Scéal Radio (Scéal means gossip, or stories, in Irish) did not look like what you might think a radio pirate would look like. Organiser Margeretta D'Arcy explains:

> Surveys had shown that most daytime radio listeners are women. If we women listen so much why can we not own and run our own station? It is not as though women do not know how to use complicated technology, being perfectly capable of controlling washing-machines, cookers, micro-ovens, electric irons. What was the taboo against women operating a transmitter? [We] obtained a small transmitter, I put an aerial on my roof, a couple of microphones and a mixer were donated, and I already had a music centre. I looked up in the newspaper and found a free airwave, FM 104 to begin with; and there was Women's Scéal Radio up in the sky.
>
> None of us had had any experience of broadcasting, let along running a radio station. We had decided that unless we went on air cold we would never have the courage to go on at all. A leap into the unknown. Organising the radio as part of a wider festival meant that radio, instead of being an isolated medium sufficient to itself, became a part of the whole creative experience and also part of the improvisational nature of our work.
>
> Our research into women's relationship to the 'Arts' had shown us that unwaged, the unemployed, single mothers, widows solely on pension and older women generally felt excluded – by lack of money, by extended family responsibilities or just because they were women of spirit from those consistent communal artistic activities . . . We were, at this stage, more interested in encouraging women onto the radio than in building up a listenership, so we did not plan programmes and any woman who wanted to could drop in for a cup of tea. If she then wished to be a part of the radio, she could be. In fact, we brought back the old rural tradition of 'visiting'. (excerpt from D'Arcy 2000 in Mitchell 2000: 169–71)

Community Media Association – from pirates to policy

One of the organisations at the centre of this movement for community FM is the Community Media Association. Founded in 1983, the CMA's mission is 'to enable people to establish and develop community based communications media for community development and empowerment, cultural expression, information and entertainment' (CMA 2005). The CMA began life as the Community Radio Association with the decided purpose of lobbying for the establishment of a third tier of community radio, alongside commercial broadcasting and the BBC. Steve Buckley, the former director, became involved in radio in the early 1980s, working with a small pirate station, Cambridge Community Radio, in Eastern England, broadcasting on weekends. There, as Buckley puts it, they would head to the top of a hill in Cambridge with coat-hangers for aerials, a little black box with the transmitter and a cassette player to play tapes with 120 minutes of pre-recorded audio programming. They were on air nearly three years, were eventually raided, and through the experience, Buckley became involved in campaigning for legalisation.

Today, the CMA is the largest member-based organisation of community media in Britain and offers support, trainings, consultancy and networking. They remain at the forefront of lobbying on behalf of the sector.

In 1983, there was a plan from Thatcher's Home Secretary to launch a pilot project for community radio, but that plan was aborted owing to opposition from the Tory backbench. In 1991, the Restricted Service Licence (RSL) scheme was created that allowed for temporary, short-term, low power stations to be licensed (Gordon 2000). These stations were important towards building a national movement for community radio and many of the new community stations have run RSLs in the past.

Finally, following 20 years of pressure, the Community Radio Order of 2004 provided for the establishment of an official third tier of broadcasting in Britain. In his evaluation report of the pilot project for 'Access Radio' in 2003, Professor Anthony Everitt wrote that community radio promised to be 'the most important new cultural development in the United Kingdom for many years.' To date, 115 new stations have been licensed, including all but one of the pilot stations that have remained on air since first being granted temporary licenses (see chapter 8).

Conclusion

Amateur broadcasters are having a renaissance. Pirate radio in Britain continues to be a force to be reckoned with, much to the frustration of law enforcement and some listeners contending with occasional unwelcomed interference. A recent survey by Ofcom showed that one in six adults regularly listens to pirate radio, with the figure even higher in some of the most ethnically diverse and poorest neighbourhoods in London. For example, North London pirate Lush FM operates as a community-run station and is involved in local anti-gun and violence prevention programmes. Only now there exists licensed alternatives for non-professional broadcasters and a sector of broadcasting devoted to ensuring a space for community voices on air. At the same time, internet radio continues to evolve and independent producers are finding more outlets through online distributed networks such as The Public Radio Exchange, Radio 4 All, The Program Exchange, and Pacifica Audio Port. Out of this activity, a network of organisers, producers, and collaborations has emerged. 'Taken together, community/micro-radio and pirate radio best demonstrate the notions of alternative media' (Atton 2004: 115). The system is not perfect as there will never be enough room on air for all the stations that would like to launch, but it is important for communities to have access to the airwaves in our analogue present as well as our digital future.

Avast ye, enter the pirates! (excerpt based on Tridish and Coyer 2005)

In the United States, the service for non-commercial, low power FM (LPFM) radio was established in 2000. However, it was curtailed almost immediately by Congress at the behest of the National Association of Broadcasters (NAB) and National Public Radio (NPR). Against findings in two separate engineering studies, Congress passed a restrictive law ('Preservation of Broadcasting Act', itself an oxymoron) limiting LPFM stations to the less-populated areas of the country based on disproven claims of broadcast interference. Since then, while 590 LPFM stations have gone on air, many thousands more have been denied or barred from applying under the arcane rules, some having yet to receive official acknowledgement of their application from the FCC though they applied in 2000–1, during the only period in which filing windows were opened. In 2007, bipartisan legislation was introduced in Congress to overturn this law – legislation pending at the time of writing.

LPFM licensing has re-opened the door for neighborhoods and amateurs to start locally owned and run stations. From 1978 until 2000, it was essentially impossible to get a non-commercial radio license in the United States. Most of the available FM spectrum had by this time been taken up, the federal government was not opening up any new frequencies for groups to apply for, and in 1978, National Public Radio successfully petitioned the Federal Communication Commission (FCC) to stop issuing small, low power, educational licenses because in some towns these stations stood in the way of National Public Radio (NPR) expanding its national coverage. In 2000, there were only about 200 community radio stations in the US, out of about 12,000 total stations nationwide.

The 1970s, were, however, a heyday for non-commercial, community radio in the US. Pacifica radio station KPFA/Berkeley was the first community station on FM. Founded in 1954 by pacifist Lewis Hill, the station was revolutionary in bringing radical voices to the air, passionate debates across ideological viewpoints on issues like communism, labour unions, and war, and the poetry and music of the San Francisco Beat Generation. Hill also developed the model of member-supported, listener-sponsorship for the station that remains the dominant means of financing for most community stations in the US. Today, Pacifica is a network of five stations and over 200 affiliates, committed to progressive politics and the peace and justice movement. They produce and distribute the award-winning public affairs and news programme *Democracy Now!*

In the 1970s, Lorenzo Milam, along with his engineering accomplice Jeremy Lansman, nurtured the community radio movement in their own eclectic way, helping build over a dozen community-run stations across the country. Their wild radio days are chronicled in Milam's *Sex and Broadcasting* (1988), a 'how to' for community radio development. In Milam's own words, they sought to create 'stations for the elite – those who wanted vigorous discussion, strong commentaries, shit-kicking interviews, and rich and controversial musical programming' (Walker 2001: 70). The wacky sensibility of the stations that emerged during this time can be found in the call letters themselves: KRAB, KCHU, WORT, KDNA, etc.

Despite the growth of community radio in the US, there was still far more demand than there were licenses being given, and the pirate radio movement took hold. Many consider the birth of this new wave of pirate radio in the United States to be in 1986, when Mbanna Kantako set up a radio station to serve the African-American community of Springfield, Illinois. The station started out as WTRA, radio of the Tenants' Rights Association, as a community organizing tool for the housing project. The station was ignored by authorities for several years, until it broke a story about what became a high-profile police brutality case. When agents came to shut it down, Kantako went downtown to the federal building and the police station and dared them all to arrest him. When authorities realized such a course of action could backfire in the tense situation, they left him alone for many years – spurring many to realize the FCC was not always ready to enforce its own regulations. WTRA is now known as Human Rights Radio and continues to broadcast without a license, even after a raid of its equipment in 1999.

Inspired by the example of Kantako, others started to test the legal limits of FCC authority, taking advantage of the increasing affordability and ease of radio technology. Steven Dunifer's 1993 case represented a turning point in the modern United States Free Radio movement. An electrical engineer in Berkeley, California, he became angered with what he saw as the nationalistic, pro-Pentagon reporting of the Gulf War. He built a transmitter from scratch and carried it in a backpack up to the hills of Berkeley, and took to the airwaves. Dunifer claimed that he did not need a license, since under the stewardship of the FCC the public airwaves had become 'a concession stand for corporate America.' After a few years of covert broadcasting, Dunifer was caught by the FCC and fined $20,000. He vowed to continue broadcasting and publicly refused to pay the fine, so the FCC took him to court seeking an injunction against him.

The National Lawyers Guild took his case, arguing the regulations were unconstitutional on the basis of First Amendment concerns. They argued the United States model of telecommunication regulations allows only a wealth-based broadcasting system – that the dominance of media by corporate interests is no accident but is inherent in the design of the current regulatory framework. They made the claim microradio is the 'leaflet of the Nineties' and that to disallow it is tantamount to censorship. Though Dunifer ultimately lost his court battle, during the four years his case was working its way through the court system winning lower court decisions, hundreds of groups across the country flooded into the gap and took advantage of the apparent lapse in the FCC's authority to regulate the airwaves.

Accurate numbers are difficult to come by, but it appears over 1,000 pirate radio stations were in operation across the country in the early 1990s, echoing Dunifer's call to see 'a thousand transmitters bloom.' They cast their defiant radio broadcasts as acts of civil disobedience against a corporate-based broadcast system that ignored the needs and interests of local communities. This movement of pirate radios grew as corporate influence suffused commercial radio, public radio became increasingly national in focus and 'beige' in sound and many large community radio stations experienced internal conflicts between guiding principles of community access and 'minority programming' versus pressure to adopt a more traditional, 'professional' style akin to the public radio stations. There were also religious and politically right-wing stations that emerged, including some stations run by white supremacists. 'What unites these microbroadcasters is the systematic exclusion of them and their audiences – who frequently are also participants – from their local media, be it commercial or public, radio or television' (Walkor 2001: 70)

The pirates of the 1990s, like Dunifer and Kantako, were different from anything the FCC had encountered before. The difference, as one professional radio engineer put it: 'We did pirate radio and we felt like we were being mischievous, that we were getting away with something. The difference with pirates nowadays is they think they're right.' Practically speaking, the pirates, like the founders of the Prometheus Radio project, also brought experience as community organizers. Organizational tactics learned in movements for social change became useful as pirate radio became a matter of policy debate. Despite the lack of funding and often chaotic organizational structures, the new pirates were unusually formidable opponents for an unpopular agency that had just experienced rounds of funding cuts at the hands of a Republican Congress. In 1998, supporters demonstrated outside the offices of the FCC with a pirate radio broadcast right from the streets into the regulator's offices. Kennard, the first black chair of the FCC, was also deeply concerned with the decline in minority ownership of radio and television stations as a result of the 1996 Telecommunications Act that lifted limits on the number of stations any one company could own across the country. His support for low power, community radio stations reflected his interest in promoting diversity in ownership and minority representation. And Kennard himself admitted that the pirates had some legitimate concerns regarding the concentration of media ownership and lack of community access to the airwaves. Robert McChesney said '[the pirates] showed the FCC that low-power broadcasting is here whether you like it or not. And that they're going to have to deal with it' (quoted in Walker 2001).

3 Alternative film, video and television 1965–2005

Alan Fountain

Introduction

A remarkable variety of alternative film, video and television was produced between 1965 and 2005. This ranged from the collective work typically associated in the 1970s and 1980s with the community video movement and left, feminist and black film and video workshops to the more individually based and formally experimental work of the avant-garde initiated by the London Film Makers' Co-op in the mid-1960s. In more recent years, the focus on globalisation issues and radical politics has been represented by Internet-based organisations such as Indymedia, FreeSpeech, *Democracy Now!* and One World. This is a multifaceted, uneven and complex history which can only be touched upon in this chapter. I will deal mainly with the UK, alluding from time to time to significant international activities which have often had a considerable, invariably inspiring, effect on practices in this country.

Enabling more people to become active producers has always been one of the primary goals of many alternative media activists. The birth of video in the late 1970s, the development of low-cost digital equipment in the 1980s and 1990s and the results of digitalisation over the last decade have all made decisive contributions to an extraordinary growth in the number of alternative producers worldwide and to the breadth, creativity and potential political effect of their activities. It is possible to read the history of participatory media in the UK, beginning with the Workers' Films of the 1930s (Macpherson 1980) and concluding with the Web-based projects of today, as a gradual widening of participation, a huge increase in individuals as well as groups able to make the transition from audience to producer.

Distribution has always been a crucial issue for politically motivated producers and has historically presented even more difficult problems than production since the major routes of cinematic and televisual distribution have for most of the time been closed to radical work. Left and radical independent distribution and exhibition organisations, such as the Other Cinema, the London Film Makers Co-op, the Institute of Contemporary Arts, Cinema of Women and Circles, played an important role in widening distribution through cinema exhibition and videotape in the 1970s, 1980s and 1990s. More recently new digital technologies are in the process of dramatically multiplying worldwide distribution opportunities.

Television companies and organisations are often perceived by alternative media-makers and activists as politically and aesthetically conservative forms of state or commercial organisations and therefore part of the structures that need to be challenged. Nevertheless, there have been television initiatives in various parts of the world which have had either alternative media at their heart (Dowmunt 1993) or a strong base at the edge of the mainstream for a period of time. The initial phase of Channel Four in the UK would be a good example of the latter since alternative media-makers were involved in the shape of a channel which for a period of nearly 20 years had a department, the explicit role of which was to work with alternative makers.

This history refers to a hugely diverse range of people and media practices which cannot begin to be brought together under one definition of 'alternative' media. The introduction to this book suggests that various attempts to define what is meant by 'alternative', 'radical' or 'oppositional' point to differing practices within particular contexts. The following characteristics are relevant to this chapter:

- critique of and challenge to mainstream media
- contestation of the media public sphere especially in relation to public service television and state resources
- transformation of people's relationship to media through participation and democratisation
- an aspiration towards relative autonomy of resources
- connection to oppositional movements and the aim of contributing to the transformation of society.

There is inevitably a relationship between media and the ever-shifting social and political context which in large part determines its form, content, modes of production, exhibition and distribution. Alternative film, video and television are by definition a response to the politics and media landscape contemporary with them. A full understanding of mainstream and alternative media between 1965 and the present would require a study of the complex and contradictory relationship between media forms and practices and the underlying social and political events and processes of the period. Such a detailed study would surely demonstrate that 'alternative media' are varied, spring from a wide variety of motivations and causes and are full of contradictions and impossible to summarise.

As an active member of the Independent Film Makers Association in the 1970s and subsequently the first commissioning editor for independent film and video at Channel Four Television in 1981 I write from an involved perspective. If this chapter errs on the side of invoking a positive and relatively unproblematic history it does so from an admittedly partisan viewpoint.

There has been comparatively little writing about this period of alternative film, video and television history in the UK and most of it has been concerned with the avant-garde and formal experimentation (e.g. Mike O'Pray 1996; Al Rees 1999; Catherine Elwes 2005). Margaret Dickinson's *Rogue Reels: Oppositional Film in Britain 1945–90* is an indispensable accompaniment to this chapter (Dickinson 1999).

Utopian dreams 1965–80?

This period, certainly to the late 1970s, was characterised by what seemed to many at the time to be momentous – even revolutionary – social, political, cultural and theoretical challenges to established order and authority. The post-war feminist movement, the birth of black political activism, the stirrings of the movement for gay and lesbian rights, opposition to the US war on Vietnam, the student movement associated most famously with the 1968 uprising in Paris, opposition to the Stalinism of Eastern Europe represented by the Prague Spring, new left political theory, the politicisation of personal relationships, radical re-thinking across a range of academic disciplines – linking much, if by no means all, of this was a renewed interest in and rereading of Marxist theory and practice.

While many of the people involved in these political and cultural upheavals in the UK were part of a relatively small educated elite, connection to far wider sections of society can be found through a phase of powerful and militant trades union activity as well as a deep rooted youth rebellion in social, class, sexual, race and cultural attitudes.

Alternative film- and video-making in the late 1960s and 1970s both expressed and drew upon this heady mix of influences and attitudes. The London Film Makers' Co-op, quite directly inspired by North American experimental film-makers like Michael Snow, Kenneth Anger and Andy Warhol, began in 1966 and became the focal point for formal and occasionally political experimentation for the next decade and beyond (Rees 1999). The Amber Film Collective was founded in Newcastle in 1968 and dedicated its work to an exploration and expression of working-class life and culture in that region (Rowbotham and Benyon 2001: 159–72). Cinema Action, a left collective which worked closely with radical elements of the trades union movement (Dickinson 1999: 263–88); the Berwick Street Collective, a left group concerned with allying formal difference with militant content (Rowbotham and Benyon 2001: 147 58); and Liberation Films (Nigg and Wade 1980: 133–63), a production and distribution group closely associated with the anti-Vietnam War movement and the women's liberation movement began their activities in 1969 and 1970. The Other Cinema was founded in 1970 and began to distribute a mix of international filmmakers including, for example, Godard, Sembene, Herzog, Watkins, Ivens and Solanas, as well as radical British work.

As these pioneering film groups began to develop their work many others were inspired to follow them. Over the next few years groups were founded not only in London but also in many regions, for example Cardiff, Bracknell, Manchester, Nottingham, Gateshead, Leeds and East Anglia. This national spread became a feature of the independent and alternative film movement throughout the 1970s and 1980s as young filmmakers aimed to create new exhibition as well as film-making centres throughout the country. *Independent Film Workshops in Britain 1979* (Stoneman 1979) lists 22 film workshops in 15 different cities.

These film workshops covered a range of differing practices. Some were dedicated to particular forms and genres, some were more closely allied to the political left than others, some were looser collections of individual filmmakers gathered around production facilities and exhibition centres. All of them were trying to establish a relative autonomy which started from control of production and editing equipment, often supported by capital grants from regional arts associations and local authorities. Virtually none of these groups or filmmakers had access to television distribution, which largely created all its own in-house production prior to the arrival of Channel Four in 1981. Hence the development of new exhibition facilities, for example Amber's cinema in Newcastle, new small cinemas in Nottingham and Cardiff, and touring programmes, for example the South West film tour which took experimental work to several locations in the West Country.

Alternative filmmaking during this period is invariably identified with the sort of collectives and groups (increasingly referred to as 'workshops' during this period) referred to above. However, that is by no means the whole picture and individual filmmakers and progressive production companies working through the 1960s and 1970s should not be forgotten in this brief survey. Individuals not associated with a group who could be described as *auteurs* within the British independent/alternative scene in the 1960s and 1970s would include Steve Dwoskin, Horace Ové and Derek Jarman. A full assessment of radical work during this period would also include those working inside mainstream television, of which director Ken Loach and producer Tony Garnett would be well-known examples. Such makers reached much larger audiences and perhaps had greater political effect and influence through television distribution than was possible for the alternative filmmakers excluded from similar distribution outlets.

The influences on alternative filmmakers during this period were quite varied and diverse and, by comparison with many filmmaking movements, the effect of theory was pronounced. New Marxist ideas, along with semiotics, structuralism and psychoanalysis, consistently featured in *Screen* magazine and events associated with it (see for example the *Edinburgh '76 Magazine: Psycho-Analysis/Cinema/Avant-Garde*) and its critique of conventional narrative and realism began to have a strong influence among many independent filmmakers. Films such as Wollen and Mulvey's *Penthiselea* (1974), the Film Work Group's *Justine* (1976), Mark Karlin's *Nightcleaners* (1975), to take only three examples, sought radically to question the process of representation.

In his article 'The two avant-gardes', Peter Wollen, a leading filmmaker and theorist, identified two distinct avant-gardes influencing UK independent film-

Figure 3.1 *Berlin Horse*, double screen installation, Malcolm Le Grice, 1970 (courtesy of the artist and LUX, London)

making, the co-op movement (direct influence primarily from the USA) and European work primarily identified with Godard, Straub and Huillet, Hanoun and Jancso (Wollen 1996). It was the work of Godard and of Straub and Huillet, along with various theoretical concerns, which most influenced what might be called the politically experimental makers. These also overlapped with London Film Makers' Co-op-connected directors such as Malcolm Le Grice and Peter Gidal (Rees 1999; Gidal 1976) who also argued in terms of left theory in their experimental work.

In spite of the theoretical critique of realism, many left filmmakers, motivated by a stronger desire to reach wider audiences unacquainted with film theory, worked in a variety of 'realist' modes. Some were positively critical of avant-gardist approaches. Amber, Cinema Action, Leeds Animation Workshop and the Sheffield Women's Film Group, as well as many other groups and individuals, aimed to work closely with and on behalf of trades unions, Labour local authorities, radical political groups and women's organisations.

By 1974 alternative filmmakers throughout the country came together to form the Independent Film Makers' Association (IFA) (Dickinson 1999), an organisation which, in its early years in particular, included not only all shades of alternative/independent filmmaking practice but also distributors, exhibitors, critics and teachers who felt part of a new dynamic left and experimental film movement. As things turned out the IFA had a relatively short life but during the mid- to late 1970s and early 1980s it played a crucial role in securing new funding policies from local authorities, notably the Greater London Council, regional arts associations and the British Film Institute. The IFA aimed to strengthen the oppositional space for its work of production, exhibition, distribution and education while at the same time mounting a critique of mainstream media and, perhaps paradoxically, fighting for finance from the mainstream.

During the late 1970s the IFA, sometimes working closely with the Association of Cinematograph and Television Technicians (ACTT) (Dickinson 1999) not only proposed a radical restructuring of the British film industry but also crucially contributed to the debate about and pressure for a new television channel. When Channel Four began in 1981 it decided not to fund this alternative sector through the independent foundation proposed by the IFA but to establish a department and budget within the channel. At that point a comparatively large amount of finance became available to contribute to the range of practices represented by the IFA, prior to which the British Film Institute Production Board had been by far the leading single funder of independent and alternative production in the country. Beginning life as the Experimental Film Fund in 1951 before transforming into the Production Board in 1966 the British Film Institute's production wing played an indispensable role in supporting a wide variety of independent and radical filmmakers (British Film Institute Productions 1977 and 1981).

While many film production companies and workshops identified and often worked collaboratively with other groups within the community or with left and feminist groups, many individuals working within the workshops did not perceive themselves as enablers but more as *auteurs*. This contrasted quite markedly with another movement which began to gather momentum through the 1970s – video makers who saw the new video portapack technology as a means by which non-professionals could be drawn into the process of production to voice their own views and campaigns directly. In general it was the video rather than film workshops which prioritised the development of what became known as 'participatory media' and which saw the 'democratisation' of media, both production and distribution, as a primary political goal.

One of the pioneers of videomaking in the UK, John Hopkins, influenced by his involvement with the development of video in New York and by the Challenge for Change programme in Canada, founded the TVX group in London in 1969. While also interested in experimental video, 'Hopkins's vision was public access and the community' (Rees 1999: 88). Many who followed Hopkins' lead in the early 1970s were already active as community or youth workers, familiar with community action around housing, pensioners' groups, political campaigns and community artists, another rapidly growing cultural force in the 1960s and 1970s. By 1973 a video group in London's Notting Hill, the Community Action Centre, which became the West London Media Workshop, was defining its role and a contemporary statement from one of its founders, Andy Porter, leaves little doubt about its objectives:

> So right from the start the video group had no intention at all to function as a specialized communications team producing polished consumer products, but was convinced of the necessity of access. They wanted to make the video skills available to as many individuals and groups as possible, so that a user's

group would develop around the equipment, capable of carrying out their own projects. (quoted in Nigg and Wade 1980: 41)

This commitment to enabling more people to become involved in expressing her, his or their own voice became the consistent and main motivation of what might be called 'video access groups' through the 1970s, 1980s and 1990s.

During the 1970s 'access' became a term which referred both to access to production and editing facilities and to access to distribution systems, most obviously television. In the 1970s video production was much cheaper than film and, although still beyond the pockets of most individuals, was increasingly acquired by newly established video groups, community groups, local authorities, colleges and schools. Graham Wade estimated that by 1980 there were up to 100 projects using video in the UK (Wade 1980) with some very well-established video workshops such as Albany Video, the West London Media Workshop, Fantasy Factory in London and groups in Sheffield, Cardiff, Glasgow, Manchester and Belfast. Together they produced a wide range of work well beyond easy definition:

> Community video – or street video, political video, Xerox television, punk video, local arts video or guerilla video – has many faces. It can be used to promote international causes, like the Chile Solidarity Campaign, tape punk bands, record street theatre performances or fight against the closure of a hospital. The common theme is its progressiveness. All of these uses are concerned with building up people's awareness of what is going on around them – constructing a picture of the real world, often with a view to changing it. It is about getting people to help themselves and decide their own futures rather than having their lives controlled for them by external forces. (Wade 1980: 5)

Comparable aspirations motivated a radical group of programme-makers to persuade the BBC to establish the Community Programme Unit in 1972. A weekly programme, *Open Door*, enabled a variety of community groups to gain access to television distribution through making programmes under their editorial control and supported by BBC technological expertise. This was a significant breakthrough since it represented the first use of the BBC as a means of enabling non-professionals to be fully involved in representing their concerns on national television and marked the beginning of British television's uneven engagement with 'access' (see Dovey in Dowmunt 1993 and Rose in this book).

Channel Four and a radical moment 1980–95

The arrival of Channel Four in 1981, the IFA having been a small but vocal and surprisingly influential part of the whole campaign for the new channel, dramatically increased the finance available to the independent alternative sector.

By 1988 some 44 workshops had been funded by the channel for programme-making, capital equipment or development, in almost all cases in conjunction with other funding sources. This included a unique regional spread including Newcastle, Birmingham, Sheffield, Brighton, Belfast, Derry, Penwith, Glasgow, Bradford, East Anglia, Luton, Liverpool, Edinburgh, Manchester, Cardiff and London. By this time the separation between film and video which characterised the 1970s had dissolved and many groups bore both words 'film' and 'video' in their names even if some tended to specialise more in one medium than another. By this time, too, a second wave of workshops had been developed, the most politically relevant and successful of which were those which emerged from the black and ethnic minority sector such as the Black Audio Film Collective, Sankofa Film and Video, Ceddo Film and Video Workshop, Retake Film and Video Collective and other fledgling groups in Cardiff, Liverpool and Birmingham.

For a variety of reasons, most notably the climate established by Britain's right-wing government from 1979 to 1997 and its attack on progressive ideas, trades unions and socialist local authorities, and the conservatising effect this had on television companies and executives, the workshop movement had effectively lost its funding base by the early 1990s and joined the rest of what had now become, with the loss of the former bargaining power of the Broadcasting Entertainment Cinematograph and Theatre Union (BECTU), the casualised independent production sector.

Although there are differing views about the effectivity of this brief workshop experiment (Stoneman 1992; Dickinson 1999; Rees 1999) it can be argued that there were some significant achievements: the beginnings of a regionally based alternative network which did not exist before and has not since; the conjunction of film and video makers working with the community to enable non-professionals to find a voice; an important means by which women, ethnic minority and gay/lesbian film- and videomakers could develop their voice and find a space on television from which they had hitherto been largely excluded; the production of large numbers of programmes, films and tapes, which, not surprisingly, were uneven in quality but included outstanding work. For example, Cinema Action's documentaries *So That You Live* and *The Miner's Film* combined left political analysis with sensitivity to working-class history and experience. Black Audio's *Testament*, *Seven Songs for Malcolm* and *Twilight City* and Sankofa Film and Video's *Passion of Remembrance* and *Looking for Langston* broke new ground in their exploration of black politics and formal experimentation. Amber's series of fiction and documentaries reflecting working-class experience in the North-East such as *Byker*, *Seacoal* and *In Fading Light*, demonstrated the value of working inside communities over long periods of time. One can add to these very many programmes, often produced at the grassroots with a variety of community groups, which aimed to analyse and intervene in contemporary political struggles and debates.

In appraising the value of Channel Four to alternative and radical voices during this period it is also worth bearing in mind that the independent sector

Figure 3.2 Still from *Seacoal*, Amber Films' 1985 feature film. (S.-L. Kontinen: Amber)

described in this history made a significant but by no means the entire contribution. For a period Channel Four enabled many radical voices to find space.

Although this chapter concentrates on the UK this period witnessed significant and varied alternative and radical film and video practices across the world. This was a period during which advances in technology, particularly the rapid expansion of video as a means of lower-cost production and distribution, enabled thousands more people to become active participants in the production process. Clemencia Rodriguez (2001) and DeeDee Halleck (2001) describe and analyse a myriad of participatory, or in Rodriguez's words 'citizens', media projects in Latin America and many other parts of the world which occurred, generally, in very difficult and invariably underfunded situations, throughout the 1970s, 1980s and 1990s.

In the 1970s and 1980s many and varied features and documentaries were produced by the movement known as the 'New Cinema of Latin America', for example such films as *The Hour of the Furnaces* and *The Battle of Chile*. These were part of a radical anti-imperialist movement with continental and global impact. During the same period some similarly politically relevant feature films were produced in mainly Francophone African countries.

While Channel Four was, in retrospect, perhaps inevitably a focus for radical work in the UK during the 1980s and 1990s there was significant autonomous production and distribution taking place which was only indirectly supported by the channel and other contributors to workshop finance. As noted earlier, many workshop and independent producers developed close relationships with organisations in the labour and women's movements as well as with elements within the gay and black communities and this resulted in a flowering of production and distribution within these movements. Perhaps the outstanding example is the Miners' Campaign Videotapes produced by a collection of production groups and workshops in conjunction with the National Union of Mineworkers. Interestingly this not only involved obviously politically motivated filmmakers but also 'artists collaborating with trades unionists and the miners themselves' (Elwes 2005: 118).

Distribution of alternative film and video through, for example, the Other Cinema, Cinema of Women, Circles, Albany Video, the London Film Makers' Co-op and London Video Arts, as well as one or two international sales companies (of which the most notable was Jane Balfour Films), ensured that the circulation of radical work, mainly through hire and tape sales, made an important contribution to non-mainstream culture.

Miners' Campaign Videotapes

During the first months of the 1984–5 miners' strike a group of film workshops, film technicians and journalists from the Association of Cinematograph and Television Technicians and the National Union of Journalists collaborated to produce a series of tapes directly supporting the miners and intended for use within the wider labour movement. The tapes were made with the objectives of winning and consolidating support for the strike and to serve as a means of fundraising to help the strikers and their families fight for the future of their communities.

Five areas of the National Union of Mineworkers (NUM) endorsed and sponsored the project with the support of other trades unionists and contributors to the tape project included Platform Films, Films at Work and London Video Arts (London), Trade Films (Gateshead), Amber Films (Newcastle), Nottingham Video Project, Cardiff Community Video Workshop, Active Image (Sheffield) and the Edinburgh Film Workshop. This wide geographical spread meant that the project had a national coverage of the coalfields with contacts within the NUM and support groups at local level.

The three tapes each included two short programmes – Tape 1: 'Not just tea and sandwiches' and 'The coal board's butchery, Tape 2: 'Solidarity' and 'Straight speaking', Tape 3: 'The lie machine' and 'Only doing their job' – and dealt with issues such as the employers' policy and strategy, the voice of the miners' wives; support from other trades unions; media coverage of the strike; and the police, the law and the miners.

The tapes were distributed by Trade Films in Gateshead and Platform Films in London, through miners' lodges, other trades unions and various support groups and individuals. Some 120,000 leaflets and posters were printed.

Tapes went free of charge to the NUM and its support groups and were hired and sold according to the circumstances of other groups and individuals.

The response to the tapes was overwhelming. Over 4,000 were distributed in the UK. Internationally the tapes went to France, Germany, Australia, Denmark, Sweden, Italy, Ireland, the USA, the Netherlands, Greece, Canada and Belgium and raised considerable money for the miners and their families. A two-week tour of Australia raised £20,000 and Danish dockers who dubbed Danish voices over the tapes raised £40,000.

In 1985 the Miners' Campaign Tapes won the prestigious Grierson Award.

New technology/new horizons 1995–2005

The political impact of the Conservative governments (1979–97) dealt a heavy blow to progressive political movements and ideas which emerged from the 1960s, 1970s and early 1980s. Not surprisingly many of the media and cultural activities associated with them had also disappeared or had been considerably weakened by the late 1990s. The organisational strength of the alternative sector, represented both by the Independent Film and Video Association (IFVDA) and elements of the trades union BECTU which had played a crucial role in the development of workshops, had vanished.

In spite of these difficulties some of the outstanding filmmakers of this broad alternative movement have managed to survive and continue their work. While few of the workshops survive in their original form, Amber have continued to do so while the work of the Black Audio Collective and Sankofa has been developed with great success by John Akomfrah and Isaac Julien respectively. Interestingly, also, some of the politically radical companies which were never formally part of the workshop movement, for example Faction Films, Parallax Pictures and Platform Films, continue to produce significant oppositional feature and documentary work.

The experimental avant-garde stretching back to the 1960s and the London Film Makers' Co-op has in some respects managed to survive and even to revive with the rise in interest and popularity of video art and art galleries, perhaps most clearly represented by the Tate Modern and its support for video installation and new media work. The Lux cinema, which regrettably did not last long in the 1990s as the leading cinema for avant-garde work in London, has successfully migrated online, with support from the Arts Council, to find new worldwide audiences for its extensive catalogue of artists' film, video and new media.

Participatory media projects which grew out of the video workshops of the 1970s and 1980s largely now take place online and look to sources of finance outside the film and television mainstream. For example, Hi8us Projects is an organisation committed to participatory media practices which had its roots in the video workshops, was for a while producing innovative television programmes and is now supported through European and national social funds to work primarily on online projects in the UK and, more recently, with a network of European partners.

It is the new worldwide distribution possibilities that seem promising to film and videomakers in a period when global television is, on the whole, very conservative and difficult to access for all but leading names. Accessible equipment and distribution means that the long struggle, dating back to the 1930s, for self-representation through participatory or citizens' media has been and will be able to take decisive steps forward. Radical activist media projects devoted to global political activism and the spread of counter-information have already made considerable impact. Much, if not all, of this work takes place outside and has little connection to mainstream media (Indymedia's slogan is 'Don't hate the media – be the media') and many of these activities have the sort of autonomy from mainstream funders which radical media-makers found difficult, if not impossible, to achieve prior to the mid-1990s.

Undercurrents began in 1993 as a radical media project to 'offer support to grassroots direct action campaign groups' (www. undercurrents.org/history/index-htm) and over the next decade originated an alternative news video production and distribution system. Undercurrents now has a very much more developed distribution system running from its website and currently offers distribution of many radical videos, a range of online activities and links to a loose network of radical media groups in the UK and the rest of the world which continues to grow. The latest development, Undercurrents TV, will also dramatically extend its distribution capability. One World began as an online project in the mid-1990s and has dramatically expanded with active groups across five continents with the aim of 'bringing together the latest news and views from over 1600 organisations promoting human rights awareness and fighting poverty worldwide' (www.oneworld.net). Similarly, Indymedia has rapidly grown over the last ten years and now has hundreds of groups throughout the world closely identified with anti-globalisation struggles. These organisations, each of which is linked to thousands more, already run streaming video services from their sites and are well positioned to develop more sophisticated global distribution to accompany evolving technology.

Distribution of film and video productions remains a key concern for radical makers throughout the world. For example, with the exception of larger-scale documentaries with theatrical potential such as *Fahrenheit 911*, *Supersize Me* or *Darwin's Nightmare*, the impressive range of progressive documentaries to be found in festivals around the world gain television screenings in a small number of territories with internationally minded public service television organisations and cinema screenings for a day or so.

Faster downloading and the building of powerful alternative distribution networks hold the promise of a twenty-first-century solution to the greatest problem

Figure 3.3 Undercurrents team filming in Sri Lanka following the 2004 tsunami (Paul O'Connor, Undercurrents)

of the twentieth century for radical media producers. There have already been several examples in which individual films have been marketed for DVD sales with remarkable success – *Outfoxed: Rupert Murdoch's War on Journalism* (www. outfoxed.org) and *Walmart: The High Price of Low Cost* (www.walmartmovie. com) being two outstanding examples. The use of social networking communities such as YouTube (www.youtube.com) and MySpace (www.strandvenice.com) has also demonstrated completely new ways of alerting a specialist audience to new work both for distribution and for fundraising for new projects. These new ways of thinking about audiences and how to build relationships with them is just beginning and should result in a considerable expansion of audiences for radical and alternative work.

New video documentary in Argentina   Michael Chanan

An extraordinary new movement of young documentary-makers working closely with the social movements which arose from the political and economic crisis has been taking place in Argentina. This movement is very largely the product of the film schools which mushroomed in Argentina during the 1990s – including new departments in state universities, as well as half a dozen private schools in Buenos Aires and others in regional cities like Rosario and Córdoba. All this was the ironic result of the same neoliberal economic policies that eventually produced the collapse of the banks, but began by allowing people to buy the latest video gear relatively cheaply, and to pay for courses in how to use it.

Came the bank collapse and the *Argentinazo* of December 2001, and the result was that documentary was boosted by an explosive reality, as young filmmakers, now in full possession of the means of production, needed no funding or commissions to go out on the streets and film. Spontaneous and often uncredited videos, recording popular mobilisations and *cacerolazos* (the extraordinary protest marches of housewives and old women bashing their pots and pans), were sold on the streets from stalls piled with copies.

Some groups were already at work before the *Argentinazo*, when the country defaulted on its international debt, and then got through five presidents in 12 days. After that, they grew exponentially. Within a year there were 40 such groups, working closely with the *piqueteros* – the picketers who make their voices heard by blocking roads and bridges – the popular assemblies, the women's movement, and the workers' co-operatives who took control of bankrupt firms, all of whom came to function with a dynamic which is not usually found under capitalism.

Collectively known as *cine piquetero*, the first thing to be said about these videos, which range from short reportage to full-length documentaries, is that they share this dynamic, and taken together they present a vivid panorama of the extent of popular action and its sheer inventiveness. Second, they make a strong contribution to a parallel and alternative public sphere outside the channels and tributaries of parliamentary democracy, which is rooted instead in the popular movement itself. Video does not just allow no-budget production. It allows the work to be projected in meetings and assemblies, in parks and on the streets, bypassing the official media entirely and still reaching their audience. Third, the result is that the people in them are representing themselves (and telling their elected representatives to leg it: '¡Que se vayan todos!', 'Let them all go!') with consequent effects on the form of address which these videos elaborate. Instead of 'I talk to you about them', even those which have individual credits take the form 'we talk to each other about us'. This is not unlike the indigenous video movement which began in Brazil in the late 1980s and now encompasses several countries, where indigenous communities use video to speak to each other, and sometimes to their Others, in a direct mode of address.

Like the indigenous video movement, the new political video in Argentina covers a wide range of styles and forms, from short reports on particular events to the music video, but the basis is what might be called 'participant reportage': fluid hand-held camera, direct sound, street interviews, the same ingredients as television reportage but differently put together – often without commentary, cross-cut with found images taken from television and the press, edited with a sense of irony and deconstructive intent and often backed by the new Argentinian rock music. In short, the pervading spirit of the dynamic of popular protest on the streets, especially the *escrache*. This is a *lunfardo* or slang word, for a kind of fiesta of public shaming and denunciation. The practice was begun by the organisation HIJOS (Children of the Disappeared), who would suddenly turn up outside the house of a former military torturer, for example, and mount a kind of performance in the street, with several hours of drumming and slogans, music, parades, pamphlets, even street theatre. Some of those being denounced, the *escrachados*, hid themselves away, others fled, some responded with bullets. After December 2001, *escraches* began to be mounted against politicians, banks and the mass media. The extraordinary atmosphere of the *escrache* can be seen in several videos, but it could also be said that the pervading style of the whole movement could be called *video escrache* – a style which brings to the screen the same energy and popular feeling, the same mixture of elements and symbolic gestures. The world's eyes, or rather, the global media, quickly turned away from Argentina's plight, but not the new documentarists, for whom their cameras were once again weapons in a struggle of survival which testifies to resistance in the face of adversity.

Television and alternative media

The development of international television over the last 40 years is a complex story which is only recently receiving the sort of detailed study necessary to begin an effective analysis. Specific political, financial, regulatory and aesthetic contexts have to be the starting point for understanding how to define 'alternative' and the relationship between alternative media and the institutions of television.

Mainstream television worldwide, whether public service, state-controlled or privately owned, tends to be conservative and, historically, has found little space for either politically alternative or formally experimental work. However, there have been and continue to be exceptions to this broad rule.

In the context of highly state-controlled television in the Middle East, Al Jazeera is a 'normal' television station in structure and approach but in relation to the limited perspectives of most television companies their coverage of the Middle East and the Arab world offers a distinctly alternative view and indeed has been criticised from that perspective for broadcasting statements from 'terrorists'.

European public service broadcasting, which varies considerably between countries, has often provided space for various forms of alternative media. Such broadcasters, for example, in Scandinavia, France, Germany and the UK, currently commission or acquire and broadcast documentaries which offer a radical or alternative analysis. As noted earlier the BBC began its access programming in the 1970s while Channel Four supported a considerable output of a wide variety of alternative work during the 1980s. Within the ever-changing shifts in the precise application of public service television in the UK, both channels continue this commitment but to a far lesser extent reflecting political and cultural changes in the last 20 years. There are signs also that both tend to use new minority digital channels such as More 4 and BBC 4 sometimes to include work which can be variously described as 'non-mainstream', 'alternative' or 'radical' with the consequence of reducing the audience reach of such material.

In France in the mid-1980s a new cultural channel, La Sept, which subsequently became a Franco-German channel, ARTE, was similar to Channel Four and offered some new space for experimentation and radical political, social and cultural views and voices often co-financing Third World features and documentaries with Channel Four, ZDF and WDR (Germany). ARTE remains a beacon for many non-mainstream fiction- and documentary-makers in Europe and other parts of the world.

The attempt to go beyond intervention into the mainstream to create more autonomous alternative television distribution was a major preoccupation of media activists in many parts of the world during the 1980s and 1990s, by which time many groups were able to own or access production equipment but had little access to distribution beyond videotape libraries and small distribution and sales companies. Clemencia Rodriguez (2001: 25–64) offers an excellent summary of many and extremely varied initiatives throughout the world.

The struggles of indigenous peoples in many parts of the world over the last half-century have been accompanied by huge efforts to create their own media. Often based around issues of language and identity, sometimes survival itself, indigenous people in, for example, Australia, Canada, Mexico, Brazil, the United States, New Zealand and Chile have all achieved various forms of television distribution but not without lengthy campaigns to do so and often with contradictory results (ibid. 2001: 27–32).

Most recently Maori Television (www.maoritelevision.com), launched in New Zealand in 2003, has a primarily public service remit with a special role to broadcast primarily in the Maori language, although the often broad objectives of indigenous television services appear to raise questions around their political definition. Philip Batty's 'Singing the Electric', an insightful analysis of Aboriginal television through the 1980s (Dowmunt 1993: 106–25), explores the difficulties of maintaining control over content once finance has been raised from exterior sources and points to the importance of self-determination from within the community.

Private companies have dominated television in the United States throughout its history and the regionally devolved public broadcasting system has led to a situation in which particular companies, for example Channel 13 in New York and WGBH in Boston, have occasionally been more open to various forms of what can be called alternative work (Halleck 2002: 263). However, politically and aesthetically radical makers have also historically sought alternative means of production and distribution.

Perhaps the most significant and far-reaching has been the creation of a national public-access television system through which many hundreds of local cable stations throughout the country were contractually obliged to offer production facilities and airtime to groups and individuals within their community. DeeDee Halleck's pertinent assessment of the strengths and weaknesses of the system (Halleck 2002: 97–109) notes the fact that such open-access channels do not become spaces for alternative or radical work alone but can, nevertheless, be a public space in which radical voices and views can be expressed. New York-based Deep Dish TV is an excellent example. It has been able to achieve autonomous national satellite distribution, making use of the access centres associated with hundreds of cable stations around the country. Deep DishTV describes itself thus:

> The first national satellite network, linking local access producers and pro-grammers, independent video-makers, activists, and other individuals who support the idea and reality of a progressive television network. While commercial networks present a homogenous and one-dimensional view of society, Deep Dish thrives on diversity. Instead of television that encourages passivity, Deep Dish distributes creative programming that educates and activates. (www.deepdishtv.org)

Founded in 1986, this has been an impressive informal movement of radical media activists who, typically, decide on a particular series subject or issue and put out a call to video- and filmmakers around the country who then contribute work back to the centre in New York. The programmes are edited and distributed via satellite back to the access centres, which in turn transmit the programmes on their local cable system, of which there is now a network of over 2,000. Many programmes have been produced, including the 1990 *Gulf War Project*, *Lockdown US* (an ongoing series covering many aspects of the prison system), and, at the time of writing, a series of thirteen 30-minute programmes centred on the war in Iraq, *Shocking and Awful*.

If there have been problems in finding the appropriate terms in relation to 'alternative', 'radical', 'experimental' and citizens' media, the same has become the case for 'television' itself. As viewers are increasingly able to watch audiovisual material on several different platforms and more and more organisations of various types offer downloadable and streamed programmes – tapes, films, logs, blogs and vlogs – the centralised dominance of major broadcasters offering conventionally scheduled programming is inevitably changing. Organisations such as *Democracy Now!*, Our Media, One World, Indymedia, Deep Dish, Witness and

Undercurrents all offer what can be called 'alternative television' and with further technological development these and hundreds of similar activities will be able to offer users and viewers worldwide distribution systems that are a massive improvement on what was possible to similar groups even in the very recent past.

4 The alternative press

Angela Phillips

Introduction

This chapter is about the alternative press, which, for longer than all other forms of media, has provided a voice to those on the social or political margins. Nancy Fraser, in her essay 'Rethinking the public sphere' (1997: 124) argues that publications of this kind form part of a 'subaltern' public sphere which continually interacts with the mainstream to create what she terms 'emancipatory potential'. When voices of dissent catch the wave of a mass change in consciousness (such as the period between 1967 and 1973) they are capable of transforming speech into action. Indeed their organising functions become a major part of the reason for their existence.

However, as Stuart Hall argues, 'We all write and speak from a particular place and time, from a history and culture which is specific' (Hall 1990: 222). Alternatives arise from movements. They do not create movements. Nevertheless dissenting voices do not die away when the moment of social change dissipates

The offset litho revolution

Private Eye looked cheap and it was. It was printed using offset litho, a photographic technique that allowed pages to be set on a typewriter. It was smudgy, and what pictures existed were indistinct and blurred with virtually no grey tones, but the alternative to offset litho was expensive letterpress which was inflexible, technically difficult to master and really only suitable for relatively large print runs. Sue Miles working on *It* remembers what that was like: 'You couldn't get plates made. Censorship was really heavy; you had printers ringing up and saying – "I'm not printing words like this – I've got women working here!" and that kind of stuff. The printers still had to lay it out – we didn't know what to do' (quoted in Green 1988: 118).

Designer Pat Kahn worked with a women's collective in the early 1970s using offset litho which in many ways prefigured the internet revolution: 'everything I learned I taught myself.' For the first time it was possible for the writers to be the producers. As Offset Litho became more sophisticated it also allowed far more flexibility than letterpress. Magazines could become visual representations of the 1960s. Richard Neville of *Oz* wrote about discovering the joys of offset litho: 'Visuals no longer required costly blocks, so Sharpe could decorate the pages at the last minute, often on the floor of the office while waiting for the courier. *Oz* going Offset was like Dylan going electric; Mart and I flipped out on the new-found freedom' (Neville 1995: 43).

Figure 4.1 Jimi Hendrix (1967) from *Oz* magazine

because the need to speak, to be heard and to belong, are powerful impulses through which we create our sense of ourselves individually and collectively. Indeed Graham Murdoch (1994: 3–19) sees this need to hear and be heard ('communicative rights') as 'central to any definition of full citizenship in a complex democracy.'

The music zines which arose in the late 1970s with punk, the football fanzines of the 1980s (Atton 2002a) and subcultural style and music magazines of the 2000s such as *Vice*, have no particular relationship with mass movements. Indeed, perhaps they have more in common with the satire movement of the 1950s and 1960s – a challenge to an existing orthodoxy. Nevertheless they can have 'emancipatory potential'. They are capable of pushing the wheel of social change, and nibbling away at the complacency of the establishment. Some of their ideas (and indeed their authors) are taken up by the media – ever-thirsty for novelty – and become absorbed but only to make way for new ideas emerging from the margins.

James Curran and Jean Seaton (1997), John Downing (2001) and Chris Atton (2002a) all provide far more detailed and broader descriptions of the radical press. This chapter looks at a brief fragment in the UK, Australia and the USA since the 1950s and charts the way in which publications arose out of moments of social change or survived political downturns. It will trace the lifecycle of some publications, demonstrating the connection between the life of the publication and the sense of identification between speakers and spoken-to (writers and readers) (see Atton 2002a: 25; Duncombe 1996: 315). It will also look at how these publications approached issues of finance, technology and distribution.

New voices

The *Village Voice* was born in 1955 from a message posted in a Greenwich Village bar, a few meetings, a couple of drinks and some cash put up by Norman Mailer and Ed Fancher (see Fountain 1988). To start with it hardly made a ripple, selling only 2,000 of the expected 10,000 copies in the first week. But it gradually found an audience among a steadily widening circle keen to identify with a new anti-establishment post-war culture.

Six years later, in London, a bunch of ex-public school boys who met at Oxford University, started the satirical magazine *Private Eye*. Within a year circulation had increased to 35,000. It had smudgy pictures and messy copy but it published stories that no one else would touch (often heavily coded and inscrutable to those not in the know) and became a must-read for anyone interested in politics.

By some definitions neither of these publications was truly 'alternative'. Neither could fulfil Downing's (1984: 17) criterion of privileging 'movements over institutions'. Nor did they blur 'the distinction between producer and consumer' (ibid. 1984: 17) – unless you count the financial support *Private Eye* got from its readers for the many libel actions it has had to defend. Yet they represented a new voice which would go on to redefine post-war attitudes towards authority.

Youth quake

The next generation, learning from the *Village Voice* and from *Private Eye*, provided a voice for the new music scene while joyfully mocking the establishment, but it was the call for liberation from sexual puritanism that sparked *Oz* and the 1960s alternative press into life. Helped by the adept publicity-seeking of editor Richard Neville – a kind of Mick Jagger of newsprint – the Australian magazine *Oz* sold 6,000 copies within half a day of hitting the streets and went straight into a reprint. The magazine was rude and racy but it had a serious side too. It was 1963, the year Kennedy was assassinated, and in keeping with the mood of students at that time it opposed the Vietnam War and supported civil rights. Abortion was illegal and for a generation embracing the new sexual freedom – without the advantages of the Pill – campaigning for abortion to be legalised was high on the agenda (Neville 1995: 26). *Oz* was twice prosecuted and sales boomed on the back of the publicity the trials generated.

When Neville arrived in London two years later his reputation had gone before. Writing in the *Oz* anniversary issue five years later, David Widgery said,

> *Oz* was to provide, if not the first, or the best, one of the fiercest and most compelling cries of rejection of the choice offered the young within welfare capitalism. It seldom said exactly what they thought but it did express how they felt. With a voice alternately cracked with passion and hoarse with laughter. (Widgery 1971)

If Greenwich Village had been *the* place in 1955, by 1966 London was the place to be. The magazine *It*, a child of London's emerging cultural 'underground' movement, was launched in October 1966 at a party at London's Roundhouse where actors mixed with musicians, and poets with drugged up hippies. Soon-to-be mega-bands Pink Floyd and Soft Machine were on the bill along with light shows and movies. It was like a firework shot into the night sky in defiance of London's dreary, home-after-the-pub-at-11 pm, mentality. The next year the UK edition of *Oz* was launched, followed by *Friends* (relaunched later as *Frendz*).

Barry Miles was one of the founders of *It* but he could be speaking for them all when he said

> We did begin to believe that we could change the world . . . There was a lot going on: in fashion, rock'n'roll, theatre, movies, poetry, literature. What we wanted to do was put these people in touch with each other; there was actually a need, quite a strong need, for some sort of vehicle for their ideas. That was what we were preaching at the time. (quoted in Green 1988: 113)

The new left

The inchoate mixture of sex and politics could not contain for long the contra-dictions brought about by the rise of feminism and the new left. By 1968 it was no longer enough to write about 'free sex, free drugs, being able to look weird and not being thrown out of your flat because you had long hair' (Sue Miles in Green 1988: 113). *Oz* saw revolutionary politics coming. January 1968 was the 'Revo-lutionary Issue'. It was the year of student demonstrations in Paris and the end of the Prague Spring; Vietnam was high on the agenda and so was civil rights – brought into sharp focus by the assassination of Martin Luther King. In the US, *Rolling Stone* had hit upon the winning formula of rock and roll and politics.

Later that year, in the UK, a group of left-wing activists launched *Black Dwarf* – an avowedly Marxist newspaper edited by Tariq Ali. It was quickly mired in left faction-fighting but nevertheless an important signal of a change in direc-tion. Neville was also in discussions with others about launching a new, left-wing, weekly newspaper to be called *Ink*, and *7 Days*, hoping to be a left-leaning *Picture Post* for the 1970s, was also waiting in the wings. By the early 1970s alternative publications were springing up in every university town in the country – produced on a shoestring. One of them, in Birmingham, was *Grapevine*. Mike Flood Page was a student when he first got involved: 'There was the building workers' strike, car strikes, demos and meetings, flying pickets, the miners' strike. The Commu-nist Party was in control of Longbridge (the car factory) and the Socialist Workers Party was snapping at their heels. I loved it' (interview 2005).

Distribution problems

Distribution was a major problem for alternative papers in the UK. British libel law implicates the seller of anything libellous or obscene and the larger news-agents and distributors were wary of being sued so national publications had problems finding (and keeping) distributors. Party papers (*Socialist Worker*, for example) had an army of party members to sell the paper. For smaller-circulation independents, delivering papers to 'hippie shops' and street selling was part of the job. *Alarm*, in Swansea, distributed 4–5,000 a week in the late 1970s via a hundred or so pubs (Minority Press Group 1980a). In the late 1970s an alternative distrib-utor (Publications Distribution Co-op) set up a distribution network supplying a wide range of radical publications to independent bookshops (Minority Press Group 1980b). PDC worked successfully for a while but without a mass move-ment behind it the enthusiasm for carrying round bundles of papers for very low wages started to ebb.

Feminism

Feminism was to the 1970s what youth culture had been to the 1960s. It was the voice of dissent among the dissenters. Sheila Rowbotham had been the only female editorial member on *Black Dwarf*. She left the publication in December 1969 with a letter of resignation in which she asked her (mostly white) male comrades to: 'Imagine you are black, not white, imagine you have cunts not cocks' (quoted in Fountain 1988: 101). It caused a sensation but little action.

Then early in 1970 women in New York took over the February edition of *Rat* magazine in protest against a cover that depicted a woman hitch-hiker lifting her skirt to get a ride. *Rat* was never edited by men again. *Oz* recognised the coming of women's liberation – with an edition entitled 'Pussy Power'. By the end of 1971 the women of the underground had had enough. Marsha Rowe working at *Oz* and then *Ink* says:

> There were women on the alternative press but always in a service role. Even with the exceptions, like Germaine Greer, their contribution was always sexual – like Germaine's Cunt Power edition of *Oz*. In fact the underground press was even more exploitative than the straight press. If I had wanted to progress I might have done better to stay on working for *Vogue*. (interview 2005)

Rosie Boycott was at *Frendz*. 'The underground . . . pretended to be alternative but it wasn't providing an alternative for women. It was providing an alternative to men in that there were no problems about screwing around or being who you wanted . . . women were the typists, men were the bosses' (quoted in Green 1988: 409).

A meeting was called late in 1971 and Rowe and Boycott got together to start an alternative magazine for women. It was the high point of the women's liberation movement. Starting with donations of only £2,000 the first print run was 15,000 rising at its peak to 30,000 and read by many, many more. Says Rowe, 'I have met lots of women who said that their only contact with the women's movement was through *Spare Rib*' (interview 2005).

Downing (1984: 23; 2001: 72) writes of a 'pre-figurative politics' in which those running alternative publications attempt to live the politics they preach. This reached its peak in the UK feminist publications: *Shrew* (produced by women's groups on a rotating basis), then *Women's Report* (run collectively). After the initial few months, *Spare Rib* also went collective. Hierarchies dissolved and decisions were discussed at collective meetings (which were often far from harmonious). To begin with it was hard to find women who could write – most on the underground had been confined to administrative jobs. Rowe remembers, 'established journalists couldn't write the "new" way. I had to work intensively with people who had never written before.'

The boundary between reader and writer started to dissolve. Readers wrote articles and then rang up to complain trenchantly if a word was tampered with. It was exhausting but exhilarating. Staff members were paid, but wages were very low. The level of self-exploitation excluded many people who could have made a contribution – my own (part-time) involvement ended with my first child. I simply could no longer afford it.

The contradictions of capitalism

By 1973, with the exception of *Spare Rib*, which lasted for 20 years, most of the nationally distributed alternatives had gone under. *It* died in 1972 and *Oz* in 1973. *Ink* barely lived before it sank under the weight of its debts and *7 Days* turned out to be based on a delusion. Around the country the community papers bloomed and then shrivelled like flowers in a field. Staff costs were covered by student grants, unemployment benefit or part-time work in other organisations. Perhaps the longest running was the Leeds *Other Paper* which owned its own print shop and subsidised the paper via jobbing printing. According to a Minority Press Group survey (1980a: 17) about 70% of the alternatives were running at a loss. One exception was the *West Highland Free Press*, which established itself on the Isle of Skye as a left-wing newspaper providing a traditional community service and still thrives today.

Nationally there were too many papers chasing the same group of readers. At its peak *It* had a circulation of 40–50,000, and with only *Oz* as a rival, both could stay afloat on the basis of sales and a certain amount of voluntary labour. By the time *Ink* and *7 Days* appeared, the market was oversaturated and fragmenting. The papers were also competing for the same advertising but, by the early 1970s, even the record companies could find more reliable places to advertise their wares than the now über-serious left press. One such place was London listings magazine *Time Out*. Launched in 1968 as a folded sheet, it relaunched as a weekly magazine just in time to prevent *Ink* from moving into the listings market – a major blow for *Ink* which would have then been able to rely not only on a steady readership but also, critically, the film, music and book advertising which comes with it.

It was different in America. By the end of the 1960s alternative newspapers were selling five million copies, attracting plenty of advertising and turning profits. John Wilcock (one of the founders of the *Village Voice*) was concerned about the growing commercialisation of the alternatives back in the early 1970s. Writing in the *Oz* fifth anniversary issue he said,

> The Freep (*The LA Free Press*) cut its teeth during a time of social upheaval in the mid-sixties and built up a vast readership with a combination of subversive social comment and racy sexist ads. Before long Trotskyist Kunkin [Art Kunkin who started it] was buying expensive homes in the hills, driving a telephone equipped roadster and milking the paper to finance a printing plant and a chain of bookstores. (*Oz* issue 40, page 6)

There are currently 118 publications in the Association of Alternative Newsweek-lies (AAN) and they have a circulation of eight million between them, paid for entirely by advertising. Rodney Benson (2003: 111–27) argues that, in spite of this, most of the US alternatives maintain a 'critical oppositionist stance'. But then 'being critical' is in itself a selling proposition in a country where the concentration of newspaper ownership ensures that only one mass-circulation newspaper survives in most American cities, providing a narrow, motherhood-and-apple-pie view of a world dominated by local concerns. Given the broad definition that Benson uses it seems likely that in the UK the *Guardian* newspaper, owned by the Scott Trust, could be seen as 'alternative' and in a sense that partly explains the difference between the UK and the US experience.

In the late 1960s the UK was being liberalised and abortion was partially legalised, as was homosexuality. The alternatives could campaign against the Vietnam War but they were not actually fighting it so that it was not the mobiliser that it continued to be in the US until 1975. The cultural underground had by now gone overground. A crowded national newspaper market was competing for new readers and needed new ideas. In 1972 Richard Neville himself was offered a column on the *Evening Standard*, a conservative-leaning daily.

One UK publication that did survive from the 1970s is *Time Out*. As the other papers collapsed, *Time Out* absorbed some of the displaced staff, providing, for a time, a financially sustainable, alternative in the US style: radical news pages and features at the front paid for by restaurant and movie listings at the back. In keeping with its 'hippy' roots it paid the receptionist the same as the editor. But the ownership structure was far from alternative. As the 1970s wore on, its proprietor, Tony Elliott, became increasingly irritated with the political slant of the magazine. In 1980 he did away with the equal-pay agreement. Most of the staff left, taking their radical politics with them. *Time Out* rejected any connection with radical politics, leaving London without any alternative press at all.

Small voices

By the 1980s the political mood in the UK had changed. The labour movement was in retreat. In this climate attempts to launch and sustain independent broad-left print publications have struggled. *Marxism Today* (Pimlott, in Curran et al. 2000: 193–211) flowered briefly, in the 1980s, under the editorship of Martin Jacques. From being a rather dull theoretical publication which was supported by the Communist Party, for a short period this magazine became the 'must-read', for certain sections of the liberal and left establishment. As a party publication *Marxism Today* does not entirely fit under the rubric of an 'alternative' and yet, under the editorship of Martin Jacques, the magazine became virtually independent financially and editorially. Party funds gave it a base and a readership, from which it grew into a stylish and, more importantly, intellectually adventurous publication.

Like *Oz* in the 1960s, *Marxism Today* was right at the centre of a changing political tide. This was not a mass movement, it was a realignment of the British left and Jacques was to politics what the magazine *The Face* (at that time an independent magazine which was then bought up and subsequently closed by East Midlands Allied Press) was to style. Both magazines recognised that the politics of Margaret Thatcher had opened the door to a new kind of consumerism. The magazines looked good, they accorded design the same centre place that *Oz* had done in the heyday of psychedelia, and they recognised that the rising generation of young professionals (even those on the left) could be reached through their pleasure in consumption.

Jacques also had the contacts and the charisma to encourage well-known journalists and academics to debate in the pages of the magazine. Broadsheet newspapers (in particular the *Guardian*; see Curran et al. 2000) used the magazine as a source of authoritative information and from time to time reprinted articles. In turn the higher profile of the paper made it a worthwhile place for professionals to publish articles which were not quite acceptable for the mainstream. The magazine's readership rose in response. This virtuous circle started to attract advertising. At its peak 40% of income came from advertising and over 50% from sales, but its circulation never rose above 18,000, mainly via subscription (Pimlott 2000: 199). As the debates on the left gradually resolved themselves with the development of New Labour, interest in *Marxism Today* began to wane. The star writers could earn more by writing for the national newspapers and subscribers could read them there. By 1991 *Marxism Today* had stopped publication. It had been absorbed by the mainstream.

Red Pepper (established in 1995) is currently filling the niche for a radical left, political voice. Says editor Hilary Wainwright,

> It has helped to give the radical left a regular voice in the mainstream through persistent interaction with the more open of this media. In keeping with the international character of the new 'alter-globalisation' movement it is now part of a growing network of radical magazines across Western and Eastern Europe, exchanging articles and producing an occasional supplement in several languages. (personal email)

UnLimited Media

Three Weeks is the magazine of the Edinburgh Fringe (the innovative aspect of the Edinburgh Festival). It was started in 1996 by three Edinburgh university students – Chris Cooke, Geraint Preston and Alex Thomson – and a bunch of friends who were passionate about the arts and wanted 'to discover, champion, support and enable cultural innovation' (interview 2005). They reviewed the shows, interviewed the artists, published the paper and drove it around to distribution points. In time the friends drifted away and like every alternative magazine they were left with the problem of sustaining their project. They solved it by encouraging students to join them for a month each year, allowing them to provide saturation coverage of the Fringe.

The founders of *Three Weeks* went on to establish *UnLimited Media* which aims both at arts audiences and music industry professionals, and also acts as a media consultancy. At the heart of the company lies the relationship with their audience most of whom they are in regular contact with by email. This inter-activity operates both ways. It brings the audiences into a direct engagement with the media 'channel' (print, web or podcast) and many of those who use the website (or read the paper) also contribute to it. At the same time this involved audience provides information which can be fed back to music and arts produc-ers via the UnLimited consultancy. For this company, interactivity is part of the core business. Chris Cooke explains:

> Companies will pay us to advise on the ways they should be engaging those audiences, or to run programmes involving those audiences. That said, we are always very upfront with our audiences when we are work-ing with brands – this is crucial, because much of the value of our brands is in our credibility, which would be damaged if we were seen to be secretly working with corporate brands (interview 2005).

Three Weeks (published by UnLimited Media) is providing for the Edinburgh Festival in Scotland the kind of service *Time Out* provided in the 1960s. Like *Red Pepper*, *Three Weeks* needs enthusiastic young contributors, who will work for the buzz of it. Both publications have established reasonably sized audiences and, perhaps more important, both provide an element of training. The standard of writing is therefore reasonably high and contributors get something back for their involvement. In both cases the motivation is to provide an alternative view: of politics on the one hand and of the arts on the other. Neither could really be described as part of a mass movement but both provide a challenge to existing orthodoxies.

But *Red Pepper* struggles and, according to Natasha Grzincic, ex-deputy editor of *Red Pepper*, it is in a state of constant financial crisis, without a viable business model, kept alive by supporting subscriptions often paid for as a goodwill ges-ture by left-leaning professionals, many of whom (she suspects) probably do not read it. There is a sense, she feels, in which the magazine has lost sight of the con-nection with its readers that every alternative publication requires to be viable and has not fully taken on board the possibilities offered by convergence. Editor Hilary Wainwright disagrees. She feels that *Red Pepper*'s problems lie with the unique disadvantage of the British distribution system:

We are a business – a social business, but it is difficult to be a business when the distribution system in Britain, in contrast to say France and Italy, makes it almost impossible for the alternative press to be available in magazine racks. Mainstream magazines either pay thousands of pounds to be on the shelves of monopoly distributors, W.H. Smith and more recently the super-markets, or they have huge advertising budgets. This lack of availability means that *Red Pepper*'s public profile with our target markets is not easily translated into sales. Consequently we are one of the growing number of magazines whose business model is based on subscriptions. Seventy to eighty per cent of subscriptions are renewed each year, and the number is steadily rising especially as a result of our widely used website. (personal email)

For *Three Weeks* and UnLimited Media, the contact with contributors and audience is vital and the service offered is designed to make use of all the different 'media channels' by which such audiences can be contacted. *Three Weeks* is print (though it also has a website) because it works better for a festival where people are out and about. The paper attracts sponsorship and advertising which, in turn, funds the website. *CMU* (*College Music Update*) is distributed by email subscription but also has its own website. New ventures will use whichever media channel seems most viable, the dominant form providing an income stream to support the others.

Summary

People producing alternative publications are still impelled by the need to create solidarity with like-minded people. It is this sense of solidarity and engagement between those who write and those who read that most clearly separates alternative publications from single people writing blogs or commercial publications.

New technologies have enabled alternatives to break down barriers between writers (and designers/artists/photographers) and readers. At each change in technology the level of technical expertise required for publication has diminished. The introduction of offset litho, followed by computerisation and then by the Internet, have enabled those who wish to speak out to be heard without the need for vast armies of intermediaries.

However, most alternative publications are hampered by the lack of an independent and reliable income stream. If they are subsidised (by advertising, grants or political parties) there is always the risk that they will lose sight of their relationship with their readers and rely on pleasing their funders. If they have no subsidy they must either recoup their costs via sales – a relationship which works best during periods of political change when readers are thirsty for alternative views – or be subsidised by the labour of contributors, or both. It is this built-in competitive disadvantage, in comparison with mainstream publications, which means that few publications out-live the enthusiasm of their founders. The exceptions to this rule are those weeklies that have cornered the market for listings and advertising of a cultural nature, though whether they retain their 'alternative' edge remains open to question.

Conclusion

Control of the means of production and distribution is now available to anyone with access to a computer – bypassing many of the problems faced by the alternative print media. But in the end it is not technology, or better distribution networks, or advertising, or grant aid from political parties or public bodies, that really matters – it is genuinely reflecting the voice and concerns of the moment. Marsha Rowe says, 'You have to go to all the conferences, you have to feel part of a bigger, wider movement.' Barry Miles, remembering the heyday of *It*, speaks of 'Staying up all night, rolling up issues in brown wrappers and labelling them. It was almost a religious thing, to get the stuff out. It's almost impossible to imagine any more. To have that kind of excitement and enthusiasm and belief in what you are doing' (quoted in Green 1988: 127). It is the need to speak, to be heard and to belong which will always be the motor of the alternatives, wherever and however they choose to deliver their message.

5 A brief history

The Web and interactive media

Chris Atton

Introduction

The history of alternative media on the Internet is brief; after all, the general availability of the technology itself is barely 20 years old. Even so, in this short time we have seen thousands of media projects, far too many to deal with in this brief introduction. Instead, we will look at a handful of key moments and major projects in an effort to identify some unique features of alternative media on the Internet. Below ('Alternative media in practice' in chapter 6) we will come right up to date with developments and in particular examine how alternative media on the Internet are helping us rethink media and journalism in the twenty-first century.

Two of the earliest Internet-based media projects were PeaceNet in the US and GreenNet in the UK. Both were founded in 1985 and together they formed the Association for Progressive Communications, which became the host for other organisations dedicated to social change. The early 1990s saw the appearance of activist mailing lists and other email based groups on the Internet such as ACTIV-L (general activism), ACT-UP (AIDS Coalition to Unleash Power mailing list), PROG-PUBS (progressive campus publications), SAPPHO (lesbian and bisexual women) and SEACnet (Student Environmental Action Coalition). The invention of the World Wide Web (WWW) in 1989 not only widened access to information on the Internet, it also improved the presentation and downloading of information. Some of the earliest alternative media sites to take advantage of WWW technology included EnviroWeb, the clearing house for all online environmental information (mainstream and alternative), and NativeNet, providing information on indigenous peoples around the world on other WWW sites, gopher sites, mailing lists and newsgroups.

Anarchy on the Internet

Anarchist publications were among the first alternative print media to move to the Internet. The American journal *Practical Anarchy Online* was the first anarchist periodical to become available solely in electronic format, replacing its original paper version in 1992. It also offered a form of subscription: its editor would send subscribers an email alerting them to the appearance of a new issue on its website (now a common practice in Web serial publishing). Others might be located on websites that must be browsed in order to discover whether a new issue has appeared, posted to discussion lists such as the Anarchy List or emailed directly to subscribers (of course, a periodical was often 'published' simultaneously by all these methods). Another US journal, *Wind Chill Factor*, based in Chicago, declared in 1993 that 'the cost of printing 5000+ copies per issue [per month] on newsprint is prohibitive' (cited in Atton 1996: 121). It decided to publish quarterly in print, and to issue electronic 'Info-Bulletins' in between as necessary.

Pre-eminent among alternative media sites in the early 1990s was the anarchist site Spunk Press (now known as Spunk Library), which archives many anarchist journals and acts as a distributor for numerous anarchist news services. Its significance and value to the anarchist community does not stop there. Established in 1992 in the Netherlands, but with an international editorial group, its avowed aim was 'to act as an independent publisher of works converted to, or produced in, electronic format and to spread them as far as possible on the Internet . . . free of charge' (Spunk Library Manifesto, available from Spunk Library at www.spunk. org). Spunk Library's catalogue contains essays, speeches and lectures from prominent anarchists, both historical (Bakunin, Goldman) and contemporary (Bookchin, Chomsky). Works by 'dissident' anarchists such as Hakim Bey, Bob Black and the Situationists will also be found here. In common with numerous sites established by new social movements (GreenNet, PeaceNet, McSpotlight, sq@t!net, contrast.org), Spunk Library demonstrates multiple and simultaneous functions at the same time as it exhibits few of the characteristics of a publication, or even those of an institution. Its 'membership' (contributors?) is diffuse, in many cases anonymous – whether for reasons of (perceived) personal security or because personal identity and circumstances are deemed irrelevant. It occupies no single physical space – neither an office nor a library, nor a meeting-place. Such features are of course common to many net-based 'organisations' – what is striking in the case of Spunk Library is the extent to which a given technology is able to be fully integrated into anarchist praxis.

The Internet and new social movements

The most widely cited example of radical Internet use by new social movements is that employed by the Zapatistas in their struggle for the Chiapas region of

Mexico. This has been considered the 'radical ideal' by alternative media commentators and social scientists alike. Manuel Castells' (1997: 79) term for their campaign – 'the first informational guerrilla movement'– is arguably over-technologised. After all, their struggle remains at its heart one for land, and for political and cultural recognition, fought in a number of arenas, only one of which is the informational. Yet the significance of the Chiapas movement's deployment of the Internet has had global reverberations as 'an arena for radical inclusivity' (Ford and Gil 2001: 220). The cross-cultural dialogue that the Zapatistas encouraged through the publishing of their communiqués on the Internet, the support they built up across the world, the visibility their message enjoyed in the mainstream media: all grew out of the deployment of an international communications medium for a project of local resistance. In microcosm, the Zapatistas' struggle represented the burgeoning anti-capitalism movement, itself a development of the holistic tendencies of the environmentalist movement, coming together with groups and movements campaigning for Third World debt relief, human rights, employment rights and social justice.

The Internet did not only publicise the Zapatistas' local struggles but also their methods of political communication and organisation. Their local struggles were effected through the Internet, through a radical internationalisation that most significantly involved anarchist groups in the West. Inspired by the Zapatistas, hitherto separate groups began not only to act in solidarity with each other, but to act together, publishing and protesting as networked 'affinity groups' (Bookchin 1986), as an anarchist model of organising. It is as an electronic complex of informational and communicational possibilities – itself linked with other complexes of previously existing technologies (face-to-face communication, print, music, political demonstrations)   that the Internet holds out such potential for oppositional groups. Since Chiapas we have seen a range of groups, movements and causes based in actual struggle, but having at their communicational, informational and organisational heart the deployment of information and communication technologies (ICTs), using them to present mobilising information, alternative news reports, video and webcam feeds, Internet radio, archives, discussion lists, chat rooms, bulletin boards and sound files.

McSpotlight

Early uses of the Internet by anarchist groups had been more or less fragmented assays into small-scale electronic media production. These saw only small increases in the circulation and reach compared to their print precursors and experienced chronic difficulties in sustaining their media projects economically (Atton 1996). By contrast the development of the McSpotlight website in 1996 demonstrated a more successful strategy based on international networking, a broadening of the protest agenda and the participation of numerous local groups (Atton 2000). The site provided a non-hierarchic centre for a range of diffuse and only informally connected groups and individuals – Bookchin's affinity groups in action. As the site grew to involve more groups, opportunities arose to expand the interests of the site to cover not only the 'McLibel' trial, but the practices of multinational corporations in all countries, and their links with governments and supra-governmental bodies. The site was set up to raise awareness of what became the longest trial in English legal history, when the fast-food company McDonald's took members of the anarchist group London Greenpeace to court for publishing and distributing a leaflet allegedly containing defamatory statements about McDonald's, claiming that the company was responsible, *inter alia*, for the destruction of rainforests to provide land for beef cattle, infringing workers' rights, cruelty to animals and promoting unhealthy eating.

McSpotlight represented a huge advance in the information and communication strategies so far used in the campaign, which had previously relied on small-circulation radical newspapers and magazines, and on the distribution of flyers and pamphlets produced by London Greenpeace. The communication networks that typify the culture of new social movements had already been advanced by the overlapping, various uses of telephones and fax machines. These were used as both intra- and inter-communication devices for movements, as well as weapons for direct action – such as the practice of 'blockading' a target organisation with telephone calls and faxes. Freed from the constraints that these technologies placed on the construction of networks beyond the local, the Internet was able to significantly extend the opportunities for networking beyond the ephemerality of telephone call and fax paper.

McSpotlight was initially termed an 'online interactive library of information' by its founders, expanding the idea of the library to become a space where information was exchanged and created, not merely stored and consulted. The site contained two major archives: one the full trial transcripts, the other an attempt to exhaustively archive print media references to McDonald's. It also hosted a 'debating room', a discussion list, DIY protest guides and campaign leaflets ready to print out 'in over a dozen languages' – even a compressed version of the entire site 'to help ensure that McDonald's will never be able to stop the dissemination of this information.' The site was constructed by a network of volunteers working from 16 countries and called for volunteers: 'HTMLers, programmers, typists, researchers, artistes [*sic*], people with skills we didn't even know we needed till you contacted us' (all references from www.mcspotlight.org/help.html).

The site's purpose was not exhausted by the end of the trial: it continued to campaign against McDonald's, as well as becoming a 'protest node' for a number of campaigns against anti-environmental corporations. McSpotlight not only connected activists to information, it enabled communication among them. Like the Zapatistas, the site's content was grounded in actual struggle. A primary aim of the site was to publicise the McLibel trial in the face of a largely disinterested national media, yet it also delighted in citing those media in its own publicity (the site claimed to have the 'most press coverage of any website' and referred visitors to its extensive press citations and awards). This ambivalence, coupled with the mass media's own fascination with the form and use of the site (over and above its content) complicate the site's characterisation as alternative media, particularly in terms of its processes and its relation to the mass media. What first attracted the mass media to the site were its processes, not its content – it was through this publicity that the content of the site came to a prominence that political and media lobbying might never have reached.

The use of new communication technologies, specifically the Internet, by new social movements can thus be viewed as a double response to informational capitalism and neoliberalism. First, the embedding of Internet practices in a wider socio-economic struggle against the internationalisation of capital can be considered as a globalised, radical-democratic struggle against globalised finance. The anti-capitalist movement's aims and praxis are fundamentally global in reach, while demonstrating the significance of local struggles, not only for those in that locale, but for those who might learn from those struggles. It recontextualises the strategies and tactics of others at the same time as drawing moral, economic and political support from them. Second, the deployment of new communication technologies offers new social movements prefigurative methods of organising (Downing 2001), in particular through the radicalisation of production, to a degree not seen in previous manifestations of social-movement media.

The Internet and popular culture

The Internet is not only used for political ends, of course. It also offers those interested in cultural activities the means to declare and share their passions. Nowhere is this more conspicuous than in the world of fanzines, or ezines, as their electronic equivalents have become known. Ezines and fan-run websites offer opportunities for the creation, maintenance and development of taste communities that cut across geographic boundaries. They act as locations for the celebration of specific genres and artists; they even encourage and enable the creative activities of the fans themselves. It has been claimed that the use of the Internet by fans 'allows greater access to information and association for fans than was ever possible with print fanzines' (Smith 1999: 96–7). Distinguished by the amateur nature of the contributions, editors and writers are autodidacts, obtaining and developing their knowledge through informal, non-institutional means, though specialist roles may arise with fans displaying their knowledge in different domains of expertise. We may think of ezines as 'cultural fora for the exchange and circulation of knowledge and the building of a cultural community' (Fiske 1992: 44–5). These communities often develop to such an extent that ezines appear to stand in for meeting people face to face. Sharing not only information and opinion about a passion, contributors construct and share their own identities with each other. They 'authorise' themselves to speak, validate their lives and make their voices public – at least the parts of those voices that otherwise would not get heard. In the case of ezines, it seems that for many these social acts are constituted wholly through the Internet.

We have also seen the use of the Internet to broadcast to community groups and political activists alike. Irational Radio (http://www.irational.org/radio/) supports information on a range of radio initiatives. It supplies information and contacts for setting up analogue pirate radio as well as DIY guides and software links for webcasting with RealAudio streaming software. Internet radio (usually 'net.radio') encourages a variety of strategies. This need resembles conventional radio only in the notion of broadcasting sound. Using streaming software, only encoding software is required to convert music or spoken word into streamed audio files. Jo Tacchi (2000) has called this technology 'radiogenic' and asks us to consider its products as 'radio.' Some webcasters couple it with live FM transmission; some capture other stations' streamed audio and broadcast that as FM radio. Irational Radio recommends two further options: webcasting another's live stream as part of one's own programming and using archives of streamed audio to build up one's own programmes (just as we have seen new print media constructed from existing print media through strategies of anti-copyright and open distribution; Atton 2002a). The Open Radio Archive Network Group (ORANG, at http://orang.orang.de/) offers hundreds of hours of such material for webcasters to upload and stream as part of their own programming.

Resonance FM, a station broadcasting to central London, began in 1998 under the British government's Restricted Service Licence scheme. While Resonance FM is permitted to broadcast only to listeners in central London, it also streams its broadcast on the Internet in RealAudio and mp3 formats. In one respect, then, it is simply an analogue community radio station with potentially global digital reach. Established as London's 'first art radio station', its general remit is to present music and sonic art operating from the creative fringes. It presents contemporary 'serious' music, free improvised music, electronic music, sound poetry, 'avant rock' and a wide range of sonic art projects that exist even beyond these specialist genres. It seeks to present music from across the globe and to this extent might be thought of as a global radio station in terms of its sources. By twinning its local analogue output with an Internet stream it is able to reach the globally fragmented, minority audience for such music.

Many of these projects have their roots in the subculture of computer hacking. Campaigns of 'electronic civil disobedience' have become increasingly common methods of protest. The use of mass emailing by protesters to governments and corporations has been termed 'Internet guerrilla warfare'. Mass email campaigns can overload Web servers and result in 'denials of service', where Web and email facilities can be immobilised. Even where such blockades do not disrupt access the protest has a publicity function, drawing attention to the cause being supported, or towards the policies and practices of the owners of the targeted website. The Electronic Disturbance Theater's sit-in of the Mexican president's website in 1998 also reveals a creative dimension to such protests: the site's access log was filled with the names of people killed by Mexican government troops during the Chiapas uprising. The electrohippies freely distribute blockading software to enable protest groups to set up their own digital resistance projects, such as ClogScript, FloodScript and Web Script. The Cult of the Dead Cow works on projects that aim to redress the imbalances of opportunity, access and provision of Internet services. For example, the group has worked on methods to email Web pages banned by the Chinese government back to Chinese citizens.

Radical approaches to copyright and creativity have also been tested on the Internet. An example of this is the operating system Linux, established under the notion of 'copyleft'. Copyleft encourages software developers to adapt the Linux system as they see fit, as long as they do not establish it as proprietary. Consequently, Linux has been developed by many authors on a social basis. Linux demonstrates the possibilities of the Internet to be employed for the purposes of social authorship. Other forms of social authorship can threaten the intellectual property rights of commercial organisations. Nowhere is this threat more conspicuous than in the legal and commercial struggles that have been taking place over the development of peer-to-peer (P2P) file-sharing networks such as Napster, Gnutella and Freenet.

A small but growing number of independent musicians are establishing models of social creativity. Like Freenet and Gnutella they take their inspiration from the co-operative and communitarian ventures of the open-source and free-software movements of which Linux is a part. For such musicians, though, the point is to release and distribute not software, but the music itself, using radical copyright licences. The free-music movement explicitly draws on the rhetoric of the free-software movement in its desire to 'free' music for personal copying, distribution and modification through sampling or remixing. The open-source record label Opsound has developed its vision of a digital music commons using a copyleft licence. Opsound invites musicians to contribute their sounds to an online 'open pool'. The copyleft licence allows anyone to copy and distribute the work, or to make derivative works from it through sampling or remixing.

All these initiatives, in their intertwining and redefining of media forms, in their blurring of creator, producer and distributor, suggest hybridised forms of media production particularly well suited to the multimedia possibilities of the Internet and the World Wide Web.

Part II
What's
happening now

6 Radical journalism

....

Introduction
....

Radical journalism is as old as the printing press. In 1776, Thomas Paine helped foment the American Revolution through the distribution of his pamphlets, most notably *Common Sense*, an incendiary piece of radical journalism advocating independence from Britain. And in the decade prior, British MP John Wilkes started a radical weekly publication, the *North Briton*, to lobby criticism at the country's leadership and landed social elite. Wilkes was twice charged with seditious libel for his printed attacks on the king. The second time he was sentenced to jail. Crowds in their thousands gathered outside his prison chanting 'Wilkes and liberty' and other slogans, until soldiers opened fire, killing seven people and leading to disturbances all over London. His case, coupled with electoral and popular support, and the introduction of juries in libel actions, eventually brought about the right of the press to comment, critique and report on parliamentary debate. And in this period, there also existed a dynamic sector of radical newspapers in Britain. These were working-class, largely underground publications that were widely read and read aloud – and played a crucial role in the development of political organisation and critical perspectives for working people.

Radical journalism is decidedly not a new phenomenon.

But what does it mean to talk about radical journalism? We chose to title this section as such to distinguish alternative media practice with a decidedly political purpose, primarily rooted in social movements. Radical journalism as a field, however, covers a wide range of projects across media (both traditional and convergent), from the well-established international papers like the *Nation* and the *New Internationalist*, to *Red Pepper*, *Squall* and *SchNEWS* (featured later in this chapter), to underground radio stations operating during times of civil war and conflict such as Radio B92 in Belgrade and Radio Venceremos in El Salvador, broadcast programmes like *Democracy Now!*, and film and television collectives like Undercurrents, Paper Tiger TV, Big Noise Tactical.

Radical journalism can be seen as reporting from the subject position of someone with an unabashed political perspective, whose ideology is laid bare from the outset without the pretext of distance from their subject. It is not about objective journalism; in fact, it is embedded in a media movement that argues it is mis-leading to presume there is such a thing as unbiased or objective journalism. They argue corporate media are not without bias as they take a subject position rooted in the selling of products in the free-market economy, and have as their primary motivation profit maximisation for company shareholders. These media are unlikely to run a story that challenges the ethics, practices or interests of their advertisers or corporate owners. A Pew Research Center study of the US news media reported that

> they [journalists] fear more than ever that the economic behaviour of their companies is eroding the quality of journalism. In particular, they think busi-ness pressures are making the news they produce thinner and shallower. And they report more cases of advertisers and owners breaching the independ-ence of the newsroom. (Kovach, Rosenstiel and Mitchell 2004)

Nor are commercial or public service broadcasters immune from government inter-ests despite their operational independence.

Out of these critiques, we can trace the rise of 'citizen journalism', a practice of amateur news reporting that is gaining currency well beyond activist media circles. Citizen journalism is a form of participatory media-making whereby 'cit-izens' play an 'active role in the process of collecting, reporting, analyzing and disseminating news and information' with the intention to provide 'independ-ent, reliable, accurate, wide-ranging and relevant information that a democracy requires' (Bowman and Willis 2003).

This kind of journalism scares some people. The factualness of such report-ing is often called into question over fears that it is impossible to be passionate and truthful at the same time. Samuel Freedman argues against this kind of reportage:

> To treat an amateur as equally credible as a professional, to congratulate the wannabe with the title 'journalist,' is only to further erode the line between raw material and finished product. For those people who believe that edit-orial gate-keeping is a form of censorship, if not mind control, then I suppose the absence of any mediating intelligence is considered a good thing.

Citizen journalism – and radical media (they are not the same thing) – asks us to rethink what values we ascribe to professionalism, and what makes a news outlet trustworthy – or, what makes us as individuals trust one media source over another.

In this chapter, we focus primarily on Indymedia. While we could have provided an overview of different radical media projects, Indymedia offers a worthwhile case study across media, utilising a variety of tactics, technologies and forms of participation that can be built upon and aspects replicated for other movements. We begin with a piece from Chris Atton that contextualises both the Indymedia phenomenon and online blogs. His examination provides a useful juxtaposition of both individual and collective projects, through which a fascinating picture emerges of radical journalism in an online world. We then turn to a piece written by Indymedia organisers in the UK who describe the process of creating temporary multimedia centres during mass mobilisations, in this case, surrounding protests against the meeting of the G8 leaders in Gleneagles, Scotland. They offer a valuable and unique insight into the 'on the ground' organising within Indymedia – an important piece of the Indymedia story that is often overlooked. The chapter ends with an excerpt from Brighton-based, alternative newspaper *SchNEWS* that offers an insight into the actual process of creating a regular radical print publication that is as much tongue-in-cheek as it is a portrayal of alternative media in practice.

6.1 Alternative media in practice

Chris Atton

The Indymedia network

Earlier in the book we looked at McSpotlight, which we can consider one of the precursors of the Indymedia network, thought by many the latest and most significant phase of alternative media on the Internet. In this chapter we shall examine some current practices of alternative media using both Indymedia and the more recent phenomenon of blogging as examples. The network of independent media centres (IMCs), also known as the Indymedia network, became a highly visible feature of the media landscape of the global anti-capitalism movement at the turn of the millennium. The Indymedia network came to prominence during the demonstrations in the American city of Seattle against the World Trade Organization summit meeting there on 30 November 1999. The Seattle IMC acted as an independent media focus for the broad coalition of social-justice groups, trade unions, anarchists, socialists, communists, environmental groups and others – a coalition that has come to be known as the anti-capitalist movement. In Seattle the Centre had both a physical and a virtual presence. Its virtual presence on the Web enabled its small core staff to distribute streaming audio and video footage of the demonstrations, as well as written reports, across the world. Technically this was achieved through the use of open-publishing software, where any independent journalist (any activist, for that matter, though the two were often the same) could upload their reports using a pro-forma on the IMC website. No prior approval was needed from the core group, neither was that group responsible for editing the content of reports in any way. Hundreds of hours of audio and video footage and hundreds of thousands of eyewitness reports, analyses and commentary became available to activists, supporters and detractors – to 'global citizens' at large.

Radio Rasa lives (excerpt from interview with Molefi Nolovu by DeeDee Halleck, Durban, South Africa, March 2006)

My name is Molefi Nolovu. I was born in and raised in Soweto, Johannesburg, South Africa. I got involved with the IMC Collective, the Independent Media Center, in Johannesburg in 2002. We are trying to raise awareness around community struggle, publishing on the Web some of the issues that are facing activists, both in the community and in academic institutions. Last year we got a chance to consider the idea of a low-power radio station through equipment donated by various sources including the global network of the IMC. We were able to secure a low-power transmitter and antenna and some microphones.

We called a meeting to get ideas not only from members of the social movements but also the broader activist strata in general that included artists, students, NGO workers and we started to talk about the possibility of low-power radio as a way of organizing and extending some of the IMC initiatives. RASA FM became part of that possible imaginative space where people could not only speak about their problems and social issues but also participate in creating some of the alternatives, making their imaginations come to life and thus the power of RASA FM. The interesting thing is that the radio station drew in quite a lot of young people interested in the issue of access to education.

None of us had been involved in a radio station, let alone producing things for a station. It meant that people had to go into libraries, read up on how you do a program schedule, find out how to interview people, sort out how to find information in the libraries.

We launched the station on June 16, 2005, the national holiday which is the anniversary of the Soweto Uprising, which celebrates the attainment of liberation by youth. We thought to use the session to argue that the conditions of young people have not really changed that much, especially if they are black and are from poor backgrounds. It was good for us to have a theme because it meant that we were able to schedule people for live interviews and discussions, and make the day go smoother.

Most of us ended up sleeping at the station for at least three weeks prior to the launch. There was so much to do. We were panicking about the timing, about whether the transmitter could blow off. So most of us slept at the station writing out scripts, preparing the show, finalizing the program schedule for the day.

When we started broadcasting it was something close to magic. There was no feeling that could ever describe it. It felt like we switched on something that had never been switched on before. The whole area was just abuzz with the 'surround sound' effect of the station. We had phone calls from everyone, saying we are getting it in one part of Soweto, others saying we are finding it in another part. People who had been working so hard to get the station started were gaining the confidence and the knowledge that what we have started is quite amazing. You could see it amongst us. Whereas we had planned to broadcast for four hours we ended up going all the way until midnight! That's the scope of the demand. We couldn't get people out. The people in the neighborhood, the aunties got so excited when they heard the voices of their sons and daughters on the radio. They would come there with all their grandchildren and send their dedication.

When we first imagined it, we thought it would be a mouthpiece for the social movements and things like that. But what ended up happening was that the station started defining its own character. It defined it through the interactions and the voices and expressions from many different people. It generated an identity of its own, something that would be equivalent in commercial or mainstream thinking as 'branding'. In this sense it was an identity that wasn't linked to an issue of exchange.

One afternoon a van from ICASA came. ICASA is the regulatory authority that looks out for licensing and frequency allocation and things like that. This was after six months of successful broadcasting through many difficulties. They didn't just come and say 'you are illegal, get out!' The authorities worked on the psychology of the community as well. The authorities used the licensed radio stations, they used the newspapers, they used all forms of communicating to the generally nervous population which began to see us as a bit too radical and too illegal. Because of its pirate status those that associate with it are criminals and therefore should be locked up in accordance with the law. That's the argument that ICASA pushed.

It became more urgent for us to start speaking about RASA not only as a radio station. It was quite clear that as a radio station they can just turn off the power and that's the way it ends. But RASA was more a calling – something that was calling to arms for people. The airwaves are ours. Communities have the right to produce things that they deem relevant to them, that express their desires, that also speak to the sort of life they would like to live.

Low-power radio can be an alternative radio, not just in terms of quotas and percentages, but real physical participation of people. Ultimately we were shut down and ICASA said that if we were operating in any way, touching any of the equipment, they said they would fine over a million rand for contervening their regulation.

This system manages to shut down peripheral voices by isolating them and individualizing them. However, there are many of us, all over the world, all over the country. There are far more of us than there are of those who want to shut us down. The lesson that we have learned is that the idea is not dead. RASA is not dead. We've been able to create friendships, friendships that are beyond just rhetoric: real friends. We feel we were part of something special, something that was never done before, that has explosive potential, that thousands more people can do and can improve on. The fact that we were there and we chose to take the risks that we did and we maintained it for the length of time that we did even with all the odds against us, sort of solidified the ties amongst us. You can talk with anyone from RASA FM and they will tell you that RASA is still very much alive. The thing now is to think about how do we learn from the experiences we have had, but also how can we spread it as well.

Such independent accounts provide a powerful counter to the enduring frames of social-movement coverage in mainstream media. A study of the framing of the women's movement by US print media (Ashley and Olson 1998) presents what have become standard responses in the mainstream media to social-movement actors, their aims and their ideologies. Ashley and Olson found dominant patterns and emphases on surface details, the delegitimisation of feminists and their depiction as disorganised and riven by conflict. Framing devices were used to minimise ideological threats by representing the actors as deviants on the margins of society (a tactic which also exaggerates such threats to the status quo and to 'reasonable' people). These frames are widespread in mainstream coverage of social movements. The ideologies and practices of social-movement actors become simplified and homogenised; mainstream framing devices render deeper explorations of social-movement activity unavailable. By homogenising varieties of dissent the mass media reify protest and limit the richness of ideologies and actions, often through a crudely simplified single example, such as we saw during the Genoa protests in July 2001, where a photograph of a masked protester, standing defiantly on an overturned car, was reproduced throughout the mainstream media to represent the entire protest movement. By contrast, social-movement ideologies and practices are complex and internally contradictory (or so it seems, with socialists working with greens, anarchists with socialists, the different hue of green politics, organised groups working with grassroots individuals) – social-movement activity is a process, not simply a series of events – it is 'a network of *active relationships* between actors who interact, communicate, influence each other, negotiate, and make decisions' (Melucci 1996: 71; original emphasis).

Since Seattle, the Indymedia network has expanded. There are now more than 150 IMCs across the world. The concentration remains greatest in the US and Europe (15 are in the UK). Other regions are far less well represented. There are none in India and only three in Africa. The network operates a unique form of editorial control. While reports may be uploaded from or by any source, the editorial group reserves the right to remove contributions judged unsuitable. The 'Publish' page of Indymedia (www.indymedia.org/publish.php3) states that 'The Independent Media Center is a collectively run media outlet for the creation of radical, *accurate*, and passionate tellings of the truth' (author's emphasis). Towards this aim the collective state that 'while we struggle to maintain the news wire as a completely open forum we do monitor it and remove posts.' The large majority of these posts are removed for 'being comments, not news, duplicate posts, obviously false or libellous posts, or inappropriate content [such as hate speech].' Indymedia do, however, still make these posts available in a separate page titled 'hidden stories' (www.indymedia.org/search-process.php3?hidden=true). While editing does take place, it does not prevent voices from being heard, nor prevent users from accessing that content. Neither does this quasi-editorial function of the core group extend to the editing of individual pieces of work: if they do not breach the criteria set out above, then pieces will remain on the 'open' pages of the site. These limitations apart, Indymedia enables any activists to contribute their work. The use of open source software bypasses the need for an editor or webmaster to upload contributions: writers and producers may do this themselves, using the pro-forma on the 'Publish' page.

Each IMC is run by a small collective who know each other well and who tend to share tasks and responsibilities. However, we should not think of this as an elitist group, a command post that directs the work of others. The features of its organisational structure – broadly collective, egalitarian, non-hierarchical – it shares with many alternative and radical media projects. John Downing (2002) locates such features in a continuing tradition of socialist anarchism, finding a tendency to organise on an 'anti-mass' level, privileging local affinity groups connected informally through international networks of solidarity and resource-sharing. From the perspective of both producers and consumers (often the same people when we are talking about activists) Indymedia functions as a content-aggregator of independent journalism, organised by country, issue and medium (text, audio, video, multimedia). Not only do journalists place original, previously unpublished work there, IMCs themselves will often link to already-broadcast or published reports. To consider Indymedia as an organisation is to consider it as a network of independent, collectively run 'nodes' through which independent journalists may circulate their work, largely unimpeded by the gatekeeping of those collectives.

Indymedia journalists offer news and narratives from the point of view of activists themselves: the journalists are indeed activists themselves. Throughout their history alternative media have privileged amateur journalists who are writing from a position of engagement with the event or process that is their subject (Hamilton and Atton 2001). 'Amateur' here has everything to say about commitment to radical intellectual and social practices; it has nothing to do with the common notion of the amateur as the ignorant, self-deceived dabbler. These amateur journalists – explicitly partisan – report from the 'front line', from the grassroots, from within the movements and communities they thus come to represent. The reporters' active, lived presence within events, while no guarantor of impartiality, enables the production of news that tells other stories from those reported in the mainstream: 'our news, not theirs.' (It is noteworthy that the

international network of alternative media scholars and practitioners calls itself
OurMedia.) This is a radical process of reporting where activists become journalists, and where grassroots reporting and analysis take place within movements
and communities. The work of grassroots activists exemplifies the passage of participants in a demonstration to activist-journalists, while remaining positioned as
'rank and file' within those movements.

Blogs and blogging

A more individual, but often no less radical, form of alternative journalism is the
blog. Blogs (originally 'Web logs') are personal Web pages used for a number of
purposes: to post commentaries on mainstream news; to enable discussion with
and among visitors to their sites and, significantly, to originate their own news.
Blogging is, if you like, a less networked and less social-movement-minded version of the global network of Indymedia, applying similar principles of activist
reporting, media critique, discussion and dialogue among its writers and readers.

The blog has become a focal point for much mainstream media attention,
perhaps due to its personal roots, enabling mainstream journalism to develop
human-interest stories around its creators rather more easily than it can explore
the more abstract, political goals of networks such as Indymedia. During the
Gulf War of 2003, mainstream media attention was drawn to bloggers posting
from within Iraq during the conflict. 'Smash', the pseudonym of an American
military officer serving in Iraq, posted chronicles of his experiences – along with
critiques of the conflict – on his website (Kurtz 2003). Blogs were also posted
by professional journalists 'moonlighting' from their day jobs. These included
BBC reporters such as Stuart Hughes. The BBC and the British *Guardian* newspaper established 'warblog' sites during the conflict. Blogs were also employed
by NGOs such as Greenpeace as well as by those claiming to be Baghdadi residents, such as 'Salam Pax'. The US journal *New Republic* ran an online diary by
Kanan Makiya, a leading Iraqi dissident. Despite this range of voices Matheson and Allan (2003) find common features. They note that even the professional
reporters tended to eschew the established standards of objectivity and impartiality, preferring instead a style of address that has more in common with what
has been termed activist or 'native' reporting (Atton 2002a). That is to say, they
wrote from direct, personal experience about that experience and emphasised
their independence from organisational or administrative constraints. From their
interviews with professional journalists who maintained blogs during the war
Matheson and Allan find that it is these aspects of their writing that the reporters believe resonated with their readers; it was the direct, 'authentic' account of
personal experience that counted in the midst of mainstream coverage dominated
by the carefully controlled output of 'embedded' journalists. It is, they argue, the
transparency of such methods (just as we have seen in other examples of native
reporting) that establishes trust between writer and reader. It is this relationship,

developed from subjective modes of address, when coupled with disillusionment and scepticism towards the mass media, makes the blog a valuable site for reimagining news practices. For the weblog, trustworthiness springs from the setting up of a subjective position from which to write about one's own experiences – it is less to do with the facticity of the reporting. It is, as Matheson and Allan show, the connectedness that a sharing of personal experience between writer and reader can bring that is emblematic of this 'new' journalism.

This journalism is less focused on the journalist as expert and the report as a commodity produced by a news organisation; instead it proposes a relationship between writer and reader where epistemological claims may be made about the status of journalism and its practitioners. This has less to do with the novelty of the knowledge being produced (a focus on uncovering 'hidden' stories); rather it suggests new ways of thinking about and producing journalism (a focus on what kinds of knowledge are produced and how readers and writers may come together to make sense of them). Arguably such practices are not new – writers such as Jack London and George Orwell had performed similar styles of native reporting in their literary journalism (Atton 2002b). What distinguishes the present examples is the space in which they take place; the medium of the Internet enables the publication of such reports outside the channels of the publishing industry or media corporations. It is arguable, though, that the work of the Iraq warbloggers came to public attention precisely through these channels and thus came to be considered within the established techniques of media framing as 'celebrities.' This only remains a problem, however, if we insist on some kind of 'purity' (or isolationism) for a field of alternative journalism. If the most powerful outcome of these new practices is to challenge the existing means of news production, then it is of less significance how we come to learn about such challenges. (Just as this book is the product of commercial, industrial arrangements, yet is able to inform us about methods of media organisation and production quite different from its own.)

The emergence of blogs offers individuals the opportunity to create their own news sites, though in the main these tend to personal commentary and opinion. However, in times of crisis and as circumstances permit, bloggers are able to offer us eyewitness accounts. We see here a deployment of various radical journalism methods, encompassing first-person native reports; radical critiques of government policies, government actions and the mass media; the occasional use of mainstream and 'radical mainstream' sources; and the creation of spaces for discussion and debate. The picture of radical online journalism thus presented is one that is heterogeneous, flexible and responsive. Above all, it offers a challenging critique to dominant news values and practices.

6.2 Indymedia and the politics of participation

Reporting the G8 in Scotland, 2005

'Sam and Annie'

> I've heard it described as feeling like you're walking in to a big collective brain. Everything pulsing this way and that, information rushing around, spreading out and taking in information. It's a high tech temporary autonomous zone. (Evan, personal interview, 2001)

The miracle of alternative media – the politics of participation

During the protests against the 2005 G8 Summit in Scotland, amidst the largest police and security operation in the UK since the Second World War, people marched in the hundreds of thousands, blocked roads and motorways, partied on bridges, created community gardens and eco-camps, held counter-conferences and fought with riot police. Some faced surveillance, harassment, dirty tricks, mass detentions and violence from police; some waved flags, attended concerts, lobbied MPs and signed petitions. And yet there is only one place where you can see an almost complete archive of these events: a place called Indymedia.

During the protests, over 2,300 photographs and hundreds of written reports were published on the open-publishing newswire of the indymedia.org.uk website, creating an in-depth record of the various mobilisations that sought to challenge the legitimacy of the G8 and the policies it represents.

The front-page Indymedia article on the opening day of the G8 Summit linked directly to 93 reports, including 36 photo essays and ten video reports. It covered events across Scotland in Edinburgh, Glasgow, Stirling and Gleneagles, each of them with their own up-to-the-minute timeline, while international solidarity actions were reported from eight cities in six different countries.

That day, the Indymedia UK website recorded 1.5 million hits, with at least one million on each of the other protest days. During big mobilisations, many

G8

The Group of Eight is made up of the leaders of the eight most powerful states and meets annually. The official G8 Scotland website is www.g8.gov.uk. For critical analysis, see International Financial Institution Watch at www.ifiwatchnet.org.

people are logging onto the Indymedia websites to get the news direct from the streets – raw, radical and unfiltered by the restrictions of mainstream media.

This is the public face of Indymedia. It's what most people see – an alternative news website, providing counter-information and coverage of the protests. But the real story of Indymedia is what happens behind the smooth surface of the computer screens: the people, the places, the technology, the infrastructure, the networks, the organising – the Indymedia politics of participation – and how the whole G8 reporting operation was achieved for around £3,500 – less than the cost of one professional TV camera.

In the Second Declaration of La Realidad in 1997, the Zapatistas called for the creation of an 'intercontinental network of alternative communication'. This is the real story of the Indymedia network, complete with online and offline communication tools and meeting spaces, and a commitment to non-hierarchical organising, consensus decision-making and openness.

In writing about our G8 experiences, we hope to convey a glimpse of the raw, on-the-ground reality of setting up and running an independent media centre for a big mobilisation. But if you really want to know about Indymedia, you are best off getting in touch with a local collective near you, and learning through doing.

Free software, open publishing and the pooling of resources in the global Indymedia networks

In today's age of universal blogging, the self-publishing of your own text or photographs seems easy, but in 1999, the software to do this had to be built from scratch. Thus an important point of reference for Indymedia is the Free Software Movement which generates software that is free for studying, copying, changing and distributing. The code that enables Indymedia to run a system of 'Open Publishing' is free software, and is shared across IMC collectives throughout the world.

The sharing and distributing of resources is a powerful practice for every local Indymedia collective. Each of the almost 150 local nodes can draw on a global network of skills. We share technical infrastructure (servers, bandwidth, technical skills) as well as many other resources ranging from expertise in media-making or non-hierarchical organising to operating video cameras.

Since 1999, Indymedia UK has grown from a single small collective to become the 'United Kollektives'. It now has local nodes in 13 cities and regions from Scotland to Brighton. For the G8 reporting operation, we really benefited from this network of nodes because it allowed reporting to exist in a decentralised fashion, both technically and organisationally.

But it is not just those who identify themselves as hardcore Indymedia volunteers that make it all happen. Sometimes the name Indymedia is just a convenient banner under which media activists gather and co-ordinate. In Scotland, the G8 reporting saw collaborations with numerous media groups including Beyond TV,

Figure 6.1 Indymedia centre

Bristol Wireless, Camcorder Guerillas, KanalB, Leith FM, Pilton Video, Psand, *Red Pepper* magazine, *SchNEWS*, Undercurrents and the *Variant* magazine, to name just a few.

Setting up independent media centres – temporary autonomous zones in the midst of global protest

The set-up sounds simple: find a space, get enough computers, connect them to the Internet, then people will come and write their reports, post their pictures and phone in to the news dispatch centre to report what's happening in the streets and at the protests (see http://docs.indymedia.org/view/Local/ImcUkG8Dispatch).

In practice there is always more: rewiring the mains electricity circuit; sourcing enough power cables (and then tables to stick 50 computers on and chairs to go with them), finding transport for all the kit, making sure phone lines and cables are working, juggling with printer drivers, sourcing smoke detectors and fire extinguishers, making banners and flyers, publishing the reporting telephone numbers, finding safe places for people to sleep, liaising with a dozen different groups, sticking maps of Gleneagles on the wall, getting enough coffee and food to keep people going, holding meetings to involve people and to decide on opening times and access procedures, designing information flows, making exhaustive lists of events to cover, identifying tasks and making rotas, and dealing with the police . . . all this before even opening the doors.

Every physical independent media centre that has been built has differed in its size, shape and the level of organisation and co-ordination. Some have been just a room to meet up in and plan coverage, like in Prague for the International Monetary Fund (IMF)/World Bank meeting in 2000. There, media activists used public Internet cafés to work from, making it almost impossible for the repressive Czech authorities to shut down the IMC operation. In the US, several media centres have had serious financial funding, running to tens of thousands of US dollars, allowing for the creation of more elaborate infrastructure.

Every centre is an experiment in on-the-ground horizontal organising, in participatory media-making – and in reporting the truth often obscured by the mainstream media.

Fighting a media war

Most of the early independent media centres were first set up to report the emerging large-scale mobilisations of the movement against neoliberal globalisation. They were set up to counter what activists saw as the mainstream media's refusal to accurately cover either the reasons why people were protesting or what was actually happening at the protests themselves.

The first Indymedia website in 1999, covering the Seattle WTO protests, published pictures and footage of riot police firing tear gas and rubber bullets at point-blank range into crowds of peaceful protesters – while the major TV news networks were still denying that police were attacking people. Indymedia UK was set up following the 18 June International Carnival against Capitalism protests in 1999. Many UK newspapers were demonising campaigners, some running ludicrous horror stories claiming anti-globalisation protesters planned to attack police from the London Underground ventilation shafts, using samurai swords!

While public dialogue on issues of climate change, poverty and global trade has become more commonplace since then, the 2005 G8 represented a massive media coup for the UK Government – and by default, the G8.

Previous G8 summits had seen united protests by all sections of the political spectrum, with huge marches held alongside spectacular mass civil disobedience. But, for 2005, a joint strategy hatched by the major developmental NGOs along with Prime Minister Tony Blair and Chancellor Gordon Brown, succeeded in dividing the mobilisation.

In short, the 'Make Poverty History' coalition headed by Oxfam sought to capture public concern over global inequality by supporting the UK government's position on aid and debt at the G8. They scheduled their massive demonstration to take place the weekend before the G8, thus legitimising the summit itself and distancing themselves from any other form of protest. 'When the Chancellor publicly backs a G8 protest you have to wonder what's going on', noted one television commentator. They also capitalised on the 20th anniversary of Live Aid, with celebrity stars Bob Geldof and Bono staging massive publicly hyped pop concerts.

'Why anyone would want to protest against the G8 is beyond me,' said Tony Blair after appearing in a photo call with Geldof, much to the annoyance of many of the smaller national and international NGOs. In fact, the 'Live 8' concerts got more newspaper column inches than either the protests or the issues behind them, including the Make Poverty History march itself, and the coverage of the actual summit negotiations and outcomes.

It is worth noting that even the major NGOs later realised they had made a public-relations mistake. The G8 finished without anything near the outcomes they had desired, while Geldof, without consulting them, declared the G8 a massive success for the world's poor.

In terms of the media war, the UK Government had succeeded in dividing the opposition into 'good' and 'bad' protesters, and in doing so obscuring the more critical NGO voices. It was the 'bad protesters' including the 'Dissent! Network' of grassroots direct action groups from across the UK and 'G8Alternatives', a coalition of smaller Scottish NGOs, trade unions, anti-war and Trotskyist groups, that most used Indymedia to tell their stories.

Making media on shifting grounds: geography, locations and logistics in Scotland
....

Since the violent confrontations at the Genoa G8 Summit in 2001, the G8 has retreated from urban environments and instead been hidden away in relatively rural or isolated places. For 2005, the exclusive Gleneagles Hotel in the Scottish Highlands was chosen as the summit location, protected by a concrete and steel cordon, helicopters and thousands of police supported by the military. This retreat makes it difficult to voice dissent anywhere near the G8, let alone report about those protests that do happen.

In Scotland, we wanted to set up a media infrastructure that would allow protesters to tell their own stories straight from the action, rather than running an exclusive media operation staffed by 'professional protest reporters'. To achieve this, we knew Indymedia had to be located wherever the protesters themselves would be: in demonstrations, crash spaces, campsites and convergence centres.

It became clear that people would gather and demonstrate in several different locations, both rural and urban. But until the last moment nobody knew the exact locations. Protest plans kept changing and several negotiations for the main convergence campsite fell through at the last minute due to police interference, as is the case with many Indymedia operations: the ground keeps shifting

What's a Wiki?

'Wikis' are online content-management platforms that encourage collaboration. They can be edited via a Web browser, without knowledge of mark-up languages like html. A wealth of experiences is documented on the Indymedia Wiki at: http//docs.indymedia.org/view/Local/ImcUkG8.

and changing each day and plans have to be flexible to take account of each new development.

In an attempt to be true to the slogan 'We are everywhere!', we accumulated enough equipment to set up physical media centres, or at least public Internet access points, in as many places as possible, connected through the collective use of IRC (Internet relay chat) channels, mobile phones and roving reporters. We bought 50 Pentium III computers and two local computer-recycling charities lent us the same number of monitors. Tables and chairs were borrowed from a local trade union. Many people brought their own equipment, and others lent some expensive kit. 'Blagging and borrowing' has always been a maxim for Indymedia, multiplying the value of goods by sharing them.

Urban IMC spaces and technologies in Scotland

The main spaces that Indymedia operated from were quite diverse, both in locations and technologies.

In Glasgow, a few activists from Germany grabbed a bunch of equipment and set up public-access reporting computers in a former hat factory turned squatted convergence centre. Internet bandwidth was borrowed wirelessly from a supportive neighbour: dirty lo-tech DIY media at its best.

The core backbone of the Indymedia operation was set up in a spacious nineteenth-century chapel in Edinburgh's centre. Owned by a charity, it was home to 'the Forest', a volunteer-based arts café and bar, and an existing hub for creative and alternative culture within the city.

With the Indymedia Centre on the first floor, it became one of the main communication nodes for the G8 protests, complete with a social vibe. Sharing the building with the Forest Café meant liaising closely with its collective of volunteers, carefully negotiating boundaries, responsibilities and working out how to co-operate in what we knew was going to be a hectic period. One great moment was a 'spontaneous' street party outside the building on the first day of demonstrations. The café removed its front windows to make a stage for bands and DJs. The Infernal Noise Brigade's drums echoed off the surrounding buildings, while people danced late into the night under an Indymedia banner written in Gaelic.

The IMC space was open to everyone wanting to produce grassroots media coverage. As is often standard Indymedia practice, mainstream media were banned, as all too often they simply pitch up and ask, 'Where's the riot then?' We had confirmed reports of mainstream TV crews candidly stating, 'We're only interested in filming the violence'.

Interestingly, the *Guardian* set up its own 'independent journalist media centre' by hiring a small central internet café, making it available for 'bloggers' as well as the updating of 'independent news websites'. The National Union of Journalists (NUJ) supported the creation of a small centre to encourage media coverage of the main counter-conferences. It seems the idea of temporary ad hoc 'independent' media centres is spreading . . . though the replications fail at the most important hurdle: participatory and transparent organising.

'Field Indymedia' Stirling: frontline reporting at the eco-village

Most people engaged in direct action such as road blockades were staying in the rural convergence eco-village campsite ('Hori-Zone') in a field outside Stirling. The Indymedia presence here was a mix of high- and low-tech. A satellite truck from mobile media veterans Psand provided Internet connectivity, while 20 old Pentium I laptops from Bristol Wireless were 'regenerated' with free open source software, and used as open access internet terminals in a big marquee. More modern computers were used to upload picture reports and to stream audio coverage. Power came partly from solar panels, but mostly from an eco-friendly bio-diesel generator – which was how much of the camp was powered.

While the level of co-ordination here was lower than at the Edinburgh centre, the atmosphere was more frenetic and infectious. Field Indymedia Stirling was frequently surrounded by riot police, and helicopters droned constantly overhead. A small Indymedia team at the campsite was reinforced by a wider group of volunteers coalescing around the computers, from the US, Australia, New Zealand, Spain, France, Austria, Germany, the Netherlands, Ireland, and several cities in the UK. From the feedback report: 'Some really fucking fantastic people came forward to help . . . People who had never even considered doing this type of work came forward and rose to the challenge.'

The Edinburgh backbone: reporting and co-ordination

Almost 1,000 people registered to use the Edinburgh media centre over the main week of protests. When the doors opened, we had around 25 public terminals providing access to the Internet, hubs for people to plug their laptops into, and dedicated workspaces for video, audio, photo, and the core function of news reporting

Figure 6.2 Inside and outside the IMC tent

known as 'Dispatch'. The Dispatch team received news via phone, chat, or face-to-face from eyewitnesses. In close collaboration with Indymedia volunteers in other countries, it ensured that reports were confirmed, processed and published.

The Radical Radio Coalition set up a studio within the IMC. They streamed live news and pre-recorded content over the Internet. Using open source audio software, they fully recorded and published some of the counter-conference events held by the more progressive and radical NGOs. The content was being used by FM radio stations in the UK, Spain, Italy, US, Germany and Africa, in addition to internet radio stations. Prior to the G8 itself, radio activists had worked with local groups to produce programming that aired on local community radio.

A team of experienced video activists ensured that all major events were covered by video cameras. They helped people coming into the centre with their own footage and edited short rushes for daily publication on the Web. In total the video teams published 72 segments of video reports. Highlights were burned onto CD or DVD for screenings and distribution at the various activist centres, so that people could see what had happened in all the locations.

A photo desk provided a speedy drop off point where people with cameras could dump their memory cards and get back out on the streets as quickly as possible to carry on reporting. Volunteers helped people publish their pictures, and advised them on legal and safety issues. Organising production into teams worked well and ensured a higher than average standard of published material.

Edinburgh IMC: service provider or participatory project?

The tension between the twin functions of setting up technical infrastructure to allow people to report their own news during a big protest and that of encouraging non-hierarchical mass participation has been with Indymedia since its inception. Dedicated Indymedia activists sometimes get frustrated at 'being reduced to running a glorified internet café' or spending endless hours administering the websites instead of getting out on the streets, protesting and reporting. Indymedia has become an element people expect to see at any large mobilisation. They expect to find online and offline facilities up and running ready for use, without necessarily feeling the need to contribute to the overall running of the spaces or infrastructure.

So what is Indymedia? – an alternative service provider or a participatory project? An almost professional news service, or a dirty, punky DIY project? The answer keeps shifting from one extreme to the other, but for the most part it is often to be found somewhere in the grey area, around the middle – and that's how we like it.

The first casualty of war . . .

'The first casualty of war is truth' runs the saying. An emergent pattern at large international protests, including previous G8 Summits, has been that Indymedia itself became a target. Media Centres have been raided by riot police, sometimes firing stun grenades and tear gas, our equipment has been smashed, our footage seized, and reporters beaten by plain clothes police dressed as black bloc rioters. Sometimes telling the truth can be a dangerous pastime.

The backend electronic infrastructure of Indymedia has also been targeted. In 2004, one week before the European Social Forum, two IMC servers in London hosting over 20 Indymedia websites, were seized under international jurisdiction. Then, one month before the 2005 G8 Summit itself, IMC Bristol's server was seized by police and one Indymedia volunteer arrested.

In the UK, Indymedia has been defended and supported by journalist organisations, electronic privacy and civil liberty groups, including the NUJ, the International Federation of Journalists (IFJ), Reporters without Borders, the APC Network, Privacy International, Statewatch, Article 19, Liberty, Amnesty and IFEX. Even so, those of us planning the G8 media centres were taking issues of security very seriously. Backup locations were organised to continue reporting in case the media centres were raided, and safe locations for important footage or photos were found. In fact, the Edinburgh IMC was the first European G8 media centre not to be violently raided by the police. But the constant presence of the police Forward Intelligence Teams (FIT) outside the building, photographing, stopping and searching, and sometimes arresting people, served a similar purpose: to intimidate and harass those using the Media Centre.

Internet connectivity was a constant problem at the centre. The existing connection fluctuated wildly, to the point of becoming unusable. Orders for additional ADSL lines were mysteriously delayed until after the protests. Luckily, in today's multi-connected world, it is almost impossible for companies to cut off Internet communication to a whole building - local geeks came to the rescue and erected a powerful wireless antenna on the roof.

During big protests, mainstream media tends to rely on the police as their primary information source, while Indymedia relies on protesters and campaigners. During the G8 2005 in Scotland, Indymedia reported on a host of dirty tricks employed by the police. On the main day of action against the G8, the police announced that the organised protest march at Gleneagles had been cancelled. This was then relayed by much of the mainstream media. Within minutes, however, a statement from the march organisers taken over the phone by Indymedia volunteers was posted to the Indymedia website confirming the march was still on. At the same time, Indymedia reported that police in Edinburgh were preventing people from boarding coaches destined for Gleneagles, and stopping those already underway.

Prior to the main day of action, Indymedia reported how police were targeting volunteer street medics and legal observers for arrest. In an underhand tactic that could only be described as 'chemical warfare by proxy', police refused to allow sewage trucks into the Hori-Zone campsite to empty the toilets – two stories you could only read on Indymedia.

After the mobilisation

While many protesters go home after the day's events, Indymedia keeps working, often long into the night. After the G8 the task of reporting continued: making sense of the huge amount of content; arranging it into chronological order; archiving audio, pictures and video; writing up summaries and feedback reports; following up on the criticisms of the official G8 outcomes; and getting updates on the 700 or so people who had been detained or arrested.

The buildings and campsites needed to be cleaned and cleared, and borrowed kit returned. Almost all of the 50 Media Centre computers were donated to local Indymedia groups and social centres, and Indymedia Scotland were left with a good deal of equipment and a usable media space.

Evaluations about what was achieved, with lessons learnt and recommendations

Additional articles on Indymedia

There are too many articles to name them all, check the IMC Essay Collection: http//docs.indymedia.org/view/Global/ImcEssayCollection. We particularly like the account in Chris Shumway's thesis and the interview in *We Are Everywhere*.

for future media centres, were written up. These texts, together with pictures of the media centres, are available online (http://docs.indymedia.org/view/Local/ImcUkG8).

This was the largest and most ambitious alternative media operation organised by the Indymedia UK Network to date. It was tremendously successful in terms of the quality, variety and number of reports. More importantly, people reclaimed their own media, and volunteered their time, energy and expertise for free, truly living up to the Indymedia motto 'Don't hate the Media, Be the media'.

6.3 SchNEWS at ten

(Excerpted from *SchNEWS* 10th anniversary edition)

SchNEWS was born in a squatted courthouse in Brighton in 1994 as part of Justice? – Brighton's campaign against the Criminal Justice Act. A few bright sparks decided to start reading out the news. Some of those bright sparks then decided to put some of it on paper – nearly ten years later and we're still printing! From the anti-road protests at the M11 in London to the Newbury Bypass to the big Reclaim the Streets events of the 1990s, *SchNEWS* was there. From workers' struggles such as the Liverpool dockers and fights against privatisation of public services to reporting on social centres and sustainable futures – week in week out *SchNEWS* reported the news from the direct action front lines.

Then in February 1998 some of the crew went to Geneva to the first ever Peoples' Global Action conference. Here we met people involved in grassroots movements from across the world, swapped stories, made friendships and began to see the bigger picture, and with many others who had been involved in localised direct action campaigns, our attention now turned to also attacking the corporate carve-up of the entire planet while supporting the diverse small-scale alternatives. The first signs of this new shift were in May 1998 when mass demonstrations were held world-wide simultaneously against the G7 Summit in Birmingham, then again on 18 June 1999 (J18). But it was the mass protests against the WTO in Seattle in November 1999 that really brought this 'movement' to the world's attention.

It is impossible to know how many people read *SchNEWS* every week, particularly now with the Internet. Out of the 2,000 that get printed (more for big festies and demos) 650 get posted out each week to everyone from subscribers to bookshops to around 50 prisoners around the world who get it each week for free. Add to that over 11,000 email subscribers, many of whom get it as a pdf file (so it looks exactly like the real thing). While many photocopy and distribute their paper copy locally, pdf files allow people all over the world to print out *SchNEWS*, and distribute it, before it has even hit the streets in Brighton! We often hear from people who print out pdfs and distribute each week – at infoshops or wholefood shops, on campuses and out on the streets, all over the world. Added to that, popular sites like Urban 75 mirror *SchNEWS* each week, while A-Infos news service email it out internationally to subscribers, and the odd issue gets translated into other languages – someone has even put a *SchNEWS* site out in Russian! So as well as the fourteen thousand or so who visit the *SchNEWS* site each week, it is hard to work out how many we reach altogether. Our Party and Protest section is the most popular feature on our website, updated every week with a mishmash of festival dates, meetings and demos as well as a section on where to go if you want to find out radical contact points around the country. Our DIY guide has useful tips on everything from setting up your own newsletter to making your own bio-diesel. We also try to continually update our contacts list – currently listing over 800 useful grassroots organisations.

So who funds all this?

SchNEWS is run on a voluntary basis – no one gets paid – though we do manage to blag free into gigs and festivals (to spread the word of course) and when our treasurer's not looking, raid the petty-cash tin for biscuit money. Our stories originate anywhere from anarchist literature to the dodgy *Financial Times* (no, really), from conversations in the pub to the Internet. While we always try to be as accurate as possible and chase people up to verify the stories, the idea behind *SchNEWS* is not to believe the printed word, but to get up off yer arse and go and see for yourself. So articles are often first-hand accounts from trusted sources or ourselves as we storm all over the country causing trouble/saving the world/having a laugh.

Wake up! wake up! – it's yer typical SchNEWS week . . .

* Monday/Tuesday evening: We get well over 500 emails a week, and a few people have the job of going though all these, answering queries and deciding which ones might become stories.

* Wednesday: Start writing and researching *SchNEWS*, go through all the mail, decide roughly what we are going to cover this week.

* Thursday: More writing, except it's usually a bit more frantic 'cos we've got to get it all finished and last minute updates come in. Writers go to pub.

* Thursday early evening: Desktop publishing (DTP) crew come in and do their stuff, somehow managing to crush a tonne of information into two bits of A4. DTPers usually make it to pub.

* Thursday bit later in the evening: Web crew come in, *SchNEWS* gets put on the Web and emailed out to thousands across the globe. Web crew never get to pub. Honest.

* Friday 9 am: Hot off the press. A bleary-eyed person prints up the *SchNEWS* at the Resource Centre for distribution round Brighton and back to the office for . . .

* Friday afternoons: The mail-out crew sends it out to all our paper subscribers.

* Weekends: Depending on the weather/time of year you might see us at festivals, gigs or conferences or handing out *SchNEWS* to passers-by in the street.

As for who keeps us going . . . Well, since our office rent was introduced we reckon to be spending around £24,000 a year on rent, printing, stamps, telephone, computers, envelopes, stationary, email accounts, (biscuits) . . . we rely entirely on subscriptions, benefit gigs and our readers' generosity to keep us afloat.

Finally, *SchNEWS* is an open collective; we are always looking for new people to get involved. So if you like reading the news the mainstream tends to ignore (or at best turns into a crap lifestyle feature, rather than why an action is going on) take a look in the next column and see if anything grabs your fancy.

Don't let the fact that *SchNEWS* comes out every week lull you into a false sense of security! We constantly need more people to get involved. We guestimate *SchNEWS* reaches around 50,000 people a week.

Not bad for a scrappy no-adverts no-compromise bit of A4, eh?

7 Experimental forms

Introduction

The previous chapter focused on alternative media as the suppliers of information and opinion that are unavailable in, and excluded by, dominant media. This is perhaps the most obvious and, many would say, the most vital function of alternative media. It is, however, not their only function. This chapter focuses not so much on the issue of alternative content, as on the 'alternative' ways in which that content can be delivered.

Isaac Julien argues that a radical filmmaking practice needs to encompass not only the 'representation of politics' but also the 'politics of representation' (Julien 2006). One of the implications of this is that any truly 'alternative' media work will need to transform the medium itself, change the way in which it is used, and find alternative styles and different languages in which to express itself, if its 'alternativeness' is to be maintained. In fact most alternative media over the years have involved a degree of this sort of experimentation, as we saw in Alan Fountain's exploration of the film avant-garde (chapter 3) or Angela Phillips' look at the explosive visual effect of offset litho in the alternative press (chapter 4). We have also seen how radio, as the earliest broadcast medium, has historically been a space for experimentation in sound and wireless technology (chapter 2), and we also look in more depth at the emergence of Resonance FM, a community radio station in London dedicated to creative exploration of sound and audio art (in chapters 5 and 8).

However, many alternative media activists share the fear of Paul O'Connor (of Undercurrents), that 'many "arty" videos soon end up staying on the shelf if the message isn't clear' (quoted in Waltz 2005: 53). David Garcia believes that this suspicion of 'art' has recently produced a

> deep split which has opened up between many of the activists at the core of the new political movements and the artists or theorists who, while continuing to see themselves as radicals, retain a belief in the importance of cultural (and information) politics in any movement for social transformation. Although I have little more than personal experience and anecdotal evidence

to go on, it seems to me that there is a significant growth in suspicion and frequently outright hostility among activists over the presence of art and artists in 'the movement', particularly those whose work cannot be immediately instrumentalised by the new 'soldiers of the left'. (Garcia 2006)

This split has always been there, in different degrees, over the last few decades, but the common ground has too. It is evident that the subversive and exploratory tendencies of some contemporary art movements frequently push artists into territory covered by our definition of 'alternative media'. Cate Elwes shows how video artists were involved both in making the Miners' Campaign Tapes in the 1980s (Elwes 2005: 118) and in the alternative media activity that arose in response to the AIDS crisis in the same decade (ibid.: 65–8). Mitzi Waltz also devotes a chapter of her book to what she terms 'Artistic Impulses' (Waltz 2005: 67–76), in which she looks at work encompassing print, radio, television and performance. Also, groups like the Critical Art Ensemble effectively straddle the art/politics divide. They explain on their website that they are exploring the 'intersections between art, technology, radical politics and critical theory'. They use a tactical-media model, which they describe as 'situational, ephemeral and self-terminating', to 'create molecular interventions that contribute to the negation of the rising intensity of authoritarian culture'. For instance, their Child as Audience project (2001) was a package designed primarily for teenage boys, which included instructions on how to hack a GameBoy and a pamphlet on the oppression of youth.

David Garcia makes the case for more exploratory uses of media through the example of the activist group Women on Waves, whose

> most celebrated achievement . . . is the Abortion Boat, a large floating clinic that tactically exploits maritime law, anchoring the boat just outside the 12-mile zones of countries where abortion is forbidden. Women can be given information, and terminations are performed by a team of Dutch medical practitioners on Dutch 'territory'. Along with the practical intervention of the Abortion Boat, Women on Waves also use art and design as part of their global campaign for abortion rights: for instance, the *I Had an Abortion* installation consisting of vests on wire coat hangers printed with this statement in all European languages. On their website a diary can be found of a Brazilian woman relating her experiences of wearing one of these T-shirts . . . how the message on these T-shirts was preferable to something like 'Legalise Abortion!' that might have read like earlier forms of agit prop. These T-shirts function 'not' she declares to 'make myself a target. That was not the point; it was to give all those women without a face a support. As to say, don't worry, it's all right, you're all right.' (Garcia 2006)

It is also difficult to separate the impulse to experiment formally in alternative media, from the desire to play with and transform the media technologies themselves. In the first essay in this chapter David Garcia and Lennaart van Old-enborgh explore how the issue of 'controlling your own transmission platforms' has been crucial in the development of alternative television.

In the second piece Manu Luksch and Mukul Patel describe their work with ambientTV.net, which combines the politics of surveillance with the expressive possibilities of TV and the Internet, at the same time as pushing formal bounda-ries. In the third piece Katie Haegele looks at how zines produce material that is much more formally experimental than is usually found on the mainstream news-agents' shelves.

7.1 Alternative visions of television

David Garcia and Lennaart van Oldenborgh

Introduction

Our subject is not alternative video but alternative *television* (or as some of us prefer *tactical* television). Many artists, activists and indy journalists have used video, but a far smaller number have taken the steps to control their own trans-mission platforms. This chapter aims to focus on those groups that will help to identify both the origins and guiding principles from which the alternative tele-vision movement emerged. We have sought to do this through a number of snapshots and case studies which capture something of the technological, legal and social conditions that must converge if a vibrant alternative TV scene is to arise.

Alternative television makers have always included many artists in their ranks. Often these artists have seen their role as political, part of a much wider move-ment of activist culture or 'cultural politics'.

Art's fragile claim to have political significance is based on its historical con-nection to a certain idea of freedom, along with the caveat that the spiritual freedoms and possibilities for self-articulation enjoyed by artists are not simply for the author but are the rightful legacy of all human subjects. In the words of art historian Thierry de Duve, 'the drive of every avant-garde or modern utopia has been founded on the basis that the practice of artists was to liberate a poten-tial for art-making in everyone and shared by humankind as a whole. A potential whose field was aesthetic but whose horizon was political' (*Duchamp After Kant*, De Duve 1996: 289).

Although this chapter will concentrate on alternative television's recent history we should not overlook origins of this movement within art and cultural politics as a whole. The beginnings of television's alternative history lie in 'naturalism', specifically the *empathetic* strand of naturalism developed by a number of the

French painters and novelists of the nineteenth century, such as Zola, Courbet or the best of Renoir, in whose works the subjects, far from being objectified, are transfigured by the artist's empathy, placing the qualities, concerns and predicaments of the subject rather than those of the artist (or the patron) at the heart of culture.

In the art of the twentieth century radical formal experimentation overtook issues of representation as the concern of the most dynamic artists. This lasted until late in the century, when a consumer electronics revolution started to transform art and media in general. Widespread access to high powered tools for capturing, processing and disseminating the facts of the observed world, in real time, such as camcorders, personal computers and the internet introduced a new dimension to the concept of a *subject centred naturalism*, giving the subjects of history greater possibilities than ever before to speak for themselves and control their own representations. For better and for worse, citizens' media became a reality.

Alongside the undoubted gains of a wider, deeper and more expressive popular media literacy we also have seen the emergence of a voracious new domain of exploitation and commodified subjectivity through the advent of reality TV. The successful and progressive appropriation of many of the core tactics of alternative media makes the recuperation of the underlying values and the history of the emergence of these values a matter of great urgency.

The technology of immediacy

For an alternative TV movement to emerge a number of conditions, technical, legal and social, have to converge. A better understanding of the technical conditions requires a brief look into the history of television.

When television began regular national broadcasts (in 1936, by the BBC from Alexandra Palace) it was an exclusively 'live' medium, and featured variety and music hall along with official announcements. Video recorders and their magnetic tape did not arrive until 1956 (2-inch reel-to-reel videotape). Whatever technological developments have come along since (including the digitally enhanced effects of the MTV era), television's distinctive characteristic remains its unique sense of *immediacy*.

The television or video camera is one of the earliest 'real-time' media tools, and television the first medium in which the maker (and the subject) were able to see, on a monitor, in real-time, exactly what is being captured. In contrast to the distancing effect of film, the video camera collapses the space between data capture, data management and data delivery. The current dominance of so-called 'reality TV' is evidence of the fact that television's distinctive quality of appearing to deliver a forensically factual immediacy remains as central to the medium as ever. In fact the global networks combined with continuing broadband roll-out ensure we are rapidly becoming universal eyewitnesses of our own intimate and public histories.

From a technological standpoint, a truly alternative television movement could not arise without the combination of (relatively) cheap production tools with accessible transmission channels. In the 1960s this combination appeared in Canada and the USA when access to cable (and sometimes satellite) television was combined with the first generation of affordable video production tools.

The initial breakthrough came after the introduction, in 1967, of the first truly portable (and relatively affordable) video rig – Sony's half-inch, reel-to-reel CV Porta-Pak. Artists and alternative makers seized on this tool for expression and investigation. But alongside the arts the availability of affordable video also had a profound effect on many of the behavioural sciences, particularly fields like anthropology and developmental psychology.

An alternative TV movement requires more than production tools; it requires a distribution platform, and in Canada and North America this platform was cable television. In addition to the available technology there had to be a willingness (and ultimately a legal requirement) for cable operators to provide access. In the US the real victory for the public access movement occurred in 1972 when 'the FCC issued its Third Report and Order, which required all cable systems in the top 100 US television markets to provide three access channels' (Olson 2000).

From the mid-1980s onwards a more conservative climate in American politics have progressively weakened these achievements. But for many years the widespread presence of a nationwide network of public access channels *as a right* functioned as a powerful backdrop for developing one of the most vibrant alternative television scenes in the world, despite the fact that the US is also the home of television at its most voraciously commercial.

The reflexive turn

Despite the power of the US community access movement, the systematic use of cable TV for alternative television began in Canada. The guiding ideals of this movement are rooted not in video but in film. They can be traced as far back as 1922 and the revolutionary film *Nanook of the North* in which film maker Robert Flaherty follows the life and times of 'Nanook, chief of the Ikivimuits', an Inuit hunter (played by Flaherty's friend and guide, Allakariallak). Although regarded by many as the first documentary film, *Nanook of the North* reconstructs the life of 'Nanook' as it would have been at the time of the first contact with Western industrialised civilisation.

The most remarkable feature of this film, for its time, was the fact that the film's subject Allakariallak, alias Nanook, and other Inuits were active participants in the making of the film. This makes *Nanook of the North* a key moment in Anthropology's reflexive turn, a moving away from the stance of studying our fellow human beings as objects. This principle of reflexivity spread throughout art and alternative media culture. It is one of the ways in which we strive to become the subjects as well as the objects of modernisation.

In the 1960s, *Nanook of the North* served as a key inspiration for a group of idealistic Canadian film makers who developed the Challenge for Change series of projects, in which poor communities worked in partnership with filmmakers to lobby for specific changes to their lives. Challenge for Change was part of a wider campaign, the Canadian government's 'War on Poverty'.

Seeking to build on these achievements of community film, two filmmakers, Dorothy Hénaut and Bonny Klein, introduced Sony's early portable video tools into the process. In 1970 the attempt was made to merge Porta-Pak video equipment with cable TV for a civic organisation. But lack of general support 'and charges that radicals controlled the project doomed it to failure' (Olson 2000). From these and other experiences lessons were learned and the ideas and principles of citizens' television began to spread.

Running in parallel to these initiatives during the 1970s the Inuit Tapirisat, a pan-Inuit activist organisation began independently agitating for a licence to establish their own arctic satellite television service. The Inuit Broadcasting Corporation (IBC) was eventually granted a licence in 1981. According to Anthropologist Faye Ginsburg 'the IBC – a production center for Inuit programming of all sorts – became an important development in the lives of Canadian Arctic people, as well as a model for the repurposing of communications technologies for indigenous people worldwide' (Ginsburg 2002: 42).

Low media: high ambition

The American subcultures of the 1970s were quick to adopt the expressive possibilities of the new generation of accessible production tools. Utopian artists, media makers and activists translated these possibilities into a vision of a decentralised and democratised media. This vision was articulated by Marshal McLuhan and even more explicitly, in manifesto form by Michael Shamberg in his book *Guerrilla TV* (Shamberg 1971). Under the influence of these and other radical thinkers media came to be seen as a key zone of contestation that would act as a catalyst for wider movements for social change.

Top Value Television (or TVTV) provides an indication of the scale and ambition of the alternative television movement of that era. In 1972 TVTV broke new ground with the video documentary *4 More Years* (Boyle 1997: 57–64). The documentary was made with a crew of 19 media activists armed with Porta-Paks moving around the largely unsuspecting Republican Party's national convention. The resulting documentary produced a more revealing insight into the workings of American party politics than anything previously seen on US media. The success of the early TVTV documentaries led to national interest and assignments for US national broadcaster PBS.

In retrospect this early flowering of US alternative television was also its most optimistic phase. A period in which many of those involved in both underground and mainstream TV believed that they were witnessing some kind of profound restructuring of the political and media landscapes.

Homeopathic TV

In 1981 the formation of the New York based collective, Paper Tiger TV, signalled the arrival of a very different atmosphere. From the outset Paper Tiger's approach was a repudiation of mainstream television and its 'seamless' production values.

Paper Tiger's classic early style of the programmes combined challenging and thought provoking media critiques with simple (even crude) production values, deliberately rejecting slickness and above all *seamlessness*. Their deliberately 'hand-made look' make it one of the pioneers of DIY media as aesthetic and politics.

Importantly, Paper Tiger began working at a time in which the simultaneous rise of MTV and museum based 'video art' had led to adulation of media effects and 'professional' production values. In an unsympathetic environment, the network of artists, activists and educators working with Paper Tiger at different times (Martin Lucas, DeeDee Halleck, Joan Braderman, Bill Tabb, Amy Goodman, Martha Rosler, to name just a few), represented values that worked against the prevailing current of the time. They staked out important territory for later generations to occupy. The tactical media movement that followed in the 1990s were happy to adopt Paper Tiger's quick-turnaround DIY aesthetic, but in contrast to Paper Tiger later movements were less worried about incorporating the impurities and hedonism of popular culture to political ends.

The art of campaigning

Later in the 1980s a pervasive sense of crisis engaged the energies of activists; the war against AIDS. The Reagan administration's policy of denial, a homophobic media and a conservative health care system provoked the rise to AIDS activism, and most notably ACT UP (The AIDS Coalition to Unleash Power), a brilliant and ferociously effective activist movement. Much of its power came from the leadership of those who had the most at stake, people with HIV and AIDS. Many of those involved in AIDS activism not only a means to bring about actual material change but also a space for empowerment through the expressive power of art and media. To look at the media work of AIDS activists is to be reminded of the importance of the power of art and the expressive dimension it brings to activism.

AIDS activist television not only deployed the facilities and experience of the well established public access tradition, it also added a uniquely expressive combination of media analysis, grief, joy, sexuality and anger. From this mix it forged a new kind of activism and with it the articulation of a more powerful cultural politics.

One of the most important examples of New York AIDS activist television was the series of programmes called *Living with AIDS*, produced by Jean Carlomusto from 1987 as part of her work for the Gay Men's Health Crisis (GMHC). The programmes carried advice and news about the epidemic that was simply not available in the mainstream media. Carlomusto described how 'So much stuff on TV was horrible. There was a total exclusion of people living with AIDS, and that sent me out onto the streets'.

But the vital work of Carlomusto and the *Living with AIDS* TV project must not be seen in isolation. Jean Carlomusto was part of a complex and volatile network of media collectives who despite very different backgrounds, tactics and aesthetics would nevertheless co-operate and share video footage. The catalyst and centre of gravity that made this level of co-operation possible was the extraordinary campaigning group: ACT UP (AIDS Coalition To Unleash Power). Galvanised by a unique emergency and ACT UP's intrinsic dynamism, an incredible variety of collaborative practices were explored. The wide range of professional backgrounds from which AIDS activism drew its members ensured that the boundaries between alternative television and media activism were rendered extremely porous.

Along with the *Living with AIDS* TV series it is important to mention two other collectives, Testing the Limits and the 'official' ACT UP media affinity group, DIVA TV. Despite applying very different approaches, these groups nevertheless pooled the hundreds of hours of footage captured at the ACT UP meetings and demonstrations.

The technology of the time contributed to the sheer volume of footage. This was no longer the era of the cumbersome Sony Porta-Pak, this was the era of the *camcorder*. It made AIDS activism the most documented political movement of its day. AIDS activism has left a powerful legacy (and for those who participated, perhaps a burden) of thousands of hours of video recordings.

The 1980s was also the era of the music video and many of the activist tapes bear the MTV imprint. In the early phase, groups such as Testing the Limits set their sights on a screening on the national broadcaster PBS. DIVA TV on the other hand, placed less emphasis on production values than in their role as ACT UP's affinity group, making fast and furious programmes, reflecting the movement back to itself, practically in real-time. Here we see the power of the reflexive turn deployed in the art of campaigning.

Of course the characterisation above is a sketch of a movement that was as fluid and swift as a river. Those involved frequently worked with different collectives and it is hard to do justice to the vibrancy of a movement whose intensity profoundly transformed the possibilities for cultural and media politics.

Amsterdam cable television

The community access to local cable TV in Amsterdam has (in the European context) quite a unique history. The Netherlands was the first country in Europe to build a nationwide, cable TV infrastructure in the 1970s. Unlike in most other countries cable was not considered a luxury but a utility like gas, water and electricity. But in those early days cable was simply used to improve picture quality and as a way to import broadcast channels from other European countries (and later global channels).

This was the so called era of 'post ideology', when people were more likely to be politicised through issues than grand historical narratives. In New York the issue was AIDS, but in Amsterdam it was housing and it was the squatters movement that mobilised political energy. The squatters were not only concerned with housing: they built their own culture including their own media. And cable television was like empty buildings, there to be occupied.

Thus it was cable TV pirates who were the first to (illegally) use the cable network to disseminate local content. Technically it was simple: they just set up transmitters near the large parabolic dish used by the cable operator to import programmes from abroad. Then they beamed in their illegal transmissions, which were then automatically spread citywide. The pirates ran a full spectrum of content, from pornography interrupted by hand-drawn advertising for furniture, to highly innovative, and highly political broadcasts made by some of the squatters' pirate stations, most notably PKP, which later became StaatsTV Rabotnik, and, much later, De Vrije Keyzer. In addition, a number of artists started to explore the potential of the cable network: a notable example was the Underpass, organised by a number of artists including David Garcia and Annie Wright, in which a pedestrian underpass was turned into a month-long public-access television studio transforming both the street and local media.

The popularity of Amsterdam's alternative TV makers made it clear to the city authorities that a legal framework for access would have to be created. The framework that emerged, unique (even in the Netherlands) to Amsterdam, was the so called Open Channel, which was to be administered and regulated by a government appointed organisation, SALTO.

Its statutory obligation was, and still is, to make the open channel culturally representative; in other words ensure that the main ethnic and social groups and movements are visible. It is this approach that distinguishes community access from public access, which is open to anybody and is based on a simple first-come first-served principle. Public access is the dominant system in the US, and is also the model followed by the Berlin Open Channel, one of the few other major European cities with an extensive and far reaching public-access television policy.

Experimental forms

The unique local TV climate in Amsterdam spawned a rash of experimental forms of television, some driven by the former pirates, and others by artists and activists. StaatsTV Rabotnik was a weekly fixture on cable TV for many years, providing alternative and highly acclaimed coverage of local elections and other events. In the heyday of the 1990s there were several artist-run programmes such as Kanaal Zero, Park4DTV, De Hoeksteen, TV3000 and Almanac. Non-profit production houses like Bellissima brought a variety of alternative programmes such as CNSYNC, while Beurs TV and Smart TV experimented with cable TV as a medium for electronic citizenship.

Park4DTV and De Hoeksteen, both artist-run organisations, have had a similar trajectory although in terms of concept and content they could hardly be more different. They both still exist but Park4DTV has turned exclusively to webcasting instead of cable TV since 2004, whereas De Hoeksteen continues with its unique live 'all night' format, and continues to cover political and cultural events in the same improvised, anarchic way.

Park4DTV

Park4DTV is entirely based on the idea '1 hour, 1 thing, pure image and sound', which would be transmitted weekly, and later daily, late at night on the Amsterdam cable. This basic format was established in 1992 and is still at the heart of their concept. It encourages formal experimentation, but their strictly modernist conception of art on television has meant that Park4DTV is a relatively traditional modern art organisation with a structure that is close to an artist-run exhibition space. There is an editorial board that acts as 'curator' of the one-hour slot, soliciting works by artists as well as working with an open submission system. Most of the funding goes to actually paying the contributing artists for showing their work, along a conventional property rights model.

The organisational structure is described as loose and 'non-institutional'; the editorial board is at the heart of the organisation and also divides the practical tasks among themselves, without any paid permanent staff. This structure could be described as one of dedicated amateurism.

As with most Amsterdam cable initiatives, there is a strong tendency to expand laterally, bringing more programmes to more people in more places, and into other media (the 'raudio' project into radio and sound work is an example), rather than to focus more resources on the core activity and achieve growth in 'depth' and quality. One could argue this keeps the activity in the experimental sphere, but similarly one could see this as a failure to develop the main idea into something more durable.

De Hoeksteen

De Hoeksteen is truly a form of no-budget television. It is essentially the brain-child of Dutch-Colombian artist Raul Marroquin, who, after a season of producing diary-style taped programmes for cable TV, hit upon the possibility to broadcast live from the publicly accessible SALTO radio station early in 1991, and has never looked back since. The broadcasts take the form of an anarchic chat- and phone-in show, entirely produced on cheap consumer technology with only minimal editorial planning. As opposed to Park4DTV, the live broadcasts are events in themselves, and (in art terms) are to be considered 'the work'.

Behind the scenes, experimental practitioners and artists like Mauz and Bart Oomen not only keep the show running technically, but also bring in experimental additions mainly to improve the 'interactivity' of the show. Consumer conferencing equipment has been incorporated, allowing live TV connections both to other cities in the Netherlands and also to other parts of the world: connections were made to the Gertrude Stein Institute in New York and to The Hypermedia Centre in Westminster University, among others. Already in 1993 they were taking not only phone calls but also faxes and emails from viewers, long before mainstream Dutch television (most notably Endemol) started using similar technology. They have used BBS, consumer mobile phones and other gadgets to experiment with interactivity, taking the freedom to try things live on air and refusing to bow to any kind of pressure to produce a seamless viewing experience. In fact, even in the improvised landscape of Amsterdam open access TV, De Hoeksteen still managed to offend some viewers with its barely controlled chaos.

But as important as technological experiment and innovation is to De Hoeksteen, it is primarily personality driven: from the outset it could attract celebrities. The combined social talents of Marroquin and its former chief anchor man, Otto Valkman, ensured that anyone from Philip Glass to a cabinet minister was likely to turn up.

The essence of the programme is an atmosphere of unpredictability; anybody can show up, and anyone who does can get a camera pressed in their hands and press ganged into the production unit. On one occasion the chief anchorman responded to a request (or a dare) from a late night phone-in by pulling out his dick and measuring it on screen. It is how one might imagine Warhol's factory (before Valerie Solanas) as a platform for the city's extremes of exhibitionism and voyeurism: an all night party with a continuous stream of gate crashers. But unlike the Factory, which comes down to us as film and photography, Marroquin's studio goes out on live TV, with the possibility of instant feedback. At the same time, Marroquin has been quick to point out that 'Warhol didn't have mainstream politicians'. He describes De Hoeksteen as 'a political programme with a cultural supplement' – more accurate to describe it as media theortist Geert Lovink did in conversation as 'low media for high society'.

Figure 7.1 De Hoeksteen composite (Photo: Raul Marroquin)

After privatisation

In 1995 the KTA, the Amsterdam cable operator, was put on the market and soon after sold. Shortly before the handover, SALTO launched a second open channel, 'A1', and the privatisation deal included guarantees for the continuation of the open channels. However, as was widely predicted, soon the commercial operator (currently UPC, a division of Liberty Global) began to put restrictions on access by introducing additional costs for the programmers, re-branding the Open Channel as 'A2' and, on more than one occasion, changing the local channel frequencies without prior notice and without adequately informing the public. The number of experimental programmes have dwindled as a result. Some are still going: apart from De Hoeksteen, Bellissima still produces regular programmes, and De Vrije Keyzer is the last of the squatters' groups to maintain a presence, even though they were late converts to television (up to 1998 they broadcast exclusively on radio).

Others have turned to the internet, including transmissions within the virtual world Second Life as the new 'free space', which with the arrival of broadband became fast enough to webcast moving images. What this fails to realise is that some of the unique qualities of local cable TV are not easily reproduced online: the localness, the 'liveness', and the intimacy. Most promising of all are the emerging hybrid models, and the most exciting of these in the Netherlands is Outloud.

Outloud began in 2003 when a group of students from the Art Media and Technology department of the Utrecht School of the Arts were asked to create a system for Amsterdam's open channel to be called 'Pauze TV'. The idea was to fill the empty time between the scheduled programmes with some kind of semi-automated TV project. Outloud has been described as a 'cross media juke box'. The system allows people to upload clips via the Internet to the Outloud server whereupon the clips are transmitted on to Amsterdam's open TV channel where it is possible for viewers to determine the extent to which the clips are played by voting. The clips can also be viewed on the Web. The result was Outloud which is one of the few sustainable fusions of grassroots broadcast TV with the Web.

Micro-media and the Italian exception

An example of a new set of hybrid tactics can be found in a fusion of the Internet with micro-television transmissions into new kinds of networks of collaboration in the Italian movement Telestreet. Telestreet is a network of close to 200 pirate or semi-legal television stations operating in Italy, since 2002.

Telestreet are literally street TV-makers using small transmitters to send programmes that mostly reach no more than a few blocks. Telestreet groups range from making their own local items to capturing the programming from the commercial satellite operators (such as big football matches) and re-broadcasting them for free on Telestreet networks. They operate between the legal and technological cracks of the Italian media landscape, occupying what are called the shadows or blank spots, which occur when terrestrial broadcasters cannot reach a certain area because of topological obstacles leaving a 'shadow' on the broadcast spectrum.

But Telestreet is not just traditional pirate media. It has exploited the latest Internet developments to scale up to a national level. Working with a group of activists, New Global Vision, they use the high-speed file transfer protocol Bittor-rent to enable the material developed by local Telestreets to be shared nationally. Hundreds of hours of video material are made freely accessible in a single loca-tion on the New Global Vision website as a common resource. They currently have the space of five servers, stocked with around 300 videos, with new material being added at least once a week. This system enables Telestreets to share their content and transforms tiny local media initiatives into a national movement. This is a new media hybrid in which 'television must be considered a new prosthe-sis of the Net which has avoided becoming simply another alternative "ghetto"; the horizontality of the Net is combined with the immediacy and "socializing" power of television' (Garcia 2004).

Orfeo TV in Bologna is believed to have started the Telestreet ball rolling when it began transmitting in 2002, just a few blocks away from the site of the legen-dary Radio Alice, and has since been described as her 'bastard offspring'. What began in Bologna with a few transmitters was soon 'joined in a circulation of struggle through a network of websites; they are now connected through "tac-tical television" to other Italian micro-broadcasters like *no-war TV*, *urban TV*, and *global TV*.' In all there are now more than 200 Telestreet micro-broadcasters operating across most of the major Italian cities and many of the smaller ones throughout the country.

The Telestreet phenomenon can be seen as another splinter from the legacy of the Italian Autonomous movement of the late 1960s and 1970s, a politics which brought down on itself the wrath of both the right and the Italian communist party by privileging desire and expression over either market forces or party dis-cipline. But more contemporaneously it was a reaction to the political climate of the Berlusconi years, in which media control was concentrated in the hands of an authoritarian regime which many on the left characterised as fascist.

Globalise our alternatives

Telestreet reminds us of the need for alternative media not to remain trapped in the comfort zone of their own self-imposed ghettos, it suggests the need to scale up, both in size and ambition. Some voices within the Telestreet network would like to see it gain its own national frequency, while others would prefer local autonomy to prevail, with each Telestreet extending and intensifying the process of expansion through networking and the sharing of content. New experimental versions of micro-transmissions are also springing up outside Italy: in Japan, the Netherlands, Switzerland, Brazil and in Argentina.

Initiatives like Telestreet work because they represent a new kind of global media from below, bypassing the corporate platforms like YouTube. These kinds of practice represent the emergence of a situated globalism: a movement embed-ded in local histories which nevertheless uses the net to develop active connections to affinity groups and initiatives elsewhere. Rather than imagining that global internet TV networks simply make borders disappear, we see how new ways of organising locally and connecting globally lead us beyond the category of alternative media, towards a global media from below and something like a 'global sense of place'.

7.2 ambientTV.net

Manu Luksch and Mukul Patel

ambientTV.net came into being as an experimental hybrid-media hub and website in 1999, emerging out of founding artist–activist Manu Luksch's long-standing interest in extending the medium of film using the Internet. Under the codirectorship of Manu and Mukul Patel, it has since developed into a crucible for independent, interdisciplinary practice, producing critical works that encompass sound, video, net- and software art, dance, documentary, installation and cuisine. Techniques and effects of live data broadcasting and transmission provide theme, medium and performative space for many of the projects. While much of the work has international dimensions, ambientTV.net maintains a physical base, 'ambientspace', in East London as a production studio, workshop, salon and artist residency.

A film always has an end while reality continues

The first ambientTV.net project was the feature-length documentary *Virtual Borders* (2000–3), which traces identity issues of the Akha people who live in the highland border regions of the Mekong Quadrangle. A camera followed the journey of an Akha elder from his village in Thailand to a cultural conference in Yunnan, China. From there, the project crew transmitted recordings of conference proceedings by Internet back to a minority radio station in Thailand, for broadcast to Akha villages. *Virtual Borders* set the trajectory for later ambientTV.net productions by integrating data transmission and broadcast into the structure of the work, and not merely deploying them for distribution.

You call it art; we call it independence

While the *Virtual Borders* project established a temporary media channel in rural South-East Asia, a more enduring and wide-ranging network came into being in 2001 in the heart of London. The East End Net is a data network that links buildings using open-access wireless networking (WLAN). The initial impetus behind East End Net, and similar initiatives in other cities, was the high entry cost and delayed rollout of broadband, coupled with the excess capacity of individuals who did have a connection. The location of ambientspace (on top of a seven-storey industrial building) made it ideal as a node in this network. While this efficient sharing of resources and do-it-yourself approach was not inimical to ambientTV.net's ethos, the possibility of establishing an independent media infrastructure was of greater significance. A network connecting buildings to each other – but not necessarily to the Internet – could potentially form a city-wide channel for creation and dissemination, a locus of resistance to the increasing legislation and surveillance of the Internet. As well as managing a network node, ambientspace hosted antenna-building workshops and collected and distributed obsolescent computers that could be reconfigured for use in the network.

Breaking the frame

Breaking the 'safety' of the screen borders, extending the dimensionality of the piece, increasing the degrees of freedom – all these approaches serve to transform passive viewer into active user, to allow deeper reflection on a work stripped of its traditional framing device. Where data networks are involved, the possibility arises of incorporating process in a novel way. For example, the *Telejam* series (2001–2) distributed the creation of live works across several cities. A single beat or frame in one location might loop and feed back through remote studios and venues, setting off spatially and temporally extended series of events. In *AV Dinners*, mealtimes in various cities were co-ordinated by data streams carrying processed images and sounds from a kitchen, a poet's evocation of the smells and flavours emanating from it and a host's commentary on the technological recipe (in the style of a TV cookery show).

Disturbing slowness in speedy times

Some projects hijack transmissions on exisiting networks and re-edit them into new narratives. *Broadbandit Highway* (2001), a live, online road movie premiered on the internal TV system of London's Great Eastern Hotel, is a true piece of ambient television that exploits the live broadcast possibilities offered by webcams. After porn and weather cams, the most prevalent cameras online are those that show traffic conditions. For *Broadbandit Highway*, a computer program hijacks images from these traffic surveillance webcams and sequences them into the movie. Now over five years long, the piece will end when the last webcam known to it fails or is taken offline.

Figure 7.2 You call it art. Manu Luksch

Scan – jam – hijack

ambientTV.net's approach involves bringing a critical perspective to bear on the technologies used. A project may reveal stealthy characteristics of the technology it employs, or show how the technology can be deployed for productive rather than consumptive ends. Myriorama (2004) was a dance/theatre performance that wove location-aware (GPS-enabled) mobile phones into a narrative of omniscience and paranoia. Inspired by Italo Calvino's short story, 'A king listens' (in which a palace shaped like an ear leads all sounds to the king's throne), in Myriorama the king's court is inside a venue where 40 people are granted an intimate audience, reclining on floor cushions and surrounded by sound and projections. A citizen of the kingdom wanders through the neighbourhood of the venue, equipped with a mobile device that transmits his thoughts (as text messages) and location to the venue.

Inside the venue, the wanderer's thoughts are projected as architectural structures, revealing his path through the city. The king reads these thoughts and plays with the projected structures, transforming and juggling words by his gestures (via a wireless motion sensor system). A dialogue is built up between wanderer and king, and as the thoughts become threatening, so the king's omniscience gives way to paranoia, and the effects of his gestures become chaotic. At the height of the paranoia, the wanderer arrives at the venue, putting an end to the king's reign, only to take over the throne himself. In the midst of the hype surrounding next-generation mobile services (3G), Myriorama draws attention to the increasingly revealing data traces that such devices leave behind in use.

'Quis custodiet ipsos custodes?'

In response to real or fictitious threats, twenty-first-century societies have developed the habit of continuous recording (of image, by surveillance cameras, but more significantly, of data transmission in general). This move suggests a concomitant shift for the image-maker away from the intentional shot, to the trawling of the sea of recorded data. *Faceless* (2006) is a science-fiction thriller shot using London's extensive network of CCTV security cameras. Footage is obtained under the terms of the UK Data Protection Act and other image-rights legislation, which gives anyone caught on camera the right to a copy of the recording. Although the final means of distribution is a video format, the medium of this work could be said to be a set of legislation, the rights and obligations it extends to those concerned, and the communicative processes involved in obtaining what is rightfully owed. Extending the Duchampian idea of the *objet trouvé* into the legal realm, and driven by a manifesto for filmmaking with a network of cameras that is already in situ, *Faceless* exemplifies the critical, process-based work produced by ambientTV.net. As we increasingly rely on mediated (and monitored) communication technologies, who exactly keeps watch on the data traces? And who watches the watchers?

7.3 Zines

Katie Haegele

A 'zine' is an independently published magazine, a photocopied booklet, an alternative newsletter, a DIY journal – it is a hard concept to pin down because it can encompass many different things. The name comes from the word 'fanzine' or 'magazine' and is pronounced 'zeen'. Today's zines are heirs to the punk fanzines of the 1970s and the riot grrl movement of the early 1990s. Riot grrl zines were mostly feminist and political, using cut-and-paste collages from fashion magazines and a wicked sense of humour. These days zines can be about anything: comics and graphic novels, fiction, poetry, zines about knitting and other crafts, sex and health, cooking and food, spirituality and religion, as well as a tremendous range of 'perzines', or personal zines. If something strikes a would-be zinester as a good topic for a zine then, by definition, it is.

The majority of zines are typed, handwritten, or computer-printed, then cut and pasted up, photocopied, and stapled into booklets. Some longer zines are taken to a print shop and printed on newsprint. Most zines are written, designed and constructed by one person, but they certainly can have multiple contributors and still be considered zines; literary zines or music zines featuring CD reviews often have more than one contributor. In some cases the medium is simply a vehicle for the words, but in others the publications themselves are 'made things' – i.e. art books, some of them limited editions that are numbered and signed. The more handmade among them are printed on specialty paper or paper made from brown grocery bags, bound with twine; fastened with metal brads, plastic garbage bag fasteners, rubber bands or duct tape; and adorned with stickers, glitter, photographs or rubber stamps. As far as I know there is only one zine, 'Ker-bloom!', that is hand-printed entirely on a letterpress printing press. Each issue is an original piece of art.

Zinesters sell their creations for around 50 cents to three dollars, some give them away for free, and almost all of them will happily trade for a copy of someone else's zine. Because they produce their work outside the publishing mainstream, zinesters must find alternative distribution channels as well. Personal writing on websites and blogs abounds, yet print zines are thriving, and old-school zinesters do make use of new technologies to sell and promote their work. Networking sites like Live-Journal and MySpace allow zinesters to build free pages to promote their work and meet lots of other people doing the same thing. The distro Fall of Autumn (www.fallofautumn.com) produces podcasts of zine writers reading their work, which can be downloaded or streamed into online radio shows, and are producing a a wiki, or open-source online encyclopedia, about DIY publishing (www.zinewiki.com). (See chapter 16 [16.3.9] for more practical information.)

The point of all this is that writing and creating zines is a way of producing printed matter that does not fall under the aegis of an increasingly stringent and impenetrable publishing mainstream. Zines are a way for people to express minority opinions and a space for people who are not 'writers' or 'artists' to write and make art. But theirs are not voices in the wilderness; today's zinesters are producing work to an already established and growing audience. The people who make and read zines do not fit easily into any one demographic group. For starters they are teenagers, college students, grad students, teachers, home-schoolers and autodidacts with library cards; they are radical single moms, girls who dress and pass as guys, childhood-abuse survivors, and sex workers; librarians, caregivers, illustrators, humorists, activists, tattoo artists and organic farmers; dumpster divers and squatters, nine-to-fivers, award-winning writers, bored people in rural settings and anxious people in big cities. My friend Sage (a tattoo artist who home-schools) once made a zine with her five-year-old daughter. I recently produced a collection of my poems as a zine, even though I have published or tried to publish them elsewhere, because submitting poems for consideration in other people's journals is a lengthy process that is often unsatisfying, even when the poems are accepted.

It is worth noting that, while flaming and bullying are common nuisances for online self-publishers, negative feedback is rarely a concern for those in the print zine community. They are probably too busy peeling glue off their fingers.

8 Access to broadcasting

Introduction

The right to communicate is at the heart of democratic society. This includes the rights of 'citizens' to collectively or independently create their own media. Alternative media production is, then, a democratic principle in and of itself, and an important means through which freedom of expression is enacted.

So what does it mean to talk about access to broadcasting? By access, we mean both content – independent producers providing alternative programming to existing networks such as the BBC – and infrastructure – the opening up of the airwaves for community groups to legally create their own radio and television stations. As we saw in chapter 2, the history of radio is a history of the fight by everyday people to gain access to the airwaves. If we consider the airwaves to be public domain, then the role of broadcast regulators should be to ensure that decisions made regarding who gets access to airwaves are in the public interest. Instead, most countries privilege commercial, state or even public service broadcasting interests over that of community voices. Public service broadcasting is vital to ensure a more democratic and pluralistic media system, but in Britain, for example, when the BBC monopoly was broken, it was in the name of local commercial interests rather than local community needs. In the United States, media consolidation in radio, with the standardisation of its programming, homogenised texture and reduction in local news and public affairs, sparked a low power radio movement that rose from marginal beginnings to become a formidable opponent of powerful media corporations. But the desire for community-based media is more than merely a reaction against flaws within the system. Community media has come to represent a different model of broadcasting, one centred on participation and access rather than profit or professionalisation, and thus, is increasingly recognised as a necessary part of democratic, pluralistic media systems. Community radio is not the only means of accessing the airwaves, take for example the continued popularity of pirate radio. These broadcasters may be doing 'community broadcasting' or 'public access broadcasting', but they share a desire to keep some of the airwaves as a commons. And the fight for greater public access has sparked a political movement in and of itself, centred on the need for media policies that ensure broadcast spectrum licensed by governments better reflects local needs and interests and the public's right to use.

This chapter is divided into two sections – radio and television. In the first piece, on radio in Britain, Kate Coyer offers an example of the diversity of community radio stations by examining three very different stations all within London. It is followed by a poetic account from Charlotte O'Neal in the village of Imbaseni, Tanzania, of what their community station has meant for their village. Later, in chapter 13, Michael Meadows and others provide an interesting look at audience research and the impact of the community radio sector in Australia. The section on television will be introduced at its start.

8.1 Access to broadcasting: radio

Kate Coyer

Miners in Bolivia, rock musicians opposed to Milošević in Belgrade, rebels in El Salvador, aboriginals in Australia, Muslims in Nottingham, hip hop youth in Tanzania, rural farmers in India, women in Jordan, artists in Ireland, environmentalists in Maryland, neighbourhoods and universities in communities across the globe. These are among the thousands of people who have organised community-run radio stations and have fought for their own access to the airwaves.

Community radio is a phenomenon that has been charted in virtually every country, regardless of its primary system of broadcast – state, public service or commercial. There are countries with well-established community radio sectors (South Africa, Ireland), but many more where community radio is still not recognised (Thailand, Croatia), and those that have only recently created formal sectors for community radio (UK, India). Where there is not licensed community radio, there often exist thriving landscapes of unlicensed community micro-radio stations, and these 'pirate radio' stations operate even if there is legal community broadcasting, owing to the fact that there will always be needs and interests not met by any regulatory system as well as those wishing to operate outside state infrastructure, either for ideological or practical reasons. By contrast, some community radio stations operate under threat of harassment in highly volatile and sometimes dangerous conditions, some continuing to broadcast at constant risk of imprisonment and closure.

One might ask why – in an era of potentially limitless Internet stations and podcasts – is there even a need for access to traditional analogue broadcasting spaces? Activists argue that broadcast policy must reflect the value of community access, regardless of the means of delivery; i.e., we can't expect our digital future to include the space for independent voices in broadcasting if we can't actually make room in the present. And while internet and satellite radio listening is clearly on the rise, it still represents a fraction of regular radio listening.

Moreover, analogue radio remains the primary means of news and information for the majority of the world. Its low cost, ease of use, minimal equipment requirements, and near ubiquity as a medium around the globe make radio the most globally accessible and relevant broadcast medium, even in our increasingly digitised world. There remains an intangible quality of radio's intimacy and immediacy. As one community FM radio listener put it,

> When you hear your neighbors volunteering on the air, you feel like you know them even if you don't. I'm gung ho on the Internet, but it remains to be seen if it can foster that same feeling of intimacy . . . Why should you use the Internet to broadcast the fact that the local church is having a bake sale or that someone's dog is lost? It just doesn't make sense. (Markels 2000)

What is community radio?

Community radio is more than just radio. It is a means of social organising and social engagement. Zane Ibrahim of Bush Radio, South Africa asserts, 'Community radio is 90 percent community and 10 percent radio.' There is no one definition of community radio; however, it is generally understood to encompass stations that embrace participatory, open, not-for-profit practices, and made by and for the community primarily by voluntary labour values. It is a source of local, neighbourhood-based news, entertainment and information. It is radio run for its own sake, for the benefit of the community, rather than for the profit of station owners.

Community radio – radio community Lilja Otto

At a book talk last week, the introductory speaker wanted to know who had come that night to be inspired. Almost all hands went up in the air. And yet, though the book was funny and informative, and suggested ways for change, I left tired, feeling somewhat anxious about the problems this country faces. Little of the talk's energy carried over into my week ahead.

There is something that these talks, conferences, and seminars lack. They rarely make the step from contemplating change or action to making it happen right here, right now.

A different format for community events, and a recipe for inspiration, is now being used by the community radio movement: Go do something you are really good at and that you enjoy, add a group of friends and inspiring new acquaintances, a pinch of play and another of political activism, and finish off with the feeling of having accomplished a major, highly relevant task. Now look in the mirror: see somebody with sparkling eyes and rosy cheeks?

That's what we all looked like at last month's *radio barnraising* in Woodburn, Oregon, a participatory community event organized by the Prometheus Radio Project. When Oregon's largest farmworker and tree-planter union, PCUN, received a low-power radio license, community radio advocates from the region and the continent came together to set up the radio station. In one weekend, working and learning around the clock, we installed the antenna on top of a nearby water tower and software for audio production, we dug ditches for broadband cable, set up high-tech equipment, and taught and learned radio production skills from each other.

The excitement about being part of building the radio station infused everything people did at PCUN that weekend. The belief that everybody has expertise, is capable, and has something to offer is built into the basic structure of the event. And that changes the energy. With everybody's sleeves rolled up, the lines blur between speakers and attendants, experts and newcomers, and a community of equals forms in just a few days. Nothing is more inspiring than a concrete act of solidarity. And few things forge stronger bonds, foster new skills so quickly, and encourage action beyond the event than working together on a common project.

As one participant pointed out: I am never again going to a conference without a power tool in my hand.

Try it. See Prometheus Radio Project for more info on community radio at: http//www.prometheusradio.org/ and PCUN's website for more info on their activities and a detailed account of the barnraising at http//www.pcun.org/

Community radio UK

It is only very recently that the British government has formally created a third tier of broadcasting for community radio. Following the success of a pilot project and 20 years of pressure from the Community Media Association (CMA), 144 new community stations have been licensed since 2005. The legislation, as set forth in the 2003 Communications Act, has as much to say about social policy as it does about broadcasting. The application itself is heavily weighted towards questions asking applicants to detail how they will serve their community, involve local residents in the programming and organisation of the station, and develop a meaningful space for community voices to be heard, over technical queries about antenna placement and transmitters (see Everitt 2003a).

In Britain, as elsewhere, different motivations for starting a community radio station are held by different people: those with a passion for the medium of radio and a background in broadcasting, those for whom radio was come to by chance and is a means of promoting larger causes; and those for whom radio is a primary means of personal empowerment and self-development (Everitt 2003a). Some have stronger institutional affiliations than others (New Style Radio in Birmingham is a project of the Afro Caribbean Resource Centre, for example). Licensing in Britain allows for stations that serve both geographic communities (like Forest of Dean Community Radio, the only local service broadcasting throughout the Forest) and 'communities of interest' (like Takeover Radio in Leicester, the first children's station in the UK). In his report, Everitt cites this broad approach as one of the strengths of the British model: 'The growth of individualisation and "active consumption" means that we tend to make opportunistic use of multiple communities to construct a confident, customised sense of ourselves, as distinct from defining ourselves in terms of a fixed community of which we are full paid-up members' (Everitt 1997 quoted in Everitt 2003a: 30). The licensing criteria for community stations included evidence of social gain and/or public service broadcasting, not-for-profit status, accessibility for people living within the area, training and community participation, and engagement with disadvantaged and underserved people and communities (see Everitt 2003a).

Here, I wish to focus on three community stations in London with different missions and audiences, each well-respected and individually recognised as strong models for community broadcasting. Together they represent a cross-section of community radio. Each of them had previously been on-air as a short-term Restricted Service Licence (RSL) station and was part of the recent pilot project, and they have since obtained renewable five-year licenses. These stations include: Desi Radio in Southall, West London, a Panjabi station broadcasting Panjabi music, news, cultural and talk programming; Sound Radio in Hackney, providing access to numerous cultural and ethnic groups from the area to broadcast music, news and speech in a variety of languages; and Resonance FM in Central London, broadcasting experimental sound, music and arts programming.

Sound Radio, Hackney

Sound Radio had previously run four short-term RSLs and is based on the Nightingale housing estate in Hackney, East London, an estate with a history as one of the more volatile in London that has also been home to a number of pirate radio stations over the years. The station opted for an AM transmission that meant nearly double the start-up costs and higher yearly transmitter fees but provides wider transmission coverage as they are using less-crowded bandwidth. Sound's mission is to serve the many multi-cultural communities in East London. With so many new expatriate communities participating and broadcasting news from the various homelands, Station Manager Lol Gellor describes Sound as 'a local world service' (Everitt 2003a: 39). The station's slogan is 'A Positive Voice for East London'.

Consequently, there are over 15 languages being broadcast on Sound in any given week. The station is for everyone, but not necessarily at the same time: 'the thing about being a broad church is that it sometimes frustrates people because people want to relate to single models that are easily identifiable. Community radio offers the stuff that's in the gaps and that's absolutely what it should be' (Gellor 2005). Many programmes embody both global and local relevance and there is often a strong connection between individual programmes and the home countries of show-presenters. The Ugandan music hour, for example, is rebroadcast in Kampala. A local listener in Stanford Hill phones in to the station during the Brazilian music show, and her voice on air is heard by her mother listening via the Internet in São Paolo.

The station draws the boundaries of free speech as broadly as possible in its efforts not to interfere with content, while attempting to ensure no programme makes claims to ethnic or religious superiority and that people have 'the right to reply' (Everitt 2003a). As an example, during an earlier RSL, the station juxtaposed two programmes back to back: *Yids with Attitude* and *Talk Black* featuring a spokesman from the Nation of Islam. Rather than limit who has access, Sound chose to position different perspectives back to back with the hopes that both listeners and presenters might have their own views challenged. In a separate programme, a young host entered into a discussion of offensive music by playing songs with sexist and homophobic lyrics, followed by a discussion of the issue and his own criticism of the songs. Gellor explains his programming philosophy:

> Let's be generous without being patronising. How are you ever going to engage with someone in conversation about a particular issue without becoming engaged with them? If you just stop people from coming in the door, they remain excluded. Are you doing a social inclusion project, or are you just kidding yourself? (Gellor 2005)

Sound provides training for volunteers and youth. The philosophy at Sound, however, is that the real learning takes place on-air (Gellor 2005). Sound's approach to training is to focus on the technical skills, but decisions on how to put together a programme need to come from the producers and, significantly, that new possibilities for what radio can sound like will only emerge through such an approach. Gellor asserts that community radio is different from commercial radio and the BBC explicitly because there are multiple approaches all converging on any one station: 'I don't think it's for me to tell the Bangladeshis what kind of content they should put out and how it should be structured. The whole point is that they're going to do it in a different way' (Gellor 2005). This is the essence of Sound's hands-off approach and of the freedom offered to their programmers – to speak for themselves rather than conform to a particular kind of sound or style.

The success of Sound has its downsides, particularly the inability to offer every group all the airtime they would like. Deciding how airtime is balanced between interests and what group gets to 'represent' or 'speak for' their particular community is inherently problematic, for there exists no one single 'voice' for any group of people. There is a growing Latin American community in East London and Sound is one of the first stations to include Spanish-language programming.

Three new Colombian groups are now producing programmes on the station following the success of the sports programme. One of those shows, *Voice of the Kidnapped*, is a programme clandestinely delivered to 109 community stations in Latin America. The demand exposes the need for more local stations in London to reach the growing underserved populations and languages.

Resonance FM, central London

Resonance FM is a project of the London Musicians' Collective (LMC), which has run numerous RSLs over the past decade. The LMC is itself a networking organisation founded 27 years ago and run by musicians whose mission is to support 'improvisation and other adventurous musical activity' through live events, publications and the radio.

Resonance is a space for a kind of experimental music, sound and art that has no other place on the radio dial. The station is known for its eclectic and avant-garde programming, openness to new ideas and adventuresome approach to the possibilities provided by the aural medium of radio. Their mission statement exemplifies this philosophy:

> Imagine a radio station like no other. A radio station that makes public those artworks that have no place in traditional broadcasting. A radio station that is an archive of the new, the undiscovered, the forgotten, the impossible. That is an invisible gallery, a virtual arts centre whose location is at once local, global and timeless. And that is itself a work of art. Imagine a radio station that responds rapidly to new initiatives, has time to draw breath and reflect. A laboratory for experimentation, that by virtue of its uniqueness brings into being a new audience of listeners and creators. All this and more, Resonance104.4 fm aims to make London's airwaves available to the widest possible range of practitioners of contemporary art. (resonancefm.com)

Though the station has had a number of New Deal work placements and 80% of its volunteers are on low incomes, 'Resonance . . . is not concerned to address disadvantaged communities in the ordinary sense; rather its aim is to enable people to engage in culture in the most practical and successful ways. Its community comprises "artists, disaffected critics and other cultural workers"' (Everitt 2003a). And its community reaches far beyond those in its FM listening range. Not only is their listening audience online quite global in scope, but also many producers themselves come from the wider London area, as well as across Britain, Europe and elsewhere.

Some Resonance shows have drawn a fair amount of attention for their quirky style, such as *Headroom with Rob Simone*, who explores unexplained phenomena and the supernatural; the 'guy who talks backwards' on his show *Xollob Park*, which is 'Krap Bollox' spelt backwards and where everything is done backwards, including records and sound collages, thus making its own mark on sonic

You Are Hear Magz Hall

My interest in radio art was sparked in the formative days of Resonance FM in London. The idea we could truly experiment with on-air radio content and format was pure liberation, I quickly threw away the ladder of 'BBC' values instilled into me on a traditional radio course, I was coming up for air.

The month's RSL broadcast in 1998 was a hands-on education in avant-garde radio. My contribution to this avant academy involved installing the Sonic Catering Band to cook popcorn over the ether and putting laughter therapy across the airwaves.

Hearing Gregory Whitehead's 'Pressures of the unspeakable', Sabine Breit-sameter showcasing the depth of European radio art, live snoring on a Fluxus programme and contributing to a Negativland show catapulted my interest into overdrive.

I immediately started teaching radio at a local college, joined the Commu-nity Media Association to spread the word about the radio arts community and helped successfully lobby for full time community radio stations in the UK, and a huge breakthrough came in 2002 when Resonance went on air full-time.

SLRA was set up by myself and Jim Backhouse to promote radio arts activity. Initially our energies went into *You Are Hear*, a freeform music and arts show.

We organised and promoted music and radio-related events: Circle of Sound, a DIY sound exhibition featuring fellow radio producers /sound artists; 'Flatpack Antenna', an 'anti-curated', pay-to-play fundraising LP for Resonance FM; and live events.

I had long been encouraging fellow artists, with no previous experience of recording or editing audio, to make experimental guest shows. In 2006 free SLRA radio art workshops were held to give people hands-on production skills to make their own creative radio.

Podcasting has aroused my DIY instincts – being able to dispense with media gatekeepers and broadcast totally independently on demand is liber-ating, although the immediacy of live radio is lost. It has certainly moved niche broadcasting forward, but there are still battles to be won against current pro-hibitive music licensing legislation. It's a real headache in terms of paperwork, having to get written agreements from all artists' labels and publishers for any track I wish to podcast; this certainly affects the range of music content on my podshows, steering me to mostly podcast new artists' live performances and stream the radio show separately via alternative Internet stations such as totallyradio.com.

creativity in the process; and a woman broadcasting live via mobile phone as she ventures through the streets of London switching between playing her saxophone, describing her surroundings, and interacting with strangers she meets. There is a programme inspired by Studs Terkel's *Working*, in which 'everyday people' talk about what they do during the day; *Bike*, a weekly show 'delving into the art, science, politics and transcendental pleasure of cycling'; and *The 8-Bit Adventures of a Bored Office Worker*, where listeners can 'expect to hear fresh joints from your favourite obsolete computers and consoles and moans about work. 30 minutes of bleeps from the world's best 8-bit musician' (Resonance FM 2006). Resonance features teen and children's programming, and *Calling All Pensioners*, a show featuring professional crank and social critic 'Old Harry', whose timely rants and salty jokes open up each programme.

Resonance also broadcasts the *Indy Global Report*, a news programme produced by Indymedia London focusing on underreported global events and local activist news; radio drama; *Speaker's Corner* (recorded live at London's famous free-speech locale in Hyde Park); and collectively run programmes like series from Deptford Community Radio, *Middleast Panorama* and *London Na Biso* from Congolese Londoners; and Bigos Planet featuring Polish music and storytelling.

One place where the station's mission comes into practice on a daily basis is the *Clear Spot*. For a segment each weekday, a space is reserved for one-off or short-term programmes, in essence giving virtually anyone with an interesting idea space to try it out. The success of each *Clear Spot* varies widely, and there is no shortage of 'misses' along the way. 'Ultimately, the *Clear Spot* is the clearest way to programme without administration and editorialising. I like to think of it as a conduit straight to air' (Weaver 2005). Recent *Clear Spots* have included highlights from a unique day-long broadcast in Glasgow targeting hairdressers, barbers and salons ('there's something for everyone, from the carefully coiffured to the bedraggled bed-head'), live recordings from the Adventures in Modern Music Festival, and Tim Hodgkinson in conversation with Sardinian composer Alessandro Olla. Resonance takes an equally experimental view towards scheduling programmes, relishing a kind of 'expect the unexpected' in terms of what might be on air next. They reject the traditional broadcast structures of 'drive time' or 'breakfast shows': 'we want to create some social mutations. You want to take the lid off the Petri dish and let things really flourish' (Thomas 2005).

Recently, Resonance took the step to cancel some shows that had been on air since their launch in 2003. They feared programmers would be irate, and were surprised when most agreed it was time to take a rest. Even more significantly, Resonance has restructured their schedule so that most shows broadcast on revolving fixed-term slots. In other words, most programmes will operate six to twelve weeks on, take a break, and then come back to air again for another fixed term if they so choose, which producers are encouraged to do. The idea is that it gives programmers a chance to revive shows, keep concepts fresh and avoid burnout, and build a system where there is always room on air for the ever-increasing number of people seeking to produce shows. They hope people will come back time and again with new ideas, and with renewed energy and excitement over the prospect of limited-run engagements.

Resonance operates on one of the lowest budgets of the initial pilot stations in Britain (£60,000 compared with upwards of £100,000 per year for some other stations). This is largely because *Resonance* does not provide formal production training courses and operates with a staff of only two station managers. At present, they do not air commercials, though they are entitled to air a certain number under the terms of their licence like most British community stations (see Ofcom 2007 or the Community Media Association 2007 for these exceptions). Overall, their attitude is one of 'doing things on our terms. If people come to us with sums of cash we would see beyond that and see what they are asking for' (Weaver 2005). At the same time, 'we don't allow ourselves to be bound by our resources' (ibid).

Like Sound, the station acknowledges it is not for everybody, 'nor should it be' (Weaver 2005). Resonance has been criticised by some for airing such challenging sound art that the station is at times difficult listening. Station manager Weaver justifies their ethos: 'We do put things out there that are tough to listen to but it's stuff that hasn't been done on a radio, not just 'cos it's tough to listen to. You know, at the end of the day, you have this box you can secretly transmit into people's homes and you should really explore this from all artistic angles' (ibid. 2005).

Desi Radio, Southall

Desi Radio is a Panjabi station located in Southall, West London. The station is a project of the Panjabi Centre, a local charity whose mission is to promote the Panjabi language, culture, and history. 'Panjab' is Persian for 'the land of five rivers' and the region sits along the border between India and Pakistan; in the 1947 partition of India, the region was divided between India (East Panjab) and Pakistan (West Panjab). The station was started by brother and sister Ajit Khera and Amarjit Khera, who became involved with radio as a community project, not because of a particular interest in wanting to run a radio station, but because it was a useful and engaging way to bring together Panjabis living in the area. 'The radio was just our tool. The whole idea of community came first – the radio came afterwards . . . Through Desi Radio, we've recreated the homeland' (Khera 2005).

Desi Radio's programming has been created with this framework in mind. With regards to their news programming:

> When we give news, we talk about East Panjab and West Panjab. We don't talk about the political states [of India or Pakistan]. We're giving news across the border as if the borders don't exist. We talk about Panjab. Can you imagine? This is very radical and very subversive with a little 's'. (Khera 2005)

The majority of Desi Radio's programming is music, but the station also airs news briefs throughout the day and an assortment of public affairs programmes focused on health, local issues, available resources and cultural events, scheduling similar styles of programming at the same time each day even though presented by different people. They feel that this engenders familiarity and is immediately recognisable and knowable to their audiences, thus helping them better build audience, and that it reinforces the sensibility of the station as a singular entity rather then a collection of many.

The primary requirement is that the language of the station is Panjabi, including music which must be sung in the Panjabi language, whether the music is Bangra (Panjabi dance music), spirituals or ballads. For example, the weekday morning shows are spiritual programmes hosted by different presenters each day. What is unique in this approach is that rather than have each morning focused on a specific religion, the morning programme features spirituals from among all of the religions of the Panjab. The response the station received from many listeners was not favourable at first:

> People said: 'what are you doing?' Take a poem, what we call a hymn, one that is identified as a Sikh hymn, and we will play it on the air and say simply 'namaste', 'as salam' – addressing it to all Panjabi communities irrespective of religion. People would ring back and say why are you saying 'namaste', you are addressing Muslims as well. Well, why not this also for Muslims? But this is religion. This is ours, they would say. We would say no, it is not just yours. It's a common heritage to all the Panjabi . . . [W]hen you hear the same language, the same music, this whole religious identification disappears . . . Fortunately, on radio, they never see you. They don't see your colour or your caste. (Ibid.)

Despite initial resistance to the station's attempts at developing cultural cohesion through their programming philosophy, the music remains one of the strongest bonds between listeners and the station. Listeners have contributed what has amounted to box-loads of music that has never been housed in one place before, building a remarkable library of all varieties of Panjabi music, music that risked being lost.

Station organisers comment that one of the most positive outcomes of Desi Radio is how it has challenged some of the patriarchal gender norms within their community. The station prides itself on creating a space where men and women are equal, has brought many women out of the home into the public realm and, as a result, has boosted their self-esteem. Part of this has to do with the training programmes the station has developed and the numerous volunteer opportunities at the station, but it is also a statement about the warm and inviting environment at Desi. There are always people around, cups of tea on offer and home-cooked food for volunteers and guests. The station is very much a social space as well as a broadcast studio.

Additionally, the station has a strict policy of addressing everyone by their first names – 'an important innovation in the context of the familial hierarchies of Panjabi families' (Everitt 2003: 50). Guests are asked not to thank individual presenters or producers by name but to thank only Desi Radio. 'It is a means by which Desi addresses the disproportionate attention afforded those most visible and the lack of recognition for the behind-the-scenes people who keep the stations running. Such a policy also serves to reinforce the focus on the station as a collective entity, rather than the project of individuals' (Khera 2005).

Desi Radio's annual budget is approximately £90,000 per year. Like other UK community stations, their funding comes from a combination of grants such as the European Social Fund, as well as other local and national grants; local advertising up to the maximum allowed by the licence; and individual contributions and monies raised from fundraising events and programmes. Desi would have no problem attracting more income from advertisers but are limited by law as to how much commercial revenue they can take.

In terms of other creative ways to raise revenue, the station has adopted two interesting practices. One is its programme to raise small, individual donations from listeners in the form of 'sponsoring' an on-air dedication or greeting to a loved one during the morning spiritual programmes. The mentions are offered without the requirement for anyone to pay for it, but it has become a means by which individuals have chosen to support the station through small contributions that total around £10,000 each year. A group of women who volunteer at the station have formed an informal troupe that performs at small gatherings for a sliding-scale fee. The purpose of the performances is in part station fundraising, but also more significantly, to provide an outlet for this group of women to come together and to build confidence by doing so, according to Amarjit. The women's events contribute £6–7,000 a year in revenue. Social events and an annual dinner-dance bring in an additional £14–15,000 each year. The station does not undertake on-air fund-drives.

A 2005 survey commissioned by Desi indicates that 85% of Panjabi speakers in their licensing area listen to the station. Critics say it is exclusionary for a licence to be awarded for one ethnic community when resources are so scarce, but for Desi, the community aspect of the station exists because of its intimate relationship, bringing together one language and region.

Conclusion

Community radio in Britain, as elsewhere, continues to be a growing, vibrant sector. The most pressing challenges remain issues of sustainability, both financial and organisational, including the complexities of running stations on voluntary labour. But as these three stations help demonstrate, there is no one model for how to run a community station or what it should sound like. Local needs must be balanced with the allocation of resources and spectrum. Decisions by regulators must be made and inevitably, there will not be enough room for everyone.

The Internet addresses the issue of scarcity, but now and in the near future fails to resolve the fact that people want listening options on the devices they have all around their homes, offices and cars – namely analogue radio.

In short, though the technology changes, the impulse for community radio will remain. Rosie Parklyn tells the story of being at AMP FM on the north London housing estate where the station was located when a story appeared in the *Evening Standard* written by a journalist who claimed to have lived on the estate for a week. His story described his awful experience and the terrible conditions people lived in. Parklyn speaks of how different it was bearing witness to the reaction from the inside: '[it] had a really detrimental effect on the people living there. If you tell people they come from the worst hell-hole on earth, then, you know, that sort of informs their behaviour in the future' (2004). It is thus the value of self-representation for neighbourhoods and people with collective interests and/or tastes that lies at the heart of community radio.

8.1.2 Community radio: *milango* for lives

Charlotte Hill O'Neal

I bet we had one of the most unique radio barn-raisings that our workshop leaders from Prometheus Radio project had ever witnessed! Drums beating; women ululating; elders and youth dancing and singing and generally kicking up the dust that lay a light film of softness on just about everything. As we planted trees to mark the occasion, I overheard one of the youth say, 'this radio is going to really be a *milango* for our lives!' (*Mlango* (singular) and *milango* (plural) mean 'door(s)' in Kiswahili, the language widely spoken in East Africa.)

I was both touched and elated that that youth 'got it' . . . they understood that our community radio would indeed open up many doors, *milango*, for so many people both in our village, Imbaseni, in the heart of WaMeru homeland outside Arusha, Tanzania and for those in the urban areas in reach of our broadcasts.

To serve as a *door opener* is exactly why we wanted to have a radio station!

We had decided from the very beginning that our mission at UAACR (United African Alliance Community Radio) FM would be to 'encourage and foster the holistic upliftment and development of the community that we serve by providing quality broadcasting with a focus on meaningful and relevant education, creative stimulation and entertainment that speaks to both the elders and youth in our community through a unique fusing and integration of traditional radio with new media technologies and the Internet'.

We have daily classes here at UAACC in English, Spanish and French; computer studies; arts and crafts; building construction; community theater; HIV/AIDS awareness; filmmaking; music production; and so much more, but we are limited as to the numbers of students who can participate in these free classes both because of space and volunteers. We all knew that the radio programmes would be the answer to our prayers to be able to reach and serve the many people who are simply thirsting for knowledge in our community.

Because of so many youth who don't have the opportunity to further their education at primary school level and because of adults who wish to upgrade their education (the vast majority of whom also have not been able to go beyond primary school) there is a great demand for instruction that can be fulfilled by our radio station acting as a community intermediary between our listeners and educational programmes found on the Internet.

And yes, through our computer classes, so many had discovered the magic of the Internet and knew that our radio station could become a strong example to other communities that the integration of knowledge from the Internet with radio is possible and essential in today's world of learning.

For us, it wasn't so much about giving a voice to a protest movement or political dissent, though we envisioned that the radio station would become a catalyst for community discussion about development and accountability issues. In our minds the radio station would afford us the opportunity to motivate non-formal education among elders and youth while bringing within easy reach of the community topical information in areas of agriculture, animal husbandry, social welfare, education, health and the environment . . . things highly relevant to people in our area.

It wasn't so much about giving voice to a *feminist movement* per se, but it *was* about giving voice to those women who have strongly felt opinions on polygamy or the female circumcision still widely practised in our area.

It was about providing information on health and nutrition for those many, many mothers who still think that *uji* (a cornmeal porridge) is enough for a growing baby or that stretching dried powered milk a few more days by diluting it with more water is not harmful.

It was about addressing the needs of growing numbers of youth who don't have jobs or much hope for employment in the future. We knew that we could offer programmes that might become the catalyst for the creation of networks for cottage and village industries, especially among women and youth, and that these programmes would offer income-generation ideas to help in reducing poverty in the community.

Since many of the teachers in our district have had very, very limited materials for their classes such as books, lesson plans and topical, creatively presented information, we knew that these teachers would benefit from our educational programme broadcasts, especially in areas of science and technology.

Because of the rapid spread of a worldwide *Coca-Cola culture* that is strangling the indigenous communities of the planet, we knew that through interviews with elders in our community we would be an effective instrument for the timely preservation of indigenous knowledge and the active promotion of arts and culture in our community.

Arts and culture in our community emphatically encompass and embrace the fast-growing kinship of artists in both the hip hop and rasta families of musicians, drummers, singers, spoken-word artists and designers.

Our radio station will strive to put these youth voices *out there* . . . and we will make sure that their talents and community works are honoured and widespread. These are the youth who are making a tremendous impact on the AruMeru community and Tanzania at large and UAACR FM will definitely serve as an effective means to get their positive messages out there.

And in a nutshell, that is what having a community radio station means to us . . . a *milango* for education and enlightenment for our community!

8.2 Access to broadcasting: TV

Tony Dowmunt

Introduction – a true creative dialogue?

Television – despite the proliferation of channels on an expanding variety of delivery platforms (digital, satellite, cable, mobile phones), and the consequent fragmentation of its audiences – remains a very centrally controlled, exclusive medium. There are still very few opportunities to participate in production for those of us excluded from the 'charmed circle' of professionals who run the channels and make programmes. 'Reality TV' and formatted 'documentary' shows like *Wife Swap* or *Big Brother* have obviously opened up television to a wider range of people as the subjects of programming, in terms of class, ethnicity or sexuality, for instance. But this is a limited openness. The power to define its limits remains firmly in the hands of the broadcasters, and these new subjects are still objects for them to manipulate, not subjects who can represent themselves in any full sense. So this chapter is about exceptions to this rule, about how genuine and relatively free access to programme-making – the power to represent themselves – has been won by 'outsiders', and about some of the new forms of television this has produced, at national and local levels.

First, Mandy Rose looks at two projects – Video Nation and Digital Story-telling – from the BBC. The BBC, as the UK's national broadcaster, is clearly not an 'alternative media' institution, but the Community Programmes Unit, which it housed and which Rose describes briefly below, was for a long time a kind of alternative 'cell' in the mainstream organisation, providing access to BBC resources for outsiders. However, the BBC lost interest in the concept of access during the 1990s, to the point where Giles Oakley (who ran the Community Programmes Unit until 1998) could comment that '"access" as a word has become like "socialism". It's better to keep the term hidden at the same time as getting on with the work' (quoted in Dowmunt 2000: 189). So it is hardly surprising that the unit was closed in the early 2000s. Nevertheless, Mark Thompson – when newly appointed as director general of the BBC in 2004 – could still say, 'We look forward to a future where the historic one-way traffic of content from broadcaster to consumer evolves into a true creative dialogue in which the public are not passive audiences but active, inspired participants' (Thompson 2004: 4).

More recently, in a press release about their creative future initiative, the BBC acknowledges that

> Increasingly, audiences of all ages not only want the choice of what to watch and listen to when they want, they also expect to take part, debate, create and control – as partners with the BBC and in their own communities – real or virtual. Interactivity and user generated content are increasingly important stimuli for the creative process. (BBC Press Office 2006)

So the word 'access' may be dead (replaced by 'user-generated content'), but the concept of active participation remains alive, and we would say, along with Mark Thompson, that a 'true creative dialogue' with its audience is still a crucial part of the BBC's remit as a public service broadcaster. It could be argued that much of their interest in 'user-generated content' derives from it being a cheap way to generate programme content, rather than from a genuine enthusiasm for democratic participation. 'We are encouraging viewers to send us film of extreme weather', said David Holdsworth, head of regional and local programmes for BBC West Midlands where they have been running a 'local television' experiment. 'The aim is to open things up a bit' (Brown 2005: 8). Soliciting sensational material from viewers to bolster conventional programming may save the BBC money, but it is hardly opening up the institution in terms of real democratic access.

All the same, it is clear that the BBC, as the national public service broadcaster, does feel obliged to find a new role in a context in which the tools for creation are now ubiquitous, and the corporation's current interest in 'user-generated content' is a meaningful response to this obligation. The degree to which the BBC permits and encourages 'user autonomy' – genuine participation in, and power over, programme-making by people outside the institution – will be a good measure of how well it is functioning in a truly democratic way. For that reason, the kind of work described by Mandy Rose below is crucial to a broad understanding of the BBC's current role and potential in alternative media work in the UK.

8.3 Video Nation and Digital Storytelling
A BBC/public partnership in content creation

Mandy Rose

When the London transport system was bombed on 7 July 2005 the iconic images
of the events shown on BBC websites and TV were captured not by BBC journalists but by members of the public, on mobile phones. Recent technological
developments have produced a quantum leap in the way that the public can contribute content to the BBC, but forms of public participation in BBC output
are not in themselves a new development. Two projects I have been closely
involved with – Video Nation and Digital Storytelling – have entailed a partnership between the public and the BBC in content creation. The projects provide a
bridge between the access TV model which developed in the 1970s, and the contemporary context of New Media where content by the public – 'user-generated
content', as it is called – is a staple element – from Amazon book reviews, to
entries in Wikipedia, to Blogs.

On 7 March 1994 a two-minute programme was transmitted on BBC 2 under
the Video Nation logo. Colonel Gordon Hencher spoke to camera in an under-
stated but powerful way about ageing, and the gap between his image and his
self-image: 'One doesn't feel old, you know. But it's a ghastly thing, to look and

Figure 8.1 Colonel Hencher on Video Nation site

see your face, what it is now, and what you feel it should be, inside you' (Hencher 1994). It was the first of 1,300 Video Nation Shorts made for BBC 2 between 1994 and 2000 from material recorded by members of the public, which has now been reborn as a New Media project. The TV series became a household name, influenced a raft of other factual programmes and was also a critical success. Five years into the project Polly Toynbee puzzled over why the participants 'all leave us with a feeling of warmth and empathy'. Her explanation was that the series 'is not about observing ordinary people as jokes or characters the way docu-soaps do. It's about letting the camera climb inside people's skin to see the world through their eyes' (Toynbee 1999: 20). In my view it was key to the success of the project that the subjects were making their own recordings, were the subjects not the objects of their filming, and enjoyed control of the material. So how did this experiment in public-access TV work? Why did it happen?

Video Nation started with an unusual if not unique commissioning arrangement. The project was given the green light in 1992 on the basis of the concept rather than programme proposals. The idea was that a broad cross-section of people across Britain would be selected, given camcorders and training and that programme ideas would be generated in response to the recordings received from them. Video Nation was partly a response to a recognition of the increasingly diverse nature of British society. The notion of a consensus among the 'general public' had, by the early 1990s, clearly become an anachronism. The BBC needed to find new ways of reflecting the wide range of views, attitudes and lifestyles that were out there, and the Video Nation project was one way of doing that.

Programme-makers at the BBC had first experimented with what came to be called access television in 1971 and in the mid-1970s the Community Programmes Unit was established with an access remit. A production team including a producer would work with members of the public, often groups with a political argument to make, for the long-running *Open Door* and later the *Open Space* series. When lightweight camcorder technology became available in the late 1990s it made it possible to place the recording equipment directly into the hands of the 'accessee'. The Community Programmes Unit responded with the *Video Diaries* series – 50-minute programmes recorded by members of the public. These had an immediacy and intimacy generally considered to be a breath of fresh air within British documentary. Video Nation was conceived as a fusion between *Video Diaries* and Mass-Observation, the anthropology of Britain begun in 1937, specifically Mass-Observation's establishment of a national panel of volunteers – the Mass-Observers – who were invited to write diaries about their own lives.

In the spring of 1993 the Video Nation team assembled and started to look for the first 50 people to take part in the project. We put out trails on BBC TV and radio and then set about sifting through the over 3,000 application forms that came in and meeting potential participants. We wanted the contributors to reflect the diversity of life in the UK so we established some demographic principles to guide our selection. We would then go to see people at home, taking a camcorder along, to find out more about them and get a sense of the world we would see on camera if they took part. Once we had selected the 50 diverse people who would become the first Video Nation cohort we brought them together in groups of eight or so for a weekend's training. We taught them how to use the camcorders and microphones. They learnt approaches to recording modelled on the *Video Diaries* experience. We ran through the administrative systems of the project, and talked about safety, copyright and contracts.

Regarding editorial control, we decided to offer a right of veto whereby nothing would ever be transmitted without the contributor having seen and approved the edited version. In retrospect I think this arrangement was a cornerstone of the project's success. It gave contributors the confidence to record freely, knowing that they would have the opportunity to decide later if they were happy for the material to be shown on TV.

After the training that first group of contributors went home with their camcorders and an open invitation to record aspects of their world during the course of a year. We urged them to record things that bothered them and things that they wanted to celebrate. We encouraged them to record significant moments as they occurred. We tried to counter their diffidence about the ordinariness of their own lives, emphasising that what seemed obvious and everyday to them was unique and of interest as part of the mosaic we were hoping to create through Video Nation. We were optimistic but we simply did not know what would happen. On *Video Diaries* the diarist had an intense working relationship with the producer for some months. Here was a small team looking after more than 50 people. Would they have enough support and feedback to feel motivated? Would they settle with the camera? Would they tire of the project or run out of steam after a few months? Would they exercise their right of a veto in a way that made programme-making impossible? More fundamentally, would their recordings be interesting and throw new light on everyday life?

As the tapes began to arrive in the office it soon became clear that the project was tapping into a rich seam. We each worked with around eight contributors, watching their tapes, giving them feedback, keeping in touch with them. Their material was a revelation. At a literal level each tape was a series of surprises; you did not know what would appear next. The recordings revealed the people themselves to be surprising, multifaceted, sometimes contradictory. They refused to conform to preconceptions. The emotional world of the recordings was unexpectedly rich; it opened up private worlds of thought and feeling and felt very different from rushes shot by a professional director.

Over the years we tried a variety of approaches to making programmes from the Video Nation material. We intercut around themes in programmes on money, spare time, community and housework in the *Coming Clean* series. We tried to combine a sense of everyday and national life by interweaving the diaries of contributors in *Nation Weekly* and *Nation Goes to the Polls* – which followed some undecided voters in the run-up to the Labour victory in 1997. We even ran rushes in real time in the late-night *Video Nation Uncut* series. But the most significant programmes that came out of Video Nation were the Shorts – two-minute slices of life or opinion that found a home on BBC 2 at 10.28pm just before *Newsnight*. The first ten Shorts shown included the colonel's discomfort confronted by his ageing face; a junior doctor, visibly exhausted, having just come off an 84-hour shift ('If they took a rapist or a child-killer and made them work these hours there'd be an outcry, and yet doctors have to do it every weekend', Mackenzie 1994); an Asian student, shaking after a night-time street encounter with some racists ('They were throwing chips at me. It was really scary. Why?', Vaid 1994); and a BT engineer painting a room and bemoaning Britain's loss of prestige ('Even the Australians don't want to know us, and they're the descendants of bleeding British!', Martin 1994). Perhaps because of their brevity the people and situations proved vivid, thought-provoking and memorable, and these interstitial programmes developed into Video Nation's core output. Between 1994 and 2000 Video Nation was annually recommissioned to make five Shorts a week for 40 weeks of the year plus three hours of longer format programmes.

The strength of the Shorts was their unabashed subjectivity, but this coexisted uneasily at times with the BBC's commitment to balance. After some debate we agreed with BBC editorial policy to preface Shorts with a presentation announcement explaining that the programmes represented 'personal views'. When a piece contained an explicitly political argument we undertook to balance it with an alternative position at a later date.

There were some complaints about the Shorts to start with – from viewers who seemed puzzled by these sudden glimpses into one individual's world, with no explanation or guiding perspective. But as the audience became familiar with Shorts, complaints about the form stopped (though complaints about particular views and lifestyles portrayed in Shorts continued to arise). It seems that most viewers began to recognise that these brief programmes were intended to add up to a kaleidoscopic picture of contemporary life, that sometimes they might recognise something of their own world, sometimes not. Research showed that most of the audience who had seen the previous programme would stick around for the Short even if they then turned the TV over or off. Hence Shorts would frequently have an audience of half a million. Once or twice, when they followed a major football game the audience reached five million.

Even with their right of veto we were concerned about how the experience of being involved in the project, and in particular being on television, would impact on Video Nation contributors. However, the evidence suggests that it has largely been a positive experience. Contributors have clearly felt affirmed by taking part, having the opportunity to be heard in the public sphere: 'I had a hard upbringing. My parents forced me to give up school at 16. I had no qualifications, not one. Doing Video Nation has given me massive lift. The BBC actually listens to me' (Conrad Gorner, quoted in France 1999). People say that by and large the responses they get from their family and community are supportive: 'Some of them still imagine I've got a whole camera crew with me, helping me film everything. But when I say "No – it's just me and a camera", they say; "That's pretty good. Not just what you've said but the technical side as well"' (quoted in Thumin 1999). They welcome a structure within which to reflect on their own lives. Some contributors find that the camera has a therapeutic function. Fisherman Ian Mackinnon took part in Video Nation for five years. Working at sea, 'the camera becomes a great listener. It's become a friend almost. A friend who doesn't answer back' (quoted in France 1999). He thinks cameras should be given out on the NHS – 'free therapy'.

After five years on BBC 2 Video Nation was decommissioned in 2000 by Controller Jane Root, whose programme strategy involved reducing documentary output. Chris Mohr took on the question of what to do with the Video Nation archive – both the programmes and the rushes – and, with BBC New Media, created a website to make Video Nation Shorts available on demand. I researched the potential of New Media for taking this kind of work in a new direction and in spring 2001 I moved to Wales to take a new post with the BBC. One reason for the move was to get involved in a project already in development at the BBC in Cardiff – Digital Storytelling.

The Digital Storytelling project started life in 2000 when Professor Ian Hargreaves and Daniel Meadows of the Centre for Journalism Studies at Cardiff University took the idea to BBC Wales. At the time Daniel was lecturing in photojournalism and new media. Alongside his academic career Daniel Meadows is a photographer. In 1973 he had taken his camera on the road, travelling round England on a bus, taking photographs of the people he met. In 1995 he retraced his steps, returning to photograph some of the same people 20 years on. On his return visit one of his subjects questioned his right to take and show his photo. That challenge chimed with Daniel's own disquiet about the power relations embedded in the relationship between the professional image-maker and his subject. It started him on another journey: to find the tools and a methodology that could enable non-professionals to tell their own stories using rich media. That journey took Daniel to California and to the Center for Digital Storytelling which had been running workshops since the mid-1990s. There he found in Digital Storytelling a methodology that he felt could unlock the stories which all of us carry in our heads, and tools that, with some expert guidance, anyone could utilise.

Ian Hargreaves and Daniel Meadows presented Digital Storytelling to BBC Wales Controller Menna Richards. She was quick to embrace the idea. Recently appointed, she wanted to use new investment that had been made in BBC Nations and Regions following devolution, to make a more direct connection with the audience in Wales: 'I believe very strongly that the BBC has to be about the audiences it serves and that what we as a broadcaster must achieve is a sense among the audience that the BBC is for them. And it isn't just about being broadcast to or broadcast at, it is about participating in the process' (quoted in Kidd 2005: 12).

Wales faces specific challenges which Ian Hargreaves addressed in his original proposal for the project. Wales has a poorer and somewhat older population than the UK average and at that time had lower Internet take-up than anywhere in the UK except for the North-East of England. Hargreaves argued that Digital Storytelling could offer a variety of benefits: access and training for Welsh people in new media tools, a boost to the Welsh creative economy, and raising community

self-esteem by asserting a self-defined identity. He made a case that Digital Storytelling should be developed in a form that was sustainable so that long-term
benefits might be derived. This would entail working with partners, an idea that
Menna Richards supported and which became part of the way the project was
developed.

Digital Storytelling found a home in BBC Wales within the New Media Department, and I became its executive producer. The project, which we christened
Capture Wales was piloted in 2001. That summer Joe Lambert and Nina Mullen
from the Center of Digital Storytelling came to Wales from Berkeley, California
to run a workshop as a way of passing on skills to the BBC team. In the autumn
Daniel Meadows led a BBC Wales team on pilot workshops in Wrexham and
Blackwood, developing and customising the America model. Taking a portable 'digilab' on the road and delivering the first workshops was challenging, but
feedback from participants and the power of some of the first stories suggested
that Digital Storytelling had great promise. In early 2002 the project was commissioned to run for three years and Daniel was seconded from Cardiff University
as creative director, to work alongside the BBC team. Since 2001 the team have
run monthly workshops in communities across Wales – some in English, some
in Welsh. Over 450 diverse people have attended and made short multimedia stories. Additionally the BBC team has mentored a number of organisations across
Wales who have delivered workshops to over 300 storytellers.

The BBC team at a workshop ideally consists of the creative director, a script
facilitator, two trainers and a musician who works with storytellers on their
soundtracks. Ten volunteers are selected after attending a Capture Wales public
meeting or filling in an application form online. The group is chosen to be diverse
– in terms of social background and existing computer skills. They give five days
of their time. In exchange they are guided through the creative and technical process of turning an idea into a brief first-person documentary. They use new-media
tools – low-cost digital cameras, scanners, image manipulation and non-linear
editing software on laptop computers – familiar to some who take part, totally
new to others.

At a presentation by Capture Wales they are shown examples of digital stories
and invited to think of a personal story that they would like to work on. The workshop process then consists of a number of steps. Day One is the 'story circle' in
which participants are guided through the process of developing the story, transforming their idea into a script of no more than 250 words. They then gather the
images they need to illustrate it, typically stills. They draw on the family album.
They take pictures of key places, people or objects. At the 'image capture' session
these are uploaded to a laptop computer. The heart of the process is the three-
day production workshop that follows. There the participants record their story
as voice-over, and create and edit it inside their computer using Adobe Photoshop
and Premiere.

The production process reflects the roots of Digital Storytelling in community
arts and oral history. Daniel Meadows describes digital stories as 'radio with pic-

tures' and situates the project within the BBC in a tradition of 'listening to the voice of the people' – a project pioneered in radio by Olive Shapley in the 1930s and continued after the Second World War in the Radio Ballads of Charles Parker.

Making the stories is challenging for all the participants, daunting for some. Most people have strong feelings about the story they have chosen to tell so they can feel vulnerable exploring it and a pressure to get it right. Many have little confidence in their creative abilities. Some are extremely nervous of computers. There is a lot to do in a short space of time if the stories are going to be finished, and the BBC team decided early on that completing the stories was a crucial requirement. Yet despite all this, or perhaps because of the satisfaction of overcoming all the hurdles, participants generally give very positive feedback about the process.

Huw Davies attended the pilot workshop in Blackwood and later joined the team as a trainer. He has made a story about the workshop process to show potential participants. It expresses something of the enjoyment, commitment and community spirit which the workshops engender:

> You've got just five days to make a digital film of broadcastable quality and if you're in the same position as I was at least half of the software is totally unknown to you and it's got BBC attached to it so you're a bit scared to start with. Ten minutes into the 'Story Circle', Day One of the workshop and you're falling about laughing with people you've never met before, because everyone's a bit uptight and it's a relief to discover that it's going to be fun and nothing like a classroom experience. Computers come next: the team managed to explain enough and give you enough time at your own machine for you to feel excited by its incredible capabilities. By Day Three most people have to be dragged kicking and screaming from their machines just to take a coffee break. (Unpublished interview, Davies 2003)

It is an expression of the power of the process that not one of these volunteer filmmakers who has started a workshop has failed to complete their story. Participants' written feedback forms suggest that the experience works on a number of levels. For many there is satisfaction and confidence gained in getting to grips with the tools of new-media production and using them to create a piece of finished work: 'Daunted at first, I was quickly put at ease as the team explained the procedures I needed to create my digital story. I was thrilled to have the opportunity to use the technology'. 'It was a life affirming, very emotional experience. I learnt new technical skills, and ways of telling accessible, engaging stories. I feel quite evangelical about the whole process'. Being heard in the public arena – on the website or on TV – is also very powerful: 'It was a peculiar and wonderful feeling to sit in my living room last night and see a story that I made (albeit with a huge amount of help from "the team") going out live on national television'. There can be a significant sense of achievement: 'I accomplished more in these four days than I did in five years of college!' And, as on Video Nation, participants often mention a therapeutic function: 'I had an absolutely great time making my film and learnt a great deal . . . Besides new IT skills, it has given me an opportunity to exorcise a demon in letting go of the past.'

The finished digital stories are as varied as the people who make them. Subject matter has included the death of a child, metal-detecting, community feeling during the 1984 Miners' Strike, father–son rivalry as expressed through fishing, the experience of exile. Some stories are funny, some sad, some surprising, many are very moving and give the viewer a feeling of privilege to be invited to share another individual's (sometimes hard-won) sense of life's meaning.

Once the story is finished workshop participants are given a right of veto regarding publication, as on Video Nation. If they are happy, and the story conforms to editorial and legal requirements, it is uploaded to the BBC's Capture Wales or Cipolwg ar Gymru websites where it will be available on demand, organised according to theme alongside some commentary provided by the storyteller. Stories are also published by place on BBC Wales regional Where I Live websites.

While feedback from participants is extremely positive, the BBC has to justify the project in terms of its benefits and reach to a wider audience. Though growing, reach via the Web is still limited so from the start we have pursued outlets for digital stories on other platforms. A natural home is BBC Wales digital zone BBC 2 Wales and digital stories now regularly appear in its schedules – sometimes singly, sometimes grouped around themes. Additionally some of the most powerful stories have found slots on BBC 1 Wales, particularly when they have topical resonance, bringing them to a wide audience. On occasion stories are shown within the BBC Wales early evening News show *Wales Today* which reaches one-third of the adult population of Wales each week. We have also worked with radio colleagues and some stories have been transmitted as audio only; others have been created in audio-only workshops for Radio Wales and Radio Cymru.

In 2005 Digital Storytelling and Video Nation have come together in a new initiative on interactive TV called Your Stories. Video Nation had found a new lease of life in 2001 when BBC English Regions invested in the project as a way of producing content by local people for their new Where I Live websites. When Video Nation was commissioned in 1993 the media landscape looked very different from now. Video Nation injected the subjective voice and an 'amateur' aesthetic into the heart of the mainstream schedule at a time when terrestrial broadcasters enjoyed a privileged role in mass communications, which has been rocked by technological developments since. Most British viewers then could receive four channels, now they can potentially receive hundreds, and on-demand delivery is coming of age and threatens to make TV schedules themselves a thing of the past. The Internet makes it possible for anyone to be a publisher. As the BBC seeks to redefine itself in this new technological climate the idea of acting in partnership with the public on content creation has moved from the margins to become a strategic priority at the BBC.

Most of these initiatives work on the assumption that users have the media literacy and tools to get involved. Many people do. Yet many others do not. The motivations which triggered Digital Storytelling still apply. Some people lack access to the tools for economic reasons. Others do not feel competent or confident in using them. And very many – from all sorts of backgrounds – have no experience of shaping their ideas editorially. This is where Video Nation and Digital Story-telling do something particular and important – unlocking untapped creativity by offering simple media forms within which, with facilitation, anyone can tell a story.

Thanks to: the Video Nation team (1994–2001) – in particular my co-Producer Chris Mohr; Video Nation Editors (2001–) Carole Gilligan and Rosemary Rich-ards and Executive Producer, Bob Long. The Capture Wales team (2001–) Creative Director; Daniel Meadows, Producers Karen Lewis and Gareth Morlais, Story facilitator Gilly Adams, Trainer Huw Davies, Researchers Carwyn Evans and Lisa Heledd, Team Assistant Lisa Jones, Associate Producer Melanie Lindsell.

Video diaries

The video diary format, first developed by the BBC's Community Programmes Unit as we saw above, has proved an enduring way for radical filmmakers all over the world to work with subjects to portray alternative realities.

'Videoletters' is a TV series devised by Katarina Rejger and Eric van den Broek, two independent filmmakers from the Netherlands. In 20 episodes of 25 minutes each, former friends, lovers, colleagues or neighbours separated by the war in the countries of the former Yugoslavia exchange 'video letters' with each other, with the aim of re-establishing what once were close relationships. Some, after seeing each other on video, meet again for the first time since the war.

The series was filmed between 1999 and 2004, then shown in 2005 by all the public broadcasters in the countries of the former Yugoslavia simultaneously. For the first time since the war, millions of viewers across the region were watch-ing television together with, and at the same time as, their former enemies.

The project is continuing independently of the TV series through a website (www.videoletters.net). A media bus equipped with internet connection and web-cams has travelled through the countries of the former Yugoslavia, helping people to record their own video letters and post them on. There are also static internet facilities installed throughout the countries involved in the project, enabling others to record and post their video letters or to look for lost friends on the website.

Video diaries are now commonplace in all kinds of 'reality TV' programming, from the Big Brother Diary Room to more 'serious' documentaries. They remain a way for 'non-professionals' to represent themselves, in the best instances in a relatively unmediated way in mainstream media. The Prisoners of the Iron Bars is a Brazilian feature-length documentary in which the filmmakers gave inmates camcorders to record their own view of life in Carandiru, a notorious prison in the city of São Paulo. In one sequence, 'The night of an inmate', the film features the occupants of one particular cell, trying to, in their words, 'show you about this place, especially at night . . . It's hard with words. Maybe it works with images, right?'

The sequence conveys an impression of the lives of these prisoners which would have been impossible for a professional crew who could go home at the end of their working day. The prisoners film their morning and evening routines, photos of their families and homes, distant commuter trains passing, and fireworks exploding far away in the dark night outside their cell window. They show how they communicate with a woman in a block of flats opposite the prison, using hand signals, and, in a remarkable scene from the early morning, how they use a mirror arrangement to see more outside their cell window: 'This is how we can see what the bars prevent us from seeing . . .'

Figure 8.2 Prisoners' stills

In the US access to, and participation in, TV broadcasting has been primarily achieved through the community-access cable movement. In stark contrast to the public service tradition exemplified by the BBC, public broadcasting in the US has been relatively weak, and television dominated by commercial interests. In this context the struggle for access has been fought for since the 1970s, through successful citizens' campaigns to secure channels and funding from the commercial cable companies, as Martin Lucas points out below in his piece from New York. As Garcia and van Oldenborgh described above (p. 95) this has produced an extraordinary tradition, currently under threat, of grass-roots television programming produced over more than 30 years throughout the US, from the East coast to Hawaii (Waltz 2005: 51).

8.4 Manhattan Neighborhood Network
Challenging monocrop monotony

Martin Lucas

Manhattan Neighborhood Network, the public-access network for the borough of Manhattan, is one of several thousand community-access cable stations that cover America. While the world of public access suffers from a *Wayne's World* image of irrelevant ineptitude, the reality is that a broad cross-section of America's citizenry uses public access, and it is a home for alternative opinions in hundreds of cities across the United States. The Alliance for Community Media currently suggests that an astonishing 1.2 million Americans are involved in producing community television (Haasch 2005: 1). At a time when mainstream media are consolidating globally, and national public broadcast systems are coming under more direct political pressure, the world of public access bears consideration as an important home for civic discourse, offering a grassroots army of citizen producers who have the training, the equipment and the platform to create audiovisual messages.

The stations vary in size. While many access centres feature one staffer, and a single channel, MNN is the largest, with a staff of over 40 and four channels that air programming 20 hours a day. The producer base includes about 2,000 people. The 60,000 shows they make a year run the gamut from political satire to hip-hop, from cooking shows to cyberart.

The history of public-access television goes back to the 1970s. As America got wired for cable, media activists joined citizen groups to demand a 'setaside' of a percentage of cable bandwidth for community, educational and government use. The basic legal framework was established, and MNN, like most access stations, came to be through a franchise process where city government grants media companies, such as Time Warner in the case of New York, the right to lay video cable under the street, and make money in a monopoly framework from citizens. In return the cable company gives a small percentage of the viewers' monthly fee back to the community cable access system, and provides the channel space for those shows to air.

MNN is far from being one of the oldest access stations in the US. While many local communities have operated their own stations for 20 years, the New York cable operators retained control up until the late 1980s, when a variety of community interests converged around franchise renegotiation and forced the cable operator to provide support for a real community-operated cable access centre. The legacy of this history, in a city already known for oversized egos, is that the individual-producer model played a more defining role in local cable culture than in many other cities where the local access centre plays a central role in creating community.

Manhattan, with its million and a half residents, and dozens of languages, hardly qualifies as a single 'community'. On the other hand, the breadth of MNN's programming reflects the amazing diversity of cultural groups who live and work in New York, as well as highlighting the lack of real representation on the other hundred-plus channels available to New Yorkers. Where else can you find shows like (picked at random) *Urban Spelunking, Italian-Americans' Midlife Crisis, Pothedz Couch, Life in Babylon, If Jesus Is Mine I'm Going to Give Him Time, Biker Billy Cooks with Fire, Modelando con Carolina, Raregrooverevolution*, and over a thousand others? (MNN 2005)

In fact, a large number of MNN producers come from communities under-served by mainstream media. MNN is home for much black and Latino program-ming on topics including public affairs, religion, music and fashion. There are programmes in languages from Albanian and Spanish to Chinese, Hungarian and Haitian Creole. From New York's arts community come experimental video, soap operas, burlesque shows and political satire.

How do thousands of non-professionals manage to make programming that challenges mainstream content in terms of diversity the way a Central American rainforest challenges the monocrop monotony of a modern agribusiness farming operation?

One answer is that, while many producers make shows using their own equip-ment, MNN provides extensive training in camera, studio and non-linear editing techniques free of charge to any Manhattan resident. While in recent years the number of ordinary citizens with camcorders has increased, the expertise needed to run a control room or edit shows on a non-linear computer system still takes some learning, and MNN provides both the equipment and the training. There is also a Youth Channel, offering a venue for 'youth-made' media that is part of a growing national movement. In addition, MNN seeks out organisations from underrepresented communities to work with, providing on-site resources and training for groups involved with immigrant rights, labour, and social justice issues.

Curiously, although the regular ratings services presumably collect the statis-tics, there is a black void of 'ratings' information about public access. In a way this is fine. Comparing access to mainstream media is a false game on several levels. For one, the typical hour of access television is budgeted in tens or hundreds of dollars per hour, a trivial percentage of the figure for big producers.

In addition, the approach to information is very different. No viewer of access cable is treated as a demographic. Selling to viewers is prohibited. And access programming is part of a communicative process linking makers and viewers; in keeping with the tenets of organic farming, this is information 'produced locally, and consumed locally'. A good clue for viewership is the large number of shows with live telephone feedback.

Call-in shows are often done in one of MNN's 'express studios' – basically a do-it-yourself set-up with a camera, a phone and a titler to insert the phone number. These shows, on topics from politics to policing, from religion to health issues, draw large audiences. One of the most important local call-in shows is the housing show *Tenants and Neighbors* where the phones ring non-stop with viewers

Figure 8.3 Amy Goodman interviews Aristide for *Democacy Now!* The ex-president of Haiti was on a plane to Africa, where he first made the claim he had been hijacked by the US and forced into exile (Photo: *Democracy Now!*)

hoping to get good legal counsel for survival in New York's cut-throat real-estate market.

While most shows are local, some MNN programmes offer an 'alternative view' on a larger scale. *Gay USA*, one of our longest-running series, offers news and public affairs for a community that is still poorly represented in the mainstream media. Another broadly popular national show is *Democracy Now!*, a daily news programme presented by Amy Goodman, started on public radio, offering a progressive viewpoint more or less totally unavailable in the commercial media.

Nonetheless, it is local coverage that is the bread and butter of access. In New York, with its huge variety of public and private channels, it is still MNN that covers city council elections, for instance, and offers a chance for candidates to debate on the air.

Equally significant in a time where democracy itself is threatened, are efforts to provide coverage of local events of broad citizen interest unlikely to get extensive coverage elsewhere. Here MNN has worked with independent groups to provide coverage of anti-war marches and other major events such as the resistance to the Republican Convention. MNN operates on a 'soapbox' model based on the right of all citizens to free speech as enshrined in the First Amendment. While MNN itself does not typically produce programming, it can work with groups, including Indymedia, Freespeech TV and others who seek to use alternative community outlets to talk about issues that are typically given short shrift by the mainstream press.

Local democracy is at the heart of what community media is, and why it is valuable. As recent interim director Bob Devine put it, 'One of the key roles that public-access organisations play in their communities involves the process of bringing private citizens into public life and engaging them in active roles of citizenship within those communities. That's the secret jewel of public access' (quoted in McGregor 2003: 2).

The need for politicians to cosy up to media outlets has ensured that communications-industry points of view become law for almost all aspects of broadcasting. This power in Washington is now combining with new digital technologies to make a serious threat to the local city-franchise model upon which local access is based.

The current model of a 'cablecaster' offering viewers a variety of channels is being challenged by telephone companies, who see an opportunity to offer a similar service, but without the need to become a 'broadcaster', and without the need to get involved with franchising on a local level. Two bills in Congress at the time of writing this article will give them what they want, spelling the end for public access as we know it.

The legislative giveaway of the electromagnetic spectrum to large telephony communications firms is outside the scope of this piece. However, while new laws may make the already uneven playing field even less so for community media, new technological innovations are not totally in the hands of the corporate R & D departments. MNN is countering the threats from corporate interests, along with access stations and other partners, by developing a variety of initiatives from digital bicycling (sharing content via the Internet) to WiFi broadcasting, to video blogging and syndications of content and media news. In addition MNN was an early leader in full-time streaming at www.mnn.org and its Web 'hits' are a significant factor in viewership. MNN's young people's wing is particularly innovative, as can be seen at www.youthchannel.org.

As these innovations in viewing habits create new audiences and new ways of reaching them, will there be a home for community media? The current regulatory climate is grim, but there are indications that popular unhappiness with the hijinks of corporate media has created a backlash in the US against media deregulation, resulting in a broad citizens' movement for media reform that may save some sort of home for local non-profit media. Meanwhile, as they say, stay tuned . . .

9 Mainstream or alternative media?

Introduction

There are many thousands of political, social and charitable organisations which have oppositional or alternative perspectives to the mainstream values and politics of the societies in which they operate. By their very campaigning nature the vast majority aim to use media to advance their ideas and objectives, whether this be revolutionary change, reform or simply fundraising. The question of whether to try to use or influence mainstream media or to create forms of media under their own control or perhaps a mixture of both is a fundamental one for each organisation in the development of its media strategy.

Historically, before the Internet, mobile phones and emails became so pervasive in an increasing number of countries across the world, many organisations, especially, for example, the larger and better funded NGOs, defined their main goal as penetrating the mainstream media of newspapers, radio and television. However, there has also been a long history of organisations and radical political groups and movements establishing their own independent media in the belief that the mainstream would not report their ideas and activities accurately or, in many cases, at all.

This last point obviously raises the complex question of the analysis of mainstream media which has invariably been a contentious issue among left thinkers and political activists. Such an analysis on a global scale is a vast undertaking. While many media analysts, for example Herman and Chomsky (1988) and McChesney (2000), have convincingly argued that the conglomerates which dominate world media tend to reflect conservative values and politics and the interests of big capital, a micro-analysis of any one country at any one time can indicate a more complex picture across the mainstream media. For instance within most Western European countries it is possible to locate forms of mainstream media which do feature liberal or progressive perspectives, for example many public service broadcasters. In most dictatorships tight control of media is a political priority. So the question of whether it is worth trying to work with mainstream media if you come from a radical or alternative perspective varies considerably from country to country. To make things even more complicated, James Deane, in chapter 12 of this book, analyses a rapid expansion of media in many developing countries in the last decade or so and points to the way that the huge variety of media which has grown up in the wake of state control denies easy application of the mainstream–alternative dichotomy.

However the terms are used in analysis, establishing successful alternative forms of media is not necessarily an easy task and is very much determined by the political moment as well as resources. In his article in this chapter, João Alexandre Peschanski describes some extremely successful radical radio, newspaper and television projects which have been built in Latin America over the last decade. In each case this has been possible because each of the media projects has been part of a vibrant political movement.

Of course the 'success' of an alternative media project depends very much on the original objective, which could vary from being a means of internal communication or organisation to trying to have a significant effect on public opinion. Even with the dramatic possibilities of the Internet it appears that it has been difficult for most alternative media projects to reach comparable numbers to those of mainstream media. It is for this reason that Ivor Gaber and Alice Wynne Willson, writing about mainstream media and NGOs, take the view that

> while NGOs do produce their own websites and magazines and support the development of alternative media voices, in terms of audience, these activities tend to amount to little more than preaching to the converted. To influence decision-makers and achieve their campaigning goals NGOs must engage with international news outlets and agencies. (Gaber and Willson: 100)

While most NGOs and similar organisations will continue to target the mainstream, the whole media environment is changing rapidly and, as Mirella von Lindenfels suggests in this chapter, NGOs, as well as many other progressive organisations, will increasingly require strategies which will analyse the entire media spectrum to examine how each can be used for particular purposes and to reach specific audiences and user groups.

Also in this chapter, Natalie Fenton, discussing NGO media strategy, analyses some of the complexities and resistances of working with mainstream media and suggests that considerable degrees of compromise might be necessary in order to 'sell the story'. Writing within the Latin American context, Jaoa Peschanski takes the view that most mainstream media are so closely associated with maintaining the political and economic status quo that the creation of alternative or autonomous media associated with political movements is the only viable strategy.

Of course the majority of NGOs seek to use mainstream media as a means of influencing public opinion or to persuade it to be more open to their ideas. As noted in the introduction to this book, the notion of 'autonomous' media, close to practices Jaoa Peschanski describes in this chapter, proposes to bypass the mainstream to create radically different ways of creating and managing forms of media. One seeks some accommodation with the mainstream, the other to bypass or become involved in political movements to radically transform it.

While it is always necessary to take into account the specific conditions in any country at any one moment it is clear that, almost everywhere, we are living through huge changes in media technology and the uses to which it can be put. Mobile phones have become a crucial means of political mobilisation, digital cameras have become an invaluable tool for human rights activists and email and the Internet a brilliant means of global communication for radical groups as much as for armies, governments and bankers. While it will not be possible to rival the global media conglomerates which currently dominate without fundamental political change it is and will be increasingly possible to find imaginative ways of creating alternative media projects, which, at least for some organisations and activists, and where possible and appropriate, will be combined with finding cracks in the mainstream as well.

9.1 Getting alternative messages in mainstream media

Natalie Fenton

Popular mobilisation and the mass media

The use of the mainstream media for popular political mobilisation (often by groups that fall within new social movements) is a deeply controversial issue. This chapter reviews some of the research in this area and the issues it raises for groups that seek to challenge the status quo and gain publicity that runs counter to the dominant hegemony. There is a prevailing belief exemplified in the work of Herman and Chomsky (1988) and the Glasgow University Media Group (1976; 1980) that the organisational structure and professional ideologies of the mainstream media produce a media system that is monolithic and impenetrable to those who flout its unwritten rules (Atton 2002b). As a consequence, it is claimed that if alternative, radical or unofficial voices do find a space they do so on preset terms or run the risk of being demonised. The practical and political dilemma then becomes whether to pursue a voice in the mainstream and risk undermining your cause for the sake of accessing a large audience or to retain political purity and accept that this means low-level distribution.

As Boyle (1997) on US guerilla television notes,

> Whenever alternative video sought power over (or from) the structure of broadcasting, their more radical messages were co-opted, diluted or absorbed into the wider system of values embodied in the mainstream media. Whenever

they set themselves outside this system limiting their scope of influence and concentrating it by controlling their own modes of distribution they succeeded in articulating 'other' voices traditionally excluded by mainstream media. Their successes seem small and reach puny audiences compared to mass media but the successes may be real. (Boyle 1997: 193)

Understanding the similarities between alternative and mainstream news and the various factors that contribute to mainstream news coverage of minority voices may enable a more sophisticated debate among activists grappling with these concerns. It is important to remember that journalists working in the mainstream media do not always and necessarily follow the well-trodden path of professional codes and conventions in their news reporting. The codes and conventions of news reporting are themselves dynamic and constantly shifting, liable to disruption from contradictory internal and external forces. Alternative voices can and do access the mainstream news media. In a consideration of the distinct news agendas of mainstream news journalists and alternative news sources, Atton (2002b: 494) distinguishes between three forms of 'coming together': sometimes it is through collision with mainstream news where both news agendas come together and fulfil the requirements of each, such as protests in Seattle against the WTO; sometimes it is through incorporation, where alternative news sources are used to provide oppositional views or personal witnesses to satisfy the requirements of mainstream news for human interest and conflict; and occasionally it is through dissidence, where alternative news sources become newsworthy to the mainstream by dint of their alternativeness. Each form of news portrayal broaches different issues. When the news agendas collide there are concerns over hierarchies of credibility (Seymour-Ure 1987) with official news sources usually taking precedence over unofficial sources with their authority most often deferred to. This is not predetermined by prevailing social structures of power, rather it is gained through successful media strategies (Schlesinger 1990). When incorporation is the charge then claims of alternative news sources acting as no more than news fodder that feed the dominant news values of mainstream journalism (and in doing so further personalising politics) becomes the concern. When dissidence is the reason then misrepresentation of violent minorities comes to the fore. But there are factors other than news values to be taken into account.

In an analysis of mainstream news coverage of NGOs Deacon et al. (1995) distinguish between the nature of proactive news management on behalf of the NGO as a news source, in particular the publicity strategies and resources of organisations, and the perceptions and practices of journalists and editors involved in the news-production process.

Research into news management in NGOs has demonstrated consistently that well-resourced, professionalised organisations are both more likely and better able to provide a steady stream of news releases, publicity gimmicks and public relations material than poorer and more informal organisations (Fenton, Golding and Radley, 1995; Deacon and Golding 1994). This has a direct consequence for the amount of mainstream news coverage they are likely to receive. In other words, the ability of NGOs to impact upon the mainstream news agenda is determined by the resources available to them. These resources include the financial (the capacity to maintain a permanent office and employ specific staff), but they also include the cultural capital associated with class, professional status and expertise as well as the legitimacy and credibility gained through previous activities within the political and media fields. Voluntary organisations who espouse causes, monitor official actions and seek to offer alternative meanings to the dominant ideology will only get their voices heard if they subscribe to journalistic criteria of expertise and professionalism. They must speak the same language, be easily contactable, understand what makes a good news story to a professional journalist and be able to feed the mainstream journalist the material that suits their product.

In the UK the more established NGOs (for example Save the Children, Greenpeace, Oxfam) are experiencing increased legitimacy with the 'liberal' press and broadcasting (Deacon et al. 1995). Deacon et al. also discovered that certain types of NGOs receive a disproportionately large amount of coverage. General service-providing NGOs gain most coverage overall, comfortably exceeding the coverage given to pressure groups. Personal heroics and fundraising are also likely to attract media coverage, more so than political commentary and advocacy.

Deacon (1996) conducted important research into journalists' views of the voluntary sector. He shows how the news values of journalists and the 'hierarchy of credibility' they employ to discriminate across a heterogeneous sector play a major part in overrepresenting certain types of voluntarism and NGOs and ignoring others. He revealed that if NGOs want coverage then they must be prepared to compete for it, by providing stories that conform to the professional news values that guide the news selection process. Essentially, the less complex and ambiguous an issue is, the more readily it can be personalised and dramatised, shown to have clear and immediate implications, and if it is consonant with previous news frameworks, the more likely it is to be deemed newsworthy and reported.

Deacon (1996) also found that journalists repeatedly emphasised two important criteria that influence their decision to approach an NGO, or follow up one of its leads. These were topicality and generality. Because NGOs are not seen as a significant elite in their own right, they largely have to defer to news agendas determined

NGO media strategy Mirella von Lindenfels

As long as NGOs need to influence the mainstream political process, they will need to work with the mainstream media. It operates in parallel with, reflects and is part of the establishment which runs the world and has power over the issues of concern to civil society.

To effectively exert pressure on decision-makers, NGOs need a constituency of support whose interests or concerns they represent. Building that constituency, over the long term or around a specific issue, requires awareness-raising, engagement and dialogue through the media and platforms that the target members of the public use.

NGOs have to go where their audiences are. Traditional media, non-traditional media – the distinction is largely meaningless. If a significant percentage of any given target audience takes the majority of their news and info from blogs or podcasts, that *is* their mainstream.

Even for NGOs without a political objective, different sectors of the general public are needed to donate funds, volunteer, change their behaviour or attitudes and access services, and ignoring or failing to take the new channels seriously is a grave mistake.

Not having an effective Web presence with 'designed-for-Web' content is already a negative indicator about an organisation and how much it values interaction with the rest of the world.

As the ability to provide rich content and new platforms increases and the 'brand-leader' NGOs embrace the technology available (see: http//www.green peace.org/international/photosvideos/greenpeace-tv or http//www.christianaid. org.uk/frameit.htm?http//www.pressureworks.org), it raises the public's expectations of NGO Web communications and notches up the benchmark for the rest of the sector.

It can only be a matter of time before one of the major NGOs launches its own Internet-based broadcasting service, providing consistent, quality programming as an addition to mainstream options. It *should* only be a matter of time because this is a critical evolution for the future.

As the traditional media undergoes its own evolution in response to globalisation and new technology, audiences will increasingly fragment, making it harder and harder to reach the people NGOs need to reach, including politicians, and there is little cause to hope that the traditional media will devote more airtime to the many civil society issues requiring attention.

Providing high-quality broadcast programmes – from news to softer documentaries and entertainment – can help to fill that gap but only if it is offered as a viable and watchable alternative to what's on the Skybox.

There are no real boundaries anymore – between national and international news portals, between traditional and alternative, mainstream and new – it is all blurring and mixing and ultimately it is becoming the mainstream norm – fragmenting audiences as it does so. A new media landscape is emerging.

For NGOs there is no choice between traditional and new. The emerging media landscape has to be viewed as a whole and approached with clear, strategic objectives. Who do you need to reach and which channel will enable you to do that? That is what good media work has always been about, we just have a much broader palette to work with now.

by other institutions and events. One consequence of this is that NGOs working in areas that become topical in the news agendas may suddenly find the media very receptive to their views and, indeed, find themselves pursued by journalists. But groups working in areas that are absent or marginalised from the mainstream news agenda will find journalists far less receptive.

The second criterion that journalists use to assess the newsworthiness of a story was the test of generality, and reveals their concerns about the broad relevance of a story. Journalists are driven by a desire to talk to as wide a number of constituents as possible. This emphasis on the general applicability of news has two implications for the reporting of NGO activity. It leads to preferential initial treatment by national journalists for those organisations with strong nationwide support and it advantages those organisations who deal with issues of a general rather than a minority interest. Similarly, Atton (2002b) notes that the space activists are given to speak in mainstream news media is not under their control and is confined to matters of immediate and personal experience. This reproduces the hierarchies of access in mainstream news by insisting that ordinary people may only speak on matters they have direct experience of.

The above research reveals several difficulties in using the mainstream media to try and present non-mainstream views:

- They conform to pre-established notions of what is and what is not news.
- They are of very limited value in empowering marginalised, oppressed or exploited sectors of society because the media have become personalised and individualised.
- Because of their compromising nature, the media frequently erode the dignity of those people whose interests they purport to reflect, i.e. they conform to a professional journalistic agenda.
- They remain hierarchical and operate a hierarchy of credibility for news sources.
- They are frequently undemocratic and prefer organisations that speak on their terms and are professionalised in the processes of mainstream news management.

Although the media obviously do not put up established or hegemonic barriers that are so impenetrable that no counter-arguments appear, they do decide which oppositional voices will be included. Frequently this comes down to economics – the poorer you are as an organisation and the less cultural and financial capital you have the less likely you are to be accepted into the mainstream. Also, as Todd Gitlin has argued (1980), opposition is most often domesticated, absorbed and incorporated by popular culture with hegemony shifting slightly to maintain consent. In this way hegemony is maintained through allowing controlled dissent: 'Major social conflicts are transported into the cultural system where the hegemonic process frames them, form and content both, into compatibility with dominant systems of meaning' (Gitlin 1980: 263).

In environmental issues, for example, the fundamental terms of the debate are of industrialism and its alternatives – these have become incorporated into mainstream culture as questions such as whether or not we should recycle household waste. This becomes the accepted terrain of debate – the common-sense approach to the subject – and the more radical perspectives are left out of the debate altogether. What often happens then in alternative forms on mainstream media is that issues receive a treatment that is individualised, drawing attention away from sociological, structural or political explanations – in this manner the media hegemonically bend attention towards accounts which carry little substance (Gauntlett 1996).

A central question that arises out of this research is whether groups and individuals in civil society can intervene in the mass media public sphere and change the agenda through setting off a critical process of communication, or whether their voices simply serve to reinforce the status quo. It is for these very reasons that much of the alternative media have preferred to conduct their struggle for social change outside the dominant public sphere.

Regulating political campaigning

Despite the real concerns and issues raised above, images and arguments about the failings of public policy provided by the voluntary sector can and do inform national and local mainstream media. There are many other routes into the mainstream media than through the annals of news and current affairs. Broadcast public appeals are no longer predominantly aimed at the public purse but more frequently implore the need for social and political change. A significant commercial development has been the removal of a long-standing ban on charitable advertising on commercial television and radio in 1989. Although the anticipated stampede of large charities to colonise the airwaves never materialised several organisations have productively used television advertising, alongside other publicity campaigns, to highlight issues and raise money.

The dual approach of fundraising and campaigning has raised broader quandaries about the appropriate political and social function of the voluntary sector. Although this government and previous governments have encouraged the growth of charities and voluntary organisations, they have been less willing to accept a similar increase in their public influence (Golding 1992). Despite this governmental reticence, a broad consensus has emerged within the British voluntary sector that urges a more active, campaigning role for organisations. The report of a working party convened by the National Council for Voluntary Organisations (1990) and chaired by Lord Nathan stressed:

> Campaigning is a crucially important aspect of the voluntary sector's contribution to society. The quality of people's collective and individual decisions benefits greatly from the way in which voluntary organisations, formed

around a particular cause, contribute their distinctive knowledge and expertise. (Ibid.: 25)

This role has also been acknowledged by governmental regulators of charitable activity, albeit more conditionally. The chief charity commissioner commented, 'It is clear that charities can – and arguably should – contribute to informed public debate, including political discussions and campaigning, on issues within their own experience which are relevant to fulfilling their charitable aims' (*Guardian*, 22 June 1994: 10b).

A crucial feature of this new order in the voluntary sector, which embodies a growing awareness of the need to compound advocacy and fundraising, is a much sharper and aggressive political style. Campaigning can often take groups uncomfortably close to the terrain of party politics, which – for organisations with charitable status at least – raises a host of serious issues, as regulations prohibiting inappropriate political activities by charities are both long-standing and becoming increasingly stringent (Randon and Perfi, 1994).

Under Rule 11.3 of the ITC Code on Advertising Standards and Practice, advertisements soliciting donations or promoting the needs or objects of bodies whose activities are financed wholly or mainly by donations will normally be accepted only from registered charities, or those able to produce satisfactory evidence that their charitable status has been officially recognised, such as acceptance of the organisation's charitable status by the Inland Revenue. (The ITC has now been subsumed by Ofcom which has adopted this code as policy.)

Rule 11 and Rule 4 exclude those organisations with objectives wholly or mainly of a religious or political nature or which show partiality as respects matters of political or industrial controversy or relating to current public policy.

Also of concern to the ITC is the use of television to unfairly exploit the audience's own emotions. In October 1995 complaints against Greenpeace, Friends of the Earth, the International Fund for Animal Welfare and the NSPCC were upheld by the Advertising Standards Authority: 'Overstepping the line between presenting a possibly distressing, but accurate, picture of their cause and misinforming people about an issue by exaggeration or stretching the truth, exploits the trust that the public have in charities and certain pressure groups' (*Guardian*, 4 October 1995). The advertisement for the International Fund for Animal Welfare linked opponents of legislation protecting wild mammals with American mass murderer Jeffrey Dahmer. The advertisement by the NSPCC showed a baby in the womb reacting adversely to an argument between its parents.

Another critical limitation of these new advertising opportunities is that their availability is directly linked to an organisation's ability to pay. The prohibitive costs of television broadcast advertising exclude all but the very affluent charitable bodies, and potentially exacerbate the marginalisation of many groups in broadcast media. The small uptake for advertising on television is related to both regulative and financial constraints.

Case study

Live Aid was a multi-venue rock music concert held on 13 July 1985. The event was organised by the pop stars Bob Geldof and Midge Ure in order to raise funds for famine relief in Ethiopia. Billed as a 'global jukebox', the main sites for the event were Wembley Stadium, London, attended by 72,000 people, and JFK Stadium, Philadelphia, attended by about 90,000 people. It was one of the largest-scale satellite link-ups and TV broadcasts of all time – an estimated 1.5 billion viewers in 100 countries watched the live broadcast. As a charity fund-raiser, the concert far exceeded its goals: on a television programme in 2001 one of the organisers stated that while initially it had been hoped that Live Aid would raise £1 million ($1.64 million), the final figure was £150 million (approximately $245.4 million) for famine relief.

The concert was the most ambitious international satellite television venture that had ever been attempted at the time. At one point midway through the concert Billy Connolly announced he had just been informed that 95% of the television sets in the world were tuned to the event.

Live 8 was a series of concerts that took place in July 2005, in the G8 nations and South Africa. They were timed to precede the G8 Conference and Summit held at the Gleneagles Hotel in Perthshire, Scotland from 6–8 July 2005; they also coincided with the 20th anniversary of Live Aid. Running parallel with the UK's 2story campaign, the shows planned to pressure world leaders to drop the debt of the world's poorest nations, increase and improve aid and negotiate fairer trade rules in the interest of poorer countries. Ten simultaneous concerts were held on 2 July and one on 6 July. More than 1,000 musicians performed at the concerts broadcast on 182 television networks and 2,000 radio networks. On 7 July the G8 leaders pledged to increase aid to Africa by US$25 billion by the year 2010. The G8 made significant commitments on debt and aid in July but fell well short of what the Make Poverty History Campaign had hoped to achieve. The World Bank and International Monetary Fund took steps in September 2005 to ensure these promises are met, but there is still much more to be done to ensure delivery. (The Make Poverty History campaign is a British and Irish coalition of charities, religious groups, trade unions, campaigning groups and celebrities who are mobilising around the UK's prominence in world politics in 2005 to increase awareness and pressure governments into taking actions towards relieving absolute poverty.)

The campaign was given a high-profile launch on British television on New Year's Day 2005 in a special edition of *The Vicar of Dibley*, written by Richard Curtis, who pledged support for the campaign during 2005. His television drama *The Girl in the Café*, broadcast in the UK (on BBC 1) and US (HBO) on the same day, 25 June, highlighted the same issues.

Television advertisements also ran during Live 8, urging people to speak to their representatives about stopping poverty. However, Ofcom banned the advertisements, deciding that they were 'wholly or mainly political' in nature, since they aimed to 'achieve important changes'. The three demands of the campaign are: trade justice, drop the debt and more and 'better' aid.

In April 2005, a commercial began airing in the United States with several celebrities in black and white stating the pledge of the American ONE campaign, their version of Make Poverty History. The commercial featured 33 celebrities and personalities. At the end, Tom Hanks states, 'We're not asking for your money. We're asking for your voice.' The general goals of the ONE campaign in the United States are to end extreme poverty, hunger and AIDS. A more specific goal is to get President George W. Bush to commit at least 0.3% of the national budget, around US$30 billion, to foreign aid, and increase it further to the UN goal of 0.7% of GDP, around US$73 billion as of 2004, over the next several years. In 2004, the United States Government spent US$7 billion on foreign aid.

Live Aid and Live 8 were very different events but both received massive mainstream media coverage. In large part this was due to the centrality of celebrity to each spectacle. Not all reports were positive. In Britain some accused the campaign for not being critical enough of the UK government, seeing Tony Blair and Gordon Brown's support for the campaign as a cynical ploy to move away from criticism of the Iraq war. The slogan of ending poverty has also been criticised as empty rhetoric – a convenient sound bite used by politicians and other groups in order to promote themselves and their alleged superior morality, with no evidence that the political ideas behind these slogans will make any difference to levels of poverty in Africa or elsewhere.

Some press reports criticised Geldof for using Africa as 'a catwalk', more about reviving the careers of ageing rock stars than about helping the poor in Africa. Many noted the hypocrisy that a number of the performing artists had tens (if not hundreds) of millions of dollars of 'spare cash' lying in their bank accounts while wanting to 'Make Poverty History'. The notion of debt relief being promoted by Live 8 was also seen as giving a blank cheque to governments, many of which are plagued by corruption, and in the past have used debt relief to increase their defence spending. Some have criticised Geldof for ignoring what they hold to be the root causes of Africa's problems, the actions of Robert Mugabe being one, and seeking to solve complex political problems by simply throwing money at them. The economic principles and theories behind the event have also been subject to criticism as ill-informed and simplistic. Some citizens of G8 nations are discontented with the idea of their tax money funding developments in another continent that could be spent on their own education, health, pension and infrastructure systems.

Nonetheless these were not events that the mainstream media were likely to pass by – they fulfilled all the expectations of news values and newsworthiness noted above and reached massive audiences. They also allowed participation and the promise of a feel-good, quick-fix solution to the problems of the world.

The G8 summit in Scotland was also the subject of a coordinated G8 protest by Dissent! – a network formed in the autumn of 2003 by a group of people who have previously been involved in radical ecological direct action, Peoples' Global

Action, the anti-war movement and the global anti-capitalist movement. (In February 1998, new social movements from all continents met in Geneva to launch a worldwide co-ordination of resistances to the global market, a new alliance of struggle and mutual support called Peoples' Global Action against 'Free' Trade and the World Trade Organization (PGA). This platform is 'an instrument for communication and co-ordination for all those fighting against the destruction of humanity and the planet by capitalism, and for building alternatives.' So far, PGA's major activity has been co-ordinating decentralised Global Action Days around the world to highlight the global resistance of popular movements to capitalist globalisation (www.agp.org).) The Dissent! network has no central office, no spokespeople, no membership list and no paid staff. It is a mechanism for communication and co-ordination between groups involved in building resistance to the G8, and capitalism in general.

Prior to the G8 protest a group of people from within Dissent! took on the function of responding to, and seeking out ways of engaging with, the mainstream media. They called themselves the CounterSpin Collective (CSC). This group's main focus was to facilitate those groups within the Dissent! network who wanted help. A very comprehensive list of press contacts from around the world was built up, and translators were found that were able to translate press releases for global distribution. The groups began to try to control media interviews with positive outcomes. Protesters began to be quoted in articles. A list of names was drawn up so that when the media did make contact they were put in touch with someone in the network who had expressed a willingness to talk to the media.

Those involved with the CSC also acted autonomously in writing letters and personal responses to mainstream media contradicting the stories put forth from police and state sources. The week before the G8 Summit the number of people actively involved with the CounterSpin Collective went from around four to 20. Soon after the convergence site opened the media response group set up in a gazebo outside the site perimeter. It was set off-site and clearly marked so that it was an obvious point of contact for journalists and photographers. Here it was explained that no journalists or photographers were allowed onto the site. They were told that no one could be referred to as a spokesperson for the network. They were given a press pack while other members of the media response team would go inside the camp to find people willing to give interviews.

The CSC built up a list of 'unfriendly' and 'friendly' journalists. Preferred journalists were given interviews and stories while others were asked to leave or confronted with questions as to the nature of their enquiry. On 5 July the media reception tent was full and the phone did not stop ringing. The CSC claim success in enabling protesters' voices to be heard and quoted alongside established voices of authority challenging those who sought to criminalise the activities of the protesters. This venture was not without its adversaries:

> nobody working within the media response group that grew to become the
> small GC group harboured any illusions about the nature of the work they

were doing. We were attempting to do something that some people were very uncomfortable with and in some cases, had an ideological opposition to. (http://www.nadir.org/nadir/initiativ/agp/resistg8/reflection/g82005disset.htm)

Here we see the mainstream versus alternative media dilemma played out. For many who worked within the CSC, and many within the Dissent! network, actively ignoring the mainstream media was not an effective tactic in the genuine fight for change in societies. The aim of the CSC was to proactively voice their social critiques and contextualise their actions to as many people as possible. For the most part this effort was based on the work of a small number of people with various degrees of experience in creating a communications infrastructure. Comparing the coverage of Live 8 with the G8 protest produces a generally stark contrast of the respectable/accepted face of mainstream campaigning as against the disrespectful/unacceptable face of political protest. Clearly, far more could have been achieved.

The experience of the CSC raised several questions for these political activists applicable to many protesters working outside the mainstream voluntary sector:

- The mainstream media are generally interested in spectacle and mass mobilisations are in some part about spectacle. Is it possible to manage the mainstream media and better reflect the aims and ambitions of the movement/mobilisation?
- How can concepts of direct action, non-hierarchical organising and self- and collective empowerment be made meaningful and interesting outside activist ghettos?
- Who should take responsibility for interacting with the mainstream media and how can this be delegated alongside the political desire not to re-create power structures of leaders and or representatives within a network?
- How can conflicts be resolved when the ideology of some parts of a mobilisation is at direct odds with others, such as with the internal conflict about whether or not to work with the mainstream media? (http://www.nadir.org/nadir/initiativ/agp/resistg8/reflection/g82005disset.htm, December 2005)

Conclusion

The research conducted on NGOs and pressure groups in the media shows, on the whole, that the mass media permeate – and may be experienced as part of – the daily life of civil society insofar as they appear to present a range of voices and debates, but as large corporate industries which are in varying degrees subject to state power and operating within established professional ideologies they also reside within the steering systems of modern society. They are, in other words, to a great extent beyond the reach of citizen practices and interventions. This partly explains why many oppositional groups have preferred to conduct their struggle for social change outside the dominant political public sphere occupied by mainstream media:

> The indirect approach of media manipulation using a spectacle of disobedience designed to muster public sympathy and support is losing proposition. The 1960s are over and there is no corporate or government agency that is not fully prepared to do battle in the media. This is simply a practical matter of capital expenditure. Since mass media allegiance is skewed towards the status quo, since the airwaves and press are owned by corporate entities and since capitalist structures have huge budgets allotted for public relations, there is no way that activist groups can outdo them. A soundbite here and there simply cannot subvert any policy-making process or sway public opinion when all the rest of the mass media is sending the opposite message. Any subversive opinion is lost in the media barrage, if not turned to its opposition's advantage through spin. (Critical Art Ensemble 1999, cited in Terranova 2001: 107)

Instead, Terranova (2001) notes, the Critical Arts Ensemble (CAE) point to the need for decentralised flows of micro-organisations that challenge societies based on the controlled sovereignty of the nation state, preferring a politics that presents itself in cyberspace and is directed by the desires of the multitude. This deliberate shift from the mass media into alternative media has not happened with all NGOs. Some acknowledge readily, albeit reluctantly, that the mainstream mass media are as important as, if not more important than, new media. Their role as agenda-setters is vital to policy-makers and public opinion. But the symbolic trade-off has been too high for many. The dilemmas invoked are both political and practical and unlikely to go away.

9.2 Communication of the oppressed
Alternative media and their political impact in contemporary Latin America

João Alexandre Peschanski

'Resignation breaks down humaneness; rebellion reinforces it'. (Paulo Freire)

'¡Que se vayan todos!' This statement – 'They must all go' – was repeated over and over in Ecuador in April 2005. Protests had spread out in major cities. Daily rallies took place in Quito. Hundreds of thousands of people were marching. They were demanding the resignation of the entire government, led by Lucio Gutiérrez. Much of the strength of this movement, which finally overthrew the president on 20 April, came from the broadcasts of a radio station, Radio Luna.

Since his election in 2002, Gutiérrez had been negotiating free-trade agreements with the United States of America and was pursuing neoliberal policies, such as privatising natural resources and increasing taxes, which were thought by many to harm the interests of poorer people. Foreign corporations were given privileges to exploit petroleum resources, which account for 40% of the country's export turnover, and to import agricultural goods. The production of crops is the basis of survival for the indigenous peasants who represent 80% of Ecuador's 13.5 million inhabitants.

In spite of the widespread anger against Gutiérrez's policies, no organisation had been able to unite the discontented. While most parties remained aligned with the government, the opposition limited itself to creating institutional obstacles for the president, without showing any intention of truly representing the voice of the poor. The leftist organisation Pachakutic was not sufficiently well organised to galvanise protesters. Political confusion reigned.

Resistance to the government was self-organised by people through an independent radio station. Every day, hundreds of people would go to queue for hours in front of Radio Luna's office, just for a chance to have their voice heard. Children, the elderly, blue-collar workers, students and peasants all spoke out on what they thought of Ecuadorian politics. Rude language was not spared.

Radio Luna, until then a small popular education station in Quito, was transformed in April into the epicentre of a continually growing protest. Demonstrations were publicised, repressive measures were revealed, actions of revolt were encouraged. The station reached the top of the Ecuadorian ratings. Mainstream media, closely connected to conventional and institutional politics, were simply overwhelmed.

Ecuadorians had discovered that their opinions and ideas mattered, and that most people agreed with them. Silence had been broken. Radio Luna had become the bridge for joining the discontented. It gave space to poor people to express their creativity and imagination. No editor would censor ideas or reproach anyone for the use of inappropriate language. In a country where headlines were normally addressed to the richest, communication was now from the poor to the poor.

On some occasions, politicians and corporate officers attempted to use Radio Luna for their own benefit by trying to control and direct events. Their voice was heard, as was everybody else's, yet their aims failed. The demonstrations belonged to the people, not to politicians, parties or oligarchs, insisted the broadcasts.

During the protests, Paco Velasco, member of the Popular Education Center and director of Radio Luna, admitted he was no longer in charge. 'The people have taken over the radio. It is theirs. They are free to do as they please with it. Those who thought them unable to understand communication techniques have been proven wrong, and defeated', he said in interviews (Velasco, 2005).

On 15 April, conscious of the damage Radio Luna was doing to his image,

Gutiérrez ordered the shutdown of its office. When his supporters arrived to carry out these orders, they encountered a human shield blocking the entrance. People had been informed of the president's aim and had been mobilised to defend what was now theirs. Radio Luna – and the Ecuadorian people – stood firm.

Mainstream media

Communication has become a strategic space for social struggle. In general, the mass media control which messages will be given space and which are to be neutralised. In an attempt to influence public opinion and decision-makers, social movements and organisations strive to obtain time or space for their ideas in mainstream media. Many organisers formulate their protests with media coverage in mind, adopting dramatic or creative styles to make the maximum impact.

As elsewhere, mainstream media are far from constituting a neutral position. Collective actors, even those who habitually present a contentious posture, are often 'tamed' or distorted by mainstream media attitudes and practices. Those who insist on making their voice heard, as in the case of the Ecuadorian dissenters, are pictured either as objects of derision or as dangerous to democracy, whichever image happens best to suit the defence of the communications monopolies.

Mass media ownership is highly concentrated. Media companies often have holdings in other business sectors or are themselves part of a diversified group. No more than ten or so corporate entities are at the origin of all news destined for worldwide presentation. This high degree of concentration automatically makes every media outlet the mouthpiece of other comparably powerful economic interests. The agendas of social movements and organisations are given positive coverage only to the extent that they are in tune with these interests.

In Latin America, communication companies have interests in common both with other corporate entities and with traditional oligarchies. Mainstream media have a clear agenda: defending the elite values and political control – *coûte que coûte*. Journalistic objectivity and neutrality are sacrificed when protests begin to present a challenge to the domination of the rich. When the poor begin to demonstrate mainstream media quickly become an expression of propaganda while continuing to preach their credibility and impartiality.

Corporate journalism has invented a number of stratagies in order to render popular dissent ineffective. This array goes all the way from curtailing coverage of the demonstrations, probably counter-productive as it ends up playing into the hands of those who eventually manage to break this silence barrier, to leaders being coopted and to divisive tactics. The most frequent technique, especially in Latin America, is criminalisation: participants in social movements are depicted as outlaws seeking nothing but disorder, and motivated by irrationality.

The creativity displayed by mainstream media in creating obstacles to the progress of protest movements has no limits. In Latin America, as elsewhere, the current *mot d'ordre* is satanisation. When they were first given television coverage in the mid-1990s, Argentinian *piqueteros*, a neologism that stands for those manning barricades, were treated as demons. Faces were intentionally made to appear red. There were scenes of extreme violence, hardcore music, vandalism. All the ingredients were there of what Argentinian spectators commonly associate with evil. Mainstream media coverage had proclaimed itself the guardian of morality, and chosen the good and bad guys. Social movements were placed among the latter, in a way similar to the treatment of 'terrorists' by the United States government.

Why were *piqueteros* protesting? What were they demanding? Who actually were they? These questions were not on any mainstream media agenda, simply because the exploration of such issues was not in their interest. Argentinian television broadcasts were intent on defending the policies of President Carlos Menem which resulted in a major economic crisis in 1998 and a recession in 2001. The *piqueteros*, mostly unemployed from impoverished neighbourhoods of the capital, Buenos Aires, were the first victims of calamitous public-policy decisions. This was clear to media owners, who wanted to make sure that the explosive potential represented by the protesters was effectively defused. But as with the movement in Ecuador, mobilisation by the poor succeeded in breaking through stonewalling and misinformation by mainstream media. By 1997, the *piqueteros* had become a national movement.

New media paradigm

Activists would be naive to complain that mainstream media ought to be more democratic. They cannot be. They will never be. Only a few acts of mobilisation manage to cross the obstacle represented by the media. Yet even those who do become tainted. Communication must be perceived as a political arena in which social actors and forces struggle to achieve cultural hegemony in a community. Therefore one must ask oneself on which side he/she is. Whose interests is he/she advocating? Journalists need to be conscious of their political choice. In the face of oppression there is no possible neutrality. If one does not denounce and endeavour to correct injustices, one has chosen the oppressor's side.

Leaders of the Ejército Zapatista de Liberación Nacional (Zapatista Army of National Liberation – EZLN), based in Southern Mexico, have broken the corporate communication paradigm by adopting a strategy of giving no interviews to mainstream media. This movement is made up of native Mexicans from the region of Chiapas, where certain towns are already self-organised by small farmers. Leaders have pinpointed instances of ideological bias on the part of the mass media, portraying them as outlaws, not as legitimate social organisers. Since adopting this no-interview policy, EZLN's public announcements are made directly to media which stand up for indigenous interests, especially to *La Jornada* (The Journey), an alternative newspaper founded by themselves which is currently the most widely read daily in Mexico.

Latin American alternative communication relies on certain principles, first enunciated in Paulo Freire's pedagogy of the oppressed (Freire 1972). Initiatives of popular media have all developed similar means of attributing value to popular experience, even though no continental paradigm has ever been formulated. The main strategy has been to deconstruct dominant values. In Latin America, for instance, the adjective 'popular' commonly signifies cheapness and tackiness – popular cars (low in cost), popular culture (poor in quality). Alternative media, as does Freirean education, aims to contest this logic and to enhance the dignity of popular knowledge.

To recognise popular culture as valuable is to perceive communication as an action having political intentionality. When one talks about alternative media in Latin America, one is immediately referring to the defence of the oppressed. Nevertheless, according to Freire's teachings, popular communicators must refrain from dogmatisation, meaning a switch from the truths that embody elite domination to top-down revolutionary instruction. They must not simply extract the knowledge from the people, give it a proper format (free of grammatical mistakes or redundancies) and then publish their articles. The communication of the oppressed is horizontal: peasants and blue-collar workers are not to be perceived as mere sources, but as co-producers of information.

Vanguardism must be rejected in the same way as any doctrine postulating a full adoption of popular practice, or basism. Popular communication must be based on dialectical action, bringing together popular concrete reality (humiliation at the work place, lack of infrastructure in the neighbourhood, high cost of seeds), with broader issues (corporate profits, conspicuous consumption in elite households, lack of governmental policies in support of small farmers) introduced by a communicator. Neither of these categories of information is more relevant or significant than the other. They must engage in dialogue. By themselves, the oppressed might not perceive their difficulties as resulting from political domination, and simply blame their misfortune. Without bonds to the people, communicators work for their personal enlightenment and doctrinal position. Both humanise their existence by exchanging experiences.

Straightforward dialogue, however, is not enough. Communication is the synthesis of the two categories: the reflections of the oppressed and of the communicators. Achievement and dissemination are the task before both participants. Both are to communicate the synthesis of their political dialogue, which contains a subversive and utopian core. It is important to highlight that I do not talk of 'journalists', but of 'communicators'. Journalists view themselves as specialists, the only ones capable of writing and editing stories. They generally manipulate the information obtained from their sources – for good or evil – and exclude the poor, especially the illiterate, from the opportunity of speaking freely. Popular communicators maintain a horizontal relation – the dialogue – with others, stimulated by them to become communicators in turn. By doing so, they resist domination.

This dialectic communication, the communication of the oppressed, rejects pamphleteering media. Its practice relies on experimentation and critical reflection.

Each and every dialogue produces new pieces of information. Social transformation is all about creativity. From this perspective, media are an instrument not for spreading doctrine, but for stimulating critical reflection and for fostering new popular communicators.

'Possible dreams', using Freire's lexicon, feed this new media paradigm. They compel communicators to think about their daily practices, setting before them a tangible goal. These dreams may come through simply because people who free themselves from oppression walk in their direction. They contain a utopian element which denounces an unfair society and simultaneously enunciates the possible dream of, at the very least, one that is fairer.

Democratising and networking

Since the mid-1980s a multitude of popular communication initiatives have popped up on the Latin American stage. Most, despite their dynamism and political energy at birth, end up fizzling out without leaving any lasting trace. The great challenge facing alternative media within capitalist societies, within which the industry is dominated by a few major corporations, is how to extend their life expectancy.

Those who control the media leave nothing to chance. Whenever the opportunity arises, these corporations put to good use their relationships with government and their advertisers to destroy popular initiatives at birth. Community radio stations, created in most cases with modest means in poor neighbourhoods, become the target of frequent police actions. Equipment is confiscated, announcers are handed in to the local police precinct and occasionally even thrown into jail. This repression is inspired by the major radio stations, worried by the competition for audience represented by the alternative content of such nascent media. They justify this violence by raising their voices against so-called 'piracy'. Alternative stations, so they allege in printed pamphlets, create wavelength disturbances for other broadcasts.

In an attempt to fend off the criminalisation of their activities, communicators denounce the concentration of ownership and content generation within a small handful of major corporations. In 2004, social movements throughout Latin America, gathered at the Americas Social Forum and founded the Continental Campaign for Communication Rights. The objective was to draw public attention to the empire of corporate media and to promote popular participation in communication. The campaign, moreover, formulated a political agenda for alternative media, ranging from requiring accountability from the majors, to pressuring the state to put some of its weight behind the newly created media, with at its core a true shift in the way journalism is perceived.

The difficulties faced by alternative media do not only originate in attacks from corporate media, but are also caused by the very dynamics of popular communication initiatives. Many of these, having had their origins in mass protest, are subsequently taken over by some oligarchy or by a particular faction, to the exclusion of others, and then disappear. Continuity for these alternative media must feed on a continuous political source, on a Freirean dialogue with the masses. Media are power, and the more the political influence of even a popular vehicle keeps growing, the greater the number of individuals or groups who attempt to stamp their control over its ultimate destiny. Thus a media initiative that may have been democratic at birth may subsequently become bureaucratic and conservative, inexorably moving an increasing distance from its origins and, ultimately, to its disappearance.

It may be costly, exhausting and lengthy, but only democratic practice, according to the precepts of dialectic communication, can ensure the survival of a popular media entity. This concern was present at the birth of the Brazilian weekly *Brasil de Fato* (Brazil as It Is), launched in 2003 during the 3rd World Social Forum. At the origin were a number of organisations such as the Central Única dos Trabalhadores (Workers, Central Union – CUT), the largest labour union federation, the Movimento dos Trabalhadores Rurais Sem Terra (Landless Workers Movements – MST) and the Marcha Mundial de Mulheres (World March of Women – MMM). The objective of this weekly was to keep social-action agendas present in public discussion, as well as acting as an instrument of pressure on behalf of other grass-roots organisations such as neighbourhoods or local associations. *Brasil de Fato* has become the main popular means of communication on the Brazilian media scene.

Brasil de Fato had to face a variety of material obstacles. First, was the invective of the major media, which published articles criticising the paper, termed a mere pamphlet, and strong-armed the news-stands into boycotting its distribution. Plus, evidently, there were cost factors such as paper, printing and postage. Despite all this the weekly paper managed to build a countrywide network of collaborators, often writers denied space in the mainstream press who found in the new paper a place for their contributions on oppression by the media and their experience with attempts at resistance.

The main difficulty experienced by *Brasil de Fato*, however, was the crisis originating from the confrontation between the expected goals and the attitude of Luiz Inácio Lula da Silva's government. Lula, a former metalworker, honorary president of the Partido dos Trabalhadores (Workers' Party – PT), had been elected in 2002 on a 'change Brazil' ticket. The weekly's first headline, which coincided with the inauguration of the new president, read 'Lula needs courage'. The various social movements remained faithful to their alliance with Lula, in the expectation of far-reaching changes for a society perceived as one of the most unequal in the world. But the changes never took place. The government kept its distance from the organisations. Party members and cabinet ministers were cashiered under suspicion of corrupt practices. The Brazilian left was thoroughly demoralised and had suddenly lost direction.

The new weekly became hostage to the political situation. Many readers criticised *Brasil de Fato* for being too pro-government, and left. Others cancelled their subscriptions for exactly the opposite reasons: the paper was seen as a mouthpiece for anti-Lula interests. Disagreements broke out among different social movements represented on the editorial board. The political crisis seemed to be leading towards the demise of the paper, as well as to that of the Brazilian left itself – formerly seen as one of the most powerful in the world, having been at the ideological and organisational origin of major anti-globalisation meetings such as the World Social Forum.

At first, *Brasil de Fato*, unable to become a uniting force for the diversity of left-wing tendencies, became a hodge-podge of stories, mainly concerning the government but also international and environmental issues. Initially, somewhat aimlessly, in part because the paper was being viewed with distrust by several social movements, adjustments were gradually made to its editorial line. It succeeded in becoming not simply a halfway house between those in favour of the PT and those against, but a vehicle carrying popular agendas in general. Prior to this, a hostage to the crisis experienced by the left, it had managed to become a rallying point and debate forum for the various scattered tendencies. It certainly served as a foil for the agendas of the right, as always in their hegemonic positions within the major media, and, if nothing else, prevented them from becoming even stronger.

For an alternative media venture there is no magical recipe for success – or even survival – but the Latin America experience shows that networking is all-important. Once a media initiative appears to congeal, and sheds its capacity to build links to a multitude of social sectors – not restricted to those who were present at its creation – it is headed for extinction. *Brasil de Fato* was conceived organisationally as a network in which its various elements all had their say. But the weekly in turn was itself a member of other networks, principally of Minga Informativa de Movimientos Sociales (Social Movements Information Pool), a continent-wide network constituting a unifying platform for popular communication experiences. Minga members are peasants, unions, women's organisations, alternative means of communication – from all the Latin American countries.

Minga has no intention of imposing its own line on its communicator members, aiming to become more of a venue for the interchange of experiences and the forging of common strategies. The ultimate aim is to create its own communicational fabric, capable of facing up to the hegemonic major media. The aim is to stimulate new communication initiatives and nurture those already in existence. The continent is witnessing a fight over antagonistic actors and destinies.

One of the main centres in the struggle between mass media and alternative communication media is Venezuela, where Minga has been concentrating much of its efforts. Hugo Chávez, president of this oil-producing state since 1998, is in the process of challenging the local bourgeoisie. Four years after the election, Chávez was the target of an attempted coup, masterminded by the major television networks – Venevisión, Radio Caracas Televisión, Globovisión and CMT – and by nine of the ten widest circulation dailies, including *El Universal*, *El Nacional*, *Tal Cual*, *El Impulso*, *El Nuevo País* and *El Mundo*. Their monopoly over the sources of information had allowed the media to take over from the traditional political parties.

Ever since the election of the Chávez government, these media made daily, concerted efforts to challenge its legitimacy, and to destroy its popular support.

Neighbourhoods from which the government had received most of its votes, were presented as 'dangerous shanty-towns, filled with communists, prepared to start a civil war in order to establish itself as a dictatorship' (from a 2006 newspaper article). In actual fact it was the mass media owners themselves who were conspiring to overthrow the government. The coup took place on 11 April, organised by businessman Pedro Carmona in league with the media owners plus the United States government, and managed to unseat Chávez. The latter was sent to an undisclosed prison. Meanwhile, a forged letter of resignation was widely circulated.

Once in power, Carmona dissolved Congress and revoked both the Constitution and 49 laws that enhanced government control over the economy, and the Supreme Court was dismissed. None of this was aired by the television channels. Newscast announcers claimed that Chávez had flown the country. But via the 'bush telegraph' and through alternative means of communication, such as independent radio stations and union broadsheets, news began to circulate among the population that the president had in fact been taken prisoner. Demonstrators began to march towards the presidential palace. During two days demonstrators besieged the seat of government demanding the return of Chávez, which took place on 13 April.

Back in power, the president made no move to close down any of the corporations or mass media that had organised the coup, despite recommendations to do so from some of his close advisers. On the contrary, his decision was to challenge the media at their own game, stimulating alternative media and helping create public television channels. He founded Telesur, a Latin America-wide network open to both Venezuelan communicators and those from other countries. This channel still suffers from certain teething problem, such as the adoption of formats that resemble the major networks too closely, but it has shown itself to be open to dialogue.

And the various movements, both in Venezuela and elsewhere, are now aware of the opportunities for using this new means of communication as an instrument for emancipation. All the while the majors have kept up their attacks on the government, but on the sly. They defend their own interests. But they are surely aware that their position of hegemony is not only under threat but beginning to crumble.

Acknowledgement

My writing of this section would not have been possible without the inestimable help of Anita Pollak, Albert Hahn and Flávio Bassi Jr.

10 Culture jamming

In the last chapter, Natalie Fenton considered the paradox of alternative messaging within the mainstream media. Here, we switch tactics to examine the ways in which existing media and culture are themselves transformed into commentary, often through parody, satire and the re-purposing of mediated images (such as advertisements), through which new critical forms of alternative media are created. These are alternative media that defiantly seek to expose cracks in our culture.

> We have facts for those who think, arguments for those who reason; but he who cannot be reasoned out of his prejudices must be laughed out of them; he who cannot be argued out of his selfishness must be shamed out of it by the mirror of his hateful self held up relentlessly before his eyes. (Wendell Phillips, American abolitionist, 1853 in sniggle.net)

In short, culture jamming does not have to be complicated. Simple actions by individuals can have a strong visual impact and the use of humour and satire can go a long way. Lisa Anne Auerbach turns the traditional handcraft of knitting into political protest, creating a knit skirt worn at the Republican National Convention emblazoned with 'Bush is a Turkey' (www.stealthissweater.com). Joe Decker and Ryland Sanders create the website 'God Hates Shrimp' (www.god hatesshrimp.com), drawing attention to the hypocrisy of those who use biblical verse to justify their opposition to gay people, citing lines in the Bible where the eating of shellfish is called an abomination in equally strident tones. Reverend Billy and the Church of Stop Shopping descend on an unsuspecting Walmart or Starbucks to proselytise their message to consume less (www.revbilly.com). And culture jamming is not only a tool for street activists. The State of California commissioned ads as part of their anti-tobacco campaign that played off the macho cowboy image of the iconic Marlboro cigarette ads, with the silhouette of two cowboys heading into the golden sunset, one saying to the other, 'I miss my lung, Bob.'

Graham Meikle begins this section by placing in context various forms of DIY mischief-making under the category of 'culture jamming'. Meikle is clear to point out that the term is by no means a universal catch-all, but rather one that offers us a useful way to consider forms of alternative media practice that are rooted in creative uses of *existing* media and cultural commodities. Culture jamming is thus about the manipulation and (re-)creation of existing cultural images in a way that results in images with a decidedly different, alternative message. Drawing from a wide range of projects, Meikle offers up important historical context around what it means to talk about culture jamming, and provides examples representing different models of possible intervention, from the subversion of advertisements, to *Escape from Woomera*, a video game in which players take on the character of an asylum-seeker in a remote immigration detention centre.

The second piece in this chapter picks up on the theme of video games as an accessible site for creative interventions. Sue Scheibler offers us a glimpse into the 'guerilla semiotics' of video games, demonstrating the sheer breadth of activity around video game jamming. The popularity of video games and the interactivity among players make them natural targets for manipulation, Scheibler argues. The amount of attention drawn here in this chapter to video games speaks to the ways in which culture jamming works best – by juxtaposing the familiar with the unexpected.

Within this chapter, we will also examine excerpts from two 'pranks' – one elaborate and one quite simple. In his introduction to culture jamming, Meikle mentions the antics of the Yes Men, a group that has made its mark impersonating world trade representatives at public speaking engagements and in the mainstream media. In this excerpt from their book, *The Yes Men*, we see a first-hand, diary-esque account of one of their pranks. All of their pranks have been well-documented, evidence that the event itself is only a part of the prank. It is in the ensuing use of the media – their own storytelling – and in their documentation of the events recounted for the rest of us in their book, their documentary film, and their website, that the depth of their impact lies.

Hacks, cracks, and pranks: fear and goofing on the internet, in the basement, and at WTO meetings Steph 99

Hey, guess what? Not all hackers are evil, pimply, lurking teenagers with a poor sense of fashion and a great sense of disaffection. They are also not criminals by default, not necessarily computer geniuses, and some of them might even be people you'd have over for dinner. Conversely, some of them are one or more of those things, but consistently, they are easy, sexy targets for a sweaty mainstream media, jonesing for the next hot lead.

So what is a hacker? A hacker, in the broadest, and perhaps truest sense, is someone who makes things do stuff they weren't intended to do. Hardware hacking can be as simple as retooling garbage into art or workshop gadgets, or as heady as tinkering with consumer electronics to circumvent the restrictions of digital rights management. Social engineering is a way of hacking human nature – of using people's assumptions, confidences, suspicions, or desires to gain information or access that would normally be off-limits. Hacking in a computer software and security context is based on the same idea, and can be used to violate and destroy, experiment and explore, or protect and repair. Thus computer hacking itself is as ethically neutral as a hammer, a pen, a bulldozer, or any other tool.

A crack is a step below a hack. Maybe it's less clever, less original, less elegant, less repeatable, but in the meritocratic economy of hacker culture, its value tends to be lower. But sometimes it's the right tool for the job, and sometimes it is as simple a reusing a well-known hack. 'Crack' is also a verb meaning to discover an encrypted password, and also the name of a computer program that attempts to do it by repeated guessing. Password cracking is used by both intruders and security professionals, to break in or discover weak passwords to prevent break-ins, respectively.

To my mind, a prank combines the strengths of both cracking and hacking, and puts them into a performance context to satirize or spotlight the target of the prank. Pranks combine the sense of humor and desire to push limits, as well as a sense of intellectual meritocracy. A good prank points out stupidity or ignorance on the part of the target, and the best pranks make the target a public laughing stock without them ever knowing what was going on. But perhaps the BESTEST pranks are the most subtle ones, where neither the target nor the audience know that it is a prank. The Yes Men pulled off an extremely elegant culture-jamming prank when they convinced an audience at the Certified Practicing Accountants Association of Australia in Sydney that the WTO had decided to disband and re-create itself as a new entity, the Trade Regulation Organization, which would focus on making corporations accountable to all people, not just the economic elite.

Of course, ask a hacker, cracker, or prankster, and you might get a different answer. These terms are loose, and hacker linguistics are subject to a kind of hyper-evolution as common typing mistakes make their way into the parlance, as grammar that sounds mangled in standard English is used for humor or emphasis, and as definitions shift along with frames of reference. Hacker culture is extremely varied as well, from intellectual libertarians who abhor 'stupid people' and take the value of meritocracy to an extreme, to 'hacktivists' who aim to open up technology to as many people as possible, especially communities on the underserved side of the digital divide, or even use cracks and pranks to break up social institutions they find philosophically repugnant. In the middle are a lot of normal people who happen to have some nerdy interests and enjoy finding like minds. What is common across the culture is rabid curiosity, a high premium placed on the strength of collaborative effort and sharing information, and a sense of intellectual ownership. Hackers demand the right to take apart, understand, and modify their tools to their liking. Thus, hackerism and the Open Source movement go together like solder and flux.

In each of these cases, people used the tools that were available to them, thought creatively about technology and social messaging, and demonstrated that often-times the media around the act can be as important as – or more important than – the act itself. And it should be noted that in each of these examples, those involved were well armed with knowledge about their intended targets and dem-onstrated a well-articulated understanding of the issues involved. These were no empty gestures.

10.1 Stop signs:
an introduction to culture jamming

Graham Meikle

'Read-only.' Passive recipients of culture produced elsewhere. Couch pota-toes. Consumers. This is the world of media from the twentieth century. The twenty-first century could be different. This is the crucial point: It could be both read and write. (Lessig 2004: 37)

Introduction

The Yes Men pose as representatives of the World Trade Organization and pro-pose the reintroduction of slavery. Graffiti artist Banksy hangs one of his own paintings inside New York's Metropolitan Museum. DJ Wax Audio releases a mash-up recording of George W. Bush 'performing' John Lennon's 'Imagine', while collage artists Negativland distribute a video mash-up of scenes from *The Passion of the Christ* set to their song 'Christianity is Stupid'. Adbusters produce a sophisticated parody of Calvin Klein's 'Obsession' ad campaign, with the new image showing a bulimic model wrapped around a toilet bowl: 'The beauty indus-try', it says, 'is the beast'.

Each of these is an example of culture jamming (although perhaps not every-one above would be keen to accept the label). It is a term that has achieved a good deal of currency in recent years – but what exactly *is* culture jamming? What is the concept that such disparate examples illustrate? And why might it matter? This chapter will examine some definitions of the term, introduce some of its key figures, and provide some context. It will introduce some of the prehistory of culture jamming (the ideas of the Situationist movement) and show how it fits into wider contemporary developments in the media environment. It will also use one detailed case study – the *Escape from Woomera* computer game – to ground all of the above; one reason for choosing this case study is to show that jamming is a concept that can usefully be applied to a wider range of media examples than just those engaged with advertising.

The most commonly recognised manifestation of culture jamming is the subverted advertisement – an example which is often confused with the concept it illustrates. Culture jamming is better understood as a broader phenomenon than just the reworking of commercials into an anti-consumerist message. Jamming is an important index of the ways in which developments in communications technologies are enabling shifts in the line between creators and consumers. To appropriate a line from Negativland, jamming is what happens 'when a population bombarded with electronic media meets the hardware that encourages them to capture it' (1995: 251). A useful analysis here is that of Henry Jenkins, who shows how anyone can now participate 'in the archiving, annotation, appropriation, transformation, and recirculation of media content' (2003: 286). While many might be tempted to identify all of this with the arrival of the Net, Jenkins traces deeper roots: the photocopier, whose adoption by small presses, alternative media groups and fanzine publishers enabled a broadening of subcultural expression; the VCR, which allowed audiences to exploit broadcast material (building personal libraries, editing their own amateur productions); the camcorder, which enabled amateurs to create footage for documentary production; video games, which fostered a sense of immersion, participation and engagement with media stories; and digital cameras and photo manipulation software, which, as with music sampling and editing programs, made possible still more new forms of production (Jenkins 2003: 286).

Culture jammers rework existing media images and media forms, to make a political or cultural statement. What kinds of statement? Most often jamming is self-reflexive media activism, in that it uses the media to address a media issue (the influence of advertising, for example). And it is often intended to draw media attention to that issue. We can summarise all of this by saying that culture jamming is the practice of taking familiar signs and trying to transform them into question marks.

Credit for the term 'culture jamming' is claimed by the experimental rock group Negativland, who used it on their 1984 record *Jamcon '84* (Dery 1993; Joyce 2005). Negativland are perhaps better known for their legal adventures with U2's record company than for their music itself (they were sued for uncleared use of a sample and for releasing a single in a cover that made it appear to be a U2 record: see Negativland 1995; Baldwin 1995). In Craig Baldwin's film about the U2 affair, one member of Negativland defines culture jamming as 'going in where you're not supposed to be on the airwaves and screwing everything up'. Such an approach sees jamming as obstruction – blocking, interfering, calling a halt – and this is one way to think about it: culture jams turn regular signs into stop signs. It is worth noting, though, that the musical sense of the word is also useful here – from this perspective, jamming would denote collaborative creation around an existing theme: experimental, exploratory, and above all, playful.

An early influential discussion of jamming was a 1993 pamphlet by cultural critic Mark Dery, who described jamming as 'guerrilla semiotics' (1993: 11), and as the shape of 'an engaged politics . . . in an empire of signs' (1993: 6). Dery provides valuable context by placing jamming in a historical timeline which includes covert underground publishing and radical journalism, satire and sabotage, and literary experiments such as William Burroughs's 'cut-up' collage method of composition (as Burroughs himself explained this, 'Cut-ups establish new connections between images, and one's range of vision consequently expands'; 1982: 264). Dery also identifies Situationist *détournement* as a key precursor to jamming.

The culture jammer's project of engaging with media images by deploying media techniques, in order to draw attention to what may otherwise go unnoticed, is directly drawn from the theoretical positions of the Situationist International (Knabb 1981; Debord 1987; Marcus 1989; Sussman 1989; Plant 1992; McDonough 2002). This small group of theorists, writers and artists, who were active from the mid-1950s until the early 1970s, sought to undermine what their key theorist Guy Debord called the *spectacle*: the integrated, commercialised cultural space in which, in Debord's words, 'Everything that was directly lived has moved away into a representation' (1987: section 1).

The Situationists were a significant influence in the near-revolution in Paris in May 1968, when *France-Soir* wrote that the students were 'fighting advertising on its own terrain with its own weapons' (quoted in Knabb 1981: 385). One of these Situationist 'weapons' is the practice of *détournement* – lifting an image from its original context and setting it in a new one, creating a synthesis that calls attention to both the original context and the new result. (There is something of a consensus among commentators that the word is best left untranslated.) 'Any sign or word', suggested two leading Situationists, 'is susceptible to being converted into something else, even into its opposite' (Debord and Wolman 1981: 13). For Greil Marcus, *détournement* is 'a politics of subversive quotation, of cutting the vocal cords of every empowered speaker' (1989: 179).

Case study 1: Adbusters

One group who have been very explicit in their use of this Situationist idea is Adbusters (http://www.adbusters.org), who are a useful illustration of both the strengths and limitations of jamming. Founder Kalle Lasn launched the quarterly *Adbusters* magazine in Vancouver in 1989; it now claims a circulation of 120,000, with subscribers in 60 countries (http://www.adbusters.org/network/about_us.php). Asked to define jamming, Lasn says,

Culture jamming is a way to fight back against advanced consumer capitalism. I see the kind of consumer culture that we have built up over the last many years as being unsustainable. It's a culture that drives the global economy in a way that will eventually make it hit the wall. Culture jamming is a way to get this dysfunctional culture to bite its own tail. (Quoted in Meikle 2002: 132)

The magazine and website specialise in very professional parodies of well-known ads, in which Joe Camel, for instance, becomes Joe Chemo (http://adbusters.org/spoofads/index.php). 'Corporations advertise,' writes Lasn, 'Culture jammers *sub*vertise' (1999: 131; emphasis in original). One early significant model here was the Australian billboard 'refacing' movement BUGA UP (Billboard Utilising Graffitists against Unhealthy Promotions). Formed in 1978, the group tackled tobacco advertising (a prominent surgeon was among the founders); the initial impetus was to highlight the anomaly that cigarette advertising was banned on TV and radio in Australia, but was widespread on billboards. Members of this group have over the years 'refaced' many billboards, broadening their targets from tobacco to confront sexist content and other products with attached health risks (one billboard advertising beer, for example, with the words 'one for the road' was amended to include the phrase 'one for the morgue') (Thornton, Phelan and McKeown 1997: 150–5).

What is significant about this approach is that it exploits the target's own medium of choice, turning the advertisement against its sponsor, and using that platform to distribute a message of its own, at the sponsor's expense. We might note also that such activist interventions are in one important sense no different from the mechanisms of mainstream party politics and corporate communication campaigns: the media release, the interview, the photo opportunity – like the détourned billboard, each of these is an example of what Daniel Boorstin (1992) termed 'pseudo-events', events which exist in large part for the purpose of being reported.

The best example of Adbusters' work, and one of their longest-running campaigns, is the annual Buy Nothing Day (BND), an event which they promote with a TV (un)commercial. This advertisement opens with an image of a burping cartoon pig superimposed on a map of the US. 'The average North American', says a voiceover, 'consumes five times more than a Mexican, ten times more than a Chinese person, and 30 times more than a person from India. We are the most voracious consumers in the world . . . a world that could die because of the way we North Americans live. Give it a rest! November 26 is Buy Nothing Day' (http://www.adbusters.org/videos). Major US TV networks have repeatedly refused to air this advertisement: NBC's commercial clearance manager wrote to Adbusters, 'We don't want to take any advertising that's inimical to our legitimate business interests', while one CBS executive observed that the advertisement was 'in opposition to the current economic policy in the United States' (Lasn 1999: 32–3).

For Buy Nothing Day, Adbusters' website offers media images and resources (such as video clips and posters) for supporters to work into local events, and campaigns. They encourage people to initiate their own actions, their own events; to become producers and distributors of their own new media and their own new meanings (what we might call, following McKay 1998, a DIY approach). In this, Adbusters illustrate Castells' contention that contemporary social movements increasingly operate in a manner which inverts the once-popular environmentalist slogan 'think global, act local'. Now, writes Castells, 'social movements must think local (relating to their own concerns and identity) and act global – at the level where it really matters today' (2001: 143).

Each year participants from around the world send in accounts of Buy Nothing Day (http://www.adbusters.org/metas/eco/bnd/2005.php). From 2005, for example, there are reports of events from Finland, Canada and Japan, and photos from participants in Taipei, Glasgow and Pittsburgh. In one example, a report from Bristol describes how more than 50 BND supporters gave away free food and cups of tea at the city's biggest shopping centre. In previous years, BND has made the front page of the *Wall Street Journal*, and been marked by events ranging from a music festival in Panama, a dance party in New York's Times Square, and credit card cut-up ceremonies in Israel, South Korea and Brazil.

Adbusters have drawn flak for the ways in which they have branded themselves and jamming ('culture jammers headquarters', declares their website). Negativland describe culture jamming as 'a term now thoroughly and somewhat distastefully commodified by *Adbusters* magazine' (http://www.negativlandcom/riaa/negbio. html). It is true that, for the sponsors of Buy Nothing Day, Adbusters have an awful lot of products for sale, including calendars, keyrings, books, DVDs and anti-branding shoes 'for kicking corporate ass' (http://secure.adbusters.org/ orders); disappointingly, Buy Nothing Day T-shirts are no longer available.

Other commentators have criticised Adbusters for what they see as its moralistic stance on tobacco, alcohol and TV. Naomi Klein writes that the magazine can resemble 'an only slightly hipper version of a Public Service Announcement about saying no to peer pressure or remembering to Reduce, Reuse and Recycle' (2000: 325). Klein quotes Mark Dery as saying that Adbusters' campaigns against cigarettes, fast food and drinking come across as patronising, as though, in Dery's words, consumers cannot be trusted to 'police their own desires' (ibid.).

Another important group is the Yes Men (http://www.theyesmen.org), whose adventures impersonating the World Trade Organization have been the subject of a major film. Members of the Yes Men have a long history of involvement with some of the most innovative culture jams of the past two decades, beginning with the Barbie Liberation Organization (BLO), a 1993 event in which they switched the voice boxes of some hundreds of Barbie and GI Joe dolls, before returning these to toy-shop shelves, where buyers found that Barbie would bark 'vengeance is mine' on demand (for instructions, see Terry and Calvert 1997: 196–7; you'll need a soldering iron).

Excerpt from *The Yes Men*

WTO, Sydney

Having overcome a minor administrative hurdle, Mike and Andy arrive in Sydney (this time, the flight has been funded by various arts organizations, and they rely on a dozen local activists for housing and other assistance). After a day of adjustment for jet-lag, they put on fresh thrift-store suits, cut their hair, and go find the headquarters of the Certified Practicing Accountants Association of Australia.

After a good many pleasantries – the conference organizers are exceedingly gracious – 'Kinnithrung Sprat' is introduced and takes the podium with all the gravitas he can muster.

Andy and Mike have decided on an entirely new tack for this lecture, one unmarked by the bombast and lunacy of previous ones. Since parody hasn't worked, they've decided to try that old standby, sincerity.

The WTO, Andy explains, has finally understood that corporate globalization is hurting the little guy; it has therefore to shut down completely. After that, Andy explains, the WTO will relaunch as a new organization – the Trade Regulation Organization – devoted, as its name suggests, to making corporations behave responsibly towards all world citizens, not just the wealthy. Instead of serving to help businesses do business – this is the way the WTO explicitly describes itself on its website – it will henceforward make sure that business helps people.

The lecture includes nearly an hour of shocking statistics drumming home the need for this massive transformation.

The accountants rally behind the plan with excitement. They are authentically thrilled at this radical new direction the WTO is taking. At the luncheon, some of them give suggestions for ensuring that the new organization will serve the poor rather than only the rich. It is very clear that these accountants want to help the poor as much as we do.

They are not the only excited ones about the prospects of a new kind of trade organization. After Mike and Andy send out a press release from the WTO announcing its imminent improvement, a Canadian parliamentarian takes the floor to announce the good news. Andy and Mike receive hundreds of congratulatory emails from others excited about the rebirth.

Could it be that the violent and irrational consensus gripping the world, that we call corporate globalization, is maintained only through a sustained and strenuous effort of faith? Could it be that almost everyone – even those, like accountants, that we are usually inclined to think of as conservative – would immediately embrace a more humane consensus if one were presented by those in positions of authority?

The 'WTO's' press release is revealed to be a hoax, and sadly the WTO still

> does exist. The Canadian parliamentarian retracts his statement, and hundreds of people email to tell us how disappointed they are that it isn't true. The Yes Men sends another press release to clear up the confusion.
>
> Although clearly another world is possible, it will have to start from the bottom up . . .

Graffiti guerilla Banksy (http://www.banksy.co.uk) has taken the BLO tactic of 'shop-dropping' into the art world. In March 2005 he hung his own framed creations on the walls of four major New York art galleries, including the Metropolitan Museum (a slideshow of this event in progress is available on the *New York Times* website at (http://www.nytimes.com/slideshow/2005/03/23/arts/20050324_ARTI_SLIDESHOW_1.html). Another Banksy piece depicting a prehistoric cave-painting of a shopping trolley was hung by its creator in the British Museum – who responded by adding it to their permanent collection (Howe 2005). What is going on here? This too is culture jamming – Banksy turns familiar signs into questions marks, inviting us to rethink, on the one hand, our understanding of the cultural status of graffiti and, on the other hand, our understanding of the museum and gallery: *public* spaces which are defined by *exclusion*.

The claim that the British Museum kept the Banksy artwork for their collection also points to the limitations of culture jamming – radical gestures of this sort are easily absorbed into the vocabulary of their targets. There appears, for example, to be no anti-commercial gesture which cannot be commercialised: amazingly, even Negativland have been invited to provide the soundtrack for a beer commercial (Klein 2000: 330). Moreover, advertisers now commonly launch knowing guerilla advertisement campaigns that pre-empt subversion, that neutralise satire by satirising themselves first. A further problem is that jamming trades in precisely the same kind of rebellious individualism that is the currency of advertising pitches. Cultural critic Thomas Frank (2002) cuts to the heart of many such debates about the recuperation of resistance by capital, arguing persuasively that the model of resistance as independent, oppositional and counter-hegemonic is obsolete in an era when independence and radical individualism are themselves the currency of the mainstream. Frank argues that the celebration of individual agency and nonconformity is itself central to mainstream media representations, including advertising ('think different' is one slogan of the large corporation that produces the machine on which I am writing this).

Case study 2: *Escape from Woomera*

The remainder of this chapter uses a single project to anchor and extend our discussion so far. There are two components to the *Escape from Woomera* project: the game itself and the accompanying website. The game is a first-person

3D adventure, in which the player controls the character of an asylum-seeker in a remote immigration detention centre. While the game is our main focus in this chapter, it is worth noting that the website works as an independent media space in its own right, and works in a quite different way to the actual game. The website is simple, economical and clearly designed. Content is kept to a minimum, but is well chosen: as well as downloading an 'almost finished' version of the game, visitors can watch a preview trailer, view screenshots, read a pithy selection of FAQs and follow links to media coverage from around the world, as well as to related sites from within game culture, and to related sites from within the broader campaign in support of asylum-seekers in Australia. Images mix photographs of detention centres with screenshots of the game, and illustrate characters and different parts of the map; hand-drawn and computer-drawn maps of Woomera are also included. The project has drawn impressive coverage in the traditional media, including *The New York Times* (Mirapaul 2003), BBC News (Hughes 2003) and the *The Sydney Morning Herald* (Nicholls 2003). Much of this coverage is archived at the site, and all of it pre-dates the availability of the game itself – indeed, for the website to work as a culture jam, the actual game need never have been made available for download.

To appreciate the project, it is necessary to realise that the issue of asylum-seekers dominated Australian politics in the first few years of the decade. The 2001 federal election was fought on the theme of 'border protection', a topic which ignited on 26 August 2001 when the *Tampa*, a Norwegian freighter, rescued 433 asylum-seekers whose ferry had sunk off the coast of Christmas Island and attempted to bring them to land in Australia. The Howard government's aggressive response to the *Tampa* – including military boarding and attempts to deny it entry to the country – was followed by a number of other highly divisive events; these included the introduction of the so-called 'Pacific solution' in which asylum-seekers were exported to the small island state of Nauru for detention, the drowning off the coast of Indonesia of more than 350 other asylum-seekers bound for Australia on 19 October 2001, and the 'children overboard' affair in which asylum-seekers were wrongly said to have thrown their own children into the sea in order to intimidate Australian authorities.

Since 1992 all asylum-seekers who reach Australia without a visa have been subject to mandatory detention, the majority being held in purpose-built detention centres. Woomera was the most notorious of these, located in a remote area of the desert, and run as a profit-making concern by a private company, Australian Correctional Management, amidst reports of overcrowding and understaffing. Opened in 1999, it was intended to house 400 people, although within a year it was holding almost four times that number. Despite their punitive treatment, 80% of those held at Woomera were ultimately found to be genuine refugees and granted visas ('About Woomera' 2003). The Australian Human Rights and Equal Opportunity Commission recorded a grim catalogue of 'major disturbances' in the detention centres from 1999 to 2002 as detainees protested at their conditions: riots, hunger strikes, mass escapes, the use of tear gas and water cannon, extensive fires and large numbers of detainees sewing their own lips together (Human Rights and Equal Opportunities Commission 2004: 23–4). Woomera came to symbolise all of this to many Australians.

The asylum-seekers issue drew a range of culture jamming responses from artists and activists. One group projected a 15-metre-high image of an eighteenth-century First Fleet ship above the words 'boat people' onto the Sydney Opera House. Other activists circulated a stencil kit with which traffic safety 'Refuge Island' signs could be détourned: with the addition of a letter 'E', a gun, and a map of Australia, road crossings could be altered to read 'Refugee Island', their figures of pedestrians reworked as armed detainer and detainee (images of both can be seen at (http://www.boat-people.org). The *EFW* game is one of the most elaborate and inventive responses to these issues.

EFW begins with an external aerial view of the detention centre as seen through high razor wire. An onscreen text reads:

> Your parents were murdered by the Iranian Secret Service. Fearing you would be next, you gave your last savings to people-smugglers, in exchange for a perilous journey that ended on Ashmore Reef. [Click to Continue . . .].

A second screen reads:

> After lodging your application for asylum, you were taken to Woomera Detention Centre and re-named RAR-124. Following three months behind razor wire, your appeal to remain in Australia on humanitarian grounds has failed. You are to be involuntarily deported back to Iran, where the Secret Service will be waiting. [Click to Continue . . .].

A third and final intro screen reads:

> Returning home promises the prospect of torture and death. Having exhausted all official channels, you realise that you only one option left [*sic*]: you must escape from this place . . . [Click to Continue . . .].

The game then shifts to a first-person perspective, showing the game world from the point of view of the protagonist Mustafa, inside a bare dormitory lined with metal bunks. Outside, a number of non-player characters (NPCs), inmates and guards, are walking between rows of huts. To progress through the game, the player has to take part in conversations with various NPCs, gathering clues while fully exploring the Woomera complex. Items and scraps of information are fed steadily to the player, who must work out how to fit these together. For example, when Mustafa reports for rostered work duty in the kitchens, he notices an electrician at work, and takes the opportunity to snatch his pliers; talking to an NPC in the kitchen will reveal that to avoid being searched, he must hide the pliers in a rubbish bin, later retrieving them at night when the bin is left outside for collection (but only after acquiring another item, a lever which he can use to force open a gate in front of the bin). Meanwhile, another line of exploration is opened up by the arrival of a parcel from a refugee support group, which contains a mobile phone SIM card hidden inside a packet of washing powder (the latter a useful item to trade with that NPC from the kitchens who complained of not having any, perhaps?). And so on.

The *EFW* creative team (which includes an investigative journalist) drew upon interviews and media archives to re-create the camp, and incorporated real-life events and anecdotes into the gameplay. Vignettes of life in the detention centres are sprinkled through the game: one NPC, for instance, complains that a guard has thrown her copy of the Koran on the ground during an inspection. The gameplay makes it necessary for the player to pay attention to these anecdotes: the player has to listen sympathetically to this character's account of the Koran incident in order to reach the branch of the conversation in which she goes on to tell Mustafa about an abandoned escape tunnel in that part of the camp.

What issues are raised by this project? For our purposes in this chapter, we will restrict our focus to three areas: first, questions of funding and sustainability; second, questions of audience and technology; and third, the issues raised by *EFW* as culture jamming.

Funding and sustainability

Creative director Katharine Neil first thought of the project during the *Tampa* events of 2001. There had been a number of actual escapes from Woomera – including an occasion in June 2000 on which several hundred detainees pushed over the fence and marched into the township of Woomera itself – and these events were one of the inspirations for the project (another was the immediacy and engagement of the participatory journalism of the Indymedia network). Neil was to spend around 18 months assembling the creative team and arranging funding. Funding is especially interesting in this case, as in 2003 the team received AU $25,000 from the national arts funding body, the Australia Council, to complete preliminary work on the project, a grant which was immediately attacked by the immigration minister: in essence, one government agency was funding a project which criticised another arm of the same government. This funding also led to significant press coverage, including the BBC, *The Sydney Morning Herald* and later *The New York Times*. The website is also archived under the Australian National Library's Pandora project, which preserves sites of national cultural importance, see http://pandora.nla.gov.au/pan/46570/20050324/www.escapefrom woomera.org/index.html.

Sustainability directly relates to funding here – in the absence of further government or commercial input, the game has not progressed beyond a beta release. While political statements in the form of games can be made relatively simply using Flash or HTML (see, for example, http://www.newsgaming.com), producing a game on the scale envisaged by the *EFW* team is a labour-intensive and time-consuming project, and while the Australia Council funding was intended to produce a version of the game which could be used to garner further funding to complete a full version, this has not so far proved possible; the existing version available for download is, according to Neil, a 'vertical slice: a gameplay prototype, a very small part, temporally speaking, of what the full game would have looked like' (personal communication).

Audience and technology

Questions of audience and of technology cannot be easily untangled in this project. With *EFW*, the audience is restricted to those savvy enough to install the game, which requires owning a registered copy of the PC version of the game *Half-Life*, and downloading code which runs on top of it. To understand this may, for some readers, require a brief explanation of some important aspects of contemporary video games. For many gamers, actually playing the games is only part of the overall experience, along with taking the games apart, altering and extending them – not just playing games but also playing *with* games, as Newman (2005) puts it. Tinkering with the code has been a feature of games for as long as players have had computers to play them on (*The Modern Age*, 2003). But today the gaming industry operates on one level through encouraging fans to become producers. Classic games such as *Doom* have been adapted by fans, using software tools provided along with the games themselves (Manovich 2001). In the case of *Doom*, the manufacturers released it on the Net before they officially shipped it to shops in 1993, including the necessary tool-sets for players to create their own levels, and also later released the source code, giving the creative community of fans a huge engine to tinker with (Herz 2005). In this way, players can create new levels and distribute these through the online fan community, or they can create new games, using the engines of existing ones (as in the release of *Counter-Strike*, a game which competes with its commercial source material). Such player-created products are known as 'mods' (from 'modifications').

EFW is a mod for the very successful game *Half-Life*. While the process of downloading and installing this mod should probably not be described as hard, it could certainly be described as fiddly, and certainly also as unfamiliar to many; more than this, it is simply inaccessible to many people who might otherwise be interested in the project. Each element of the technical requirements (numbered below) narrows the potential reach of the game still further. Simply being able to see the game demands that you: (1) have a PC (not a Mac) with (2) decent Net access (probably broadband for a 19.7Mb download), and (3) a registered copy of (4) the PC version of (5) *Half-Life*, (6) are comfortable with installing the mod and (7) are able to cope with any bugs or incompatibilities with your own system.

It is true, of course, that the mod scene is large and established, and many gamers will have accomplished more substantial feats of design and programming for themselves (*EFW* does not require users to make a mod, just to play one), and it is true that *Half-Life* is an extremely popular game, with many copies in circulation. And it is also true that there are a great many people who meet all seven of those requirements. Nevertheless, the choice of technology here defines the constituency of the game very tightly. It requires particular kinds of literacy and cultural competence. All forms of mediated communication, of course, make particular demands in this way; but in this case the choice of technology does restrict the potential circulation of the work in quite serious ways.

Escape from Woomera as culture jamming

Why is this culture jamming? Let us recap on the main elements of our discussion above. Jamming involves the grassroots reworking of existing media images and media forms to change their meaning, to call attention to what may otherwise go unnoticed, to implicate those images in broader political issues. Jamming is self-reflexive media activism, engaged with media issues. Jamming most often works through détournement, through taking signs which should work as guides, and reshaping these into question marks.

EFW uses grassroots reworking of existing media forms to call attention to issues – it is a media product that calls attention to media problems, such as the lack of journalistic access to the camps and the dehumanising reporting of asylum-seekers as 'illegals'. It is also self-reflexive in that it uses the video game form to address the limitations and possibilities of that form: it operates on one level as a challenge to gamers and designers. The game also makes use of principles of détournement: there are two especially important senses in which *EFW* takes familiar signs and changes them into question marks, and these will be explored in more detail below – first, it détournes the detention centres themselves, and second, it questions the cultural status and uses of the media form of the video game.

First, *EFW* invites us to rethink the detention centre which gives the game its title. Such centres are closed, remote, secretive, carceral environments; their nature, structure and location combine to forbid access, and hence to deny inspection, scrutiny or knowledge. *EFW* proposes this space instead as one for exploration, mapping, awareness. In this sense, a game is the ideal media form for a project of this sort: one of the fundamental characteristics of the video game form is its creation of a navigable space (Manovich 2001; Newman 2004), mastery of which enables progress and success in the game. From *Spacewar!*, *Pong* and *Adventure*, through *Myst* and *Doom*, *Mario* and *Zelda*, and on to the entire fictional US state that is the setting of *Grand Theft Auto: San Andreas*, video games create an illusion of space, of territory and place, that the gameplay invites us to negotiate, navigate and master. In drawing upon the input of former inmates and employees to re-create the environment of the detention centre, the game takes the closed environment of Woomera and turns it over to the player as one to acquire expertise over, to open out and explore. Such simulation, suggests one games theorist, is 'an ideal medium for exposing rules' (Frasca 2004: 87). In encouraging players to explore the system of the detention centres in simulated form, *EFW* focuses attention on that system in a very different way than could be achieved in a narrative form such as a news report. Playing the game is about 'exposing rules' in Frasca's terms; it demands exploration of the system, experimentation with its limits. It turns that system into a question mark.

Second, *EFW* takes the familiar sign of the video game and invites us to re-think it as a space of political engagement, contestation and debate. Games continue to struggle with an image problem, and the industry, players and academic analysts alike have been attempting to re-frame games as a serious cultural form (Aarseth 1997; King 2002; Wolf and Perron 2003; Harrigan and Wardrip-Fruin 2004; Newman 2004). Members of the *EFW* team had been thinking about games as an art form, as a vehicle for serious topics and social-realist representation. *EFW* is part of a clear developing trend towards the creation of games which engage with political issues (a good archive of links to such games is at: http://www.selectparks.net). As one commentator suggests, there is an increasing trend towards 'games that reflect critically on the minutia of everyday life, replete as it is with struggle, personal drama and injustice' (Galloway 2004: unpaginated).

Perhaps the most remarkable example of such political games is *America's Army*, a recruitment tool and propaganda vehicle, produced and distributed by the US military. *America's Army*, available in various versions for consoles and desktops, uses a commercially licensed software engine to create a team-based multiplayer tactical military game, in which the player works their way up to combat missions from basic training exercises (be warned that if you give in to the temptation to simply shoot the drill instructor, your character ends up in military prison). The US army is not the only organisation to sense the benefits of playable propaganda: there are also first-person shooters (such as *Under Ash* and the Hizbullah-produced *Special Force*) where the protagonists are young Palestinians confronting Israeli forces (Galloway 2004).

EFW's Katharine Neil argues that game developers have an obligation to reflect on how the form itself is to develop:

> If we are to contend that games are more than just toys and are in fact an emerging art form, we are contending that games are by nature political and that, consistent with the history of every other artistic or expressive medium, the future of the game medium will be shaped by struggle. (Personal communication)

In this way, *EFW* illustrates the emergence of the video game form into the political arena, and the increasing prominence of social, cultural and political issues within video games.

Conclusion

Culture jamming, then, is not just about advertising and consumerism, but encompasses a range of uses of media products and images. What *Escape from Woomera* shares with an Adbusters subvertisement, with a Negativland audio collage, or with the Barbie Liberation Organization, is the reworking and reuse of existing images and forms to create surprising new images and connections. As Lessig (2004: 37) suggests, the experience of twenty-first-century media could be not just 'read-only' but 'read and write'. Jammers temporarily block the flow of images – *jam* the culture – but they also improvise and create with those images – jamming *with* the culture, in the musical sense. In both of these ways, culture jamming illustrates some of the opportunities and limitations of the emerging read-and-write media environment.

10.2 Culture jamming the video game way

Sue Scheibler

Taking as a starting point the discussion above, with its articulation of various definitions of culture jamming and its exploration of the role that video games can play in the various forms of guerilla semiotics, this essay will attempt to, in a very brief form, provide other examples of video game jamming. As was stated above, culture jamming applies to and occurs across a wide range of media examples. While jamming has been around for a long time, pre-dating the digital age by many years, its tools have been refined and its reach enlarged by digitally savvy jammers. With the video games industry becoming increasingly mainstream, outselling movies even as it infiltrates cultural consciousness to a greater and greater extent, it makes sense that jammers would use games as a tool while turning their eye to the media itself as well as the industry that produces it. At the same time, the interactive nature of the medium, as well as an emphasis on players as both consumers and producers (due in great part to its roots in the hacker ethos of computer culture, an ethos that led to the development of *Spacewar!*, the first computer game, as well as the permutations that followed it and laid the foundation for a video game industry that, in turn, encourages game modification as a way to extend the life of a game while identifying talented game designers), makes it a natural vehicle for jamming.

While there have been instances of subvertisements aimed at the video game industry (spoofs of X-Box ads, for example) as well as at individual games (recent actions have included stickers riffing on *Grand Theft Auto*, taking the logo and adding the words 'Sexist City' before being affixed to telephone kiosks in New

York City), our interest here is in the way that games themselves have been used to draw attention to the limitations and contradictions inherent in video games while using them and the addictive qualities of play to reach a large audience. It would seem that games are especially useful for collaborative creation and participatory engagement as each game can be further modified by its user/consumer, therefore prolonging not only the life of the game but also the manipulation of signs and possibly the power of the game as an object for political and cultural critique.

Culture jamming with and through video games can take several forms – action within online games such as the *Sims* or multiplayer role-playing games, game development and design, modification of existing games, and machinima or game-driven animated films. As advertisers pursue product placement in games, games have become a target for culture jammers. One example would be the action in 2002 when a deal was struck between *Sims* online publisher Electronic Arts and McDonald's, allowing virtual players to open their own McDonald's kiosks and improve their game stats by consuming burgers and fries. When news went out, players such as Tony Walsh of Shift.com put out a call for players to challenge McDonald's and product placement by logging in to the game and engaging in a variety of actions, including picketing the nearest kiosk, ordering and consuming the food then playing dead or emoting sickness, opening a kiosk then verbally abusing the customers, opening an independent kiosk and explaining to customers how McDonald's is hurting your business (see http://www.alternet.org/story/14530/).

While there are instances of politically informed games distributed by games companies and available through the marketplace (for example, *The Political Machine*, a satiric game released during the US elections in 2004 that takes the player through the 41-week election cycle, ending with the player watching as the electoral vote comes in), online games seem to adhere more closely to the jamming ethos, distributed as they are over the Internet and therefore available for free to anyone with a computer and a modem (and, in some instances, a mobile phone or other handheld device). Online games, usually designed using fairly easy to master Flash techniques or HTML, reflect a wide array of political sympathies, using popular game genres such as first- or third-person shooters, puzzles and quizzes, dancing and music, platform and fighting games to play with and off of the headlines and current events. The great thing about these games is that many of them are based on classic arcade games such as *Space Invaders*, *Frogger*, *Mario Brothers*, *Mortal Kombat* and *Asteroids*, creating a familiar sense of play in potential gamers. At the same time, they are quick to play and their availability over the Internet helps seduce people working at computers to turn their workplace and work-time into a space and time of play. In this sense, then, the content as well as the play itself becomes a form of culture jamming. Examples of such games would include *Dick Cheney's Texas Takedown*, a *Space Invaders*-like game created by Jade Kite in which the player, as Dick Cheney, tries to take out as many lawyers and family friends as possible before time runs out; the *Bush Shoot-*

Out game in which you play either Bush or Condoleezza Rice, shooting terrorists in the White House; *Crosser*, a rif on *Frogger* in which the player tries to cross the Rio Grande from Mexico into the United States; and *Donkey John*, a game that requires the player to guide Xanana Gus-mario as he attempts to prevent *Donkey John* from laying claim to East Timor's oil resources.

A second form of game manipulation would be mods or game modifications. *Escape from Woomera*, mentioned above, would be one example of a game mod. Game mods take on different guises, ranging from modifying the skins (appearances) of game players as well as the landscape in which the action takes place or adding new characters to the game play (for example, Ronald McDonald or other signs of corporate capitalism) to creating entirely new games using the game engine of existing games. As was mentioned above, mods are limited in their reach to players who own or have access to the original game.

The last form of video game jamming involves the creation of machinima or animated films made using video game engines (usually *Sims, Quake, Halo, Half-Life* or *Doom*) (see http://www.machina.com). Creators can choose to stay fairly close to the look and themes of the games or push them to their limits. Machinima probably began with *Quake*, released in 1996 by ID software. The game had a feature that allowed players to record their gameplay, most often used to record deathmatches. One of the earliest films took the deathmatch map from the game, added lumberjack skins to the game characters and added dialogue to tell the story of two lumberjacks, Lenny and Larry, looking for an apartment. Created by ILL Clan, Lenny and Larry Lumberjack have participated in other activities, including, most recently, running for president and vice president in a spoof on the recent US elections.

Many machinima films are designed to critique and subvert computer games, drawing attention to issues of violence, race, class, gender and ethinicity. *Blood Gulch Chronicles*, an early hit that established the long running Red vs. Blue series, used largely unaltered footage recorded from *Halo* to feature characters standing around, discussing the emptiness of violence and war as they contemplate and ruminate on what exactly they are doing and why. A more recent example is *The French Democracy*, a film about the recent riots in France. The film follows the event that started the riots, showing a young man watching the news reports, including comments by French leaders about the need for law and order as well as the containment of certain elements of society. Leaving his apartment, he encounters friends with whom he shares his frustrations about the event and the invisibility of people like him and the victims. Moving on, he is arrested for not carrying his passport and placed in jail overnight before being released in a case of racial profiling. Enraged, he vows to do something to bring notice.

From here the action shifts to Mamadou, who is turned down from a job and an apartment, both of which had been promised to him then withdrawn when his race and ethnicity became known. Frustrated, he too vows to do something to change things and perceptions. The third character is a black youth who is roughed up by a couple of white policemen for no real reason. A montage of the three characters shows each in close-up saying that 'we can't take it any longer'; a call to arms results in images of the riots – youths throwing Molotov cocktails, cars and buildings on fire, then the news reports filled with talking-head political leaders still out of touch with the reasons for the unrest. The film ends with a vision of an idealised past, a great country in which Liberty, Equality and Fraternity were valued, followed by a comment on the present in which these three ideals have been replaced by Misery, Lies and Misunderstanding.

In conclusion, it is safe to say that video games provide a viable and thriving form of culture jamming, ranging from politically themed games to modifications of existing games in order to comment on games as well as on political and social concerns, raising awareness through the games as well as related websites and links (as mentioned above) while potentially jamming work-related servers with people playing games on company time, through to machinima as a relatively inexpensive means for people to make films and put them out on the Internet, creating a more grassroots film movement for politically engaged filmmakers and activists.

Personalising your sneakers (email exchange between MIT graduate student Jonah Peretti and Nike iD from: http//www.villagevoice.com/news/0107,jockbeat,22274,3.html)

Following is an email exchange between MIT graduate student Jonah Peretti and the customer service department of Nike iD, an online service that allows customers to order personalised Nikes by submitting a word or phrase to be sewn onto the shoes, under their swoosh logo. The correspondence began when Nike declined to fulfil Peretti's order for a pair of Nikes stitched with the word 'sweatshop'. Nike has been the target of a number of hacks on the ubiquity of their logo, especially when their branded image is juxtaposed against the abysmal labour conditions their shoes are made in. Here we see not only Peretti's effort to contrast Nike's corporate image with their corporate reality, but an example of the impact of the prank laying in the rapid dissemination of the email exchange through the internet. Over the next two months, the story was recounted in the Guardian, The Independent, the Wall Street Journal, La Republica, USA Today, NBC's Today Show, and many other mainstream newspapers, television outlets and independent media. Peretti, who was at the time an MIT graduate student, had done his research and was well-armed with data on Nike's labour practices when speaking to the press.

From: 'Personalize, NIKE iD'
To: 'Jonah H. Peretti'
Subject: RE: Your NIKE iD order o16468000
Your NIKE iD order was canceled for one or more of the following reasons:
1) Your Personal iD contains another party's trademark or other intellectual property
2) Your Personal iD contains the name of an athlete or team we do not have the legal right to use
3) Your Personal iD was left blank. Did you not want any personalization?
4) Your Personal iD contains profanity or inappropriate slang, and besides, your mother would slap us.
If you wish to reorder your NIKE iD product with a new personalization please visit us again at www.nike.com
Thank you, NIKE iD

From: 'Jonah H. Peretti'
To: 'Personalize, NIKE iD'
Subject: RE: Your NIKE iD order o16468000
Greetings,
My order was canceled but my personal NIKE iD does not violate any of the criteria outlined in your message. The Personal iD on my custom ZOOM XC USA running shoes was the word 'sweatshop.'
Sweatshop is not: 1) another's party's trademark, 2) the name of an athlete, 3) blank, or 4) profanity.
I choose the iD because I wanted to remember the toil and labor of the children that made my shoes. Could you please ship them to me immediately.
Thanks and Happy New Year, Jonah Peretti

From: 'Personalize, NIKE iD'
To: '"Jonah H. Peretti"'
Subject: RE: Your NIKE iD order o16468000
Dear NIKE iD Customer,
Your NIKE iD order was canceled because the iD you have chosen contains, as stated in the previous email correspondence, 'inappropriate slang'. If you wish to reorder your NIKE iD product with a new personalization please visit us again at nike.com
Thank you, NIKE iD

From: 'Jonah H. Peretti'
To: 'Personalize, NIKE iD'
Subject: RE: Your NIKE iD order o16468000
Dear NIKE iD,

Thank you for your quick response to my inquiry about my custom ZOOM XC USA running shoes. Although I commend you for your prompt customer service, I disagree with the claim that my personal iD was inappropriate slang. After consulting Webster's Dictionary, I discovered that 'sweatshop' is in fact part of standard English, and not slang. The word means: 'a shop or factory in which workers are employed for long hours at low wages and under unhealthy conditions' and its origin dates from 1892. So my personal iD does meet the criteria detailed in your first email.

Your website advertises that the NIKE ID programme is 'about freedom to choose and freedom to express who you are.' I share Nike's love of freedom and personal expression. The site also says that 'If you want it done right . . . build it yourself.' I was thrilled to be able to build my own shoes, and my personal ID was offered as a small token of appreciation for the sweatshop workers poised to help me realize my vision. I hope that you will value my freedom of expression and reconsider your decision to reject my order.

Thank you, Jonah Peretti

From: 'Personalize, NIKE iD'
To: '"Jonah H. Peretti"'
Subject: RE: Your NIKE iD order o16468000
Dear NIKE iD Customer,

Regarding the rules for personalization it also states on the NIKE iD website that 'Nike reserves the right to cancel any personal iD up to 24 hours after it has been submitted'. In addition, it further explains: 'While we honor most personal iDs, we cannot honor every one. Some may be (or contain) other's trademarks, or the names of certain professional sports teams, athletes or celebrities that Nike does not have the right to use. Others may contain material that we consider inappropriate or simply do not want to place on our products. Unfortunately, at times this obliges us to decline personal iDs that may otherwise seem unobjectionable. In any event, we will let you know if we decline your personal iD, and we will offer you the chance to submit another.' With these rules in mind, we cannot accept your order as submitted. If you wish to reorder your NIKE iD product with a new personalization please visit us again at www.nike.com

Thank you, NIKE iD

From: 'Jonah H. Peretti'
To: 'Personalize, NIKE iD'
Subject: RE: Your NIKE iD order o16468000
Dear NIKE iD,
Thank you for the time and energy you have spent on my request. I have decided
to order the shoes with a different iD, but I would like to make one small request.
Could you please send me a color snapshot of the ten-year-old Vietnamese girl
who makes my shoes?
Thanks, Jonah Peretti

(no response)

As one email forwarder writes, 'this will now go round the world much farther
and faster than any of the adverts they paid Michael Jordan more than the entire
wage packet of all their sweatshop workers in the world to do . . . (http//home.
tiac.net/~cri/2001/personalize.html)

11 New(er) technologies

Introduction

Throughout this book we have explored a wide range of the alternative uses to which activists have put new (as well as older) media technologies. However, in this chapter we want to focus specifically on the issue of 'newness' in relation to how alternative media have developed, and how they are developing now.

We think this is important because of the explosion of activity that has resulted from the increasing prevalence of digital media in general, and the opportunities offered by the Internet in particular: 'The networking revolution has diffused very rapidly: it took the telephone 75 years to reach 50 million people, but the Web took only four years' (Sreberny 2005: 264). In addition to this rapidly increasing accessibility, there are a number of features of the net that make it appear to be, in and of itself, an 'alternative' medium. Most obviously, it is a horizontal, peer-to-peer network, rather than a centralised or vertically organised system; also, it is universally accessible (at least to those able to afford a computer and telephone connection, or who have access to a wireless network); and it is inherently participatory, a medium in and for which, potentially, we can all write as well as read, create as well as consume.

These features have certainly stimulated an enormous growth in alternative media activity, but have also inspired a certain amount of problematic utopian thinking about the technology itself, based on the notion that the net will set us free, on its own. In this 'digitopia' – as Gregor Claude calls it below – 'information wants to be free', an idealistic view that ignores the social forces and institutions that want to keep information restricted. This kind of notion has arisen before in the history of alternative media, notably when video became a more accessible and user-friendly technology. Jon Dovey has pointed out how, in a previous 'utopian moment, video was seen as *inherently* democratic and challenging' (Dovey 1996: 117), which is especially ironic given that the miniaturisation of camera technology which made the video 'revolution' possible was first developed to assist in the guidance systems of military missiles. Video was also initially mass marketed as a consumer-durable tool for home-movie making, and the Internet itself started life as a 'closed military data network' (Waltz 2005: 91) set up by the US Department of Defense and the Rand Corporation in the 1970s, to meet the need of the US military during the Cold War period for a dispersed (and therefore less vulnerable) system of communication. Only later was the technology taken up by the international academic community as an open way of intellectual networking.

These chequered histories should not surprise us. As Raymond Williams pointed out over 30 years ago, 'new technology is itself a product of a particular social system, and will be developed as an apparently autonomous process of innovation only to the extent that we fail to identify and challenge its real agencies' (Williams 1974: 136). However, as we saw in the introduction to this book, Williams also recognised the possibility of using 'the new technology for purposes quite different from those of the existing social order' (ibid.).

Unexpected applications

Mobile phones became a symbol of the People Power II revolution in the Philippines in 2001. And it was not just the phones, but the use of texting that proved key to the success of the movement to overthrow the corrupt Philippine government of President Joseph Estrada.

In short, it could be said that Estrada is the first head of state in history to lose power to a smart mob. Mobilised via waves of text messages, over one million Manila residents gathered at the site of the peaceful demonstration that had toppled the Marcos regime in 1986. Tens of thousands of Filipinos converged on Epifanio de los Santas Avenue (EDSA) within the first hour of the text message volleys. Over four days, more than a million citizens showed up.

Texting allowed information on former president Estrada's corruption to be shared widely. It helped facilitate the protests at the EDSA shrine at a speed that was startling – it took only 88 hours after the collapse of impeachment to remove Estrada. The use of mobile phones was why the mobilisation (or perhaps 'mobile-isation') was so large and so rapid and thus so decisive. Estrada himself blamed his ousting on the 'text messaging generation' (Court 2006).

Despite the relative poverty in the Philippines, there are 4.5 million mobile phones, in a country of 89 million. Text messaging is cheaper than making a phone call, and single messages can easily be distributed to large numbers of people through both organised and informal networks of friends texting friends, texting friends. During the People Power II week of protests, Philippine Mobile (ibid.) processed over 70 million text messages. Technology literally put the power to communicate directly in the hands of the people.

The use of mobile phones in political organising is not unique to the Philippines. In 2003, Iranian student protestors seeking democratic elections used their phones from the streets of Tehran to call in to an Iranian radio station in Los

Angeles to report on what was happening, and to let Iranians know where the police were and where to move to next. The station, in turn, broadcast the calls via shortwave radio from the Czech Republic back into Iran (shortwave radio is illegal in Iran, and broadcast media inside the country remains tightly controlled by the government). The one-to-one phone exchange between the caller and the receiver was amplified through a complex network of telecommunications using both mobile phones and radio across continents.

In the first essay in this chapter Gregor Claude discusses the issue of copyright in relation to digitopian dreams. He reveals how the 'enclosure mechanisms' that are being put in place by new digital copyright legislation are threatening some of the creative areas which have been opened up by digital technologies, and which have also been the playground of a lot of recent alternative media work. Adnan Hadzi's piece, which immediately follows, gives an account of a variety of projects and activities which continue to exploit digitopian possibilities, and challenge the threat of 'enclosure'.

11.1 Copyright:
the politics of owning culture

Gregor Claude

When the Internet entered public consciousness in the mid-1990s, it appeared as a new space of freedom, a digitopia promising a transcendence of the restrictions of earthly law. In John Perry Barlow's influential 1996 *Declaration of Independence of Cyberspace*, he demanded,

> Governments of the Industrial World, you weary giants of flesh and steel, I come from Cyberspace, the new home of Mind. On behalf of the future, I ask you of the past to leave us alone. You are not welcome among us. You have no sovereignty where we gather . . . I declare the global social space we are building to be naturally independent of the tyrannies you seek to impose on us. You have no moral right to rule us nor do you possess any methods of enforcement we have true reason to fear. (Barlow 1996)

Today the digitopian dream has receded. It is not that the freedom of the Internet has, or will, disappear. But neither is it the technological inevitability proposed by the digitopians. In recent years the law has returned to cyberspace, and copyright is a paradigmatic example of this process.

For Barlow and others copyright in cyberspace was dead on arrival; how could you control copying when the Internet makes it anonymous, easy and free? Up to the late twentieth century, the illicit reproduction and distribution of copyrighted material was rather difficult and time-consuming. The mass production and reproduction of cultural commodities pioneered by the cultural industries required correspondingly industrial means – a printing press or broadcasting equipment, for example. So the legal control afforded by copyright was reinforced by technological and economic concentrations of power. For the cultural industries, copyright functioned effectively as a means of enabling a clear determination of the ownership and control of particular cultural goods. Until recently copyright was capable of resolving disputes which revolved around these questions. Since the mid-1990s, however, copyright has been refashioned from a regime designed to control the copying of analogue media to one designed to control the digital. States, international organisations and cultural industries have tried to reinvent an outdated copyright, designed to protect analogue media, as a digital copyright that can enclose digital media and extend established property claims into the digital realm. What has emerged out of the contradictory trends of the openness of the Internet, and the attempt at enclosure through digital copyright, is not a simple, technological inevitability, but a contested politics of information. The central questions at stake in this politics are: who owns knowledge, or culture, or information? When are they held in common and openly accessible to all? When are they someone's exclusive property and subject to private control?

Creating: the utopian origins of copyright

Both copyright and the Internet passed through a utopian moment. The Internet was born out of apocalyptic Cold War nuclear paranoia, and had its utopian 'information wants to be free' moment in the mid-1990s. Many of the defenders of copyright today perhaps represent its paranoid moment, but it emerged out of utopian aspirations at least as potent as those of the digitopians of the 1990s. The major importance of copyright is not the legal detail (though this is important), but its principle. Copyright was not designed to enrich culture-industry executives, though this may be a big part of what it does today. Rather it began as an economic provision to support the intellectual and creative independence of writers, artists and inventors. There are some significant international differences, but most contemporary copyright legislation affords authors (and other creators) a 'limited monopoly right', saleable to a publisher (or other cultural industry), in which the rights-holder may exclusively publish and sell a given work. The origins of modern copyright laws bear the mark of the Enlightenment project of which they were an important part. The English Statute of Anne (1710) was subtitled 'An Act for the Encouragement of Learning'; the US Constitution (1789) echoes the earlier sentiment, mandating Congress 'to promote the Progress of Science and useful Arts, by securing for limited Times to Authors and Inventors the exclusive Right to their respective Writings and Discoveries'. Copyright in these early laws was a practical measure creating an incentive to write, to invent and, crucially, to make public this new knowledge. The abstract principle of freedom of speech, with its promise of intellectual independence, was complemented by a copyright which enabled authors (or at least some of them) also to achieve economic independence from the confines of private patronage.

Generally, copyright is limited firstly in time, to a certain term of years; and secondly in scope, so the exclusive control exercised by a rights-holder is not total. The limitations on the copyright monopoly are its most important features, distinguishing copyright from other forms of private property. Copyright has some proprietary characteristics, but to call it 'intellectual property' can be somewhat misleading. A copyright-holder does not have anything like the same rights as a property-holder. By law they have the exclusive right to copy and publish a particular work. They can also license some or all of those rights to others, a possibility recently cleverly exploited by Creative Commons to enable artists and authors to circulate their work under much less restrictive terms than a full copyright claim. But copyright-holders do not have the rights to determine how a particular text is used. They cannot, for example, prevent quotation, critique and parody, the resale of used books, or lending libraries. Copyright-holders do not have rights over the *ideas* in a work, only over the particular *expression* of those ideas. And once the limited term of copyright expires, the work becomes freely available to all. In creating the limited legal conditions in which content can be owned and controlled, copyright law also creates its opposite: the public domain, or the commons – a space beyond those legal limits, in which knowledge and culture cannot be privately controlled or owned.

Copying: digital media

As Jack Valenti, former president of the Motion Picture Association of America, was fond of repeating, 'If you can't protect what you own, you don't own anything'. Despite becoming *less* limited in time and scope – and thereby more like private property – through the twentieth century, copyright no longer offers clear answers to questions about ownership and control, the proprietary and the common. Copyright, as property, has become unstable. There are distinct technological and social reasons for this. At the level of technology, the Internet has had a massively disruptive effect on the copyright-based business models of the cultural industries. As computers evolved from office productivity machines and isolated gaming consoles, into a linked Web of communication-and-culture machines, cultural industries have found their ability to protect their digital assets profoundly weakened. The Internet is a vast, global copy machine. Sharing information between computers, copying data from one computer to another, is fundamentally what the Internet does, and what it was designed to do. The Transmission Control Protocol/Internet Protocol, the so-called 'DNA of the Internet', is the set of instructions that tells computers how to transmit copies of data between each other. To download a file, open a Web page or send an email is to copy information from one computer to another. It is not just that the Internet facilitates copying; rather it is that copying is how the Internet works. The simple fact of the copyability of digital media creates serious difficulties for anyone wanting to manage or control it.

Digital copying is different from copying in any analogue medium in another way. Like an analogue medium, the Internet is a physical medium of computers, routers, magnetic and optical data storage devices, cables and so on. There is no virtual transcendence of physical reality and earthly law, as suggested by much of the early digitopian hype. Like any other medium, it operates within physical constraints. The digital copy is still embodied in some material form, whether as pitted aluminium in a compact disc, magnetic fields on a hard drive or electrons in a flash drive. But whereas the circulations of paper books were identical in a predigital age, today the circulation of digital content has been separated from the circulation of the digital storage medium. We often now buy our storage media empty; the difference between a full and an empty flash drive is the presence or absence of information patterns. To copy digital media is to reproduce pattern; to buy a digital film is to buy a pattern, which is copied onto storage media. This is problematic for analogue copyright, which always protected the 'tangible expression' of a work – a material thing like a paper book or a celluloid film – rather than the work itself. The difficulty in differentiating between idea and expression was one of the reasons for the early digitopian's enthusiasm for the Internet – it seemed to promise the possibility of liberation from the messy and limited world of physical things and the untethered possibilities of a world of disembodied information and knowledge. An effective digital copyright would need somehow to distinguish between legitimate and illegitimate information patterns, and have the ability to restrict their reproduction.

Producing: collaborative culture

It used to be difficult for anyone without a printing press to violate copyright; now it is improbable that anyone with a computer does *not* violate copyright at some point, intentionally or accidentally. But technology alone is not enough to explain why copyright no longer effectively answers questions about owning culture. This is also a consequence of a shift in the way culture is socially produced and circulated. Nick Couldry (2003b) suggests thinking about this shift by looking into the new ways that people consume, produce and distribute media. He writes,

> it is, I suggest, to new hybrid forms of media *consumption–production* that we should look for change, since they would challenge precisely the entrenched division of labour (producer of stories versus consumer of stories) that is the essence of media power. (2003b: 45; original emphasis)

This hybrid consumption–production is at the heart of digital media culture. Whether it is remixing music, collaboratively developing software or creating hyperlinked websites, digital media production uses already existing media produced by others to create something new. This practice is not new, or even unique to digital media; remixing has been an explicit feature of innovative culture through the twentieth century: Duchamp's readymades in the 1910s, Heartfield and Hannah Höch's photomontages in the 1930s, the sampling of *musique concrète* in the 1950s, Warhol's commercial and celebrity appropriations of the 1960s. Digital media simply makes it easier for producers not just to be 'influenced' by previous works, but to re-purpose old copies into new works. The key raw material of new culture is already existing culture; digital media only makes the process faster, easier, cheaper and more precise. The copyright issue here is not just a simplistic consumerist dispute between an overcharged buyer or a seller suffering from theft. Rather what is at stake is the possibility of more intense forms of co-operation between consumer–producers that does not necessarily rely on proximity in time or space, or even on shared intentions.

After consumption and production, the third dimension that Couldry mentions is distribution. For new modes of cultural production, inexpensive access to the means of circulation or distribution is just as novel and at least as important as access to the means of production. Couldry's description of the division of labour could be reformulated here more specifically, as one between producers of stories *that circulate as media* and the consumers of that circulated media. The hybridisation at work is then the consumer–producer–distributor. If production and reproduction of texts once required a printing press, distribution of texts once required a publisher as intermediary between author and readers. This is one of the more intractable problems for those cultural industries whose business models rely on building up a portfolio of copyright material which they publish, promote and distribute. These intermediaries will not disappear, but they may find their dominance displaced.

Enclosing: digital rights management

The limits of copyright shape the contours of what is public, common and shared, and copyright today is limited both by traditional legal limits and by the practical technological limits of enforcing copyright on digital media. These limitations have left open a space within which a vibrant digital culture of hybrid consumption, production and circulation has developed. However, cultural industries, led by organisations like the Recording Industry Association of America and the Motion Picture Association of America, have had some important successes in extending the scope of what copyright owners can do to protect their assets. They are attempting to re-inscribe, or at least preserve, that older division of labour clearly demarcating cultural producer and cultural consumer within new digital media. In some cases the extended proprietary claims of copyright clearly threaten to interrupt the dynamic cycle of consumption–production–circulation of media at each stage. The new digital copyright can restrict the consumption of culture, it can prevent sampling or remixing and it can constrain circulation.

The latest digital copyright provisions are techno-legal hybrids. For the technological and social reasons discussed, law alone fails to create a copyright that is viable as a property asset. But just as the computer architecture discussed above facilitates copying, it is possible to create secure code layers that operate as safe enclosures, or to 'wrap' digital files in protective code that restricts how they can be used. So, for example, a song bought from Apple's iTunes music store is enclosed within a protective code shell, a form of 'digital rights management' (DRM), that restricts the number of computers or devices that a given download can be played from. Apple's DRM is mild compared with other music download stores, who use subscription-based models in which downloaded music can only be accessed as long as the monthly fee is paid. The restrictions used in either scheme would not have been legal before recent digital copyright legislation, and do not apply to music bought on compact disc. Most code-based restrictions that have been implemented by cultural industries do not survive long before they are hacked, but digital copyright laws have introduced 'anti-circumvention' provisions which criminalise attempts to disable the technological protection. In this way, a DRM-protected song is protected three times: first by traditional copyright law, second by DRM code and third by the law prohibiting any tampering with the DRM.

These new efforts go beyond an attempt to model older copyright law in a new digital form. Rather, many aspects of the emerging digital copyright regime are means to control and own information, knowledge and culture in ways never before possible. This is more than just a project to create a technological 'model' of existing copyright law; the emerging digital copyright regime is in many circumstances far more restrictive. Digital copyright and, in particular, DRM have rewritten copyright not as an incentive to create, but as an enclosure mechanism that aids the maximisation of intellectual property. They make immaterial information or culture act more like a physical object, with definite borders – information becomes governable, the clear determination of ownership is restored.

It is a mistake to interpret this situation as a mirror image of the digitopian hope of openness – a distopian projection of control. The Internet was designed as a resilient decentralised communication network, and it usually works remarkably well to create zones of openness that coexist alongside (or sometimes directly challenge) zones of control. The parallel development of the openness of new modes of cultural production and the enclosures of new techno-legal control demonstrate that the question this essay started with – when is knowledge and culture proprietary and when is it common – is not an unavoidable consequence of either technological, legal or economic power, but a terrain in which all three form the contours of new political contestation.

11.2 A2T: bridging the digital divide

Adnan Hadzi

> If the social needs of the age in which such technologies are developed can be met only through their mediation, if the administration of this society and all contact between people has become totally dependent on these means of instantaneous communication, it is because this 'communication' is essentially unilateral. (Debord 1994: 13)

Over the last few years 'Free Libre and Open Source Software' (FLOSS), a form of collaborative software development, has grown rapidly over the digital networks. 'Free software' is a matter of liberty, not price. To understand the concept, you should think of 'free' as in 'free speech', not as in 'free beer'. The users have the freedom to run, copy, distribute, study, change and improve the software.

The idea of free software still needs more acceptance from users who are not programmers. This shows a demand for technical literacy, but also the fact that FLOSS needs to be developed further for it to become 'user-friendly'.

Linux is one of the most famous FLOSS developments. Linux is a computer operating system which can be installed for free on any computer without having to pay for it, unlike the commercial mainstream operating systems like Microsoft Windows or Apple Mac OS. All its source code is available to the public and anyone can freely use, modify and redistribute it.

> A useful starting point is in the political philosophy of anarchism and Proudhon's well known formulation 'all property is theft'. But even if we accept this axiom, with what might we replace it? Murray Bookchin (1986: 50) has proposed that we consider 'usufruct' as a counter to property rights . . . usufruct should be contrasted with property. Where the latter implies the permanent ownership of resources, usufruct is 'a temporary property relationship based on utility need which meets the demands of communality' (Clement and Oppenheim 2002:42) . . . The continuing history of Linux is a significant working model of usufruct . . . It is anarchism in action. (Atton 2004: 101–2)

In the first part of this section we look at access to FLOSS with the Dyne:Bolic distribution as an example which offers a whole multimedia studio on one CD. A Linux distribution, or GNU/Linux distribution, or less formally Linux distro, is a Unix-like operating system comprising software components such as the Linux kernel, the GNU tool chain, and assorted free, open-source software. It shows how streaming technology can also run on older and slower computers. Streaming media are media that are consumed while being delivered, 'streaming audio' for radio and 'streaming video' for television broadcast over the Internet.

In the second part of this section we look at access to technology as a human right and explore how a Scottish collective, 'the Camcorder Guerillas', gives a voice to asylum-seekers and how a global network, 'Kein Mensch ist illegal' (Nobody Is Illegal), supports immigrants struggling with being illegal in 'First World' countries.

The third part of the chapter looks at access to intellectual property, through the example of the student movement 'Free Culture' which motivates people to participate in a peer-to-peer society. The Free Culture movement opposes the commercialisation of knowledge which is threatening the very idea of democracy.

By asking 'how can a democratic debate take place if knowledge is restricted to a small group of engineers and corporate interests', Free Culture argues that democracy is based on free, informed debate, and supported by cultural exchange, diversity and education. In order for a democratic system to function, knowledge has to be free. There has to be a move from the ownership society to a gift economy, from copyright to copyleft.

Access to FLOSS

> This software is about Digital Resistance in a Babylon world which tries to control and market the way we communicate, we share our interests and knowledge. The roots of the Rastafari movement are in resistance to slavery: this software is one step in the struggle for Redemption and Freedom from proprietary and closed-source software. (Jaromil 2000)

In 2000 Jaromil registered the domain dyne.org. dyne.org started as a software atelier, a lab for online development of software, a place to show the creations of programmers and to address issues like distribution of knowledge, freedom of speech and the sharing of free technologies in support of those who have less opportunities to access them.

If dyne.org is not a company, then what is it?

> dyne.org is a network, communication flows between individuals, without any hierarchy or power structures. As long as the constituting fundamental of every community is identities, defining themselves with their activity, dyne. org is a network of individuals and doesn't aim to be in any way representing neither substituting them. If you make us a collaboration proposal remember that dyne.org is not a business company: you'll need to arrange business terms with each one interested, singularly and independently. (Jaromil 2000)

The lab developed Dyne:Bolic, a bootable GNU/Linux system. Jaromil came up with the idea of creating a free and easy-to-employ operating system for radio

Figure 11.1 Self-portrait by Jaromil

broadcasting including his streaming software MuSE after he attended, in 2001, the presentation of the Bolic1 live CD distribution by the LOA hacklab, when they gathered in a hackmeeting in Sicily organised by the FreakNet medialab. In August 2002 Jaromil employed Dyne:Bolic in the independent Net-art project Farah in Palestine. After gaining the experience of the Farah project, the development was focused on lowering requisites in order to be able to use recycled hardware. Today the bootable Dyne:Bolic CD is a complete multimedia system. At the time of writing (June 2007) the Dyne:Bolic system is being used by the independent Iraqi media project Streamtime.org.

Streamtime uses the Dyne:Bolic system to broadcast radio programmes from Iraq. People can speak to the world through a hand-held microphone connected to a computer. The first streams were initiated on 14 July 2004. The broadcast was picked up by several stations in European cities such as Naples (Italy), Zurich (Switzerland), Munich (Germany), Sheffield (United Kingdom), Bern (Switzerland) and Amsterdam (the Netherlands) and broadcast directly, or in an edited version later on.

The Dyne:Bolic system is a computer operating system that gives the widest possible public access to the technology because it will run on the original Pentium series of machines with quantities of RAM that would not be considered sufficient for a basic PC these days, let alone a multimedia workstation. Dyne: Bolic also runs on a Microsoft Xbox.

> It's a core feature for Dyne:Bolic! Hardware recycling has been an important activity for the FreakNet Medialab, setting up free surf stations in a squatted building back in the early '90s . . . It is about the politics and philosophy we developed in the Hackmeeting: in solidarity with the poor, and trying to fill the digital divide since the very beginning. (Jaromil 2000)

How to use Dyne:Bolic

All you have to do is to download the disk image from http://www.dynebolic.org, burn it on a CD and reboot your computer with this CD inside. You can manipulate and broadcast both sound and video with tools to record, edit, encode and stream. You do not have to install anything because the Dyne:Bolic system can run just from the CD and automatically recognises most of your devices and peripherals such as sound, video and network cards.

Among other software, Dyne:Bolic includes the free software below, released under the terms and conditions of the GNU General Public Licence. The GNU General Public Licence (GNU GPL or simply GPL) is a free software licence, originally written by Richard Stallman for the GNU project (a project to create a complete free software operating system). It has since become the most popular licence for free/libra/open-source software.

- MuSE – multiple streaming engine is a user-friendly but powerful tool for network audio streaming.
- Cinelerra is a video editing system. Thanks to its small size it can be run on older computers and enables multimedia video and non-linear video editing access more publicly.
- HasciiCam makes it possible to have live ASCII video on the Web. It captures video from a TV card and renders it into ASCII letters, formatting the output into an HTML page with a refresh tag, or in a live ASCII window, or in a simple text file.
- FreeJ is a Vj-ing tool for real-time video manipulation. VJ or vee-jay (from video jockey, by analogy with disc jockey, DJ or deejay) is a term coined in the early 1980s to describe the fresh-faced youth who introduced the music videos on MTV. The term VJ is also used to represent video performance artists who create live visuals on all kind of music.

Access to technology as a human right

> It's about dignifying people – and the way to do it is to offer participation.
> (Camcorder Guerillas 2002)

New technology gave the ability to form communities and to collaborate both on a global and on a local scale, starting from one's neighbourhood and reaching out to the whole world.

On a local level the Camcorder Guerillas (a collective based in Scotland) are concentrating on raising awareness of human rights and social-justice issues through video. With camcorders now widely available, a group of filmmakers, artists and individuals formed Camcorder Guerillas in 2002 at an Indymedia meeting.

Camcorder Guerillas empower people and communities with technical knowledge to tell their stories and to distribute these testimonies via the Internet and throughout the media network. A strong commitment to training and education

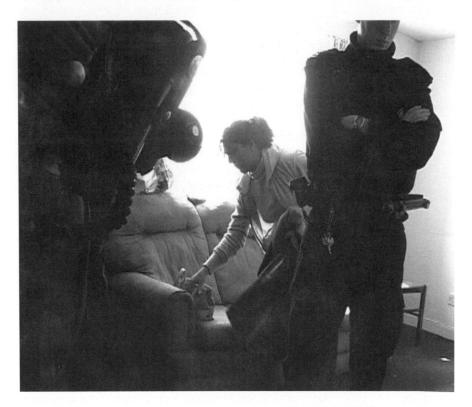

Figure 11.2 Iranian asylum-seeker being evicted from her Glasgow flat. Still from 'Welcome' by the Camcorder Guerillas

has carried on throughout the group's existence. The collective is open to anyone who shares its aims and is interested in using the moving image as a tool for activism and campaigning.

Media content like the Camcorders Guerillas' film *Welcome* is being distributed on a global level over the KEIN.org portal which came out of the 'Kein Mensch ist illegal' movement offering free publishing with the use of peer-to-peer networks and free access to information for activists. KEIN operates only on FLOSS software with open codes and is based on the V2V videofilesharing system. At the time of writing V2V distributes multimedia content over a Bittorrent peer-to-peer network. As soon as a new film is available the exact address for downloading will be published.

Excerpts of the V2V manifesto (V2V 2003)

TO WHOM IT MAY BELONG

Therefore we pose the question of intellectual property: To whom belongs an image? To the one who is mapped, to the one who produced it? Or to the one who makes copies from it? Or does it belong to everybody? We know that there is no final solution to these questions. But we have learned: New films are based on new freedoms.

RE-PLACING THE IMAGES

We believe in images with open sources: Reassessing the cinematic heritage of other generations, broadcasting the general intellect, empowering collective story-telling, changing the views, fast sharing of content, skills and resources, enabling multiple connections between creative nodes and networks.

Virtual images that everyone can edit, change, forward, rewind and PLAY.

In 1997, during the 'Documenta X', the 'Kein Mensch ist illegal' campaign had an infodesk at the Hybrid WorkSpace. Basically it came out of a network of local groups who were dedicated to helping immigrants and asylum-seekers, much like the 'Sans Papiers' campaign in France. The idea for a German and Polish border festival, an autonomous zone where artists and activists could show their concerns towards the treatment of immigrants, was born. The camp was realised in 1998.

In 2000 several camps had been organised along the borders that separate the European Union with the former Soviet bloc and 'Kein Mensch ist illegal' took place for the first time at the borders of the United States of America at the city of Tijuana, Mexico, under the title 'Borderhack!'

On one side the Malls are filled with happiness, and on the other, the wrong side, we are forever condemned to produce goods that we will never enjoy ourselves. That is, unless we are lucky enough to come by a green card. This is the border. Our border. A place where we earn pesos and consume in dollars. Where we almost live in the US. Where we can smell the future coming from the freeways, from Silicon Valley, from Hollywood, but yet we are trapped in a muddy hill with unpaved streets. To reach the freeway we need a car, something that we could never afford. The only way for us to cross the border is on foot, without a penny in our pockets. We resign ourselves to earn a minimum wage throughout our lifetimes, to looking through store windows as if they were postcards from Europe (it could be Jupiter or earth, for us it is the same), knowing that we could only reach the other side in our dreams. We are the good neighbors of the US, always here, always smiling, ready to serve the next margarita. (Borderhack 2000)

How to use Kein (V2V) filesharing

To watch content

1   Download and install Bittorrent.
2   Click on the content you want to watch on the site, a small torrent file is downloaded. Double click this file and the content will be downloaded over the Bittorrent file-sharing network.
3   To watch the file you have to install the Videolan VLC player (available for every operating system, including Windows and Mac OS X) or the mplayer (Linux).

To distribute content

By registering on the V2V site one can contribute multimedia content. You can edit your footage with the LiVES or Cinelerra video editing suite on a Linux System (see above 'Access to FLOSS'). All the video content is encoded with the oggtheora codec. For encoding your own material which is not saved in the oggtheora codec you can use an encoder like mencoder or ffmpeg2theora. Encoding is the process by which a source (object) performs this conversion of information into data, which is then sent to a receiver (observer), such as a data-processing system.

Access to intellectual property (education and culture)

The Free Culture Movement focuses on fair use and the public domain as a commons, rather than copyright as private property. Copyright is a barrier to creativity, culture and the distribution of knowledge. If copyrights were less restrictive, people would be less consumers than participants in a common culture, more able to remix and reinterpret this culture. An example is the free software movement, which develops the GNU/Linux operating system and distributes software under the GNU general public licence that allows anyone to download, use and modify this software for free, as long as the modified work itself is distributed under the same licence and the original author is credited.

The Free Culture Network is promoting the use of open licences as an alternative to copyright for cultural productions. You can find an overview of existing open-content licences in 'Guide to open content licences' (Liang 2004).

Since April 2004 the Free Culture movement has been rapidly spreading to college campuses across the United States (and from July 2005 in the United Kingdom). Microsoft chief Bill Gates called Free Culture 'digital communism'. As Nelson Pavlosky (co-founder of FreeCulture.org) stated in Keystone Politics (http://www.keystonepolitics.com/node/559), this would be like calling Bill Gates a fascist. Nelson argues that it is false to say that there should not be incentives for artists and innovators to create, but copyright today threatens to reach the point where it inhibits more creativity than it encourages.

Free Culture is inspired by the non-profit Creative Commons institution and the Electronic Frontier Foundation; other groups like Downhill Battle and Participatory Culture in the US or the Open Knowledge Foundation in the UK have joined the movement. It has lent a voice to those concerned with the current development of intellectual property. Creative Commons was set up in 2001, inspired by the free-software movement promoting an alternative copyright replacing the 'all rights reserved' with 'some rights reserved'.

As Lawrence Lessig, who defined the term 'free culture' (Lessig 2004) states,

> Creativity always builds on the past
> The past always tries to control the creativity that builds upon it
> Free societies enable the future by limiting this power of the past
> Ours is less and less a free society

FreeCulture.org (USA)

Nelson Pavlovsky, co-founder of FreeCulture.org, answered, in an email exchange questions for *The Alternative Media Handbook*:

1. The need for FreeCulture.org: why did it happen or how did it develop? What is the mission of FreeCulture.org?

We started our group because there weren't enough students my age involved in the free culture movement, which I found odd since we grew up with the Internet, and we probably understand the democratising potential of digital technology better than earlier generations. There was a need for a student movement, and we founded FreeCulture.org to fill that gap.

2. Over what period did FreeCulture.org develop and what are the significant moments?

FreeCulture.org was launched in April 2004, when Professor Lawrence Lessig came to speak at our school, attracting a large crowd for our launch. Important moments that led to our founding include the Diebold case, where we found ourselves involved in a lawsuit against a multi-billion-dollar corporation.

3. Resources, technology, participants and funding: how did it happen practically?

We've just started picking up grants . . . we've been focused on our local campus groups, so most of our members come from our campuses, and most of our funding comes from our schools, for our local groups.

4. Organisational structure: how is FreeCulture.org run? What relationships exist between projects, workers and participants/volunteers?

FreeCulture.org attempts to be decentralised . . . we have a core group of volunteers (mostly the people who have founded or are trying to found chapters) who help out on the national level, but mostly our activities take place on the local level. We do Internet-based campaigns on occasion, like Barbieinablender.org and UndeadArt.org, and we intend to do more of those in the future, perhaps with more of a local component.

5. Content and audience: what are the outcomes of FreeCulture.org and how are you distributing and exhibiting?

Outcomes? Lots of people on college campuses who are getting involved? And the aforementioned Web-based campaigns, of course. We have a blog (http://blog.freeculture.org), I suppose that's an outcome . . .

6. Sustainability: what are your main projects, long-term? Do you have any one-off projects?

We haven't figured out what our long-term projects are yet, although I suppose a couple include promoting open-source software and Creative Commons licences, and helping and encouraging people to publish their stuff online using sites like the Internet Archive or projects like Broadcast Machine, which enables you to embed a Bittorrent tracker in your blog.

7. How would readers of the Handbook *get involved in FreeCulture.org?*

The best way to get involved is to start or join a group on your college campus, but we need help with graphic design, Web design, programming, blogging and writing papers, and all sorts of other things on the national level. Just email us at newgroup@freeculture.org if you want to start a chapter, or freedom@freeculture. org for anything else :-)

FreeCulture.org.uk (UK)

The following text was written collectively on a Wiki page by members of the Free Culture UK movement.

1. The need for FreeCulture.org.uk: why did it happen or how did it develop? What is the mission of FreeCulture.org.uk?

Before FC-UK there was no group dedicated to grassroots free culture activism. We had Creative Commons UK who deal with the UK-specific licences, but they do not officially tackle more social and political issues for obvious reasons. We also had a range of digital rights organisations, but none were focusing on free culture and none were encouraging grassroots participation.

The mission of FC-UK, therefore, is threefold: first, to get many people involved in free culture activism; second, to work together to oppose those that would restrict our freedom, whether by extending laws relating to copyright, repressing new technologies or promoting a closed, proprietary future for culture; and third, to work together to promote positive alternatives that will increase our cultural freedoms, such as the public domain and Creative Commons.

2. Over what period did the FreeCulture.org.uk develop and what are the significant moments?

The idea was probably mulled over by various people ever since the Free Culture organisation in the US was announced. Possibly people thought about doing something similar for years before that. But the intention to form the group was announced in May 2005. In late June, Rufus Pollock and Tom Chance drafted the website and campaigns in the space of a few days and formally announced the launch of the group on the 28th of July 2005.

The next significant moment will be the first FC-UK Congress, where we will meet as a network to make decisions about what we will do over the next year. On 8th April 2006 the FC-UK constitution was ratified.

3. Resources, technology, participants and funding: how did it happen practically?

Rufus Pollock hosted the FC-UK website and mailing lists on the OKFN servers, since FC-UK is officially part of the Open Knowledge Foundation Network. At present all participants are volunteers and have either come into FC-UK through existing similar organisations (Creative Friends, CC-UK, CNUK, AFFS, Remix Reading, Liquid Culture) or by word of mouth from friends. We have no funding, but I suppose we may be looking for some in the future.

So how did it happen? Messily, spontaneously, as and when people found the time and energy to put some work into it :)

4. Organisational structure: how is FreeCulture.org.uk run? What relationships exist between projects, workers and participants?

FC-UK is an open, decentralised, participatory grassroots network. Buzzwords aside, we have a national network that is co-ordinated online by means of consensus decision-making and a meritocracy tempered by a democratic spirit. So decisions tend to depend upon who is willing to put in the work, but we also try to ensure every participant agrees with decisions where possible.

We also have a network of local groups, which are autonomous from the national network. They can organise themselves as they see fit, but should keep in touch with the national network and try to work in sync with the national network. This works in reality because every local group will have at least one or two participants on the national mailing list.

5. Content and audience: what are the outcomes of FreeCulture.org.uk and how are you distributing and exhibiting?

Well our content is really just the website, announcement emails and any leaflets and posters we produce. Distribution of announcements is done by flooding every mailing list, website and news organisation with announcements. Flyers and posters are put around by local groups.

We will, once we get it working, have a public domain register. People will be able to find works that are in the public domain, burn and upload the file to archive.org, then enter the metadata into our registry. We will then promote this registry heavily as the point of reference for the public when they want to know what they can share and remix.

6. Sustainability: what are your main projects, long-term? Do you have any one-off projects?

The first long-term project is to continue recruiting and involving people. After that we have our three long-term campaigns: 14+14 (reducing the length of copyright terms), Creative Commons (promotion) and Public Domain Burn (building the register). They can all be worked on indefinitely.

Within each campaign we have short-term goals. For example, we are trying to get signatures and testimony to demonstrate support for the 14+14 campaign, which can then be presented to ministers and industry figures at opportune moments. The Reading and Brighton groups are running remix projects, which encourage people in their local area to share and remix work, and which therefore have results that can be appreciated in the short term.

This way, with long-term campaigns that have short-term goals, we give ourselves longevity but also give participants and the outside world times when they can see concrete examples of our success.

7. How would readers of the Handbook *get involved in FreeCulture.org.uk?*

Visit the website and then contact either the national network mailing list, or your local group. If a local group doesn't yet exist in your area and you'd like to start one, contact the national network mailing list.

Links

Barbieinablender project http://www.Barbieinablender.org
Bittorent http://bittorrent.org
Camcorder Guerillas http://camcorderguerillas.net/
Converge Workshops: http://www.converge.org.uk
Creative Commons http://www.creativecommons.org
Downhillbattle project http://www.downhillbattle.org/
Dyne project farah http://farah.dyne.org/
Dyne project streamline http://www.streamtime.org
Dyne software lab http://www.dyne.org and http://www.dynebolic.org
Electronic Frontier Foundation http://www.eff.org/
Free Culture movement UK http://www.freeculture.org.uk
Free Culture movement US http://www.freeculture.org
Free Software Foundation. http://fsf.org/
Free software manuals: http://www.flossmanuals.net
Indymedia http://www.indymedia.co.uk
Internet Archive http://archive.org
Kein portal http://www.kein.org and http://www.kein.tv
Make Internet TV: http://www.makeinternettv.org
MPlayer http://www.mplayerhq.hu/
Open Knowledge Foundation http://okfn.org
Participatory Culture http://www.participatoryculture.org
Transmission Network: http://www.transmission.cc
Undead Art project http://www.UndeadArt.org
V2V portal http://v2v.cc
VLC Player http://www.videolan.org/vlc/

12 Alternative media in development

Introduction

This chapter looks at alternative media work in 'developing' countries, in two parts. First James Deane defines the territory, pointing out how the definitions of 'alternative media' become different when seen from the perspective of developing countries. Then Su Braden tells the story of a particular grassroots project in Malawi, which empowered a number of villages to be able to address their government directly.

Each raises the issue of how those excluded from power can use the media for their own ends, and the extent to which international NGOs involved in the development process can help this process – in Braden's phrase, 'follow a community lead'. There are numerous other instances worldwide of communities taking the lead in using media locally. Su Braden has also co-written an account of a project in Vietnam (Braden 1998) and *Insights into Participatory Video* (Lunch and Lunch 2006) is a useful and practical handbook in this area of work.

12.1 Alternative and participatory media in developing countries

James Deane

This chapter focuses on alternative and participatory media in developing countries. It is customary in guides such as this to define one's terms. In the case of alternative media, this is not necessarily an easy task. The term alternative media is one that is inherently defined more by what it is not than by what it is. Focusing on what it is not and what distinguishes it is perhaps the best starting point for any such guide, with an obvious starting question – to what are alternative media an alternative?

Alternative media in developing countries tend to have very different origins and dynamics to alternative media in industrialised societies and it is useful to state these different dynamics from the outset.

As explained elsewhere in this book, in most industrialised countries alternative media are normally taken to mean media that are rooted in, controlled by or in some way accountable to non-corporate, often community, interests, and are explicitly focused on providing perspectives that are distinct from – often discordant with – the mainstream media. They are especially defined by being independent of, and often explicitly established as an alternative to, corporate oligopolies that control large sections of the mainstream, mass market media. Their rootedness, together with their determination to avoid income sources that could compromise their independence, often mean that they are small in scale and both limited and restricted in profit-making.

Alternative media in much of the industrialised world have evolved as a response to perceptions that mainstream media invest insufficient legitimacy or provide little coverage of minority perspectives and experiences. In particular, they have sprung from claims that much of the mainstream media is an instrument of corporate and elite power, intent principally on 'manufacturing consent' of populations (Herman and Chomsky 1988).

Alternative media in these industrialised countries have a long history, but have mushroomed greatly in the last decade or so as a result of a variety of factors. The first is increasingly overt corporate power and concentration of media ownership and a perception that the diversity and pluralism of the media sector were increasingly being eroded. A second was the growth of global civil society, mass social and protest movements of the 1990s, particularly in response to globalisation, and a third was the falling economic costs of media production accelerated not only by the growth of the Internet but also by the falling costs of printing, computing and other production processes. In these countries, as seen elsewhere in this book, alternative media now take a dizzying variety of forms.

However, in most developing and former Soviet bloc countries, and indeed for much of humanity, most media could be said to be – and most would perceive themselves as being – alternative, at least compared to sources of information available just a few years ago. Fifteen years ago, most people on the planet received most of their information from one source – their government.

For most of the Soviet bloc, much of Africa and large parts of Asia including China, the mainstream media were controlled by government. In much of Latin America, most media were in the hands of large private companies that were so closely tied to government interests and ruling elites that content was similarly open to accusations of state control.

Government control – formal or informal – was especially true of the broadcast sector, with governments being particularly keen on retaining control of media that could reach all parts of their populations (with rural populations often providing the main power base for governments). For many years, the first target for any coup attempt was taking control of the government radio station.

In these countries, the growth of independent media was a response less to corporate control than to government control. It is even more difficult in such a setting to determine clearly what are and are not 'alternative' media and indeed there is a strong case to be made that media that are explicitly focused on informing and providing an airing for the perspectives of poor and marginalised peoples (often the great majority of people), should perhaps be regarded as the mainstream – certainly majority – rather than alternative media.

The fall of the Berlin Wall in 1989 had many profound consequences documented exhaustively elsewhere. As well as ushering in a wave of globalisation, it also ushered in a fresh democratisation in much (but far from all) of the developing world, and major processes of liberalisation, including of the media. As a consequence, media actors have mushroomed and flourished. In 1992, there were just two radio stations in Uganda, for example. Today there are more than 100, mostly FM, radio stations.

The extremely rapid changes and proliferation of media actors in developing countries have been called (by this author) 'the other information revolution'. Most people on the planet depend heavily on access to information on issues that shape their lives from two main sources: their own informal communication networks (family members, community discussions, travellers etc.) and the media, particularly the broadcast media. Fifteen years ago, this meant that most of their information came from government. The picture now is infinitely more complex.

We will explore this new media environment and its relevance to providing ordinary people with a voice – perhaps the most important characteristic of this discussion – below. First, it is important to acknowledge that, while this essay seeks to make some distinction between industrialised countries and developing countries, there are of course many commonalities.

There are issues of corporate control of the media in developing countries. Most developing-country media continue to depend heavily on Western news sources for their information and analysis of international events, including of news on issues that have a powerful impact on their populations, such as negotiations on trade. Agencies that have emerged to report on issues from an alternative, developing-country perspective and which have focused on South-to-South communication have often struggled. Twenty years ago there were several such agencies (Gemini News Service, Compass News Features, South Features, among others) but today the Inter Press Service is one of the few surviving such agencies in existence. There are other sources of independent information on development issues, such as the Panos Institute, One World and the Third World Network, but again these are poorly resourced.

Much of the content of developing-country broadcasting, particularly of television and cinema, is derived from the global export of cultural industries from the US and other Western sources. Long-existing debates over cultural imperialism (characterised by the wholesale domination of the global cultural industry by Western products) have transmuted into more complex scenarios where Bollywood, Latin American telenovellas and Chinese cinema (amid many other examples) assert themselves as global cultural industries. It is difficult to argue that

these are alternative media, but they are certainly creating a more complex portrait of global cultural industries. However, Hollywood and its exports still retain a dominant hold on much global content, particularly in developing countries.

Concentration of media ownership, too, is an important and growing characteristic of developing-country media environments, ranging from Rupert Murdoch's global media empire encompassing major television operations in China and India and elsewhere, through to regional media conglomerates such as the Nation Media Group in Eastern Africa. Such concentration can be expected to increase as developing-country markets grow in importance.

Despite this clear and growing element of corporate strength in developing-country media landscapes, the fact is that most 'alternative media' have not grown up in direct response to it, but for other reasons.

First and foremost, media have flourished in response to new – often hard-fought and still very fragile – media freedoms. This has taken a multitude of forms, much of it commercial. Print media have proliferated, FM radio has mushroomed and television access and viewership is exploding in almost all countries. This is a complex phenomenon difficult to sum up in the short space available here. Commercial media are dependent on advertising and there is a strong move among much media to focus on mainstream news and 'lifestyle' journalism (fashion, celebrities, health etc.) which attracts urban middle-class elites. There are arguably decreasing incentives for this commercial – and generally described as – mainstream media to cover issues of poverty or marginalisation and in this sense there are strong echoes of the same commercial dynamics that operate in industrialised countries. On the other hand, these exploding media have played a major role in many countries both in holding governments to account and in providing news for for public debate and expression for all sections of society. One of the best examples of this is the popularity of the radio talk show and phone-in, where contentious issues are discussed openly and provide new forms of public expression. In Uganda, Ekimeedza – public or community meetings – are organised and recorded by mainstream radio stations for broadcast, for example.

In this sense, while the competitive pressures on commercial media are growing, and the incentives for covering poverty-related or contentious social and political issues are arguably weakening, such media have played and are likely to continue to play a critical role in enriching the democratic life of most developing countries. Media freedom is fragile and many such organisations require outside advocacy support to survive in often hostile political environments. Organisations such as Article 19 play an important role in this.

Some organisations which can be described as alternative have sprung up to provide a measure of accountability for the media. Just as the US has the Media Channel to play this role (which also covers issues beyond the US), in India for example the Hoot exists to provide independent commentary on media issues. There has also been an explosion in online sources of news and analysis holding government and others in authority to account (examples include www.malaysia-kini.com in Malaysia and www.tehelka.com in India).

One product of liberalisation has been the increasingly vigorous commercial media. Another is a resurgent community media movement. Many hundreds of community media and particularly community radio stations have flourished, providing an increasingly important empowerment role as people have sought to make their voices heard more clearly. Community media are usually defined as media that have some form of accountability to their communities and are characterised by the objective of empowering communities through voice. They provide information to communities on issues relevant to them in forms – and particularly languages – they can understand. They provide spaces for people to discuss and debate issues in public. They provide a channel through which people in the community can make their voices heard in the public domain. And they provide forms of accountability and transparency where people in authority can be held to account by explaining their decisions and actions. Further information on community media can be found from the World Association of Community Media Organisations (known by its French acronym, AMARC). Examples of the use of community and other media and their impact can be found in *Making Waves: Stories of Participatory Communication for Social Change* (Gumucio Dagron 2001). Another important phenomenon has been the emergence of edutainment, particularly working with or creating soap operas with the explicit purpose of including socially relevant content (ranging from promoting family planning and HIV/AIDS messages to tackling domestic violence by making women aware of their rights). One of the best examples is *Soul City* in South Africa.

Despite the growth of community and other public-interest media, new information and communication divides are opening up between rich and poor, rural and urban. Urban centres find themselves increasingly saturated with media channels and rural areas often extremely poorly served. Indeed, access to media may be decreasing in many areas rather than increasing. Radio reaches far more people in developing countries than any other medium. Former monopoly broadcasters are having to compete with their vigorous commercial competitors and are consequently facing budget crises. They are often changing content to attract advertisers who are focused mostly on urban audiences. They are often cutting back on transmitter capacity, on minority-language programming and on providing content (including areas such as agricultural advice) to rural areas. The overall picture is one of changing information and communication divides rather than narrowing ones.

A section follows this one on the use of participatory communication for development, outlining in detail how the use of video was used in empowering people in Malawi. Such communication – alongside the use of oral testimony, theatre, puppetry and other media – has a long history demonstrating proven results over many years (one of the earliest examples was the use of video by Fogo Islanders in the late 1960s to identify their problems and communicate these to authority). Further information on such approaches can be found from Don Snowden (who pioneered the Fogo process) at the Centre for Development Communication at the University of Guelph (www2.uoguelph.ca) and from the International

Development Research Centre (www.idrc.ca), which has a major stress on participatory communication, as well as from the Communication for Social Change
Consortium.

Despite this long history, and wealth of experience in empowering people,
these approaches remain poorly supported and outside the mainstream of most
development policy. The role of video and other tools remains poorly recognised
by many mainstream development organisations (although techniques such as
participatory rural appraisal as developed by the University of Sussex Institute of
Development Studies have become common practice).

Donor organisations have remained lukewarm to such approaches. Most donor
organisations funding development projects require quantitative, measurable
results over relatively short time frames. They require project proposals which pre-
dict the outcome of a process and much participatory communication insists that
the outcome is determined by the process of involvement of people themselves.
They require a close correlation between investment and outcomes. They are
suspicious often of processes which are complex and where political and power
dynamics are prominent. Increasingly donors channel funding through budget
support to governments. They often have a rapid staff turnover, making long-
term engagement on complex issues difficult. For these reasons, participatory
communication has struggled to find prioritised acceptance within many donor
agencies.

There are signs that this may be changing. Donors and other development
agencies increasingly acknowledge that development is only successful if policies
command public acceptance and ownership and that poverty-reduction strategies
are informed by the perspectives and aspirations of those they are designed to
benefit. Donors have also increasingly accepted that placing conditions on development assistance has made developing-country governments more accountable
to donors than they are to their own citizens, which is economically and politically unsustainable. They are looking for new ways in which people living in
poverty can hold governments to account and can shape and communicate their
own agendas for change. It is likely to be some time still before participatory communication becomes widely accepted within development agencies, but the logic
of it becoming so is growing more obvious, and the prediction of this author is
that such logic will – despite many technical and technocratic obstacles – ultimately prevail.

As suggested above, the term 'alternative media' is not necessarily the most
helpful one in describing these phenomena in many developing countries. The
term 'public interest media' may be more helpful.

At first sight, the idea of working in alternative media, of making a career
in a profession that is poorly prioritised, chronically and persistently short of
resources and extremely fragile, may be unattractive even to the most committed
person.

However, the capacity of people to lift themselves out of poverty will depend
far more on their ability to form and communicate their own agendas for change

than it will on the amount of aid spent on them. A new phase in development may be approaching, marked essentially by the most marginalised in society asserting their rights and charting their own agendas for change. Historically such processes have been immensely powerful. Any such process, particularly if it is to be achieved through dialogue, debate and peaceful and democratic means, depends fundamentally on the role of communication – the capacity of people to access information on issues that shape their lives in forms they can understand, and their capacity to communicate their perspectives in the public domain. There is little that is likely to have a more profound impact on people's lives over the next decades. It may be the most thrilling profession to be involved in of all.

12.2 *Mgwirzano*: a case study from Malawi

Su Braden

> The video is very important because they have seen actual problems, not only reading or hearing about them. I hope that all the government departmental leaders and the district assembly members will help us because they have seen our problems through the video. They have promised us . . . face to face.
> (Samson Batwell, Village Management Committee Chairman, Kasambwe village, Salima District Assemby, Malawi, interview February 2002)

Introduction

This section gives a brief account of some of the lessons of an action research programme that I initiated. It took place between 2001 and 2004 in two African countries, Malawi in the south-east of Africa, and Sierra Leone in the west. For reasons of space I will focus here on our work in Malawi.

We set out to answer a specific question: how can communication processes and technologies overcome the barriers that prevent semi-literate and illiterate people from analysing and negotiating their own futures?

Many development organisations have virtually patented the buzzwords 'participation' and 'empowerment', but they leave the people for whom they work voiceless and without any active part in the business of negotiation with their own governments and policy-makers. Today, democracy is made a conditionality of aid by most Western governments that is largely satisfied by crosses on ballot papers. So neither Western governments nor development agencies are tackling democratic enfranchisement, in the sense of the participation of the mass of African peoples in their own government. On the contrary, an examination of the practices and underlying philosophies of development in the twentieth and twenty-first centuries reveals that the priorities and goals of the dominant players in the developed world work to the detriment of the self-determination of the poorest peoples. As a result the buzzwords of development thinking could well be characterised as follows:

*   *modernisation* – the exploitation of Third World dependency and capacity for debt
*   *participation* – the masking of the real conflicts between the poor and those in power
*   *advocacy* – the misrepresentation of the poor and the causes of poverty by jargonising elites.

The means by which economically powerful governments and NGOs relate are corrosively familiar: designing projects according to donor formats; providing salaries and funding for expatriates, elite cadres and experts, whether from the North or the South; buying into to the ethos of economic and/or cultural globalisation; producing glossy publications, evaluations and reports; and branding the poor as the advertised product of the fundraising endeavours of humanitarian organisations.

Our action research in Malawi was designed to respond to the disenfranchisement of resource-poor people, and to test a methodology. Participatory communication for development (PCD) brings poor communities into face-to-face negotiation with NGOs, donors and government and enhances their ability to analyse and represent their own development priorities. Video is used as a tool for community research to represent these needs and to carry responses back to the wider constituencies.

It works through a cycle of processes – participatory research and recordings, community alliance building, representation to government and donors, responses and feedback to the wider communities. This cycle is seen as key to establishing a practice of democratic participation, negotiation and accountability that includes the voices of the illiterate and semi-literate.

Power, or empowerment, comes through effective representation, as everyone who has lobbied in the developed world knows – and lobbying is an activity that is most effectively undertaken by groups and networks.

How was it run?

The action research was initially funded for three years by DFID (the Department for International Development in the UK).

The international office of ActionAid, based in London, was invited to participate as both partner and subject in this action research. The specific country research design for the Malawi programme was undertaken with the field staff and management of the partner organisation, ActionAid Malawi (AAM), in the autumn of 2000.

A research design workshop was organised with the AAM team and examined existing forms of communication used across the country between a wide range of government and non-government agencies, and the people they serve – variously termed 'communities' or 'beneficiaries'. One of the most interesting outcomes of this workshop was a diagram showing that 'communities' with whom AAM works are illiterate and speak a local language, while the organisations that serve them most commonly use written forms of communication in a different language, inaccessible to the majority, or speak through interpreters.

Training was given to the local team of ActionAid fieldworkers in video production, designed to help them to become technically confident, while taking care not to change their roles fundamentally from those of development workers or facilitators to video documentary-makers.

The training was organised in two parts. Part one was strictly technical and took the form of a basic five-day introduction to camerawork, sound and editing, with emphasis on developing skills such as following action that would enable the team to facilitate village participants to direct the camera. We made the decision to train the ActionAid field team, as opposed to the community, to use the camera for the following reasons:

- hierarchical leadership in the village context could mean that it was likely that only the most powerful (men) would use the camera
- conditions in the village (mud houses, rats, no electricity) meant equipment would be difficult to maintain
- cost and time: the ActionAid team would be able to respond to need and travel with the same camera to different locations
- the ActionAid team would work as facilitators and as technicians, while village residents would act as 'producers and directors'.

Part two of the fieldworker training – to facilitate local subsistence farmers to research and represent themselves with video – was designed as experiential learning. It accompanied the team through the process that was to form the structure of the action research, in the real context of village life, and through to village alliance-building and representation to government.

The process of the fieldwork training is summarised below.

1   Introductions (communities and development workers) and negotiation for the use of cameras in the village or town.
2   Participatory observation – team join in everyday activities with the community participants (it is important that the team become familiar with the way of life of the people with whom they work).
3   Facilitating and recording community research in the village or town, and community analysis via video playback each day.
4   Formation of a village or town editorial team who facilitate the community's development of action and communication plans (the action plan determines

and prioritises what needs to be done, the communication plan determines who the community needs to convince).

5   Once an audience for their communication has been decided, the editorial team works out which parts of the community's research recordings are relevant to the audience, and what other material needs to be filmed.

6   Rough editing with editorial team and playback to the whole community for checking.

7   Final edit is shown to the whole community.

8   The community takes their video and shows it in other villages or similar groups in their area and negotiates an alliance around the issues they have represented, and about which they can all agree.

9   The process (1–8) is repeated in two or three more villages throughout an area that experiences similar ecological, social and economic conditions. Again each village shows their tape and builds an alliance cluster.

The AAM team also discussed the final part of the process cycle that they would put into practice once the village alliance clusters were in place. The alliances show their tapes to each other, and if there is agreement on the issues selected by each individual alliance, they now join together as one community alliance and plan to show their tapes to chosen audiences. This planning includes analysis of key action points discussed in their tapes, and training in advocacy.

At each level of showings (to district, phase 1, and to National Government, phase 2) some of the needs are met by the authorities, and commitments made. Finally, alliance representatives take recordings of meetings back to the wider alliance membership, to enable follow-up and monitoring.

Chitsulo – key village 1

The experiential training for ActionAid Malawi's audio-visual researchers began in May 2001. Salima, a district around a small crossroads town of the same name, some 20 kilometres from the shores of Lake Malawi, was selected for the initial study. Within the Salima development area, Mwakhundi 'Island', so-called because of its isolated situation between the Lilongwe and Lithipe Rivers, with a population of approximately 10,000 people, was pinpointed for the test run. The first village they worked with was Chitsulo.

Findings about food security, but also about lack of access to public services, which had led to nine deaths by drowning in that year as people tried to reach the hospital by crossing the flooded river, confirmed what is described in the Action-Aid's Salima programme strategy paper (analysing problems and a programme of work to be undertaken by the ActionAid local teams). But village residents' emphasis on food shortages raised questions about how effectively ActionAid's inputs had been addressing these problems.

Within the first few days of work in the village, the process of recording and playing back the tapes to participants was interrupted by a series of deaths and funerals. There were four in three weeks, of which three were HIV/Aids related.

It was becoming clear that findings from this audio-visual research were likely to relate not only to the village participants, but also historically to ActionAid's own analysis and programme design at local, national and international management levels. The Salima team experienced participant observation in the village for the first time – sleeping in village houses and going to work in the fields with the people. As a result they began to reflect on the implications of four deaths in three weeks in a village of 32 households. The team confirmed that in their experience this toll was not particularly abnormal or high. They said that they knew of a further six funerals taking place in neighbouring villages. They began to consider the effect of loss of population on the abilities of the remaining children, widows and grandparents, to grow adequate amounts of food. And this discussion led the team to reconsider the issue of land distribution. A map drawn by village participants on the ground marked out the distribution of fields and showed ownership and crops grown. Many fields remained uncultivated and had been inherited by single-parent widows and grandparents, the parents of those who had died. The team asked themselves how the findings of this map related to the supposed issue of shortage of land in this area that had been noted in ActionAid's own strategy paper. What proportion of the population was physically capable of efficient cultivation, dependent mainly on hard manual labour with a hoe? The team's own reflections led them to ask the village participants more open questions about their needs. What were their own priorities?

The team's reflection on the findings in the village videotapes was an important stage in enabling them to support and encourage analysis of the problems raised, their causes and possible solutions. Discussions revealed that much of the time the village participants were sensibly trying to second-guess what inputs ActionAid Malawi might be expecting to provide, based on Chitsulo residents' knowledge of the agency's work in neighbouring villages.

Chitsulo had placed food security at the top of their list of problems to be resolved. Their solutions to the problems of food security echoed the known inputs supplied by ActionAid in the past: fertiliser, ox carts and ploughs and seed. However, the relation of food security to the second priority, the construction of a bridge to give access to Salima town, with its hospital, market, schools, maize-mill and the cash economy, required some teasing out.

The action plan

In their research videotapes the residents of Chitsulo show a village isolated from public services and dependent on agriculture, despite a workforce that is declining in numbers and physical strength due to illness and deaths, especially from HIV/Aids. They emphasise recurring and severe food shortages and yet land is under-used and badly distributed. The village ranking of the need for a bridge after that of food security may indicate not only the need to reach public services, but also literally the only way that they could see a solution to staying alive by accessing the cash economy and other forms of work. In other words, it may signal their recognition of the failure of smallholder subsistence farming.

The ranking of the bridge as the next most important thing to food security is also significant because it illustrates the broadening of discussions with residents, beyond the point where they simply reiterated a list of the inputs they might expect from ActionAid. A bridge to span a broad fast-running river is too large a project to fit within ActionAid's remit and it implies the involvement of government departments, and an understanding that there are other authorities to be lobbied. It could also indicate a change in AAM's role, from provider, to facilitator of negotiations. The bridge is seen as the major barrier to accessing to public services that the Malawi Constitution promises to make available to all its citizens.

The communication plan

To move their action plan forward and raise debates around their findings, village residents would need to communicate their analysis both to other villages in the area to form alliances around key issues, and to their local MP and district assembly. Elements of findings that had already been recorded could be used for this communication, but facilitation was needed to enable villagers to crystallise and demonstrate key issues.

The village was invited to elect an editorial team, representative of age groups and gender as well as relative wealth and poverty, to undertake organising additional things to be 'shown to the camera' and recorded for the final film. The editorial team decided to show how people were currently taken across the river to hospital at times of flood, being placed in a tin bath and pushed through the rushing water by swimmers. This was how nine people had died in the current year. They also planned linking shots explaining the research the village had undertaken to back their advocacy for food security, the bridge, education and access to public services which would also be needed.

From their planning it was apparent that the village team were developing a new kind of literacy that is close to traditional story-telling but involves the selection of images of real places and situations.

The village editorial team took these tasks on with enthusiasm and good planning. They organised presenters to 'show the camera' Salima market, where they would like to sell cash crops; the hospital; and the only existing bridge, 30 kilometres away, and they arranged for a short drama to illustrate the dangers of the river crossing for a sick child. They were able to timetable inputs and participation from other members of the community at moments and in places that fitted conveniently with their other tasks, a feat not always achieved by development workers in their participatory endeavours. Those who were to be filmed turned up on time and had thoughtfully carried whatever props they expected to need.

Finally the tape was edited, and a premiere showing to the whole village was

Figure 12.1 Gertrude Mthana, AAM participatory communication team leader, filming in Chitsulo village (Photo: Su Braden)

Figure 12.2 Gertrude Mthana filming (Photo: Su Braden)

arranged in Chitsulo one evening so that the whole population could check the contents.

The video projector was set up on the back of the AAM pick-up and a sheet was used as a screen on the wall of one of the village houses. The team explained that people should watch carefully to see if everything that was said was correct and true, because it was still possible to make changes if they were not happy. As dusk fell, a low murmur greeted the Chitsulo song and title sequence, then a movement backwards by the whole audience as the first speaker stepped to the front of the screen, then attentive silence. As soon as the showing was over, they asked to watch it again. Then they said it was good. They made one correction to a figure wrongly given for the distance to Salima market. Above all they said they were proud to have spoken, to have explained their problems clearly, and they wanted as many people as possible to hear what they had said.

Kaponda – key village 2

The initial training was now complete and the ActionAid team began to work independently, moving on to a second key village, while continuing to support regular showbacks and discussions organised by the Chitsulo village editorial team, to build solidarity and alliances around the key issues of their research, within their neighbouring village cluster. Kaponda is nearer to the existing bridge that links the 'Island' to Salima district, but still some 30 kilometres from Salima town, and access to hospitals, schools and markets.

Residents of Kaponda reviewing their situation during the period of hunger in January and February 2002, said that they felt that a new bridge would not help in the issue of food security or poverty, because it would still be too far for most people to access public services. Instead they felt they should fight for schools, markets, a maize mill and a health centre on their side of the river.

A historical time-line produced and filmed in Kaponda gives evidence that in 30 years between 1970 and 2001 the village has only three times produced sufficient food to maintain itself throughout a whole year. For the majority of the period between 1970 and 2001 the village had only produced on average 50% of what was required, and had several times experienced severe famine. In December 2001 they had been hungry for almost nine months and by January 2002 they expected to be experiencing fatal famine conditions.

This was a testing time as the Salima team watched participants they had come to know and work with closely getting thin and wasting away and sometimes dying. The president of Malawi meanwhile went to the press denying that a famine existed. The film was crucial evidence.

Mvululu – key village 3

Again, while supporting Kaponda in showbacks to their surrounding villages, the Salima team moved on to a third village, named Mvululu, situated in the forestry reserve some distance further on from the only existing bridge to the 'Island', beyond Kaponda. ActionAid had not yet worked in Mvululu and we thought it would give us a comparison with the Chitsulo and Kaponda village clusters.

In fact the findings of Mvululu reflected those of Chitsulo and Kaponda and prioritised the issues of food security, but gave strong emphasis to HIV/Aids education. The women talked openly about children being used for prostitution to help feed families.

The village editorial committee organised showbacks to their surrounding villages, despite the fact that by this time, spring 2002, the death toll from the famine throughout the area was mounting and one of the key characters in the Kaponda film had already died.

Building *Mgwirizano* (alliance) between villages and government

The rehearsal, 9 October 2002

The aim behind community participants showing their tapes and addressing policy-makers and donors is to create opportunities for them to enter into communication and negotiation on equal terms with those who make decisions about their lives. The first stage is to enable villages to agree on the areas around which they can develop alliances. It is important for both village communities and team members to understand that it is possible to agree to form alliances on some issues and not on others. Bringing issues to the forefront on which the village groups are not agreed or about which they are unclear will undermine their power to negotiate.

It is also important to continue to maintain and extend this alliance at the broadest possible level among the villages, and to include all ages, gender groups and income levels.

In September 2002 the Salima team spent time concentrating on the nature of the alliance that they hoped to build between the three village clusters that now involved over 10,000 people and the district. The first formal meeting between Mwakhundi *Mgwirizano* and Salima District Assembly, local ministry officers and NGOs was planned to take place on 10 October.

The team organised a rehearsal day for village representatives, none of whom had entered a conference building before. They met at the venue that had been booked for the actual meeting and walked and talked (and ate) their way through a rehearsal for the real day. The idea was that they should feel like confident, equal negotiators at this meeting.

The day began with an explanation of the purpose of the Thursday meeting, the meaning of the words *mgwirizano* ('alliance') and *mu umodzi muli mphamvu* ('together there is power').

The AAM facilitating team opened a discussion on the structure of local government, on the way that government works through the district assembly and how the district is supposed to link in with village management committees. None of the community members had been able to give a name to the institution of the district assembly at the beginning of the day.

There was a good debate between participants from Chitsulo and Kaponda about the relation of the proposal for a new bridge, made in the Chitsulo tape, to the issue of hunger. They agreed that while the overall problem was indeed hunger, the issue of the bridge represented isolation from all public services, including markets, which left the whole area unable to protect itself with money from cash crops against shortages at other times of the year.

This debate led the 19 community representatives to discuss and select the topics for the working groups they would convene with members of the district assembly, local donors and NGOs once they had shown their three tapes.

The *Mgwirizano* meeting between communities from the 'island' and Salima District Assembly, local ministries and donors (10 October 2002)

The seating plan for the meeting clearly raised eyebrows among the suited assembly members. They found they had not been invited to sit at the head of a conference table or on a raised platform to address an audience of villagers, but rather to sit among and between their poorer constituents, old and young, men and women, some with babies, on chairs arranged in a horseshoe.

The 75 participants were welcomed by the chair, who asked Mr Julius from Mvululu to explain how the three tapes that they were about to see had come about. Then an elected representative from each village cluster introduced their film in turn. When the viewings were over village residents summarised the main points and invited the assembly members to join them in working groups. These village-led working groups signalled a new level of debate between local government and subsistence farmers. The task for each group was to produce solutions to the problems discussed in the films and to feed these back at a plenary session where an action plan was drawn up with a time table for each task, as well as a programme for follow-up monitoring.

The commitments made by local NGOs, MPs, the district assembly and government ministries were recorded on video and shown back throughout Makundi Island, and the villages appointed representatives to monitor and follow up on the progress of the promises.

> The meeting was very, very informative because it was a grand opportunity for different people to come together, discuss and analyse issues that affect the community. In particular, one thing that has interested me most is that

the meeting has given us an opportunity as government and other key players in development to be accountable and responsible to their needs. I feel this is important. (Mr Chinyanya, chair, Salima District Assembly, interview following the first Village *Mgwirzano* meeting with Salima District Assembly)

Meeting with national government in the Malawian capital, Lilongwe

It took another year to arrange the next public meeting at which the Village *Mgwirzano* from Makundi 'Island' showed their tapes to national government and international donors. By this time some problems had been resolved, or temporarily resolved. But others remained outstanding. As one of the young village women presenters said to the government ministers, speaking now with practised assurance: 'If we are sick we go first to the hospital in Salima, but if we have complications, sometimes they tell us to go to Lilongwe. We have come to you today with our complications.'

The issue of the bridge was still outstanding despite some earlier promises by the Ministry of Works to look into costings. Meanwhile, however, ActionAid had provided a boat and some river training. But there were still problems with seed stocks, fertiliser, the recruitment of teachers and supplies to a local health post, as well as training around HIV/Aids. As a result of their meeting with the district assembly, the *Mgwirzano* representatives said that they now found it easier to knock on doors, and they had better support from local service providers, but that it was apparent that sometimes these providers themselves did not have the power or resources to solve problems. Indeed, some of these officials had accompanied the representatives of the *Mgwirzano* to Lilongwe.

The meeting took much the same form as that at district level and again the commitments were filmed and contacts were made.

Audiences and distribution of the tapes and CD-ROMS

Tapes were shown at several different levels. They were reviewed within the village involved, each evening after a research session. The completed programmes were shown first to the village concerned, and then by that village to neighbouring villages. The three key village clusters showed their finished programmes to each other and then to the local district assembly, and finally to national government ministries and international donors. All three tapes with a commentary on the process were distributed on CD-ROMS through ActionAid country offices throughout Africa and Asia. Following the Lilongwe meeting, UNICEF, DFID and the EU asked for copies of the tapes to show to internal meetings.

Sustainability

The Village *Mgwirzano* has extended beyond the 'Island' and this larger *Mgwirzano* was entirely the work of the Makundi people. There is now a membership of over 20,000. Field staff in Salima continue to work with the communities. Is it sustainable? Malawi is a poor country and this affects everything – transport, communication and people's morale. The *Mgwirzano* is driven by the perceived needs and the small successes of the experience and is clearly moving forward more or less autonomously. The Village *Mgwirzano* expanded beyond the limits of the 'Island' and linked up with other communities, but outside the ActionAid child-sponsorship development area.

Can an international NGO follow a community lead? ActionAid Malawi has plans to expand the training and development of the PCD process. But the structure of ActionAid's work in the field is based on child sponsorship in the villages where they work and, as the Chair of Salima District Assembly pointed out in the review of the action research, 'Communities within the district have different capacities. The sponsorship approach to funding specific communities could create an imbalance between communities. If we do not support all communities this could limit the potential for advocacy and learning.' He added, 'The PCD process is a good approach which can feed into the democratic society and when the people are able to "voice out" they bring us a bigger challenge than ever before.' The *Mgwirzano* is already ignoring the boundaries set by sponsorship for ActionAid's work. The question is, will ActionAid be able to follow?

For free copies of the Malawi and Sierra Leone CDs – *Participation: A Promise Unfulfilled?* – email supporterservices@actionaid.org.uk.

13 Distribution and audiences

Introduction

The opportunities for alternative media-makers to reach audiences have never been greater. The Internet and allied distribution media like DVD, podcasting and mobile phones have opened up (still relatively unpoliced) ways to transmit radical material. In this chapter we look at three specific instances of how alternative media have connected with their audiences: community radio in Australia; Lux, who distribute artists' film and video in the UK; and the distribution of *A Letter to the Prime Minister* – a film about the aftermath of the last Iraq war. However, we are aware that the potential for alternative media distribution and audience engagement is much greater than these examples on their own would indicate.

The diversity of practices and beliefs which we have seen is characteristic of alternative media is also a feature of how the question of audiences and how to reach them is addressed (or not) in the sector. There is some disagreement, both on the question of audience size and reach for alternative media messages, and on the importance of asking this quantitative question in the first place. It is almost a given in dominant 'mass' media that the larger the audience, the more effective the media artefact. The quest for audiences in mass media is about 'stimulating consumer markets . . . and certainly not about the public's social agency' (Downing 2003: 634). In alternative media the size – or 'massness' – of the audience is often seen as an irrelevant, even reactionary, consideration. It is what we say, the content, and the quality of the audience response (maybe the degree to which they have been spurred to action) that counts, rather than any abstract numerical measure of 'success': 'There is a danger of accepting definitions of alternative media which always risk requiring them to be evaluated by standards peculiar to large-scale mainstream media – and by which they are bound to fail!' (Downing 2003: 625). In many cases, the significance of alternative media (particularly participatory work with groups) is thought to be in the experience of the media activity itself, in the process of making it, rather than necessarily in the product that comes out of the activity.

When the product is seen as important, there is also an often-expressed worry that a lot of alternative media output is 'preaching to the converted', talking to a small number of people whose beliefs coincide with those of alternative media-makers, rather than reaching out and touching the lives of people who otherwise rely on dominant media. As Uzelman puts it rather more colourfully, alternative media practices could be seen as having 'little effect, something akin to pissing one's self in a dark blue suit: you get instant relief, you feel warm all over for while, and pretty much no-one notices' (Uzelman 2005: 25). It is certainly true that production rather than distribution has been the main focus of alternative media activity for most of its history, although the recent proliferation of opportunities for reaching audiences through the Internet and digital technologies is already reversing this trend.

However, the issue is rarely one of audience size and reach on their own. The products of mainstream media often encourage a more passive response from an audience than do alternative media artefacts. John Downing suggests that the users of radical alternative media will behave differently from the normal 'somewhat static, individualised – or at least domesticated – audience', because these media often overlap and interact with active social movements (2001: 9). It is also true that smaller, more local audiences are frequently more favoured by, and appropriate for, alternative media. Clemencia Rodriguez believes that 'the capacity to articulate the local constitutes a crucial component of the political potential of citizens' media'. She questions 'media activists' aspiration for their media outlets to become bigger, more powerful, to reach wider audiences, to have more visibility' because 'the consequence of losing one's ability to articulate the local is unavoidable if coverage and audiences expand' (2001: 155).

This is not to suggest that the need to connect with audiences of whatever size is not vital. As we have seen, digital technologies are making this more possible at the level of simple technical practicality, enabling alternative media-makers to bypass traditional gatekeepers. For instance the film *Outfoxed*, a radical critique of Rupert Murdoch's Fox News in the US (which we mentioned in chapter 3), was originally released on DVD only. As a result of the success of its distribution on DVD, in August 2004 it was released to cinemas in New York, Washington DC, Los Angeles, and San Francisco, and in the following weeks in other cities as well. The film eventually earned over twice its original budget at the box office, and, as importantly, remains part of an ongoing campaign against Fox News. Interestingly, the filmmmakers have also released the *Outfoxed* interviews online under a Creative Commons licence that allows others to use the interviews in their own projects without their permission.

There is also evidence of growing audience interest in other instances of alternative media. Mitzi Waltz refers to a 2004 report on news media in the US which suggests that 'alternative, ethnic and online media are the only news outlets gaining in audience numbers' (Waltz 2005: 1). Paul O'Connor from Undercurrents estimates that their tapes can reach as many as 200,000 people (Murphy 2006: 27), which is more than the reported ratings for *Channel 4 News* in the UK, and the first piece below from Australia evidences substantial audience support for community radio: for instance, almost a quarter of Australians over 15 years old listen to it in a typical week.

13.1 The power and the passion: community radio in Australia

Michael Meadows, Susan Forde, Jacqui Ewart and Kerrie Foxwell

Community radio in Australia began as an urban phenomenon and while most of its audience continues to be city-based, almost three-quarters of licensed stations are in rural, regional or remote areas of the Australian continent. It is an important indicator of a changing relationship between local, volunteer-run radio stations and their relevant communities of interest. More than 60% of community radio stations cater for a broad-based local audience. These 'generalist' stations provide access and an opportunity for participation for ordinary citizens who would otherwise have no real or recognised input into local cultural life. The remainder offer 'specialist' formats catering for ethnic, Indigenous, visually impaired and religious audiences, among others. The first comprehensive study of the sector in 2002 revealed that it plays a significant cultural role in the Australian mediascape, particularly as a source of local content. And in around 30 locations, volunteer community radio provides the *only* source of local news and information for audiences (Forde, Meadows and Foxwell 2002).

The Australian community broadcasting sector emerged in 1975 when the federal government freed up spectrum on the newly introduced FM band. Fine music and 'radical radio' led the charge, with FM remaining the sole province of community radio until commercial pressures during the 1980s saw a continuing progression of Australia's commercial radio stations making the switch from the AM band. The community broadcasting sector is now Australia's largest, with around 460 licensed, independent, community-owned and operated broadcasting services. In comparison, there are around 260 operational commercial radio licences (Department of Foreign Affairs and Trade 2005).

The sector has become Australia's most diverse, with 104 stations (including six full-time) producing more than 2,000 hours' broadcasting by ethnic communities each week. This involves around 4,000 volunteers from 125 cultural groups broadcasting in 97 languages. There are 23 full-time indigenous community radio stations and 80 remote indigenous broadcasting services (RIBS) producing 4,000 hours of indigenous programming each week. In addition, Australia has 15 dedicated radio for print handicapped (RPH) services where around 1,600 volunteers produce 1,500 hours per week of programming suitable for people with a print disability. The sector boasts 38 full-time religious radio stations and others with a focus variously on youth, senior citizens, the arts, fine music and Australian music. Three satellite-based programme distribution networks service the general, indigenous and RPH sub-sectors. There are two national news services – indigenous (National Indigenous News Service, NINS) and general (National Radio News, NRN) – and seven community television stations operate in every state except Tasmania. The sector is volunteer-driven, with more than 20,000 people participating on a regular basis, contributing the equivalent of AU\$145 million annually in terms of volunteer working hours. Around 114,000 people financially support community radio services as subscribers or members, while an estimated 8,000 people are trained in broadcasting skills each year (Forde, Meadows and Foxwell 2002).

Quantitative research

In September 2004 the first comprehensive quantitative audience survey of the sector revealed that 24% of Australians aged 15 years and older – around 3.8 million people – listen to community radio in a typical week. Monthly audience figures sometimes leap to 45%, or around 7.1 million people. The study found that one in five community radio listeners – almost 700,000 people – are *exclusive* listeners. The main reasons nominated for listening were programming diversity, specialist music or information programmes, and the emphasis on local news and information. Metropolitan areas account for nearly two-thirds of all community radio listeners. Most listeners are aged 55 and over and tune in for more than 12 hours a week. People aged 15–24 average five hours per week and audiences in the 25–54-years range average almost seven hours per week. Overall, the audience is almost equally split on gender lines with almost half of listeners engaged in full-time work (McNair Ingenuity 2004).

Qualitative research

Findings from the first qualitative audience study of the sector by the authors suggest community radio in Australia plays an important cultural role. Local radio is a central organising element of local community activity and thus an important cultural resource. Audiences have emphasised the importance of community radio providing an alternative by focusing on local rather than global or even national events. Their argument is simple: existing publicly funded organisations like the Australian Broadcasting Corporation (ABC) and the Special Broadcasting Service (SBS) already provide independent sources of news and information and have the resources to cover national and international news – so how can community radio compete?

Our research has revealed an extraordinary level of passion for community radio, with audiences describing their relationship with a local station as like being 'part of a family'. Others speak about the strong appeal of 'ordinariness' in being able to identify with a presenter or a person being interviewed on air. These are powerful indications of the varied ways in which audiences are engaging with community radio. It suggests that a high level of interaction – either perceived or actual – between audiences and producers is fundamental to the very definition of community radio in Australia, and it challenges conventional concepts of the

audience–producer barrier in broadcasting. This is particularly evident in Indigenous communities where local radio is consistently identified as providing
communities with a 'first level of service'. Audiences, both Indigenous and non-
Indigenous, have emphasised the significant role played by community radio – and
only community radio – in crisis situations like floods, bushfires and major weather
alerts; in dealing with multiple deaths in a community by offering on-air coun-
selling for listeners; in offering the alternative views of 'citizen journalists' who
challenge mainstream versions of events; in providing listeners with a sense of
community likened to being part of a family; and in rejecting globalising information processes in favour of what affects the local and the everyday lives of listeners.

Acknowledgement

This section comes from research which has been jointly funded by the Australian
Research Council and the Federal Department of Communication, Information
Technology and the Arts.

13.2 Lux

Julia Knight

Lux describes itself as 'a not-for-profit organisation that supports and promotes contemporary and historical artists' (www.lux.org.uk) moving image work, and those
who make it, through distribution, exhibition, publishing and research'. It came
into existence through the merger of the London Film Makers' Co-op (LFMC) and
London Electronic Arts (LEA) in 1999 and houses the largest collection of experimental film and video work in the UK. (LEA was called London Video Arts when
it was originally set up, then changed its name first to London Video Access in the
1980s and then to London Electronic Arts in the 1990s.)

The distribution of artists' film and video is labour-intensive, but yields relatively low levels of earned income and has thus always relied on subsidy via
low-paid/volunteer labour and grant aid. Lux currently has one major revenue
funder (the Arts Council) and a team of volunteer interns earns a modest level
of income from its core distribution activity, and applies for additional funding
on a project-by-project basis. This 'mixed-economy' model is both a strength and
a weakness. On the one hand, such organisations tend to have a fragile existence
due to the vagaries of national arts funding policy and a high turnover of staff
due to the low levels of pay. On the other hand, however, organisations like Lux
attract enthusiastic and highly committed workers, with extensive subject knowledge, who can exploit project funding and utilise volunteer labour to raise the
profile and awareness of artists' film and video on a number of fronts.

Lux's two predecessor organisations initially operated open-acquisitions policies for ideological reasons and rapidly accumulated large collections. Lux inherited its combined collections and now has a library of around 4,000 works which is added to quarterly. While the Web means that all these works can be listed in an online catalogue, it is impossible to promote effectively such a large number. Although the online catalogue can be browsed and searched, selection of a film or video depends on a customer's foreknowledge of that work. And what most distributors like Lux find is that a mere 20% of their library generates 80% of their earned income. While Lux's revenue funding allows it to maintain its large collection, of necessity it operates a selection process for new acquisitions – centred around whether they think they can effectively promote the work.

Any distributor is at one level acting in the interests of the 'producers' they distribute, but this is a defining feature of Lux which stems from its history. The LFMC and LEA were both set up and initially run by artists on a volunteer basis. Hence there was a concern to return as much of the earned income as possible to the artists. Although the royalty split to the artist had to decrease as the organisations started to take on paid workers, this concern has persisted and has made it difficult for Lux to cover its overheads and reinforced its grant-aid dependency. At the same time most alternative distributors have operated non-exclusive distribution contracts to allow artists to place their work with other distributors in the belief that this was beneficial to the artists. Unsurprisingly, artists have been reluctant to relinquish such terms and, combined with Lux's own history, this has meant Lux has resisted the adoption of more commercially minded distribution strategies and sees itself as an agency serving the interests of its artists.

Although digital technology has eroded the historical divide between film and video, many artists and viewers remain concerned about the legitimacy and quality of the viewer experience when work originated on film is screened on video or DVD. In this context Lux has an important contemporary role to play since it is often the only place in the UK where it is possible to hire artists' work in its original format. A further concern is the much-improved screening quality of DVD technology, which has meant that once sold, the distributor (and artist) loses control over how the work is used. This has made some artists reluctant to make their work available on DVD. Other artists and some distributors, however, have embraced DVD technology for this very reason in the belief that it – and the enormous popularity of the DVD medium – will facilitate access to a wider audience. In theory, Lux is well-placed to capitalise on both markets as long as the display equipment for celluloid and video remain readily available to its target audiences. At the same time, Lux is experimenting with online distribution by offering 'tasters' via their LuxOnline site (www.luxonline.org.uk).

Although alternative distributors have suffered from an inherent instability due to their funding base, this has also rendered organisations such as Lux very adept at reinventing themselves, adjusting to new circumstances and exploiting new opportunities.

A letter to the Prime Minister Julia Guest

This was a film that evolved from the concern that Jo Wilding and I had for what was about to happen to ordinary people in Iraq if the country was occupied by US and British troops. The film follows Jo on her journeys to Iraq of the last few years, creating a moving picture of the terrible impact UK and US foreign policy has had on the Iraqi people.

I managed to make three short reports for South West BBC's *Inside Out*, regional reports as Jo was a local activist in Bristol. This allowed us to show the issues around sanctions, the protests against the war and eventually the siege of Falluja on prime-time UK TV, in an unusual slot for a foreign documentary. It also helped to fund the longer film.

I funded the bulk of the production by borrowing and selling footage to broadcasters for news reports. Some of the post-production funding came from sending an email to Jo's email list asking for £100 donations to help finish the film, in return for a credit on the film and a copy of the DVD, and pre-orders of the DVD of the film for £15. The response was incredible and made the last, and most expensive, stage of the production possible. People were forwarding the message on to other lists and websites, so in the end I was still receiving donations nearly three months after the original email went out.

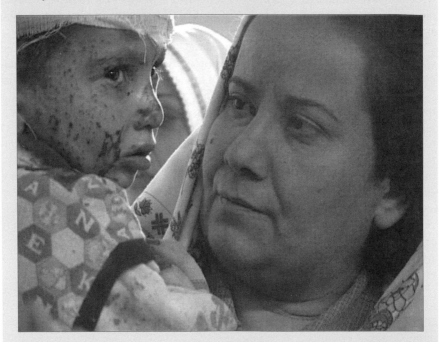

Figure 13.1 Iraqi woman and child (Photo: Julia Guest)

Funding from conventional media sources was not easy to achieve and the project had been rejected by a range of different funders, who wanted to see a proper distribution plan. For me this was the biggest learning curve, how to get a documentary into the cinema. Again no one was interested in funding distribution, so it was down to the film being networked by activist groups around the world. It was premiered at the Barbican in London in May 2005, to a very substantial audience, as it had been sold out a week in advance and we had people queuing for the returns. It has since been shown at arts cinemas around the UK, by various activist groups including Indymedia, and in the OXDOX film festival, which took it to Leicester Square. It has also been broadcast on Al Jazeera across the Middle East. At present no UK broadcaster has decided to broadcast, though it is going onto US cable sometime in 2006.

While the film has yet to meet its full production costs, to date I have sold hundreds of DVDs worldwide, and millions of people in the Middle East have now seen it, thanks to Al Jazeera, as well as thousands of people around the UK. Perhaps one day it will even get broadcast on UK television . . .

14 Student media

Introduction

Student media include radio and television stations, video collectives, film clubs and the myriad of print and online publications produced by students, from daily or weekly newspapers to quarterly magazines, literary publications, political papers, satirical and comedic zines and blogs. Some of this is political, some of it modelled on the familiar broadsheet newspaper format, some of it issue-driven, and some of it about creative, artistic expression. Student media can also play an important role in forging stronger links between campus and community.

Student media have a strong history of radicalism and affiliation with social movements, especially in the 1960s in North America and Europe. Student media played a key role in organising student involvement in the civil rights movement and against the Vietnam War, and today against the war in Iraq. They can also be a polarising force on campuses, a place for political and ideological opposition to play out in print and on air. Confrontations over feminism, race, sexual orientation, war and global warming find space for heated and often contentious debate. All manner of free speech is wrestled with. Student media are a microcosm of the wider college experience. If Western student media today can be seen first and foremost as a training ground for future professionals, they are emblematic of the increasing pressure on students to graduate with competitive industry skills and top grades, leaving them less time to engage in radical activity (or any extra-curricular activity) on campuses.

But student media today still exist at the heart of revolutionary uprisings, and at the centre of political violence. As recently as July 2006 a student radio station in Oaxaca, Mexico was attacked by gunmen. It was reported in the Associated Press that masked assailants fired into the station's windows while students were on the air. The university station had supported local protests opposing the state governor accused of corruption and election fraud, and his administrations' violent repression of dissent. In South Africa, student journalists were crucial in the struggle to end apartheid and they were threatened there for their reporting of criticism surrounding Zimbabwe's 2002 election. Student publications continue to be important advocates of press freedom, and in the US, groups like the Student Press Law Center provide legal assistance to student media in need (www.splc.org). Student media provide an important training ground for media-makers, give voice to student interests and concerns and create spaces that are largely self-organised and managed by students, for students. The possibilities are, hopefully, endless.

14.1 Student radio   *Salvatore Scifo*

Student radio can offer an important space for minority voices and promote wider campus and community participation and political activism. South American scholars (Rodriguez 1997) have emphasised the educational and pedagogic function of university radio, where stations have played key roles in student uprisings against repressive and undemocratic regimes. There remains a lively on-going continent-wide debate on the sector (ASCUN 2005, online).

The main purpose of this chapter is to highlight the creative possibilities offered by student radio, which has been described by Priestman as

> made by students for students, especially where universities and colleges are set on campuses. The scale and sophistication of student radio varies enormously, but North America and Canada have the longest experience of college radio subsidized within public education systems. There, they have been tremendously successful and often integrated into a region's mix of FM stations. In many other countries, attempts to follow this model have been constrained by a) lack of external subsidy b) more restrictive licensing and usually both. (1999: 22)

There is little academic work in this area – Sauls' *The Culture of American College Radio* (Sauls 2000) is arguably the most definitive source on this subject, providing an insight into the sector in the wider framework of the contemporary US media and cultural landscape. Sauls argues:

> The college radio station offers a true alternative to programming not commercially available or viable. The best indicator of this trend is the programming of alternative music that reflects the diverse life styles of a 'college culture'. Additionally, the 'open format' utilized at the majority of college stations also distinguishes them from their commercial counterparts. (Sauls: 1995: 3)

The main aims of a student radio are to provide training, practical skills and work experience for those who aim to work in radio and an alternative and/or complementary perspective to other media available locally, often content that is specifically targeted to students, although not exclusively.

It is not surprising then that the debate on the function of a student station has been focused around these issues. On one side, McDonald (1995: 21) argues that 'the primary function of the campus radio station is to educate and train students to enter the forbidding realm of professional broadcasting'. On the other side, the relevance of this medium is not confined to its training delivery: student radio is a tool to experiment with new formats, broadcast alternative music and give space to under-represented music genres and social groups, whose needs are not met by other local media.

> Although the purposes of radio stations licensed to institutions of higher education vary somewhat from school to school, several common ones can be identified. Most importantly, all or nearly all stations see their primary function as one of providing alternative programming to their listening audiences. (Caton 1979: 9, cited in Sauls 2000: 27)

Tower (2006), telling about his experience as a college radio volunteer, adds that 'the station was emphatically not intended for professional training, but intended as a way for students to expand their horizons and dabble in a new kind of activity that would otherwise not be available to them'. Farnsworth (2006) who has been a founding member and volunteer on-air host at New Zealand's Radio U (RDU), a Christchurch-based student radio station, argues:

> One function it should have is to represent student interests, whether this is in music programming or station output; the other, often closely allied, is experimentation; in New Zealand's context, this is the only forum or venue in which this can really take place. Audiences are more likely to accept it (and allow for it) and having secured funding through the local student's association makes experimentation possible.

The funding issue is not peculiar to New Zealand though, as the issues of sustainability can push stations towards more commercially accessible formats, as in the Americas. Finally, Sarnoff (2002: 1) evidences college radio's role in the broader media landscape in the US: 'Non-profit college radio is, by its nature, a medium dedicated to the local community and the public interest (. . .) the role of college radio lies in the bleak future of diversity and innovation that is lacking in the industry today'.

Italy

In Italian broadcasting, the involvement of politically active students has been present since the advent of the free radio (*radio libere*, or 'pirate radio') in the 1970s. Students have been an important part of radical media experiences, especially after the 1976 break-up of the local monopolies of Italian state radio broadcasting. Thousands of stations literally 'flooded' the airwaves and students joined co-operatives formed by workers, artists, trade union members and local community groups. Students joined stations like Radio Città, Radio Quartiere and Radio Alice in Bologna (see Lewis and Booth 1989), ControRadio in Florence and Radio Popolare in Milan (see Downing 2001).

Student-led social movements found in radio a tool to discuss political issues.

Students can promote their ideas and culture, as well as using the station as a method of communication during demonstrations. As argued by Palumbo (2003: 520), 'the most significant aspect of the relationship between radio and social movements has been the language . . . from the movements of 1977 a new radio-based communication was born'. This relationship refreshed the 'communicativity' of radio in Italy. Many stations born in that period are now closed. However, their legacy has influenced radio broadcasting in Italy and in other countries, where students were inspired by the Italian example.

The regulatory obstacles to student involvement in radio broadcasting existed throughout the 1980s and 1990s. Because of the commercialisation of the sector during this time, student involvement in licensed radio broadcasting at a local level was limited until recent reforms of the higher-education sector. Students were encouraged to use radio to improve internal communication inside the universities (Perrotta 2005: 33). Since the year 2000, the number of stations has grown slowly because of current Italian policy and the regulatory framework.

However, one of the roadblocks remains the high cost of buying a frequency since the regulator does not issue new licences and there is no special provision for educational or student broadcasting. Although some stations have managed in spite of the costly fee, other stations have opted for limited broadcasting hours on local radio stations or for Web radio. It is worth remarking that the establishment of media courses in Italy, as compared to the US and the UK, is a relatively new phenomenon, so there is less institutional support on campuses.

I feel privileged to speak from the point of view of a former deputy station manager at Italian's first university radio station, Facoltà di frequenza (Fdf) at the University of Siena.

At that time, I could have applied for internships in mainstream media, or opted to work for a regional or local station to learn about radio, but the opportunity to be part of a student-led station proved to be much more fruitful, giving me the chance to 'think outside the box' as I learned. Every year, hundreds of students got involved, bringing with them fresh ideas and innovative points of view, creating a lively and creative environment.

On 19 March 2003, the deadline of the US ultimatum to Iraq, Fdf gathered the sentiments of the members of the Siena community. In a special eight-hour broadcast, Siena community members' feelings were shared. All the volunteers were involved in the production process, interviewing local and foreign students, religious authorities, institutional representatives, professors and researchers. Instead of relying only on press releases, state sources and syndicated bulletins used by national and local media, the station managed to broadcast the 'heartbeat' of its community. In doing so, the station fulfilled a public service otherwise not available elsewhere in the area. Quite remarkably, for some time one of the local commercial stations re-broadcast the transmission of Fdf. Station members may have believed that such heartfelt content could be more useful also for its listeners than the usual mix of short news and Top 40 playlists.

Another programme, *Get Yourself on the Radio*, had the station giving airtime to foreign students living in Siena, broadcasting ten hours a week of non-Italian programmes. Ester, a Spanish exchange student involved in the project, describes the benefits of being involved in Fdf:

> When I arrived in Siena from Barcelona I didn't even dream to be involved in a radio station. I have had the possibility to speak about my country, my culture, and play our local artists and make them known to the public here. We had the possibility to discuss specific issues related to us, as foreign students in this city, interact with other Spanish students abroad and make many new friends. In being trained on how to use radio production tools, I feel also more empowered in having the possibility to express myself. (Personal communication, 2004)

This comment echoes some of my own experiences. Only a person who has taken part in this kind of work knows how rewarding the long hours and the endless amounts of energy and commitment can be. Overseeing and being part of an ever-changing team of volunteers is a challenging job, but getting involved will be an unforgettable experience. 'I think [college radio] is a vital and necessary part of radio today! The college scene makes us all examine ourselves as to where we are . . . What defines the norm if you do not define the edges?' (Gimarc 1994, cited in Sauls 2000: 3).

14.2 Student press   *Salvatore Scifo*

> Our scene is Cambridge, formed in the image of multi-shifting circles that overlap, but do not connect. We wish *Circuit* to enable the student mind to escape from the imprisonment of the narrow compass of academic degree requirements . . . It is not our minds but the world about our minds which makes us whirl. Hence *Circuit* attempts to offer a critical perspective of the full range of student experience and thought. We have assembled the talent, but there are many more voices we would like to hear. We hope this circuit will connect to others. (*Circuit* 1965)

> *The Colonel* is an independent student-run satire publication at the University of Kentucky founded in 2004 that seeks to scrutinize local, state, national and international policymaking through a brutally honest and sometimes irreverent voice. As much as anything else, *The Colonel* seeks to question the assumptions upon which political discourse is built and so we refuse to be bounded by the shackles of propriety. Consequently, though *The Colonel* was inspired by our sympathy for the left, we have no intention of letting

it become an apologist mouthpiece for the Democratic Party. It is necessarily an independent entity free of any political affiliation. In fact, the one theme that might unify its diverse array of pieces is the same one that Simpson's creator Matt Groening described as the principal motif of his classic animated series: a distrust of the people in power and their capacity to make decisions that are in the best interests of the people they represent. (http://www.uky.edu/StudentOrgs/Colonel/mission.html)

Student print media, just like other forms of student media, are both a training ground for a career in the professional sector and a venue for student views, experimentation, comedy, commentary, news and political reporting. While some student press is similar in style and publishing format to a local newspaper or magazine, other types of press adopt a more experimental and 'artistic' approach similar to zines. Student press is designed to educate, inform, diversify, entertain and act as a watchdog (Bouwer 2003). Students can have 'hands-on' experience in gathering information, researching, editing, working on layouts and organising, all of which are done while students are under 'real' deadlines.

The student press 'exposes everyone – students, teachers, administrators, parents – to a working laboratory of democracy' (Dardenne 1996: 9, cited in Bouwer 2003) and 'should cover as many segments of its community as possible, not to satisfy notions of political correctness, but because the press's goals of accuracy and truthfulness are impossible to meet if its coverage systematically excludes portions of its community' (Dardenne 1996: 12, cited in Bouwer 2003). Finally, Bouwer argues that 'a free student press is one of the few platforms students can use when they feel that they have been treated unfairly by any body of power. By reporting on issues such as malpractice, corruption or incompetence, such bodies can be held accountable for their actions' (Dardenne 1996: 6, cited in Bouwer 2003). An important function of the student press is also its ability to link global and local issues and demonstrate how events elsewhere are, or will be, affecting students' lives at the university and in the future. And there exist networks and organisations connecting student media.

While some papers are dedicated to news and political commentary, other student papers publish poetry, satire, comics scripts, or magazine-style prose. And others seek to reinvent the format of a student paper altogether. *Smiths* is the magazine of Goldsmiths in London, funded by the Student Union. Its approach is more experimental, both in content and in design. *Smiths* aims 'to provide a relevant and reflective contemporary voice that represents the progressive college ethos and diverse mix of students in both content and form' (*Smiths*, 2006). The issues are theme-based, for example, 'Modern life is rubbish', echoing the title of a *Blur* album. A publication like *Smiths* gives students the opportunity to experiment with another medium: graphics.

15 Media activism

Introduction

To many people 'media' are associated with production: the making of images, sounds, websites, print media. But, for alternative media-makers particularly, various questions then arise: who gets to make media, who gets to see it and how is it distributed? And these are the questions, and the issues of power behind them, which lead to some of the complexities explored in this chapter.

Media analysts and activists have pointed to dramatic inequalities of access to media production and distribution on global, regional and local levels, and have been involved in creating new alternative practices aimed at widening participation in production, and reaching audiences with alternative, often politically oppositional, views, experiences and messages. Invariably the starting point for alternative media-makers and activists is dissatisfaction with existing media and most of the activities described in this book reflect attempts to challenge or reform existing media institutions or to create autonomous or relatively autonomous alternatives.

Reform of dominant media often takes the form of trying to create spaces in which new voices can be seen and heard. For example, the creation of *Open Door* and *Open Space* at the BBC (see chapter 8, 'Access to broadcasting') or the creation of Channel Four (see chapter 3, 'Alternative film, video and television 1965–2005') can be seen as attempts to enable new sections of the community to have a voice in television and to offer a widened view of the society to audiences. As Simon Blanchard points out in his essay in this chapter, these efforts are the result of the work of activist organisations such as the Campaign for Press and Broadcasting Freedom, the Independent Film Makers Association and media trades unions. Similarly, Kate Coyer and Pete Tridish in 'Media reform activism in the US' in this chapter describe the way that a concerted and organised campaign by many organisations was able to challenge the concentration of media ownership in the US. The example also serves as a reminder of how important it is for each of us to get involved in the public process itself. The UK broadcast regulator Ofcom (and the FCC in the US) open formal periods where public input is sought and, as the American example reveals, public opinion can in fact make a demonstrable difference.

Dorothy Kidd's essay provides an excellent launch pad for getting involved in media activism since it enables you to situate your own activity within an empowering historical and global context. In 'The global movement to transform communications' she traces the development of media analysis and activism, beginning in the 1970s, which has led to wide-ranging demands for the democratisation of media and communications and the right to communicate. This globally based movement, as she points out in her introduction, has embraced demands to reform global media power and the creation of alternative spaces and systems. She also points to a third factor which is invariably crucial to successful alternative media practices or perhaps should be seen as their raison d'être – the relationship between social and political movements and the creation of new forms of media production and distribution. João Alexandre Peschanski's 'Communication of the oppressed' (chapter 9) explores this relationship in Latin America. Sometimes one person appears to embody the struggle for change on all these fronts and one such person is DeeDee Halleck (see her book *Hand-Held Visions: The Impossible Possibilities of Community Media*, 2002) who is a maker, a campaigner, a thinker, a strategist. Reading her book offers a compelling and inspiring account of the many and various aspects of media activism.

The needs of the global movement described by Dorothy Kidd are numerous and demand many different skills, ranging from academic analysis to production and from strategising to distribution. Finally in this chapter Simon Blanchard, in 'Media activist initiatives', explores the relationship between media activism and alternative media-making, but also outlines how to get involved at a practical level, prefiguring the more 'how-to' flavour of Part 3 of this book, which immediately follows. He lists a number of international and UK-based organisations that are engaged in different ways in trying to change existing media power, and suggest how to get involved yourself. You can find more organisations listed in the resources section of this book, and there may even be a group working on local media issues in your neighbourhood.

15.1 The global movement to transform communications

Dorothy Kidd

Introduction

Alternative media producers are best known for creating media, which, as this volume describes, now extend around the world, in a wide variety of stand-alone projects, as well as national, regional and global networks. Less known is the important role they play as activists in the global movement to create more just, democratic communications systems and societies. Of course, the primary activity of alternative media activists is to *construct communications spaces*, which demonstrate what democratic media might look like with alternative content, modes of operation and overall philosophy. In addition, they actively participate in *media reform* campaigns, from local to transnational levels, to make media more accessible, representative, accountable and participatory, and to take an active role in the democratisation of societies. Finally, alternative media activists provide the platform for social-change movements, whose *transnational communications networks* provide additional links for the movements to democratise media. In this chapter, I highlight some of the key historical moments, movements and institutions in each of these three dimensions: alternative media, communications and media reform and social movement communications.

A New World Information Communications Order (NWICO)

An earlier rehearsal for the movement to democratise communications took place during the 1970s in the debate over the New World Information and Communications Order (NWICO). The Non-aligned Movement (NAM) was a coalition of national governments of newly independent countries who were not part of the two Cold War blocs, the rich countries of North America and Western Europe or the Soviet Union. Buoyed by a series of political and economic successes in the 1970s, the NAM used the power of their numbers to lobby in the United Nations (UN) and its affiliate, the United Nations Education, Science and Cultural Organisation (UNESCO) for a realignment of economic and political power. They called for a New World Economic Order, a fairer system of world trade, which would be negotiated through the multilateral forum of the UN (Carlsson 2005: 197), using arguments that are still valid for many of the less-industrialised countries in current trade negotiations (Sneyd 2003).

The movement also called for major structural changes to the global information and communication systems, as part of a New World Information and Communication Order (NWICO). During this period, the military powers and large information-based corporations were developing global information networks via satellites, and the NAM countries were particularly critical of the ways that these new systems were being designed to serve the interests of the industrialised countries. They criticised the asymmetry in information flows and its negative 'impact on national identity, cultural integrity and political and economic sovereignty', a concern shared with several industrialised countries such as France, Finland and Canada (Ó Siochrú, Girard and Mahan 2002: 77). More specifically, they spoke out about the continuing Western domination of global communications technologies, in which a small number of transnational corporations dominated news and entertainment programming.

The NWICO discussion lasted almost a decade, and included extensive research documenting the inequities of the global communications system and a wide-ranging discussion about remedies from delegates of national governments. The resulting debate was fierce; the US and the UK representatives, and the commercial media industry, disagreed with much of the analysis and the remedies. The US and the UK argued that any measures to limit media corporations or journalists represented state censorship of the 'free flow of information'. However, behind their arguments was a concern that changes to the status quo would affect their considerable economic and political interests.

All the other national representatives went ahead to produce a consensus report, still worth reading for the values and principles it underscores. *One World, Many Voices* – or The McBride Report, after Sean McBride, the Irish chair – was submitted to the UNESCO General Assembly in 1980. It calls for the right to communicate, as an elaboration of the UN Human Rights Charter, and as an extension of democracy, in which there would be increased social and economic development of all nations, and citizens would be better represented as active partners in creating and disseminating the greatest variety of information and communications (Sénécal and Dubois 2005: 256). The McBride Report also recognised the role of alternative and community-based media in democratising communications, challenging the top-down or vertical nature of mainstream media and allowing more horizontal and reciprocal communications between citizens.

By the time the McBride Report was released, the window of political opportunity for the NWICO movement was closing. The governments of President Reagan and Prime Minister Thatcher withdrew from UNESCO, as part of their shift towards policies of neoliberalism, an ideological viewpoint in which the primary role of government is to ensure competitive markets for capitalist industries. Rejecting further multilateral talks, the US government began to take a more unilateral strategy, in which they promoted the rule of the corporate marketplace in communication and culture, a sector in which US firms had a dominant market advantage.

The US government also called for the globalisation of trade in audio-visual services, in the General Agreement on Tariffs and Trades (GATT), the precursor to the World Trade Organization (WTO). Opposed by France and other European countries, they instead began free-trade talks with less powerful allies – Taiwan, Canada and Mexico. They also began to deregulate and privatise public information and communication systems in the US, and supported the implementation of similar policies in other countries through their powerful voice in the International Monetary Fund and the World Bank.

In their book, *Global Media Governance*, Seán Ó Siochrú, Bruce Girard and Amy Mahan write that the main lesson of NWICO was 'that the way forward would have to be through the democratisation of media and communications, rather than through state- or industry-led efforts' (2007: 79). This principle, in which civil society takes the leading role, underscores all of the movements we describe below. In addition, many of the arguments of the McBride Commission continue to resonate today. First, although there was no global consensus about remedies, the importance of information and communications for national development was agreed by all and has resurfaced in discussions among the rich countries of the G8, at the UN, and at the World Intellectual Property Organization (WIPO). Second, the importance of culture and communications, and especially the human rights framework of communication rights, has been taken up by many transnational media reform organisations. Third, alternative media activists still use many of the same arguments, first stated in the McBride Report, to describe their role in processes of democratisation in the new transnational networks of alternative media.

Global networks of alternative media

During the 1980s, the number and sophistication of alternative media projects and networks grew around the world. Although many, such as community radio and cable access television, were based in local geographic communities, media activists began to link across their own countries and national boundaries to exchange media content and ways to improve their operations. In addition, they shared lessons for campaigns to legalise community radio, and to gain public access to cable, satellite and the newly emerging computer-linked systems. They also met to discuss common issues of technology and policy, such as the cuts to public support programmes and the shifts to digital systems and copyright rules, all of which were increasingly being decided at the global level.

During the 1980s, alternative media activists began to formalise these links in national, regional and global networks. The World Association of Community Radio (AMARC) started in Montreal, Quebec, in 1983, linking community, educational, campus and indigenous stations and radio producers. Since then, AMARC (amarc.org) has expanded around the world, holding regional and international conferences, and operating via regional organisations in Latin America and the Caribbean, Asia and the Pacific, Africa, Europe and North America. AMARC regularly shares news and other programming through the Pulsar service in Latin America, and through special theme-connected collaborations against, for example, discrimination against women, via the Women's Network, and racism, via Voices without Frontiers.

In addition to station support and programming exchange, AMARC is very involved in media reform. Through their regional organisations, AMARC supports campaigns for the legalisation and licensing of community radio stations around the world. They also co-ordinate global action responses whenever community radio stations are shut down, or otherwise under threat by government authorities, an ongoing problem in many countries throughout the North and South. For example, in April 2005, authorities tried to shut down the independent FM station Radio La Luna (www.radiolaluna.com), in Quito, Ecuador, for their support of public discussion and mobilisation during the protests which led to the ousting of President Lucio Gutiérrez. AMARC helped link the regional chain of radio and TV stations, video teams and International Media Center (IMC) sites, to media activists and human rights networks around the world. AMARC is also active in several global-level efforts of media reform described below, including the World Summit on Information Society (WSIS) and the Communication Rights in the Information Society (CRIS) campaign.

A similar network of video activists, Videázimut, was also formed in Quebec in the 1980s. Much like AMARC, they co-ordinated a series of international conferences, which exchanged programming, and discussed ways to support video producers involved in social-change projects. Although the network no longer exists, several regional organisations have stepped up to provide the same kind of support, via audio-visual exchange, training and opportunities for exhibition.

More recently, transnational networks of alternative media producers have moved to the Internet, as best exemplified by the IMC described elsewhere in this volume.

Social-movement communications

The 1980s also saw the emergence of another network of networks which form an important pillar of the global movement to democratise communications. During this decade, many social change movements began to adapt the global communication networks developed in response to corporate and military needs to create their own links across borders, to exchange information and support about common problems, and to co-ordinate common responses to many social issues and policies no longer contained by national borders. Long before the commercialised Internet, the global reach and speed of these networks dramatically transformed the possibilities for political organisation and action, providing the platform and connecting tissue for many of the new transnational social movements of women, labour, ecologists, indigenous peoples and activists organising against free trade and corporate globalisation. One key example was the network linking Geonet, Worknet, Fidonet, Econet, Greenet, Labornet and Peacenet.

In 1990, the Association of Progressive Communicators (APC, apc.org) was created to support this global network. Building on the idea of communication rights, APC prioritises the inclusion of women and rural and poor people, who have been marginalised by mainstream communications systems of telephony, the Internet, and the media. They provide training, capacity-building and collaborative research and experience about the best ways to use Information and communication technologies (ICTs) for member sites from social movements around the world. They also actively participate in the reform efforts of member groups, and in transnational media reform, in multilateral fora such as the World Summit on the Information Society (WSIS) and the World Social Forum (WSF).

Minga Informativa (www.movimientos.org) is an example of a regional transnational network of social movements operating in Latin America. *Minga*, in Kichua, an Andean language, means collective community work. Formed in 2000, Minga pools resources, co-ordinates information and actions, produces news bulletins and extends solidarity across a broad range of social movements – rural and urban dwellers; women; indigenous peoples; lesbian, gay, bisexual and trans-gendered (LGBT) activists; and those mobilising against the Free Trade Agreement of the Americas (FTAA) (León, Burch, and Tamayo, forthcoming). Minga Inform-ativa also participate in several aspects of media reform. They support initiatives for better public access to radio, TV and new ICTs throughout the region. They are also helping to widen the concept of communication rights, promoting, for example, the campaign of indigenous groups for the inclusion of the right to com-municate in the new Constitution of Ecuador; as one activist puts it, 'so this right will not be only to express or write an opinion, but also to found media, to have access under equal conditions' (León, Burch, and Tamayo, forthcoming).

South Korea's MediACT (http://mediact.org/web/eng/eng01.php) is a national centre which has always made sure to link with transnational networks of alter-native media, social-justice movements and media researchers and reformers. Based in Seoul, South Korea, one of the most sophisticated high-tech centres in the world, MediACT is funded by the Korea Film Council and run by the Korean Independent Film and Video Association. They operate as a movement-media hub, combining training and technical support with independent film exhibition, public education, policy research and media reform. With long roots in the strug-gle of Korean social movements against the US-backed military dictatorship and for democracy, MediACT prioritises the training, production support and film exhibition of the media work of labour, migrant workers, the unemployed, the homeless, the disabled, women, LGBT actionists and, senior citizens, as well as the vibrant independent media sector. As MediACT's Myoung Jun Kim has writ-ten, the 'strengthening of the media movement' requires the 'interconnection of movements' in three areas: the establishment of 'alternative systems and capaci-ties', 'political tension within mainstream media', and 'a wider public domain' to nurture the capacity for a democratic media movement in both independent and mainstream media.

In addition, MediACT participates in national and transnational media policy research and reform. Working with a national network of media activists, it has won significant victories, including the establishment of several other public-access media centres, low power FM stations and of public-access programming on mainstream cable and satellite channels. Thinking globally, MediACT has also provided the public space for ongoing international forums for alternative media producers, social movement activists and media reformers to discuss and collabo-rate on media democracy issues, ranging from media education, the protection of fair use and public access to knowledge, and the problems of monopoly control of intellectual property, to the impact of free trade agreements with the US on communications rights and innovations. At the same time, MediACT has actively participated in many of the transnational reform networks described in this essay, such as AMARC, APC, and CRIS.

Media reform

The numbers of global media reformers have grown exponentially, partly in response to the growing problems of cultural and communications inequities exacerbated by the mainstream media (discussed elsewhere in this volume), and the rising opportunities via communications networks. Although the global networks of reformers are diverse in national origin, perspective and practice, we can still see the traces of NWICO in many of them, especially in their shared concern for civil society taking the lead in democratising communications and the media. As well, as in the NWICO movement itself, and especially since the turn to market-based policies of neoliberalism, many of the groups also concern themselves with trade issues, and the commercialisation and commodification of culture and communication.

Most obviously part of the legacy are a group of researchers and advocates who kept the ideas of NWICO and the concept of communications rights alive. During the 1980s and 1990s, they continued meeting in a series of international fora, such as the MacBride Roundtables, the People's Communication Charter and the Platform for Democratic Communication, and also in the World Summit on the Information Society (WSIS), in 2003 and 2005.

WSIS

Sponsored by the International Telecommunications Union (ITU) and the United Nations (UN), WSIS was officially designed to address global communications, and particularly the digital divide, and brought together representatives of national governments, private media and telecommunications corporations and civil society organisations. It took place in two sessions, in Geneva in 2003 and Tunis in 2005, and was the first UN-level debate on information and communication since NWICO. In the 1990s, several UN summits were used by social movements and NGOs to articulate perspectives and mobilise around the environment, human rights, the rights of women and indigenous peoples, and sustainable development. However, unlike those earlier UN conferences, which privileged the participation of national governments, and where civil society had to set up counter-summits outside the main forum, WSIS offered a modicum of access and administrative support to the private sector and to formally constituted organisations of civil society.

The WSIS attracted a wide spectrum of alternative media, social-movement communicators and media reformers from around the world. Some used the opportunity of the meetings to gain international consensus on specific issues, such as the communications rights of women and indigenous peoples, or the legal status of community radio stations. Other groups, such as the Communication Rights in the Information Society, or CRIS network, sought to organise with alternative media, social-movement communicators and media reformers to use the framework of communication rights to critique the limitations of the neoliberal apparatus for communications and construct a more democratic vision. Still others, such as a coalition of IMC and anti-globalisation media activists, created a counter-forum called WeSeize (http://geneva03.org) which combined a *polymedia* lab for workshops and independent media producers, a strategic conference and a site for webcast spins around independent media activism and community media projects across the globe.

CRIS campaign

The Communications Rights in the Information Society (CRIS) campaign (cris.org) was formed in 2001 by a coalition of media activists, researchers and advocates, many of whom were involved with previous efforts to support communications rights. Their first goal was to foster civil society participation and the discussion of communication rights in the World Summit on the Information Society (WSIS). Critical of the neoliberal frame, they have worked with other groups such as the Heinrich Böll Foundation, the International Association of Media and Communication Researchers (IAMCR) and the Council of Europe to further elaborate a more pragmatic framework of communications rights based on the needs of civil society. For example, in the Geneva Summit, they co-sponsored two fora which linked communications rights to other human rights such as peace, the eradication of poverty and access to the knowledge commons.

Since the WSIS meetings, the CRIS campaign has been working to make the somewhat lofty ideals of communications rights relevant to the everyday work of alternative media activists and media reformers. They have sponsored national research teams in Colombia, Brazil, Kenya and the Philippines, to demonstrate the concrete links between ideas of a pluralist democratic public sphere, privacy and freedom from surveillance, public knowledge creation and sharing and respect for cultural diversity. The resulting handbook was made available at the Tunis meetings of WSIS and is accessible at www.crisinfo.org.

International Network for Cultural Diversity

Another global media reform mobilisation is the International Network for Cultural Diversity, made up of independent film and music producers, cultural groups and media reformers, whose aim is to promote respect for culture as a public knowledge commons, and not as trade commodities to be sold to the highest bidder. (See the Korean Coalition for Cultural Diversity in Moving Images at http://culturescope.ca/ev_en.php?ID=10206_201&ID2=DO_TOPIC and the Canadian site (http://www.cdc-ccd.org).

The network was influential in mobilising for the Convention on Cultural Diversity, which was adopted by UNESCO in 2005. Endorsed by many national governments, and especially France, Canada and South Korea, the convention is partly in response to the continuing global concerns, first aired in NWICO, about the negative impact on cultural diversity of the global asymmetry in cultural and media production.

Many media reform activists also hope that the convention will alert people to the dangers posed by including audio-visual services in trade negotiations, a continuing demand of the US government. Although national governments have been more or less able to keep cultural-protection measures, such as policies advocating national ownership, content levels and support of non-profit or independent media, out of trade negotiations, the US has been attempting to curtail these programmes in new bilateral and regional trade agreements. It remains to be seen how effective the convention will be.

Intellectual property: IP rights at WIPO

Another global campaign, at the World Intellectual Property Organization (WIPO), concerns the protection of public rights to access and circulate knowledge in digital communication, and the right to national development of less-industrialised countries. Started in 1967 to protect intellectual property, WIPO came under the UN in 1974 with the understanding it would facilitate technology transfer to developing countries in order to support economic, social and cultural development. Although intellectual property was first designed to encourage innovation, with strong measures to protect the public's investment and future interests in the public domain, since the decline of the NWICO movement and the advent of a market-oriented climate, powerful broadcasters, publishers, pharmaceutical manufacturers, plant-breeders and other commercial interests have been successful in convincing the US, Japan and other countries with rich communications resources to restrict uses of intellectual property in their own countries, and in global bodies such as WIPO.

In response, a transnational coalition of media reformers, social-justice movements and the national governments of less-industrialised countries, such as Brazil, Argentina and India, have focused their energies on WIPO, arguing that the organisation should recognise its original obligations to national development, and more broadly to the world community. So far, they have been successful in passing a Development Agenda and a Treaty on Access to Knowledge and Technology.

Ad hoc coalitions
in support of media reformers

Supporting media reformers against the backlash of government authorities or corporate media is another important dimension of this transnational network of networks. One of the best examples was the campaign in support of Thai media activist Supinya Klangnarong, the secretary-general for the Campaign for

Media Reform (CPMR). Against the backdrop of social movements mobilising for greater democracy, Supinya published an article in the daily newspaper the *Thai Post*, on 16 July 2003, criticising the conflicts of interest of the Thai Premier Thaksin Shinawatra. She noted that the huge telecommunications conglomerate, the Shin Corporation, owned by his family, had enjoyed enormous profits since he had come to power. In reaction, the Shin Corporation sued Supinya and four staff of the *Thai Post* for both criminal and civil libel, seeking prison terms in the criminal case, and a 400-million-bath ($10-million) penalty in the civil case. In Thailand, and South-East Asia, journalists, local rights groups and academics rushed to Supinya's defence. The New York-based Committee to Protect Journalists (CPJ) provided some legal counsel and funds to finance her legal battle, while the World Association of Christian Communication (WACC) and CRIS mobilised supporters in independent communications and rights groups around the world. On 15 March 2006, the Criminal Court threw out the lawsuit, and on 8 May 2006, Shin Corp withdrew the civil lawsuit.

Conclusion

The new global movement to democratise communications follows a long trajectory, from the calls for a New World Economic Order and a New World Information and Communication Order, to the current campaigns against global trade deals (the WTO) and monopoly control of information systems and for cultural diversity and the creation of public communications spaces independent of mainstream control. The movement certainly encompasses a broad and deep opposition to the entrenched media, telecommunications and intellectual property regimes that govern most of the world's communicators. However, more than a coalition of 'Nos', this movement of movements is building on the extensive global network of alternative media and social-movement communications to demonstrate that other kinds of communications are possible and are already happening.

15.2 Media reform activism in the US

The movement against consolidation of media ownership

Pete Tridish and Kate Coyer

The American media system is characterised by a gross concentration of media ownership in the hands of a few global corporations. In 2003, the Federal Communications Commission (FCC) tried to change the rules governing ownership of the media to make it possible for a single company to control the majority of all media in any one city, including print, radio and television. The last time media ownership rules were dramatically altered was in the Telecommunications Act of 1996. The big difference between 1996 and 2003 is that in the latter media activists fought back – and won.

The first round was direct action. FCC chairman Michael Powell had expressed his fervour for media consolidation, claiming that 'the market is my religion', and while speaking at a meeting of the commercial broadcasters' lobby declared, 'The night after I was sworn in, I waited for a visit from the angel of the public interest. I waited all night, but she did not come.'

Activists with Media Tank, the Center for International Media Action, Prometheus Radio Project, Indymedia and others responded in-kind: 'Since he had trouble seeing one Angel that dreadful night, on 22 March 2001, we shall descend upon him in droves. Dressed as Angels with cardboard wings and robes with tinsel on them, protesters were turned away from the FCC by police menacing with riot batons' (http://www.mediatank.org/ 2002).

This media action at the national level marked a shift in the nature of the social actors who were engaged in such battles. These activists did not have backgrounds in the traditional world of NGOs, or media policy, but were grassroots activists accustomed to taking people's personal problems and recasting them as political issues. Many were former radio pirates who had been involved in civil disobedience and were willing to take advantage of the full range of tactics at their disposal.

The second prong in the attack was to use the FCC's own formal public comment process. This mobilisation to encourage public participation in the official decision-making process proved successful at the grassroots level and, as a result, larger organisations like labour unions and the National Organisation of Women started to activate. And eventually, concern over further media consolidation reached across ideological lines and involved groups as oppositional as the National Rifle Association (NRA), who felt the liberal media kept them from getting a fair shake in the press, and the Parents' Television Council, whose leader, conservative cultural critic Brent Bozell, complained that indecency in the media was because of the unaccountable, corporate bottom-line thinking about content. Describing the left–right coalition against the new media rules, Bozell said, 'When all of us are united on an issue, then one of two things has happened. Either the earth has spun off its axis and we have all lost our minds or there is universal support for a concept' (CNN 2003).

By the end of the FCC's comment period, there had been an astounding new record set of more than 520,000 formal comments filed and millions more informal comments submitted.

Lastly, a coalition of progressive media activist organisations took their case to federal court and sued the FCC. Despite the bipartisan grassroots mobilisation efforts, the FCC continued to persist with its publicly unpopular scheme to allow

Wireless Cities

> Imagine a free wireless networking system that any municipality, company, or group of neighbors could easily set up themselves. (Network CUWiN, Free Press 2006)

Another key area of media activism in the US with resonance elsewhere is the issue of community access to high-speed Internet. The city of Philadelphia became the first city in the US to create its own low-cost, community wireless system that would compete with the expensive broadband Internet currently being offered by the commercial companies. But they had to fight one of the largest telecommunications companies in the country in order to do it. And every city in the rest of the state has been barred from creating their own community wireless network as a result of lobbying pressure from corporate interests.

Groups like CUWiN take the issue of Internet access one step forward and have created their own non-profit, open-source system for high-speed, low-cost Internet access. Their model is a way for communities to empower themselves, and to be involved in creating their own infrastructure based on non-proprietary software, and a DIY ethos. Other cities have given rise to similar projects. One of the most important things to keep in mind is that the work of groups like CUWiN is not just about helping consumers save money, but is about empowering people to create their own systems and infrastructures. Alternative media is, thus, not just about content, but about access to content and about creating alternative means by which we have access. For more, see CUWiN: http//cuwireless.net.

a single media corporation to own a majority of all major media in any one city. Activists decided there was enough popular support to keep pressing the issue. In Prometheus v. FCC, lawyers with the Media Access Project argued that the FCC had failed to give a rational justification that its decision to further deregulate media ownership was in the public interest. The court agreed and blocked these changes in media ownership from being implemented literally the day before the rules were set to go into effect.

From radio pirates to gunslingers, 'citizen activists' took full advantage of the tools at their disposal, from direct action and formal public process to the federal courts. This political acumen has only grown since then, with groups like Free Press and Prometheus poised for the inevitable future battles. And the battle is far from won. As this book goes to print, the FCC is considering presenting a different version of the same policy.

15.3 Media activist initiatives

Simon Blanchard

Introduction

This part of the book is in four short sections:

- What is the *point* of media activism?
- How to get involved in media activism.
- Media activism in context.
- Media activist organisations and websites.

What is the *point* of media activism?

Short answer: 'the philosophers have only interpreted the world in various ways, the point is to change it' (Marx and Engels 1968).

Slightly more extended answer:

1   Dissatisfaction with established media can often get stuck at critique, and – at worst – end up in a type of weird 'co-dependent' love-and-hate symbiosis, crafting ever more elaborate denunciations of the ghastliness of The Mainstream.
2   In general, the problem with Radical Critique as Vocation is that the mainstream media can (and usually do) thrive on critique, lap it up, and then carry on regardless.
3   The problems with established media are structural and systemic, and this has led radicals in two broad directions.

Direction 1

The first is to stop feeding the dinosaurs and launch radical, self-managed 'alternatives' of all kinds. The advantage of this is that it takes people into learning how to make their own media, not just complaining about the mainstream.

It also has the advantage of taking audiences' attention and legitimacy away from the mainstream. Making your own media is the best way to understand how media production actually works. It also makes radicals more aware in practical terms of the power and resources at the mainstream's disposal, and what it will take to shift them, which brings us to:

Direction 2

The second direction (which is often combined with the first) is to get involved in longer-term campaigns, policy debates and lobbying to change the structure, funding and accountability of the mainstream. The established media are full of gaps and contradictions, plenty of personally progressive people work in that arena and sustained campaigning *can* make a difference.

Whichever direction you prefer, or if you combine them, the result is new skills, experience and understanding; a chance to work with others on changing the balance of forces; and a sense of empowerment and voice in the conversation about media and social change.

How to get involved in media activism

In terms of the two broad directions above, you may feel a bit wary about how to actually 'get involved'. Here are a few basic pointers:

- Start from where you already are. Use the Web to find out whether there are any media activist projects on your doorstep. Talk to friends and colleagues about anyone they know who is already making media, and go and talk to them.
- Think about what kind of media projects most appeal to you. Use the list below to talk to existing networking bodies in that area, and try to hook up with an existing project.
- Join one of the media campaign groups, go to their events, offer to help with a local group or a new or emerging issue.
- Volunteer some time to help with one of the national, regional or local campaigns.
- Be realistic about your time and energy, and try to find others to work with you on your chosen issues or media. You will probably find that you build up your involvement gradually as you get more knowledge, contacts and support.

Media activism in context

Radical media argument has a history which goes back at least 150 years (Theobald 2006) and – as Charles Tilly has suggested (Tilly 2004) – the history of social movements since the 1750s is full of examples of what we would now call dissenting 'media' performances – petitions, pamphlets, vigils, rallies and suchlike.

Indeed, the fluctuating fortunes of the radical tradition on a global scale are closely tied to its ability to project its ideas and visions to the widest possible public, by trying to leverage established outlets and, conversely, by setting up its own media projects and networks. The radical tradition has always had to grapple with the difficult but unavoidable tension between these two challenges:

- the need to develop critiques and campaigns about the power and influence of the established media (Direction 2 above)
- the desire – in the face of established media indifference or hostility – to set up 'alternative' media channels (Direction 1).

Under the rubric of 'media activism' (Carroll and Hackett 2006) these strategic concerns have produced a rich legacy of campaigning and media activity, and a test-bed for attempts to bring ideas and action into a closer and more fruitful alliance.

Looking at the current landscape of media activist networks, we find a wide, diversified range of organisations – varying widely in terms of remit, geographical scope, accessibility, resources and profile. The listing provided below does *not* pretend to be in any degree comprehensive, but simply to provide a few of the most obvious 'points of entry' for anyone interested in contemporary media activism.

Media activist organisations and websites

The list is in two sections. I start at the broader global and trans-national scale. It is now widely recognised that many of the trends and actors in the media and communications realm operate at this scale (Sklair 1997; 2001; Braithwaite and Drahos 2000; McChesney 2001), and are now finding their agendas challenged by activists and social movements on this same ground (Keck and Sikkink 1998; Barlow and Clarke 2002; Starr 2005). In a second section I move on to list a few of the key organisations working at the UK and EU level, at which many of the same trends – and again, active resistance – will also be found (Balanya et al., 2000; George 2004).

Transnational

The Association for Progressive Communications (APC) – www.apc.org

Started in 1990, the APC is an international network of civil society organisations working on progressive uses of the Internet and information and communication technologies (ICTs). With a broad global membership and consultative status with the UN, the APC plays a pivotal role in Net and ICT activism worldwide. The well-designed website is an exceptional resource of news, policy papers and activist reports, in both Spanish and English.

Creative Commons (CC) – www.creativecommons.org

A non-profit organisation that offers flexible copyright licences for creative works. Founded in 2001, it provides ways for creators to make their works available for others to legally build on and share – a pro-social strategy that helps to strengthen and defend the public domain in creative work. Many writers, artists, musicians and performers are using CC licences, and there are local CC chapters around the world. The website provides a detailed overview of the benefits of the CC vision, and links to national and local projects.

The Free Software Foundation (FS)F – www.fsf.org

Established in 1985 the FSF exists to promote computer users' rights to use, study, copy, modify and redistribute computer programs. The FSF promotes the development and use of 'free' or 'open-source' software, and maintains a directory of over 4,000 free software packages. The FSF also helps to spread awareness of the ethical and political issues involved in the use of software. The FSF has sister organisations in Europe, India and Latin America.

The Internet Archive – www.archive.org

A non-profit foundation started in 1996, the Internet Archive is an open library of websites, texts, audio, moving images and software. It provides a vital meeting place and storehouse for media projects old and new, and is becoming a key depository for media activist work, and a source of 'raw materials' on which projects can draw. The Wayback Machine provides a unique archive of detailed 'snapshots' of the Web, now totalling some 55 billion pages.

LabourStart – www.labourstart.org, www.labourstart.org/tv

Started in 1998, LabourStart is an online news service for the international trade union movement. Maintained by a global network of some 350 volunteer correspondents, it features daily labour news and action alerts in 17 languages, and a news syndication service used by more than 630 trade union websites. The project now includes a LabourStart TV subsite, bringing together links to hundreds of trade union and social movement videos from around the world, and another subsite offering radio and music. A pioneer site in the use of the Net and Web for progressive activism.

World Association of Community Radio Broadcasters (AMARC) – www.amarc.org

Started in 1983, AMARC is an international NGO supporting the community-radio movement, with almost 3,000 members and associates in 110 countries. The website is organised in English, French and Spanish and provides a rich picture of community-radio activity across the globe, details of regional chapters, and reports on conferences and action alerts.

United Kingdom and European Union

BECTU – www.bectu.org.uk

BECTU is the union for those working in broadcasting, film, theatre, entertainment, leisure, interactive media and associated areas. It represents permanent, contract and freelance workers and has over 27,000 members across these industries.

The Campaign for Press and Broadcasting Freedom (CPBF)
– www.cpbf.org.uk

The UK's principal progressive media campaign body, with strong trade union and activist membership, and a regular newsletter. The CPBF has played a central role in defending the BBC and resisting the wider trends towards 'market' models of media policy. They have regular public events and a website which links to many key sources of ideas and activity.

The Community Media Association (CMA)
– www.commedia.org.uk

Established in 1983, the CMA is a non-profit support and advocacy body for those active in the community sector of local radio, local TV and other strands of 'social-action' media. It holds an annual festival of community media and publishes a quarterly magazine – *Airflash*. In 2004   after two decades of lobbying – the Office of Communications (Ofcom) agreed to license a new sector of 'community' radio stations, and by May 2006 there were over 100 stations licensed for broadcast, with many more planned.

European Digital Rights (EDR) – www.edri.org

EDR was founded in 2002, and by 2006 its membership embraced 21 privacy and civil rights organisations from 14 European countries. EDR works to monitor and defend civil rights in the 'information-society' era, working on issues around the Internet, copyright, privacy online, data retention, etc. Since 2003 it has been publishing the EDRI-gram, a bi-weekly newsletter about digital civil rights in Europe, available by email or on their website. The EDR site provides an important campaign resource at the European level.

Free Software Foundation Europe (FSFE) – www.fsfeurope.org

Established in 2001, the FSF Europe is an advocacy and networking body supporting all aspects of the free-software movement in Europe. FSFE has been active on the question of software patenting, Microsoft's legal battle with the European Commission and the development of a free-software culture across the EU.

National Union of Journalists – www.nuj.org.uk

The union for journalists in Britain, with 35,000 members. The NUJ works to protect journalistic rights at work, professional freedoms, and campaigns over the attacks on journalism from growing media commercialism.

Undercurrents – www.undercurrents.org

Started in 1993, Undercurrents has made a series of direct-action videos and now runs a DVD-based news network. They also provide video training for activists and an archive of protest video, and run the annual 'BeyondTV' Festival from their base in Swansea. As part of the festival they organise an annual MediAC-Tivist Awards (MISTY) event.

Voice of the Listener and Viewer (VLV) – www.vlv.org.uk

VLV is a leading media lobby and citizen action group, working for quality and diversity in British broadcasting. Founded in 1983, it organises a rolling programme of conferences, seminars and special events on broadcasting policy, and makes regular input into the media policy process at both UK and EU levels. It publishes a regular members' newsletter and organises visits to broadcasting centres around the UK.

Part III
Doing it yourself

16 DIY media-making resources

16.1 Getting started

Introduction

Whatever your reason for making media is, one of the first questions to ask yourself is if you want to create your own project from scratch or plug into something that is already out there. If you are looking to share your record collection with a wider audience, maybe you do not have to start your own radio station, maybe you just want to present your own show. But what if there is no community-oriented station in town and you have friends that would also like to DJ? Maybe you have been recording video footage at demonstrations. Should you post edited selections on an independent newswire, or should you make your own documentary film? What if you want to share your poetry with a wider audience, should you send in contributions to existing zines or start your own? Or both? It is a constant balancing act of time, resources, energy and necessity.

The intention of this section is to offer guidance on how to get started in a few different media – print, websites, audio and video; the basics of blogging and podcasting; ideas on finding distribution, training and skills resources, and tips for conducting interviews – skills useful regardless of your medium of choice.

For some people, alternative media practice may be a solitary act that involves them and their computer, and for others it is the collective act of collaboration that inspires. No matter what route you chose to take, it is useful to remember you are not alone, and that there are numerous resources available and existing networks either to plug into, or go to for support, solidarity and inspiration.

Sustainability

In most cases, alternative media projects are run on the tightest of budgets, relying on volunteer labour and enthusiasm. Infighting and tensions may occur – disagreements over direction, frustrations over vision versus reality. John Downing offers a cautionary note: 'The conditions under which alternative media is produced demand the donation of time and energy from contributors and only rarely do these publications become self sustaining independent of their contributors' (2001). One way to avoid this pitfall is to organise as a collective or be a part of the construction of a community-based endeavour through which a larger base of support has more at stake in the project's outcome. Some alternative media are criticised for their focus on the immediate, over long-term follow-up of complex stories, or on coverage of major protests that fetishises the immediate action in the streets – the bloody clashes with police – rather than deep engagement with the issues that brought people to protest in the first place. Seattle Indymedia co-founder Dan Merkle calls this the 'chasing the spotlight' strategy, or what activist John Jordan refers to as an 'obsession with the collective present' (John Jordan as quoted in McKay 1998: 11). Graham Meikle articulates the concerns with such a strategy: 'This focus on speed and immediacy, on being the first on the scene, leads to news that is all event and no process' (2003–4). For Indymedia, though they are most known for their coverage of global protest movement, it is the day-to-day reporting that sustains the network.

There is a typical life cycle for many alternative media projects: a sudden proliferation in response to important social and political events, a period of coexistence with new social movements, and then a dwindling in number as readers and writers shift into new roles (Downing 2001). So how is interest sustained beyond the initial period of excitement? What distinguishes alternative media above most commercial media is that alternative producers seek to address their audiences not as consumers but as publics. And there exists a dynamic 'alternative public sphere' that mutually reinforces alternative media production, distribution and social-movement organising. In many cities, there are autonomous public spaces for gatherings, events, meetings, parties and alternative media distribution both of print material, video screenings and radio broadcasts. Sustainability, is then, not just about financial security but is also about how your project is set up and organised, how it is distributed and who the audience is – and what other means of social support and community participation might be a part of it.

A sampling of autonomous public spaces in the UK and US

Links to social-centre network spaces across the UK can be found at: http//www.londonarc.org/social_centre_network.html

56a Infoshop

'The 56a is an unfunded 100% DIY-run space. We are a resource for local people, campaign groups and projects as well as selling books, zines, music and clothing. We have a radical archive of international info, a seed trading project and we share the space with Fareshares whole foods co-op and a DIY bicycle repair workshop. Stop by for a read, to check the squatters' bulletin board or for a cuppa': http//www.56a.org.uk/.

LARC (London Action Resource Centre)

'A collectively run building providing space and resources for people and groups working on self-organised, non-hierarchical projects for radical social change' (http//www.londonarc.org/).

RampART

The rampART Creative Centre and Social Space 'is a squatted school from which the gospel of grassroots DIY culture, creativity and participation is experienced, practised and promoted. This non-commercial private venue is just one of a growing number of such autonomous spaces emerging to counter consumerism, materialism, spectacle and apathy.' RampART emerged in the summer of 2004 in East London and hosts cultural and political events, including a community cinema, exhibitions, benefit gigs, discussions, meetings and workshops etc. The space has a large hall for public events of up to around 400 people, a makeshift stage, a small PA, kitchen facilities, library, meeting rooms, workshop space, a band rehearsal and recording room, video and audio editing, a radio studio, free community Internet access including public WiFi, and a shared office. They also host a 'hack lab' with public-access computers (http//www.hacklab.org.uk) and an ongoing radio project (http//www.radiorampart.co.nr).

Organisation

There are innumerable resources from which to learn basic skills to make media, but not many that address the question of how to organise the structure of your project. For projects that involve more than a few people, decisions will have to be made about how decisions are to be made. Some projects operate a decentralised structure where the work is broken down into committees. For example, typical collectives (or working groups) for an independent media centre might include video, audio, editorial, technical, outreach and finance. For a community radio station the committees might include programming, news, fundraising, engineering, training, publicity, community outreach and governance. When Big Noise Films co-ordinated production of a collaborative video on-site following the WTO protests in Cancún, each team was tasked with producing a five- to ten-minute piece on their agreed topic, which was then compiled by the editing producers. However your work is divided among participants, it is important to ensure transparency in all aspects of your work.

Excerpt from handbook of Los Angeles-based Internet radio station Kill Radio

Kill Radio has an organizational structure that is fairly unique in our society. No one is in charge, no one has power over anyone else, and no decisions are final until everyone is satisfied with the outcome. None of the 'Joe is club president, Jill is vice president, the majority rules and the minority is screwed' stuff that you're probably used to. An organization that lacks such hierarchy is called a collective, and this decision-making process is called the consensus model.

Basically, we take turns leading/facilitating the meetings, where the important Kill Radio decisions are made. When someone has an idea or a plan, we discuss our thoughts and concerns about the plan, and then make changes and compromises with the plan until it takes a shape that everyone likes, or at least one that everyone can live with. Granted, the process can be time consuming and difficult. Democracy can be a pain in the ass, but consensus really is one of the most fair and equitable ways for groups of people to make decisions. For more information on consensus, visit www.consensus.net (killradio.org).

There is no one model that will work for every project – some necessitate short-term individual interventions – but there is a strong appreciation for collective organising among alternative media-makers, echoing the notion that it is not just alternative content that defines a project, but alternative forms of social organising. A few things to consider when launching a collaborative media project include:

1   Create a mission statement. What are the aims and objectives of the project? Who is the audience? The structure of the project should match the values you are espousing. Even if you are blogging from home, it is useful to be clear about what you are trying to achieve and who you are trying to reach.
2   Take stock of the best (and worst) practices of other projects, and borrow ideas from what you like and think about how to avoid what you do not.
3   Solicit the support of key people or communities you hope will be a part of your project by getting them involved at the very start in a decision-making capacity. If your project's mission is to promote diversity, reach out to diverse people and engage with them in a meaningful way rather than assume they will come just because your work is clever and meaningful.
4   Outreach is the best form of publicity. Outreach is a way not only to look for active participants and volunteers, but to let people know about your work. 'If no one is there to hear a website fall in the forest, did it really make a sound?'
5   Be realistic about what you can commit and participate in ways that are in sync with the amount of time and energy you have. It can help avoid burn-out.

6   Try to avoid 'founder's syndrome' – the idea that the project will collapse if you are not there to sustain it. While that may indeed be the case, it is far less likely if you have established a network of people who are invested in the project and who are vested with the ability to make decisions.

7   Take the time to celebrate your achievements and milestones with a fundraising party or public event.

8   Remember, you are not alone! It is likely there are other projects in either your geographic community or community of interest to collaborate, celebrate, counsel and commiserate with.

16.2 Training and skills

At least in some alternative media communities, 'skills' are not seen as neutral categories. Becoming skilled or proficient technically is sometimes viewed as taking the first steps on a hierarchical ladder that will remove you from the egalitarian world of alternative media, where a rigid distinction between amateurs and professionals is seen as being as undesirable as that between consumers/audiences and producers. We too believe that skills are never neutral, and are always in the service of one cultural or political goal or another. It is also true that the status that having skills confers – particularly in the media – is often used as a spurious way of excluding and disempowering people without them. Nevertheless, we also think that their acquisition is invariably an essential part of furthering the interests and effectiveness of alternative media practice. At least a basic level of craft competence is a prerequisite for making most media, alternative or mainstream.

Added to this, 'alternative media', as we have seen, can more easily be described as a social movement than an industry, more an attitude to, and ways of, doing media than a specific medium, like television, radio or journalism. This attitude and these ways of working are also mostly in explicit opposition to mainstream or dominant industrial practices. There are two immediate consequences from this. First, there are obviously no recognisable 'industry' organisations, institutions or associations to define what the training needs of the field are, or what skills are required to practise alternative media. Second, even if such organisations did exist, it would be an almost impossible task to specify a list of skills that an alternative media practitioner needs, as the field encompasses such an enormous variety of technologies, different media and ways of working.

If you are interested in learning how to make alternative media the way around these challenges is probably to choose, and get trained in, one specific medium that appeals to you, and then learn (or teach yourself) how to apply the skills you acquire to 'alternative' ends. So in this section we will try to point you in useful directions that will help you acquire skills in a variety of different media – but these courses and resources will most likely not be teaching alternative approaches (though some may, of course). And if you choose to go a more institutional route, it would be worth asking the colleges and institutions you approach what attitude, if any, they take to alternative media on their courses.

One exception to the above is that of community and cross-sectoral arts – which could be seen as one branch of alternative (or certainly participatory) media activity, and for which there is a limited amount of formal training. Goldsmiths in London run an MA in the field, which they describe as follows:

> The term Cross-Sectoral Arts is used to categorise those cultural organisations and areas of activity whose parameters extend beyond a particular art-form sector, in pursuit of a wider agenda. Frequently geared towards aspects of social inclusion policy – and/or economic development – at both a local and national government level, they form a diverse mixed economy of public, voluntary and private-sector provision, with specific concerns ranging from rural audience development to the 'mainstreaming' of disabled artists and audiences. (See www.goldsmiths.ac.uk/study-options/postgraduate/MA-Community-Arts.php)

The Community Arts course at the University of Strathclyde is advertised as the

> only degree in Scotland which offers a grounding in arts forms and arts management, with the opportunity to specialise in music, art, dance or drama in work with young people and adults, with a bias towards those discriminated against by society. (See www.strath.ac.uk/sca/ug-info/communityarts.htm)

An additional problem may be that formal training is prohibitively expensive for those who are not likely to recoup their costs through getting mainstream jobs. You may be able to seek out community training which will give you a start in the media that interest you and provide a degree of mentoring while you try to find your feet. Look out also for part time and evening courses. Most universities and colleges with media departments will provide these. They are not prohibitively expensive and may be free if you are on benefits.

In the medium-specific sections below we give a brief idea of how to research general media courses and training opportunities that do exist (mainly in the UK), but also outline more informal approaches to acquiring knowledge and experience of alternative media – in particular through websites and other publications. There is currently a wealth of information available which makes it possible for an aspiring alternative media practitioner to be entirely self-taught. In addition we believe that – as with most media practice, but maybe more so with alternative media – the best learning is achieved by doing: so where possible we go on to outline ways in which you can get involved in practical activity, in starting to make alternative media yourself.

Learning it

The most authoritative and comprehensive source of information on training and education opportunities in all forms of media in the UK is on the website of the British Film Institute (see www.bfi.org.uk/education/coursesevents/mediacourses/). The site includes theoretical as well as practical media courses in further and higher education, as well as shorter courses in the statutory and less formal sectors, and has details of 5,511 courses across England, Northern Ireland, Scotland and Wales. Co-published with Skillset – the UK sector Skills Council for the audio-visual industries (www.skillset.org), the site has a search facility, which – unsurprisingly – does not come up with anything when you ask for 'alternative media', and makes only a couple of responses to 'community media'. However, you can search usefully for categories such as 'documentary' 'journalism' or 'website design' and find a course that may suit your needs.

For journalism you may want to check also on the sites of the National Council for the Training of Journalists (NCTJ), the Periodicals Training Council (PTC) or the Broadcasting Council for the Training of Journalists (BCTJ). Courses here have all been endorsed by the industry (which may or may not be a good thing). Some short courses are industry-recognised.

There is a wealth of media training opportunities organised at a local or regional level which you will need to do some research to find. The place to start is on websites such as www.hotcourses.com which list pretty much every type of course in colleges across the country. The websites of the Arts Council and Film Council between them cover most of the areas which alternative media infiltrate. Both of these bodies are organised regionally (as well as nationally), which is useful as this is where you will find most training opportunities.

The Arts Council is at www.artscouncil.org.uk – and has details of activities in each of its nine regions. For Scotland consult www.scottisharts.org.uk, for Wales www.artswales.org, and for Northern Ireland www.artscouncil-ni.org.

For the regional offices of the Film Council in England see www.ukfilmcouncil.org.uk/regions, for Scotland see www.scottishscreen.com, and for Wales www.walesscreencommission.co.uk.

The BBC's website offers a number of free online training production courses in addition to fee-based courses, and has downloadable writing style guides and other resources: http//www.bbctraining.com/onlineCourses.asp.

Journalists who are members of the National Union of Journalists also have access to very moderately priced courses run by fellow union members (www.nuj.org.uk). Additionally, Undercurrents video collective hosts occasional workshops (http//www.undercurrents.org/training/index.htm)

Alternative and Activist Media (Waltz 2005) is not a training manual, more a book about alternative media as a whole, but it is well worth mentioning here as it includes training exercises in the analysis and practice of alternative media, as well as references to very useful print and online resources, including, for instance, a three-page interview with Michael Dean, a US independent/alternative filmmaker who has published his own video training book, *$30 Film School* (Dean 2003).

Be the Media is an independent media encyclopedia designed to 'give you the tools you'll need to inexpensively create and widely distribute your content, and promote positive social change, by enabling people-powered, community-based, participatory media'. It 'shows how communities and non-profit groups throughout the United States are using their publicly-owned airwaves and rights-of-way to create community-run radio and TV stations, media centres, news agencies and community-controlled Internet access'. There are chapters on, amongst other topics, book self-publishing, filmmaking, radio, music-making and distribution, starting your own TV station, zines, blogs and the creative commons. It is available from www.bethemedia.com.

Jamming The Media: A Citizen's Guide to Reclaiming the Tools of Communication (Branwyn 1997) – Though some of the multimedia material is dated in this decade-old book, it remains highly useful on making your own media, covering print, zines, radio and video as well as areas like hacking and releasing your own record. Includes a range of practical tips and advice from practitioners.

Finding Voices, Making Choices (Webster 1997) is a handbook on the principles and practice of community arts by members of the Walsall Community Arts Team based in the Midlands, UK.

DIY: The Rise of Lo-Fi Culture (Spencer) is 'an ambitious history of much of the do it yourself "movement" – encompassing zines (of course), independent political magazines, bands, record labels, pirate radio, shows and events'.

Girls Make Media (Kearney 2006) traces the sites in US society where girls' media production is currently encouraged and supported, and building on her previous work on Riot Grrl, Kearney analyses girls' creative expression and identity-exploration through the zines, films, musical recordings and websites they produce.

Community Media Association UK has information on CMA trainings and links to online trainings and courses on webcasting, computer skills, Linux, radio and television production at: http//www.commedia.org.uk/learning-and-skills.

16.3 Doing it

Here we have broken the section down by medium, including the basic tools you will need to get started, some advice from alternative media practitioners and organisations who have launched their own projects, and a number of print and online resources we found especially useful (though this is by no means an exhaustive list). There is currently a massive proliferation of 'how-to' guides for making all kinds of media on the Web. Search the medium you're interested in + 'tutorial' (e.g. 'DVD tutorial') and you will get there.

16.3.1 Radio production

There is a reason radio is the most popular medium around the world – it is accessible, ubiquitous, often live and cheap and easy to produce. Whether your interest in audio production stems from the desire to produce content for FM radio, Internet radio or a podcast, you will need the same basic tools: a recording device, microphone, computer and software. A precursor to any discussion of equipment is that of cost. In general, what you spend on your equipment should be directly proportional to what you can afford. Great radio can be made with cassette recorders and inexpensive microphones if need be but, ideally, plan to spend £150–300 for solid budget equipment.

To produce a piece of broadcast-quality audio, there are four basic pieces of equipment you will need:

1 *An audio recorder.* Independent producers typically use either flash recorders or mini disc recorders (Sharp and Sony are popular brands). Though mini discs are a dying format, the availability of used devices for sale online helps maintain their popularity. Those with deeper pockets use professional quality flash recorders (Marantz recorders are becoming the new industry standard, although cheaper, consumer model recorders are always being introduced and many producers on a budget are starting with these). Both mini discs and flash recorders are digital audio recorders, but the benefit of flash recorders is that they utilise flash memory cards so that audio is stored and uploaded onto a computer the same as with a digital camera or USB memory stick. They have fewer movable parts to break and some even have professional-grade microphone inputs.

   If I mentioned specific models, this section would be outdated before it went to print. The best source of analysis on recording equipment for independent producers is Transom (transom.org). Before buying any digital recorder, do be sure it has a microphone input so that an auxiliary mic can be used for broadcast quality audio. A remarkably useful anorak site for mini discs is minidisc.org. Used mini disc recorders sell for as little as £30–70 on eBay (or £100–200 new). Now, you can spend not much more for a low cost, consumer flash recorder (£50–100), and more inexpensive flash recorders are constantly appearing on the market (Zoom, for example). Professional quality flash recorders cost around £300–500, though that price too is starting to come down. Some portable mp3 players (like some iRivers) offer high quality recording capabilities (ie recording in wave files rather than mp3 files, which can result in recordings that sound too compressed or 'thin' for broadcast). So it is wise to keep a look out for the latest – every month a new piece of gear is on the market.

What you need to bear in mind when purchasing lower cost equipment is that most consumers are using these devices to *play* audio rather than *record* audio – radio producers have taken advantage of this changing technology and reap the benefits of affordable used equipment. Thus, it is always useful to verify that the device you are looking to purchase has a record mode, microphone input (preferably with separate input volume controls), records uncompressed audio, and enough memory. But again, if all you have access to is a cassette recorder from 1970, you can still make great radio.

2   *Microphone.* You might have a top-end recorder, but if your microphone is mediocre, it will be reflected in the quality of your sound. So do remember when fixing your budget to save room for the microphone. See transom.org for reviews and sample sounds from a number of microphones. A decent all-purpose field-recording microphone should cost between £60–100. You can, of course, spend more for specialist mics.

3   *Headphones.* Garbage in, garbage out, right? But how would you know if you cannot hear what is being recorded? Spend £10–30 on a pair that blocks external noise, or use your iPod earbuds, or a cheap pair from your last transatlantic flight. Just be sure to monitor what you record.

4   *Audio editing software and access to a computer.* You could stop there and make decent radio. If you record an introduction and conclusion to your piece, your unedited interview or sound recording could be ready for broadcast. Chances are, you will want to do some fine-tuning, or if producing a news story or in-depth feature, major reconstructive surgery will be necessary. If you can use a wordprocessing program (like Microsoft Word), then you can edit audio. The basic commands are the same – cut, copy, paste. Only instead of words, you are moving around squiggly lines that represent sound waves, that in turn represent the voices of interesting people you have spoken with.

There are a number of different audio editing programs to choose from. There are commercial programs available for purchase, and Soundforge (a popular software program) has recently made its older model, Cool Edit, available for free download for PC users, and ProTools is professional grade software for more advanced editing and sound mixing. There is also

Audacity, which is a free, cross-platform open source audio editing program available for users of PCs, Mac, and Linux (http://audacity.sourceforge.net/). I use Audacity, especially because in workshop trainings everyone can be learning the same program regardless of what computer they use at home, and because I like to support open source software development. There are a number of excellent tutorials for learning Audacity (and other audio editing software) online. In general, the differences between the basic editing software programs is nominal and proficiency in one is easily transferable to another.

> When recording material in the field, capture at least 60 seconds of background audio from wherever you are recording. You might need that extra sound when editing, or recording your own introduction.

If you cannot afford a field recording kit at the moment, it might be wise to contact your local community or campus radio station (and not all campus stations require volunteers to be students, though many do). You might be able to borrow equipment, but, moreover, you might better ensure your story has a place to air. In terms of audio editing, again, consider community centres, libraries or any place with open-access computers and enquire as to the possibility of installing audio software.

In terms of distribution, even if you do not have a particular station in mind, there are numerous websites for independent producers to post their audio (prx. org, audioport.org, radio4all.net) and syndicated or national programmes you might consider pitching your story to as well (Free Speech Radio News, BBC World, individual public radio programmes, BBC local radio, etc.).

As is the case when planning any piece, best to begin by asking what are you trying to say. What is the point of the story? *This American Life* creator and long-time public radio producer Ira Glass likens the best radio to the art of good story-telling. Though your initial vision might change as you conduct more interviews, better to have something you are working towards to help guide you than not. Of course, there are narrative reasons why this is important, but there are practical ones as well. For example, knowing how long the piece is should inform the amount of time you spend and number of interviews you conduct. Do you really need five hours of interview material for a 15-second sound clip in a news report? Conversely, are three interviews enough when producing an hour-long documentary? Often, people getting started in audio production find themselves so overwhelmed with material that their story never gets produced. Better to be realistic and set achievable objectives. And better to start small and accomplish a nice, short piece than end up with a drawer full of unused recordings.

To this end, it is equally useful to consider an approach taken by many community radio stations that strive to produce quality programming, but are not afraid to have people make technical mistakes when starting out so long as the information they are disseminating is accurate. Lol Gellor at Sound Radio asks, 'So you hit the wrong button and get it wrong this time. Big deal. How'd you learn?' (Gellor 2005)

Tips for starting a college radio station

Involve your student body and administrators in covering campus issues. Interview interesting professors. Not only will they see the usefulness and quality of your programming, but your station will become better integrated into the very fabric of the college community and a source of information.

Do not stop there – interview the janitors, the kitchen staff, the grounds-keeper. Everyone has a story. And it never hurt to have supporters in the most unlikely of places.

Outreach to unlikely places – go beyond the ivory tower. Build bridges between your campus and community.

Partner with other campus media. Invite student groups or production courses to take on shows. Consider working with local secondary and primary schools.

Think of ways to keep people involved year-round. Broadcast online or host DJ nights.

Contact independent record labels and promoters. You might get tickets to give away on air or free records for your station's library – if you can demonstrate a real interest in their music and sample relevant playlists.

If in Britain, consider applying for a short-term, 28-day Restricted Service Licence (RSL) to test the waters.

16.3.2 Interviewing for radio

Aaron Sarver

In October 2003, Emily Udell and I debuted the half-hour monthly radio programme *Fire on the Prairie* on WLUW in Chicago. The show aired on college and community radio stations across the United States; an archive of the show can be found at fireontheprairie.com. The interviewing tips I offer here assume long-form radio interviews, eight to 15 minutes. Specifics will differ for print and radio news stories, but these basics apply to any type of interview.

Becoming a good interviewer takes practice; knowing when to deviate from scripted questions or when to cut someone off can only come from experience. Hopefully these tips (many of which were passed on to me by experienced radio people) will help you along in creating meaningful radio.

Preparation – when researching for an interview you can never read too much about the subject. Some people avoid reading other interviews because they do not want to ask the same questions – obviously, this should be avoided; however, asking the person to elaborate on previous answers is an effective technique.

Write out your questions ahead of time. How you use the scripted questions will vary as you become more experienced and comfortable, but writing down and organising your questions will clarify what you want to get out of the interview. The interview is about the guest, not you. Unless you're hosting a three-hour block on AM radio, avoid rambling statements and monologues. Some people like to think of an interview as a dialogue, but in my opinion, until you win a few awards for broadcasting excellence, keep it simple. Also, do not ask double-barrelled questions such as, 'what made you run for mayor and what do you hope to accomplish if you're elected.' Most likely, you'll get half an answer to both questions or an answer to the second question. Ask one question at a time.

Your questions should have an intentional sequence; an interview should have a narrative arc, opening with broad questions and then moving into specifics. A question should either build off the previous answer or logically follow your previous questions. Some breaks are inevitable, but you want to transition as smoothly as possible. Conclude with an open-ended question such as, 'so what's next for you?'

Scheduling the interview – always try to arrange to talk in person. It's difficult to establish a good rhythm during a phone conversation and it will result in a less enlightening interview. If you're not recording at a station, always let the subject choose the location. They'll be more comfortable and you'll get to see them in their natural environment (hopefully their home or place of work). This will also provide insights into the person and give you some background details to use in your lead. When you contact your interview subject on the phone (or via email) briefly give them a basic idea of what you'll be asking about. This pre-interview will establish a familiarity for the full interview. Always make sure it's clear how much time the guest has to talk when you set up the interview.

On air – one of the trickiest parts of an interview is to establish a comfortable, conversational tone. Conversations with new people are generally awkward. You do not have a sense of their pace of talking, cadences, sense of humour, etc. Take a minute or two to warm someone up before you jump into your questions. Ask them how their trip to your city is, or how the book tour is going.

Once the interview is under way, time is critical. You will have to interrupt at times, but try to avoid speaking over your guest in mid-sentence. This is one reason why the in-person interview is preferable. Use subtle hand gestures and non-verbal clues to indicate you're ready to ask another question. You do not need to gesture hysterically, but think about how you get the attention of a group when there are no spaces in the conversation to jump in. In some cases, you may need to interrupt verbally, but be polite and simply say something like, 'we're running short of time and I have a few more questions I'd like to ask'.

Uncomfortable situations – if you are interviewing someone about a sensitive or tense subject, say the death of a child, ask them if they are comfortable talking about it before you ask about it.

Being combative and hostile to a public relations (PR) representative may make some people feel righteous about confronting an evil company, but it will not result in a good interview. Try to sound neutral. A bad way to challenge a company's record is, 'why do you insist on polluting and making people sick?' A better question is, 'studies have shown that your facility has led to increased rates of cancer in the area. Why do you think there's a link between the facility and the increased cancer rates in these studies?'

Comfort, comfort, comfort – being a little nervous during an interview is normal, but if you are worried beyond that point the interview is not going to go as well as it could. Worrying about whether the batteries in your recorder will run out means you are not paying attention to what the guest is saying. If you are paralysed mentally because you do not want to ask a stupid question to the über-famous activist you are interviewing, then you are not ready to ask the follow-up question that begs to be asked. Do not let the fear of things going wrong get in the way of you focusing on the interview itself.

As I have said, the only thing that will make you a better interviewer is actually interviewing people. Beginners, or those who interview infrequently, need to practice. Get some friends, or co-collaborators in your radio project, and schedule a few mock interviews. Try to create the interview process as it would normally happen and stay in character; decide on a time limit and record the interview in the studio or place you normally have access to. Write down a list of things that distract you during interviews and work on eliminating them during your practice sessions.

If your guest doesn't have a lot of experience in being interviewed, especially for radio, there's a good chance they are a bit nervous as well. Few things make people clam up like shoving a microphone in their face. In your pre-interview be sure to ask them if they have been interviewed on radio before. If the interview will be taped and edited later, let them know they can start over again if they stumble and that they should feel free to clarify a question if it is confusing. If the interview is live assure them that you will step in if they stumble or draw a blank. A good trick is to summarise what they have said so far, repeat the question and ask them if they could give a little more detail to their answer.

Hopefully these tips will help, but I learned the most about interviewing by picking interviewers I thought do it well and trying to pick up elements of their interviewing style. In my case, Terry Gross, host of *Fresh Air*, and Steve Edwards, host of *848*, a morning news programme in Chicago, are two that stand out. When do they jump in? When do they let a guest ramble on?

In my mind, you have to be able to answer those questions in theory before you can answer them in practice.

In Chapter 17, Mark Dunford offers some sound, detailed advice on obtaining grants for your media project. Here, the Prometheus Radio Project provides a very DIY approach to launching a radio station, for projects on a limited budget that might not lend themselves to a formal funding strategy or those that might not require the same kinds of infrastructure.

16.3.3 Starting a community radio station

Pete Tridish

Haven't received that $50,000 grant to start your radio station? Two months from going on air during your community festival and still lacking the funds to buy a top grade mixing board? One of the most beautiful things about low power radio is how cheap it can be.

A professional grade transmitter and associated equipment for a 100 watt station will cost you between $4500 and $6500, if purchased new. However, a low cost studio set up using consumer grade audio equipment will cost you between $0 and $1000, depending how much you scavenge and how picky you are.

Consumer grade studio equipment is perfectly adequate, especially when you are starting out and short of cash. Keep in mind that it is generally a little noisier, less convenient to use and will break much quicker than quality professional equipment, but if you are putting things together on a shoestring, the pro gear can wait. You may need to rent studio space – but if you are doing something positive for your neighbourhood, you should be able to get a local organisation to donate a bit of studio space, at least for the first year or so. Remember, if you are doing something positive for your community and involving participation from your neighbourhood, you have access to a lot of resources and people power that can accomplish amazing things.

When most people think of what it takes to actually build a radio station, they think of giant metal towers and banks of meters and dials administered by men with funny glasses and white laboratory coats. It seems like an endeavour for wealthy corporations and electrical engineers. But radio doesn't have to be that way. There is an international movement of largely self-taught community media producers who have built small-scale, participatory radio stations. In some developing countries, groups have built village radio stations with a handful of electronic parts, plumbing scraps and cassette recorders. Although there is always more you can learn to perfect your craft of radio, getting started isn't that hard. But it means thinking about both technology and community organising. It can be an intimidating task to create a radio station that brings voice to the voiceless that is interesting and relevant. Tough questions will come up, and volunteers will have to learn to communicate and compromise with people who are different from them. It is tough but satisfying work. Above all, keep it fun and don't let the group take itself too seriously – you are running on volunteer and community power!

Radio resources: in print

Most resources for independent radio production are found online. However, there are some very useful books and graphic novels to consider.

- *The Radio Handbook* (Fleming 2002): geared towards mainstream production but with a range of very useful practical information about a variety of aspects of radio production.
- *International Radio Journalism* (Crook 1998): 'A comprehensive guide, *International Radio Journalism* explores the history and practice of radio in America, Britain, Europe and many other countries around the world. The book details training and professional standards in writing, presentation, technology, editorial ethics and media law and examines the major public sector broadcast networks such as the BBC, CBC, NPR and ABC as well as the work of commercial and small public radio stations.'
- *Radio: An Illustrated Guide* (Abel and Glass 1999): graphic novel on how to make great radio, from *This American Life,* http://www.thislife.org/pages/trax/comic/comic_base.html
- *A Popular Guide to Building a Community FM Broadcast Station: A Graphic Novel* (Enrile and Dunifer): an illustrated beginners' guide on starting your own microradio station, from what equipment is needed, to finding a location, to how to build and set up a simple antenna. In English and Spanish from Free Radio Berkeley.

Radio resources: online

- www.audacity.sourceforge.net: free, open-source digital audio editing program.
- www.transom.org: incredible resource for all things radio production, including microphone 'shootouts' and reviews of the latest recording equipment. Could include wider range for budget producers.
- www.bbctraining.com/onlineCourses.asp: Free BBC online production tutorials.
- www.fsrn.org: Free Speech Radio News reporter guidelines and writing for radio.
- www.minidisc.org: More than anyone needs to know about digital, minidisc recorders
- http://radio.oneworld.net/article/view/66913/1/: One World radio technical manual.

- http://radio.oneworld.net/section/training/publications: Training links from One World radio.
- http://www.audiotheater.com/phone/phone.html: To record over the phone from home.
- www.frolympia.org/website/index.php?module=faq&FAQ_op=view&FAQ_ id=1: how-to, basic equipment needs for microradio broadcasters from Free Radio Olympia.
- www.freeradio.org: technical resources, microradio handbooks, transmitter building camps from Free Radio Berkeley.
- http://www.dojo.ie/active/bomb.htm: *Radio Is Our Bomb*, second edition of a pamphlet which was brought out first in 1992. The first edition was concise and contained all the relevant information needed to get you interested in starting your own free radio station. The first edition was not an original idea. A magazine distributed through the anarchist press with the name, *Radio Is My Bomb*, has been very popular with those interested in setting up radio stations.

Online content sharing and independent radio distribution sites

- www.audioport.org: Pacifica Radio Audioport.
- www.fire.or.cr: Feminist International Radio Endeavours.
- www.prx.org: Public Radio Exchange.
- www.radio4all.net: Radio 4 All.
- www.radio.oneworld.net: OneWorld Radio.
- www.radioproject.org: National Radio Project.
- www.wings.org: Women's International News Gathering Service.
- www.youthradio.org: Youth Radio.

Handbooks for community radio/ community broadcasting

- www.communityradiotoolkit.org: extensive handbook from Radio Regen and the Community Media Association UK on all aspects of running and starting a community radio station. UK-focused, but relevant in any country.
- http://www.osf.org.za/Publications/default.asp?PubCatID=31: Community Radio Manual from the Open Society Foundation for South Africa.
- www.unesco.org/webworld/publications/community_radio_handbook.pdf: Unesco community radio handbook.
- http://funferal.org/mt-archive/000192.html#1b: This guide provides a short introductory overview of the issues which have to be addressed in developing a radio station for a college or community. By Andrew Ó Baoill.

Community broadcasting associations and resource organisations

- Common Frequency (US): www.commonfrequency.org
- Community Broadcasting Association of Australia: www.cbaa.org.au
- Community Media Association (CMA), UK: www.commedia.org.uk
- Community Radio Association (Ireland): http://www.craol.ie/
- Community Radio Network (India): http://www.communityradionetwork.org
- National Association of Community Broadcasters (US): www.nacb.org
- National Campus and Community Radio Association (Canada): www.ncra.ca
- National Federation of Community Broadcasters (US): www.nfcb.org
- Prometheus Radio Project (US and international): www.prometheusradio.org
- World Association of Community Radio (AMARC; International): www.amarc.org
- Worldwide links to 700 community and public-access television sites: www.communitymedia.se/cat/index.htm

Broadcast regulators (to apply for community broadcasting licences, file public comments, etc.)

- Australia: http://www.dcita.gov.au/
- Canada: http://www.crtc.gc.ca/eng/welcome.htm
- Ireland: www.bci.ie/
- South Africa: http://www.nab.org.za
- UK: www.ofcom.co.uk
- US: www.fcc.gov

16.3.4 Podcasting

Andrew Dubber

Since the mid-1990s, it has been possible to listen to audio over the Internet in a couple of different ways. Independent media outlets and enthusiastic individuals have been quick to make the most of these new technologies. Now, podcasting provides a new way of distributing programme content over the Internet.

The technology of podcasting is essentially a distribution technology. That is to say, there is nothing particularly different about the way you might record and edit your programme – but the way your audience receives that programme has changed. In a nutshell, podcasting enables audiences to receive your content automatically when it becomes available, rather than having to tune in at a specific time or deliberately find your website and click to download your programme.

Think of it a bit like a magazine subscription. When you subscribe to a magazine, you choose to receive it automatically each time a new one comes out. You no longer have to go to the shop to buy the magazine – it just turns up.

In podcasting, listeners 'subscribe' to your programmes. Each time you make a new one, their computer will automatically retrieve that programme without them having to visit your website. They can then listen at their computer, or transfer to a portable mp3 player and listen where it suits them.

The central technology at work in podcasting is called RSS. RSS stands for 'really simple syndication' (actually, that is not true – it stands for 'rich site summary', but people decided they liked the other description better). RSS was developed for news sites and weblogs or 'blogs', which are regularly updating Web pages in a diary format. RSS is a piece of code that enables website visitors to subscribe to that site using a piece of software called an RSS aggregator, so that whenever anything new is posted, they will know about it without having to visit that individual page to check.

Podcasting uses the technology of RSS and adds the feature of enclosures. Enclosures can be any media file, typically an mp3, that will be automatically delivered with the RSS feed.

Setting up a website with an RSS feed and media enclosures in order to start podcasting can be technically challenging for all but the most advanced of Internet users. Fortunately, there are services online that automate this process for you and can make it relatively easy to start podcasting.

The three things you will need to start podcasting are a website, an RSS feed and somewhere online to store your mp3s. Free services such as blogger.com and wordpress.com take care of two of those for you. Both sites offer free blog hosting, with built in RSS feeds. This will enable you to post regular information to the Internet, and provide your listeners with a feed that they can subscribe to. Next, in order to make the leap from blog into podcasting, another free service called feedburner.com will take your RSS feed and make it podcasting-compatible. If you provide a link to an mp3 file posted somewhere on the Internet within your blog post, feedburner.com will enclose that mp3 file as a podcast within your RSS feed.

There are, of course, more complicated ways to do this and more professional services that will allow your RSS feed, media file and blog post all to be hosted within your own site's domain. From the point of view of branding, this can be money well spent – especially if you have access to somebody with a fair bit of Web expertise.

There's also an even simpler way. Odeo.com is a free online service that allows you to record audio straight onto the Web or upload your own pre-recorded audio, and make that into a podcast. Odeo is an extremely good and easy-to-use service from the point of view of both the content provider (that's you) and the audience. Although provided free, it is a commercial venture and uses an embedded Flash player to contain the audio. However, aside from inserting a small promotional message about Odeo itself at the beginning and end of your podcast, the amount of commercial activity seems very slight and may not cause you any concern. The messages are only heard if the users subscribe, rather than if they simply listen from your website. If they are at your website, then they can see the Odeo visual branding. However, if they have set up your podcast to auto-download, then Odeo use the audio opportunity to promote their service.

Finally, it is worth mentioning that there are genuine open-source tools available for the budding podcaster. Podcast Generator (http://podcastgen.sourceforge. net) is a piece of code that you can put on your website that allows you to easily upload audio to a podcast, and it automatically creates and maintains the RSS feed and displays the podcast in a user-friendly manner on your website. It does require a bit of Web expertise to get things up and running, but the website allows you to test it and see if it's suitable for your requirements before you commit yourself to installing it on your own website. And there are no commercial messages to contend with.

As complicated as podcasting can sometimes seem from a technical perspective at the producer's end, it can also be quite daunting from an audience perspective. Although podcasting is hailed as a new democratising force of media production and distribution, it does represent a bit of a learning curve for most people. If you would like to create podcasts, then it's a good idea to be as helpful as possible to your audience by making it as clear and simple as you possibly can to subscribe and listen.

One of the things I recommend to audiences is to download iTunes (http:// www.apple.com/itunes), which provides what seems to be the most intuitive and simple interface for finding, receiving, managing and listening to podcasts.

A great advantage of podcasting is the convenience for the audience. They can listen at a time that suits them, in a place that suits them and in a way that suits them. They do not have to remember to go to your website with any particular regularity, or tune in at a specific time. Once they have subscribed, every time you make a podcast, it just turns up on their computer ready to be listened to.

This is also a very powerful advantage from the 'broadcaster's' perspective. While there may be a technical and educational barrier that may initially slow audience uptake (turning on the radio is so much easier), once you have them as a listener, it is easier for them to keep receiving your programme than it is to unsubscribe. In other words, it's more of an effort not to receive your programme than to receive it.

Of course, with increasing Internet speeds and improving data compression, which allows for ever-smaller files, video podcasts are becoming increasingly popular. For instance, Greenpeace produces a regular short video podcast that subscribers automatically receive and can watch on their computers. That said, the vast majority of podcasts are audio podcasts.

Some examples of podcasts you might want to check out for ideas and inspiration are Florida Soapbox, Indymedia, Organically Speaking and Under the Pavement. Again, one of the easiest ways to find these podcasts is using Apple's iTunes software, which is available free online for Mac and PC, and includes a very good podcast search function.

In short, podcasting provides a way of connecting with a geographically dispersed community and allows audiences to listen when it suits them. There is no shortage of broadcast spectrum to contend with, as is the case with radio, and in fact, the rise of amateurism in podcasting has started to make audiences more accustomed to less polished audio programmes.

Podcasts are usually judged on the quality of their content rather than the slickness of their presentation. My own podcast was recorded with a hand-held mp3 player on the bus home from work each day, and yet people seemed to overlook the obvious technical faults and listen instead to the content.

For more advice about podcasting and how to get started, there are a great many excellent fora and websites online where seasoned podcasters give help to newcomers. At only a few years old at the time of writing, this is still very new technology, and its enthusiasts are very keen to help out.

Podcasting resources: online (just a few of the many)

*   http://www.how-to-podcast-tutorial.com
*   http://www.voxmedia.org/wiki/How_to_Podcast
*   http://www.podcasting-tools.com

16.3.5 Video/TV/film production

Video is now also a massively popular medium globally, as we have seen with Radio above, and for similar reasons. It, too, is cheap and relatively easy to produce, though it is worth saying that distribution – showing videos to an audience – remains more difficult and expensive than radio broadcasting in most parts of the world. This will become increasingly less of a problem, when (and if) universal access to broadband on the Web becomes a reality, and when video streaming, uploading, downloading and podcasting are within reach for all of us.

As with radio, it is not that complicated to get hold of basic equipment with which to make videos. You can spend as little as £200 on a camcorder that will give you reasonable pictures, and spending £3,000 will get you a machine of a similar standard to that used by broadcast television companies. As with radio technology (again), it is unwise to be more specific about models and manufacturers as the information might well be out of date by the time this book is published.

However, there are some suggestions about accessories which will remain constant and relevant. For many of the reasons outlined above in the section on radio, it is important to use a separate microphone. To get audible sound in most locations, you have to get a microphone closer to the source of sound (people, mostly!) than you will want your camera to be. Also, the onboard microphones on camcorders, at the same time as being low-quality, pick up handling noise from the camera operator. It is useful also to have a way of steadying the camera for those occasions when you do not want to 'hand-hold', and/or you need a stable shot. There are a number of ways of doing this. The most common method is with a tripod. If you want to be able to move the camera while shooting (by 'panning' or 'tilting', for instance), it is essential to buy or hire a tripod with a 'fluid head', which allows you to move smoothly, without jerks. These are more expensive than regular, 'amateur' models, but worth it if you want polished, viewable material. Try them out with the camera you are using before buying or hiring one. A 'monopod' (like a tripod only with one leg instead of three) is an easier and more portable way of achieving steady shots, but not much use if you need the camera to perform complex, smooth movements. Finally there is 'steadicam' – a harness worn by the camera operator with an armature and a weight that counterbalances the weight of the camera and so minimises the effects of the operator's movements. The Steadicam was developed for heavy 35-mm feature film cameras, but there are a number on the market designed to be used with lighter DV cameras (Google 'Steadicam DV').

A great many modern computers are now sold with free editing software (for instance Apple's iMovie or Microsoft's Windows Movie Maker), which can be perfectly adequate for simple editing jobs. If you want to make more complex films, or are interested in exploring the craft of editing in depth, it would be worth acquiring a more sophisticated program. 'Leading brands' at the time of writing are Final Cut Pro for Mac users, and Adobe Premiere for PCs. Last but by no means least, there are of course the 'open-source' alternatives explored by Adnan Hadzi earlier in this book (see p. 197). If you are making video to be viewed online, something else to consider is the compression functionality of your software. While it would be ideal to be able to stream at video quality, we are not yet there. Windows Media is one of the most widely accessible media formats many people choose to compress their videos into; however, it is important to bear in mind issues of copyright and intellectual property limitations with some of the commercial programs. Additional basic peripheral equipment you will need is a firewire card and cord. And if you will be distributing copies of your video, investing in a DVD burner is not unreasonable. Possible sites for online distribution are listed at the end of this section, along with other resources.

Video/TV/film resources: in print

- *Video for Change: A Guide for Advocacy and Activism* (Gregory et al. 2005): published in association with WITNESS (www.witness.org), this is a very focused, practical guide to videomaking within campaigns and human rights advocacy work, particularly internationally. However, most of the information in it is applicable to every sort of alternative video production, in that it has very useful chapters on storytelling, filming, and editing. The section on distribution by Thomas Harding (ibid. 2005: 233–76) is a very comprehensive guide to how to 'reach, or in some cases, create, the audience that matters, and get around the traditional gate-keepers who prevent audiences from seeing your material' (ibid.: 237). Witness also produces a 'Tips and Techniques' training video and manual, available on their site.
- *The Video Activist Handbook* (Harding 2001): 'The global protest movement is growing because activists are learning to tell their own stories, to capture their triumphs on tape, and share them with others around the world. This book is about media that doesn't just cover activism, it is activism, a crucial part of the process of reclaiming public space and communities' (Naomi Klein, author of *No Logo*). *The Video Activist Handbook* includes examples of global video activism, as well as teaching the basic skills, from choosing and using the right equipment to planning when, where and how to shoot, edit and distribute tapes.
- *Insights into Participatory Video: A Handbook for the Field* (Lunch and Lunch 2006): written by Nick and Chris Lunch, this 125-page booklet is a practical guide to setting up and running participatory video projects, drawing on experience in several countries, and is described as a 'compact and friendly handbook' and 'eminently practical' by Robert Chambers from the Institute of Development Studies, University of Sussex.
- *Participatory Video: A Practical Approach to Using Video Creatively in Group Development Work* (Shaw and Robertson 1997) deals specifically with the use of video to empower active group and individual processes, which the authors see as distinct from other alternative video practices. The book describes this context, and then gives practical information on how to run workshops and set up projects, and on technical teaching and video operation in the group-work situation.
- In addition to the above, *Local Television Renewed* has a useful appendix (Rushton 2005a: 99–111) containing 'pointers for filming local TV news and short documentaries'. Michael Rabiger's *Directing the Documentary* (2005) is a very comprehensive handbook, with practical exercises, for anyone wanting to learn documentary film techniques in some depth. *The Guerilla Film Makers Handbook* (Jones and Jolliffe 2000) is 600 pages of densely packed and lavishly illustrated information and interviews on all aspects of filmmaking, and includes a 'Film Producers Toolkit' CD, with sample contract and other production forms, audio mixing software, and even a VAT calculator!

- *Guerilla TV – Low Budget Progamme Making* (Lewis 2000) is a very practical guide to television production, with useful information on, for instance, budgets, schedules and rights clearances, as well as the nuts and bolts of shooting and editing.
- *In Short – A Guide to Short Film-Making in the Digital Age* (Elsey and Kelly 2002) is a guide to short films with interviews with filmmakers, and has a section at the end on how shorts get made, as well as a list of shortfilmmaking funding, exhibition and distribution resources.
- *The Television Handbook* (Bignell and Orlebar 2005), in the same series as this book, although geared almost exclusively to the mainstream, has a range of useful and practical information about television production.
- *The Guerilla Film Maker's Handbook* (Jolliffe and Jones): 'A–Z in 660 pages on low-budget filmmaking.'

Video/TV/film resources: online

- Video Nation (www.bbc.co.uk/videonation/filmingskills/) contributors give instruction on a range of filming techniques.
- Freevlog (http://freevlog.org/tutorial/) give an online 'step-by-step guide to setting up a videoblog for free'. They explain: 'a vlog is a videoblog and you want one because, let's face it, they're not going to put you on TV. Besides, not playing that game is what makes this so much fun. You can do whatever you want'.
- Izzyvideo (www.izzyvideo.com) is run by Israel Hyman – 'a weekend videographer headquartered in Mesa, Arizona' – and has free tutorials on a range of subjects, including on how to set up your own video podcasts.
- Melt (www.lovemelt.com) distribute a very readable 'beginner's guide to the creative use and abuse of convergence media' by Andi Stamp, which gives a clear introduction to broadcast and digital media convergence, defined as 'the coming together of television, telecommunications, computing, radio, music industry and the net'.
- Witness (www.witness.org/Partners/) is an organisation that works with human rights groups, training them to use video to document abuse and create change. They have a range of ways in which people can work with them as partners and receive training.
- Links to a wealth of video production and media activist resources: http://www.videoactivism.org/resource.html

Distribution

There is currently an enormously wide range of online and print opportunities to disseminate your media work, either as an individual, or as part of a more collective enterprise or online community.

- First among these is Indymedia (www.indymedia.org/ and www.indymedia. org.uk) whose work has already been mentioned many times in this book.
- Our Media (www.ourmedia.org) describes itself as 'the global home for grassroots media publish and store video, audio, text and images that you create – share and discover independent media. Connect to a global community! Learn how to create citizens media . . .'
- Democracy TV (www.getdemocracy.com) is a 'free and open source Internet platform' which enables 'you to get your videos out to thousands of people. We have tools that make it simple and can even help you share high resolution video without high bandwidth costs.'
- OneWorldTV (http://tv.oneworld.net/) is an open documentary platform which showcases videos on human rights, sustainable development and the environment. By registering as a member of the OneWorldTV community you are able to begin uploading your video clips onto the site.
- Flicker (www.hi-beam.net/cgi-bin/flicker.pl) is a US-based 'home page for the alternative cinematic experience. Here you will find films and videos that transgress the boundaries of the traditional viewing experience, challenge notions of physical perception and provide cutting edge alternatives to the media information technocracy'. You can't upload work, but it acts as a place to exchange information.

There are numerous websites that act as distribution outlets for media content that have a less overtly alternative flavour than those mentioned above – most obviously MySpace (www.myspace.com), YouTube (www.youtube.com) and Current TV – a US/UK-based interactive cable channel where viewers send in video stories they have created to be aired on the network (www.current.tv or http://uk.current.tv): 'Current is a national cable and satellite channel dedicated to bringing your voice to television. We call it viewer-created content, or VC2. It works like this: Anyone who wants to contribute can upload a video. Then, everyone in the Current online community votes for what should be on TV. You can join in at either stage – watch and vote or create and upload. (We've also got online training to help you get the skills you need to make TV!)'

- Moblog UK (www.moblog.co.uk) enbles you to create a free moblog and post images, audio and video from your mobile phone or desktop computer direct to your own moblog. Phlog (www.phlog.net) provides a similar service, a 'way to share photos from your cameraphone or digital camera'.
- Another site worth exploring for distributing your video is Youth Media Toolkit (http://www.ymdi.org/toolkit/) in the US. Converge (www.converge. org.uk) is a UK-based organisation that assists in the publishing of alternative video on the Web.

16.3.6 Creating websites

Owen Mundy

As of this writing the Internet is still widely accessible to both receive and distribute almost any information without government or corporate interference (see savetheinternet.com for more information). Because it is possible to reach so many with so little, it is enormously important for independent media protagonists to use the Internet to make their voices heard by the millions online.

There are many ways to put information on the Web. Whether you are a beginner or more advanced the comments below should provide you with some important concepts to begin, or continue, to make use of the Web as a tool.

Think about content

The first thing to consider, regardless what other function you want your website to serve in the future, should absolutely be your content. A website can be many things – a work of art, a networking tool, a historical record. Most importantly, it should be a vehicle for the information you wish to share.

Often the information on websites is not well organised or the information architecture is lacking. This can be frustrating to users and cause them to look elsewhere in lieu of searching your website for information that they may not even find.

- Begin your website by creating a traditional outline.
- Create a navigation menu based on the main sections and display this navigation menu on every page of your website.
- Avoid distracting graphics, which impair the analysis of actual content by users.
- If a user can't find something the website has failed them. Design for everyone – regardless of age, ability and computer-familiarity.
- Create a list of things you see on other websites that do or do not work for you. Avoid replicating those that do not.

Audience

Understanding your audience can help you to create a website that is easy to use, and content that is engaging, updated frequently and worthwhile. Create a prototypical person and begin to think about ways to organise and present information to them. It is a good idea to watch someone similar to your intended audience use the Internet. For example, I often ask my grandmother to use my websites to see how well it might work for an older person. Many people use the Web in different ways. Looking at popular websites can help you to understand what people might expect from yours.

Important things to consider when designing your webpage:

1   *Create an outline.* Structure your website in an organised and clear way. Ask yourself – if you were to create an outline of your website would it make sense?

2   *Consider free services to help you master the basics.* Sites like myspace.com and other social software or networking sites, and blogger.com can provide a free site with no required knowledge. When you sign up with a hosting company for your website (whether it is MySpace or yourname.com), your domain name is what points to files contained on the Web server.

3   *HTML is very easy to learn.* HTML stands for hyper text mark-up language and is the software language used to create Web pages. Every Web page is actually a plain text document in which HTML tags are used to change the appearance of the text in the Web browser (i.e. <i>Alternative Media Handbook</i> would render the title of this book in italics). And once you know the basic codes, or 'language', you can format your information on the webpage however you see fit. To see the source code of any webpage, click 'Page Source' under 'View'. It might look like gibberish, but when you learn the basics of html, the code will start to make sense and it will feel like you have just translated some ancient hieroglyphic text. Sample HTML codes (or 'tags'):

> **This is bold text**
> *This is italics text*
> <u>This is underlined text</u>

4   *Software.* You can use any plain-text editor (such as Notepad (Windows) or TextEdit (Mac). Some software programmes include features that allow for formatting and colouring. WYSIWYG editors, or What You See Is What You Get provide a preview of how your site will look. A File Transfer Protocol (FTP) client is required to upload website. Meaning, you must have a way of taking the document that you've created using your plain-text editor and turning it into an actual website online. You can also learn to build your site in a way that will use less code which means pages load quicker, and impatient users stick around (i.e. XHTML and CSS).

5   *Email newsletters.* Put an email sign-up feature on your website. Send information to people who are interested in what you are doing, but only email those who opt-in, i.e. *do not spam.*

6   *Search engines.* Search engines like Google have complicated ways of ranking each website, which determines what websites show up and in what order when you search for certain keywords. This is important because if your website

shows up in a Google search on page 54, even if it is the authoritative source on said topic, it is unlikely many users will find you. Search Engine Optimisation (SEO) can increase your page rank, or the placement your site receives for various search queries. Using relevant search terms in the text, meta and image alt tags (alternate text that describes the image) of your website will ensure not only that your website is found by search engines, but that it will be found closer to the top of the list of websites that contain the search terms. Search engines index sites that are updated more frequently. Never pay for search engine submission. Submit your site once to Google and all others will pick it up. Sharing links (linking to other related sites and asking them to link to you) leads to more traffic, increasing the possibility that your site will be indexed by search engines and viewed by relevant users.

7 *Usability*. Consider the connection speed of your average user. Provide different versions of large files for low-bandwidth users. Users in some countries may not have access to fast computers and connections. Ask a possible user to find specific information on your website. Visit useit.com for usability advice.

8 *Web accessibility*. Ensure people with disabilities can use your website with special software that speak the text in the body and image alt tags. Learn more about accessibility via the W3 Web Accessibility Initiative (WAI) at www.w3.org/WAI.

9 *Web standards*. Ensure websites comply to pre-defined rules so browsers display them correctly. The World Wide Web Consortium (W3C) website contains tips and validation tools (w3.org).

10 *Web statistics*. Allows you to see who is visiting your site, what they are looking at, where they are linking from, what keywords they used to search for your site if they came from a search engine. Web stats tell us which browsers are most popular. www.w3schools.com/browsers.

11 *Design tips*
    (a) Picasso said, 'Good artists borrow, great artists steal.'
    (b) Look at other sites, making note of things you can use.
    (c) Form + function = ;-)
    (d) Consider how others use your site often. Can't stress that enough!
    (e) Try to use a standard navigation menu across your entire site.
    (f) Make your website 'scalable', i.e. built in such a way that it is easy to make changes and add new content.

Website resources: in print (general Internet-based media resources)

• *The Cyberspace Handbook* (Whittaker 2004), in the same series as this book, is an excellent and very practical introduction to digital media and the Internet. It has detailed and useful information on topics such as using the Internet, webcasting and digital broadcasting, and online journalism, as well as a chapter by Jayne Armstrong (ibid.: 173–88) of particular relevance to alternative media-makers, on Internet forms and radical, alternative and women's and grrrls' e-zines.

- *We the Media: Grassroots Journalism by the People, for the People* (Gillmor 2006): something of a bible for people looking to produce news coverage using blogs, chat groups, email and other digital tools. Gillmor is the founder of the Center for Citizen Media.
- *Plug in Turn on: A Guide to Internet Filmmaking* (Kronschnabl and Rawlings 2004): 'A step by step instruction manual for aspiring Internet filmmakers of all levels of experience that is both informative and irreverent.' From the creators of www.plugincinema.com.

Website resources: online

There are many websites and forums with advice about how to do just about everything on the Web. A good place to start is by forming what you want to do into a question and searching for it online.

16.3.7 Blogging

Andrew Dubber

One of the most significant developments in terms of opening the media to individuals, community groups and independent organisations has been the phenomenon of blogging. Weblogs or 'blogs' are websites presented in a diary format with the most recent entry appearing at the top of the front page. Subsequent entries move the previous post down and take top priority in its place.

Typically, blogs are used for regularly updated types of information presentation and communication. These may take the form of personal diaries, news or commentary on news, or a progression of ideas around a certain theme.

Most importantly, blogs are a very simple way to regularly update a Web page without requiring specialist website design knowledge or the input of experts. Blogs use a content management system (CMS) to enable users to easily enter new information, pictures and headings and simply publish to the Internet at the press of a button.

An advantage of blogs, apart from the ease of update, is the fact that most blogging systems allow readers of the Web page to add comments to each post, allowing a community of readers to engage in discussion and debate around a particular topic.

Add to this the fact that there are many free blogging platforms available online, and it is not difficult to see why the practice of blogging has not only proved popular but also to a significant degree challenge the dominance of major media outlets as a source of news. Citizen journalism, in which private individuals report on news items or topics that they have particular interest or knowledge of, has become an increasingly important part of the news landscape.

Of course, with the proliferation of blogging, alternative viewpoints have had much more ready access to mainstream consciousness than perhaps at any time in history.

While it is true that anybody who can compose and send an email is capable of creating and publishing a blog, there are certain useful things to know in order to make a blog that is both easy to find and worth reading once you have found it:

- Write in conversational language. Although blogs are ideally one-to-many forms of communication, people read them as if they are the only person 'listening' to what you have to say. You should keep them personal, colloquial and 'spoken' as if you were writing for radio.
- Link to external sites. Linking to pages other than your own, especially for external sources and to other people speaking about the same issues, is a good way to generate reciprocal links, which search engines to use to rank your page. Use keywords to make those links so that users will have a fair idea of what it is they are likely to find when they click on your link. Encourage other organisations with which you have relationships to link to your website with keywords that best describe the kind of things that your site is about.
- Write often. One of the most successful ways to increase readership of a blog is regularity. An ongoing conversation will not only draw an audience to the fact that your site is active, it is also likely to improve your search engine results. Google, for instance, will rank a page that has daily activity far more highly than a page that hasn't been changed for a long time, and that means more people are likely to come across your blog when using the search engine.
- Choose your headings wisely. The name of your site and the heading of each post is a significant queue for Web search engines as to how they should categorise your site. Your heading should give a very good indication of what your blog entry is about, and your Web address should be uncomplicated, easy to spell and easy to say.

There are several ways to start blogging. Many social networking sites like MySpace and LiveJournal have blogging facilities. There are also free commercial sites like blogger.com and wordpress.com, which provide both the platform and the server space for you to start your own blog after a simple sign-up process. Wordpress also provides a software platform for you to install on your own Web space so that your blog can be hosted on your own domain, rather than at 'yourname.wordpress.com'.

Blogs can also be created as part of a website with a more sophisticated content management system such as the open-source platform 'Joomla'. It is possible to construct an entire website complete with static pages, fora, news pages and blogs as well as membership sections and mailing list management using Joomla – but it does require that you use your own Web space and hosting. The benefit is that you have complete control of your site and are not interfacing with commercial companies. Commercial services like blogger.com (owned by Google) and wordpress.com, while not open-source, are both free and will provide you with everything you need to get started straight away.

Best of all, blogs give you the opportunity to keep your audience, constituency, network or friends and family up to date with what you have been up to, what is important to you and what has been happening in a way that gives them the opportunity to engage with it and respond.

Blogs also typically come with RSS feeds. RSS (rich site summary, or really simple syndication) allows your blog readers to 'subscribe' to your website. Using a blog aggregator such as the free online bloglines.com platform, readers can subscribe to any number of regularly updated pages and blogs, and be notified when there is anything new to read on any of them without having to actually visit any of the individual pages to find out.

RSS provides Web users with an effective way of managing the massive amounts of information that could potentially cross their paths each day. By being alerted as to which of the sites they like to visit have new content, and some information about what that content is particularly about, gives them the opportunity to see very quickly what they do and do not want to read. By creating a blog with an RSS feed (and most blogs automatically have them without you having to do anything), you are contributing to a diversity of information in a way that is both user-friendly and easily navigable.

Finally, a quick word about photoblogs. Photoblogs are very similar to ordinary blogs in that they are regularly updated and the most recent post is presented first. The first, and most obvious difference between a photoblog and a regular blog is that instead of a body of text, the post consists of a photograph. The other difference is that typically the front page of the website will consist only of the most recent post, rather than the last several posts in reverse chronological order. 'Previous' and 'Next' navigation buttons allow users to scroll through the chronologically sequenced photographs.

It is also worth mentioning that there exist such things as audio blogs and video blogs. There is a great deal of overlap between these two phenomena and podcasting. As we shall see, podcasting takes the idea of an audio blog or a video blog, and through the technology of RSS throws a home-delivery service into the mix.

Blogging resources: online

The indispensable and excellent *Handbook for Bloggers and Cyber-Dissidents* is available at www.rsf.org (Reporters without Borders) in English, French, Chinese, Arabic and Persian. Its aim, RSF say, is to:

advise Internet users, especially those in repressive countries, how to set up their own blogs and get them known, while preserving their personal anonymity . . . Blogs get people excited. Or else they disturb and worry them. Some people distrust them. Others see them as the vanguard of a new information revolution. Because they allow and encourage ordinary people to speak up, they're tremendous tools of freedom of expression. Bloggers are often the only real journalists in countries where the mainstream media is censored or under pressure . . . Reporters Without Borders has produced this handbook to help them, with handy tips and technical advice on how to remain anonymous and to get round censorship, by choosing the most suitable method for each situation. It also explains how to set up and make the most of a blog, to publicise it (getting it picked up efficiently by search-engines) and to establish its credibility through observing basic ethical and journalistic principles.

Additionally, the Electronic Freedom Frontier offers a valuable site on blogging at: http://www.eff.org/bloggers/lg.

Further websites on starting your blog

- http://www.emilyrobbins.com/how-to-blog: a blog on, er, How to Blog.
- http://www.unc.edu/%7Ezuiker/blogging101/index.html: Blogging 101, by Anton Zuiker.
- http://www.cyberjournalist.net: Cyber Journalist.

Global community of blogging

- Civiblog: http://www.civiblog.org/blog/BloggingResources.
- Global Voices: http://www.globalvoicesonline.org/.

16.3.8 Print publishing

Jen Angel, Clamor *magazine*

In print media, there are always opportunities for independent journalists to get involved with existing publications, either as reporters, editors and designers. Some may provide training for volunteers (such as *Red Pepper*). These publications depend on activists to keep them supplied with news and one way to get involved is to offer news about social action in your area. Print publications will be more selective about what is published due to space constraints, but larger publications will have websites with additional content beyond the print version, which creates opportunities for new media makers to get published. There are also publications like *Bulb* (www.bulbmag.co,uk), Britain's first and only global issues youth magazine. In this section are some insights from individuals and organisations braving the world of DIY publishing. One of the most frequently given pieces of advice in this section is to go get advice from others. Seek out other publications you respect for ideas and think creatively about what you do.

We have published *Clamor* for seven years and 38 issues. It was one of a growing community of independent magazines that seeks to make the world better through critique of dominant culture and support of alternatives. *Clamor* was successful in a notoriously difficult industry, and over the years we learned a lot of lessons.

First, the basics. *Clamor* was a quarterly publication. We printed between 6,000 and 10,000 copies of the magazine depending on the season, and our subscribers were primarily (though not exclusively) 18–40 years old, had some connection with the social-justice movement, and live all over North America. Like most magazines, we got our income from a combination of advertising revenue, subscriptions, and news-stand sales (sales through stores), and we also generated a fair amount of our income from donations as well as sales of other people's independent media projects through our online store. Unlike many other magazines, we were run by volunteers, except for two part-time employees who worked in the online store, processing and packaging orders.

Be able to define your project and your audience

If you are considering starting or joining a publishing project, knowing what your magazine is about and who you are creating it for will guide every decision you make, from what advertisers to approach (or even whether to accept advertising) and what types of articles and artwork to print, to what the cover should look like. Before you raise any money, solicit any writers, or think of a title, spend a lot of time clearly defining your vision.

Having a clearly defined vision also helps when it comes to working with and soliciting writing. Early on, sometime during our first year, we decided to assign themes to each issue. Even though not every article included in an issue is related to the theme, having a broad topic really helped writers be able to focus and know where to plug in. Some of our most successful themes have been things like food, crime, sex, education, and the body. Of course, we also had some not-so-good themes, like sports, which had great content, but people didn't really get. (Do stores put it in the normal section with political magazines, or with the sports magazines?)

Choose your work group carefully

When Jason and I started the magazine, we did everything except write the articles. We edited, designed, sold advertising, worked with distributors, solicited writers, sold subscriptions, and made the coffee in addition to holding down our regular jobs that paid the rent.

Being able to work with one person who you know well makes it easy to come to agreement and, unlike a large group, we didn't have to get ten people to OK decisions. That was a big plus, and I think really contributed to our sanity over the first few years.

As the magazine grew, it was just too much for us to handle, and we expanded to include section editors, and eventually to have a structure that included an editorial group that deals with content, a business group that deals with finance, and other miscellaneous volunteer staff that helped us with things like the review section and with proofreading and fact-checking.

What I learned was that especially for volunteer organisations, being able to include individuals who are passionate about your mission in the functioning of the organisation benefits you by bringing in new ideas, but most importantly by helping you get the work done. While it is essential to have a decision-making structure that allows the organisation to function efficiently (maybe not as efficiently as just two people coming to agreement), having more people helps your project.

Beyond that, creating and maintaining an independent media project is difficult, demanding work. You need to surround yourself with people who can support you in that work, who help make the project fun and exciting for you.

Find others who are doing the same thing

Not only should you find individuals who support your mission *and* who can help you with the real work of doing a publication, the most important thing you can do is turn to others who are already doing similar projects. *Clamor* gained invaluable advice over the years from our friends who publish peer publications like *bitch* magazine, *Punk Planet*, *Left Turn*, *Yes!* and *$pread*. Creating and maintaining positive relationships with peers is an essential part of running any business.

Funding

And yes, your magazine is a business. Many mission-driven projects fail because of lack of attention to finances and details. While you may not want to admit it, you need money to create your project, and you should spend at least an equal amount of time thinking about money as you do thinking about content. It is easy to underestimate how much it will take just to keep your project going, even if you run on a shoestring like we did.

Clamor started with very little money. We used a combination of personal investment, credit cards, and a bank loan to publish the first few issues. I would seriously caution everyone against relying too heavily on borrowed money, as the debt that we took on in early years was difficult to pay off.

Other than avoiding credit cards, one of the things *Clamor* learned was to diversify our income. When the magazine industry has gone through hard times, *Clamor* survived because our online store, where we sold projects produced by other people, has helped provide us with a steady income. Many success stories in the magazine world exist because those publications also publish books, organise conferences, or somehow supplement their normal income.

Although publishing a magazine is difficult, and a lot of work, it can be very rewarding, especially if you truly care about the focus and mission. Not only have I been able to see my vision come to fruition, but independent media work is also at its core empowering to individuals.

Launching a local newsletter from the Pork-Bolter: what's really going on in Worthing
(excerpt from their website: http://www.eco-action.org/porkbolter/howto.html)

1. Organise a meeting

You've talked about it down the pub with a few mates. You all think it's a great idea. There are a few more people you can think of who'd be interested. So just get on with it – it's not going to happen otherwise. Fix a date, time and venue (could be someone's house, it's not a public meeting). Leave other possibilities wide open. It's important for everyone to have had a say in the shaping of the project from the start.

2. Get it all sorted

There's no point in having your founding moment and then coming away having vaguely agreed to do something soon. Probably. When we've got our act together. The minimum you should have agreed is a name and address, which will in turn enable you to set up a building society account in your newsletter's name. We use a PO Box, which costs about 50 quid a year. We had to chip in up front to start it but donations over the next 12 months covered the renewal (just). It would probably be better to have an actual local street address, not just to save cash but so people could drop stuff in by hand and bypass the official mail system.

3. Think of a good name

OK, maybe you can't take that advice from a group with a title like the Pork-Bolter. But it is a genuinely historical nickname for Worthing people and the piggie identity has provided us with hours of puns. The main requirements are that it should be a local name and that it shouldn't put people off reading your stuff by being too overtly political. This may not come naturally to most would-be rabble-rousers, but you are addressing ordinary people here and not fellow sub-versive scum. On the same lines, there is no need to invent a separate name for the group producing the newsletter. It may well prove an own goal to declare that ON THE BOG – What's Going Down in Little Bogweed is published by the South Bogshire Emiliano Zapata Revolutionary Militia Propaganda Outreach Cell.

4. The nitty-gritty

Thinking of a name is the fun bit and may well take up 95% of your opening meeting (if you let it). But you've also got to start thinking about boring detail, like what size is the newsletter going to be, how often will it come out, how many will you get printed and so on. Without wanting to come across all sycophan-tic, we were greatly inspired by SchNEWS in our inception and had no qualms about blatantly copying their format. You'd be amazed at how much you can fit on a double-sided piece of A4. As far as frequency is concerned, once a month seems about right for us. Quantity is obviously limited by funds. Try getting 500 done to start with, then up it to 1,000 or more if your distribution is working. Another advantage of double-sided A4 format is that it is easy to photocopy and you may be able to supplement your print run with the help of office-worker vol-unteers (and various people will be busy copying and distributing them round their mates and colleagues who you won't even know about . . .).

5. Printing

Cheap photocopying/printing is hard to come by, but very useful. Don't just rush out to the nearest High Street print shop. Ask around for ideas about cheaper options. Try your local student union or college print department or local resource centre. If all else fails, why not bring out the newsletter at whatever cost and appeal to readers for leads on cheaper printing. You never know who may come forward.

6. Paying for it

You'll probably find yourselves fulfilling this role. But spread between the group members it doesn't come to much. If you meet at someone's home instead of in the pub, you'll have probably paid for the next issue from what would have been spent at the bar. Other costs may well be covered by donations/subscriptions once you've got going.

7. Getting it out

Distribution is a piece of cake when it's free. It's just a question of getting them all out into the hands of the local population. You can do that most directly by standing in the town centre and thrusting them rudely into people's hands (with a smile on your face). And you can leave them in public places like the library and town hall (small amounts but frequently – they tend to get removed). Ask in shops if you can leave a pile on the counter. And in pubs. You'll be surprised at the positive reaction to a lively local newsletter. Keen people should also be able to subscribe for a small charge to cover postage (though since they're local you could drop them in by hand and save the stamp).

8. Contents

You'd forgotten about that small detail, hadn't you? What do you put in the bloody thing? This should not really be a problem for anyone who's got as far as even thinking about doing a newsletter. First of all you read all the mainstream local papers. And then you get very angry with all the stuff the council's up to and the MP is spouting on about. And then you don't just forget about it and resolve not to read annoying local papers any more, but instead you cut out the relevant bits and bring them along to the next newsletter meeting. And everyone else says how crap the council is and takes the piss a bit and someone else has cut a bit out of the *Big Issue* which sort of fits in. Meanwhile, a person with biro-manipulating skills writes down the best bits. And lo, the contents start to emerge. Add in your own little campaigns (anti-GM, anti-CCTV, anti-negative attitudes etc.), plus titbits about worthy local groups (Friends of the Earth, animal welfare, etc., etc.) and you've got a newsletter.

9. Campaigns

Gives a positive focus amidst all the sniping from the sidelines. But obviously depends on what's happening locally. And what you're into.

10. Keep it local

Forget the recommendation to act locally and think globally. You have to start thinking locally as well. Only then can you go on to draw your political conclusions. For instance, trying to persuade people here that global capitalism is a bad thing because it is destroying the Amazon rainforests is a waste of time. But talk to them about the way that money-grabbing property developers are allowed to build all over green spaces on the edge of your town and your readers will understand why you then call for an end to the rule of greed and money over people and countryside. In your newsletter your views can clearly be seen as common sense. You are normal and the council/property developers/government are the outsiders – reversing the way radical views are conventionally presented. Use words like 'we' and 'our' a lot.

11. Have a laugh

A jokey approach makes people read your newsletter and explodes certain ill-founded stereotypes about types involved in radical political initiatives. Could be a problem, though, if your group does in fact happen to be entirely composed of humourless left-wing gits.

12. Law-abiding

Remember that you can get done for libel if you make certain claims about individuals. Get round this with humorous digs and heavy use of satire and sarcasm (think *Private Eye*, *Have I Got News for You*, etc.). It is worth knowing that you cannot libel a council – so go for it!

13. Media

You yourselves are the new media for the town, so you don't need to worry about publicity. But if they want to give a rival organ a boost, that's just dandy.

14. Carry on publishing

There will be ups and downs. New people will join your circle. Others will drift away. It might seem like nobody's taking any notice of you at all. But in fact your subversive message will be permeating the very fabric of your community. It's got to be worth it.

Writing resources: in print

- *The Newspapers Handbook* (Keeble 2005): geared towards the mainstream but carries an implicit critique of mainstream practices.
- *Good Writing for Journalists: Narrative, Structure, Style* (Phillips 2006): a critical approach to long-form writing coupled with a concern for the craft.
- *Alternative Press Review: Your Guide Beyond the Mainstream* (www.altpr. org/) (*Alternative Press Review* quarterly – online at www.altpr.org) compendium of the best of the alternative press – the first issue reprinted articles from *Anarchy*, *Covert Action*, *Fifth Estate*, Mesechabe, *Mother Jones*, *Open Magazine* and *Synthesis* among others. Full of reviews, listings and interviews.

Writing and journalism resources: online

- *Columbia Review of Journalism*, journalism tools: http://www.cjr.org/tools.
- 5 steps to multimedia reporting: http://dev.journalism.berkeley.edu/multimedia.
- *BBC News Style Guide*: http://www.bbctraining.com/journalism.asp. An excellent, witty guide on writing news for broadcast and Internet. Spends a fair amount of time encouraging avoidance of clichés and improper English! And other journalism training resources.
- Story Writing Tutorial: http://www.bbc.co.uk/dna/getwriting/module4.
- *Student Newspaper Survival Guide* (illustrated) (paperback) by Rachele Kanigel, see her blog: http://collegenewspaper.blogspot.com.
- poynter.org 'The Poynter Institute is a school dedicated to teaching and inspiring journalists and media leaders.' Has many columns on wide range of journalistic issues from practitioners.
- USC Annenberg online journalism review, useful how-to guides and discussions for online journalists, and other resources http://www.ojr.org
- NewAssignment.Net, an experiment in open-source, independent reporting by combining the work of amateurs and professionals to produce investigative stories distributed online.
- National Union of Journalists (www.nuj.org.uk).
- List of resources for journalists (www.journalism.co.uk).

16.3.9 Zines

Joe Biel

Today, people who continue producing print zines do so because of the warm, human feel or artistic elements that are only available in print. You can hand screen print zines, create 3-D pull out sections, paste envelopes onto your pages with secret contents, create textures, use different kinds of paper, and incorporate other ways that the reader will find your zine unique.

I have found zines to be most satisfying in the way that I can project some of my thoughts, experiences, or interests to a relatively wide group of people (several hundred to several thousand), and people will write honest, heartfelt, involved responses. People who are incarcerated are particularly invested in reading and responding to zines. When I created a zine about the Puerto Rican Independence Movement, I received numerous responses from former members and admirers alike, as well as those who were not that familiar or had no idea that independence movement leader Filiberto Ojedo Rios was killed by the FBI in 2005.

When I had a vasectomy and created a zine about it, I was able to share the experience as well as share information to plenty of individuals who were peripherally interested, many of whom wrote and said that I inspired them to get the operation performed as well.

The technical approach to zine making takes a backseat to what it is that you need to get out; whether it is something that you need to purge from yourself by writing and publishing it or creating art that you do not have an escape valve for or information that you feel needs to be broadcast. Zines have seen virtually every imaginable format from a letter in an envelope to a 60 page booklet where every page had some sort of three-dimensional, interactive installation to a 192 page paperback book. The only limitation is what you can conceive of. The time and materials necessary to create a zine are seldom matched by revenue from sale of zines.

Alex Wrekk offers some starting points culled from her booklet *Stolen Sharpie Revolution* (see p. 300).

Zine-making tips

- Keep a notebook handy and write down any ideas.
- Think about audience: how might the writing be interesting to people who will read the zine? Will each issue of the zine be themed?
- Revising zines: make sure the ideas are properly edited and adequately developed.
- Zine promotion. Many larger zines have zine review sections (like record reviews). There are also zines that just review other zines or are directories of zines. The Internet is a good place to promote a zine, specifically on message boards and email lists. Also, some zines sell ad space at reasonable rates or have cheap or free classified sections to advertise in. Creating eye-catching flyers, stickers, patches, and pins are also great ways to advertise.
- Start a zine library. Find a friendly community centre, library, or other public space and seek donations from other interesting zines.

Approaching stores with the zine

A store will generally want 40% of the cover price of the zine. Find a price that is high enough that it is sustainable to print as many zines as you would like to have available. A common number of zines to start out with is five or ten in order to judge how fast the zines will sell.

Distros

Zine distributions are called distros. They are normally bedroom operations run by people selling a variety of different zines. Distros are great for obtaining lots of zines by different folks in one place, as well as getting zines out to a larger group of people. There are distros all over the world that focus on different subjects and areas of specialty interest. Many distros have websites and can be found that way. Most distros (perhaps all) do not make a profit or attempt to. Distros are more of a community effort for supporting zines and related culture, independently even from bookstores. Distros actively network the same way that zines do and link to each other through their websites. Talking to zine makers about which distros they are partial to can be a reliable way to locate good zines and operators who will fulfil your requests in a timely manner.

Zines as books

In order to compile several issues of zines into a book, anthologise back issues, or put out that super thick new issue – it may be helpful to approach an offset printer as an affordable option. Approaching a printer for a book is a little different than doing so for a zine. A printer will generally have a checklist to go through before printing is done in order to minimise chances of error and minimise costs.

Places that are recommended for getting quotes are Hignell Book Printing (www.hignell.mb.ca), United Graphics (www.unitedgraphicsinc.com), 1984 Printing, Eberhardt Press, Parcell Press, and Stumptown Printers (environmentally sound printing, www.stumptownprinters.com). Different printers do things differently, so do not assume because one printer has a certain policy that another will have the same. Since the book will be printed on a printing press, set up the artwork so that it fits evenly onto the size of the press. Talk to the printer about this, and find a good size and coordinate page count.

Generally after the book is sent to the printer, they will convert everything to films and print a sample copy before they go ahead and print all of the books. Since the total cost of the project will most likely come to a few thousand dollars, make sure to go through the sample copy for any final graphical, spelling or grammar mistakes. Make sure that the cover of the book is visually appealing.

If the book is being created on a computer, most printers will not accept MS

Word files and will want the final product setup as a PDF, Indesign, or Quark file. Check with the printer before laying out the pages; especially if there are extensive artistic layouts. To make the book available to the public, the most efficient strategy is to contact book distributors. One of the primary advantages of working with distributors is that they will most likely have more luck getting the books into stores.

Zine resources: in print and DVD

* *Stolen Sharpie Revolution: A DIY Zine Resource* (Wrekk): a hard-to-find but immensely useful and engaging guide to starting a zine. Includes tools, layout, copying, printing, trading, promotion, ordering, mailing, distribution, and more.
* *A Hundred Dollars and a T-Shirt: A Documentary about Zines in the Northwest* (US DVD): 'Culled from 64 hours of footage (and interviews with 70 zine-makers), this 83 minute film (with 20 minutes of bonus footage) provides a cultural analysis of what causes zine makers to tick, what the hell zines are, why people make zines, the origins of self-publishing, and the resources and community available to zines.'
* *Make a Zine: When Words and Graphics Collide* (Bill Brent and Joe Biel) Microcosm Publishing, 2008
* *Notes from Underground* (Stephen Duncombe) Verso, 1997
* *Zines, Vols. 1 and 2* (V. Vale) Re/Search Publications, 1996
* *Whatcha Mean, What's a Zine?* (Esther Pearl Watson) Houghton Mifflin

Zine resources: online

* BrokeZinesters mailing list: http://www.groups.yahoo.com/group/Broke Zinesters
* Grrl Zine Resource: www.grrlzines.net
* Zine Book: www.zinebook.com
* Zine Scene on Livejournal: http://www.livejournal.com/community/zine_scene
* Zinesters MessageBoard: www.zinesters.net
* Zinestreet: www.zinestreet.com

Places to read zine reviews and have your zine reviewed

* Almost Normal Comics Members: tripod.com/almostnormalcomics/id181.htm

- Alternative Press Review: www.altpr.org
- Artella Magazine: http://www.artellawordsandart.com
- Bibliotheque: http://www.lunar-circuitry.net/bibliotheque
- Broken Pencil: http://www.brokenpencil.com
- The Comics Journal: www.tcj.com
- Factsheet 5: www.factsheet5.org
- Livejournal: www.livejournal.com/community/zinereviews
- New Pages Zine Rack: www.newpages.com/magazinestand/zines/dcfault.htm
- Poopsheet: www.poopsheetfoundation.com
- Punk Planet: www.punkplanet.com
- Razorcake: http://www.razorcake.com
- Ten Page News: http://members.aol.com/vlorbik
- Utne Reader Associate: http://www.utne.com
- Xeroxography Debt: www.leekinginc.com/xeroxdebt
- Zinethug: www.zinethug.com

16.3.10 Culture jamming

In chapter 10.1, Graham Meikle considered some ways in which people have used new media like the internet and video games to subvert the dominant discourse around issues like asylum seekers (*Escape from Woomera*) and global capitalism (Yes Men), and how groups like AdBusters rework popular advertisements into alternative messages. In the same chapter, Sue Scheibler delved into a broad exploration of culture jamming and gaming. Here, we wanted to include a few additional ideas about how to get started creating your own pranks, hacks or culture jams. In thinking of the examples from Meikle's chapter, it is also worth bearing in mind the creative uses of the Internet either as sites of documentation or dissemination of the prank (Perretti's email exchange with Nike), or in some cases, the site of the prank itself (gwbush.org).

In his book *Jamming the Media* (1997), Gareth Branwyn offers some practical advice, with emphasis on the fact that most pranks are driven by content. What it is you have to say should determine the medium best suited to your action.

You have to have something to say and you decide what media channel to send it down. There are, of course, situations where the medium itself is the proverbial message – pranks designed to call the media's attention to itself and its predatory nature. Sometimes, opportunities present themselves that just beg to have a prank built around them. [Pranks] are almost as much fun to conceive as they are to actually do . . . Fear of getting caught and of getting arrested can sometimes shackle the pranksters, encouraging them to keep the prank safe in the realm of fantasy. Luckily, real pranking has a thrill to it that makes it worth all the risks . . . Pranks, both real and imagined, are also therapeutic. They act as an antidote to the helplessness, anger and frustration that comes with full critical awareness of the insidiousness of mainstream media. For those who feel hustled, brainwashed, talked down to, and marginalized by mainstream media (and media seems to be synonymous with culture these days), pranking is a way of fighting back, through parody, humor, and absurdist gestures. (Branwyn 1997: 272–3)

There are three key areas to consider: planning, execution and documentation (ibid: 272–7). In terms of planning, it is important to think through the logistics of what you are actually looking to do. Consider what tools you will need, the level of detailed preparation required, the number of people needed. Your plan may involve a reconnaissance or scouting mission as part of your advance preparations, perhaps even taking photos of the location or other surrounding details. Do you need costumes or other materials that may take time to construct? You must also consider safety concerns. If you are looking to 'redesign' a billboard, or engage in some form of social engineering or hacking, there are risks to you and others who may be involved or affected that must be considered, including safety concerns.

Another area to think through is the question of intended audience. Who are you trying to reach? Will they see or take part in the prank, or do you need coverage in mainstream or alternative media to 'get the biggest media bang for your buck'? (Branwyn 1997: 275). Thinking through the impact your hope to achieve will be important. When the Women's Action Coalition was organising pranks in the early 1990s, they relied heavily on media coverage and planned actions accordingly. They developed an extensive database of media contacts and sent out press releases (no more than one page!) for every public action. Their goal was to reach as broad an audience as possible so media outreach was an important piece. When they rented a plane to fly over the Super Bowl with a banner reading 'Stop Violence Against Women' they were armed with data about the rise in domestic violence reporting on Super Bowl Sunday so that when the press asked questions, the activists had something substantive to say.

Of course not every prank will involve aircraft. Postering a neighbourhood, stickering boxes in a store and redesigning advertisements with subversive messages may be the best tools to accomplish your aims. Part of the fun, of course, is in thinking up new ways to infuse public life with the unexpected. Thus, along with alerting the press to reach a wider audience, documentation will also be key, whether it is emailing photos, blogging about your action or documenting the event on video or audio.

Anyone who's involved with performance art or other process-oriented forms of art will tell you that documentation is everything . . . These events are fleeting, and while that's part of their charm, they can have a more lasting impact and greater reach if recorded. The more media antennae you can deploy, the better: cameras, video, audio, written accounts, whatever. (Branwyn 1997: 276)

Yo Mango, a collective in Barcelona, Spain has some excellent examples of public performance as culture jam that have been turned into video documentary shorts (www.yomango.net).

Ted Stevens: senator, fisherman, meme-maker Steph 99

Summer 2006 was all about tubes, thanks to US senator Ted Stevens, a Republican from Alaska, and chairman of the Senate Committee on Commerce, Science, and Transportation. Teh Intarwebs asploded with lol's (Internet slang for, 'The Internet exploded with laughter'), when Stevens, whose committee chairmanship gives him some clout over Internet regulation, stuttered through an incoherent explanation of how the Internet works. He was arguing against a bill that would enforce the concept of 'net neutrality', which would make it illegal for telecom companies and internet service providers to allow content providers to pay extra for faster delivery. It was a popular bill among people who see the Internet as an inherently decentralized, organic communication network, and feel that degradation of net neutrality is tantamount to the sanctions of a pay-to-play Internet that would effectively ghettoize independent content. In a hilariously botched attempt to explain bandwidth limitations, he famously stated about the Internet: 'It's not a big truck. It's a series of tubes.'

This set off a social domino effect that Richard Dawkins first termed a 'meme' in 1976. He posited that ideas propagate through societies the way physiological characteristics spread via genes, passing from one participant in culture to the next, evolving and growing along the way. Urban legends, fashion trends, and skills passed in an 'each one teach one' model, are all examples of memes. Internet memes are trends or fads that spread, morph, and die at lightning speed, like online quizzes, animation styles, and song parodies. An early example is the Dancing Baby, a widely circulated animated 3D rendering that originated around 1996. It was popular enough to exceed the escape velocity of Internet humour, and became a recognized image on television commercials and series, including as a recurring hallucination on the TV show Ally McBeal. One of my favourite Internet memes is 'Owned!' or 'Pwned!', which is hacker slang for 'defeated' or 'busted'. The meme features photos of people or animals in compromising (or compromised) positions with some mutation of the word 'Owned!' in large, bright print. The images range from a child holding a marker next to a child whose face has been scribbled on, to a photo of a minivan in a pool. It is a good example of a meme that is easy to participate in, and whose potential for expansion is unlimited.

The 'Series of Tubes' meme was a big winner. Within days, blogs, message boards, and instant messenger conversations were awash in links to commemorative works. Stevens' speech was chopped up and set to a techno beat, parodied in a folk song, celebrated on a T-shirt design with vacuum tubes, elucidated in a Powerpoint slideshow, and more, all riffing on tubes. One of them happened to be a shirt design spearheaded by yours truly and an unruly gang of West Philadelphia hooligans, featuring a series of fallopian tubes. These shirts were a big hit at the Hackers on Planet Earth (HOPE) conference, and made for an interesting techno-feminist interjection when all of a sudden, hacker boys were walking around with uteruses on their chests, making a statement about freedom on the Internet. One wonders if Senator Stevens took away from the skewering a better sense of how email travels, and the power of unintended consequences on the Internet.

Culture jamming resources: in print

*   *DIY Screenprinting: A Graphic Novel* (Isaacson 2006): 'A fascinating graphic "novel" that details the art and science of screenprinting from inception to printed t-shirts.'
*   *Digital Resistance: Explorations in Tactical Media* (Critical Art Ensemble): a collection of tactical and persuasive essays – 'a veritable user's manual and toolkit for the intelligent cultural hacker, artist, and hacktivist. Herein you'll find some trenchant how-tos: How to build a graffiti robot. How to think recombinant theater. How to make collective actions. How to pervert GameBoy.'
*   Art and Science of Billboard Improvement (Billboard Liberation Front): 'Everything you wanted to know about how to rearrange that offensive advertisement.'

Culture jamming resources: online

*   *Make Magazine*: http://www.makezine.com/ – ultimate resource for DIY anything.
*   *Culture Jammers Encyclopaedia*: http://www.sniggle.net/
*   Ruckus Society: www.ruckus.org

Additional DIY resources

The following resources are on topics not directly covered in this book, but aspects of alternative media production that are important to rethinking the breadth of what is considered alternative media production, from bookselling and music production, to strategic communications on getting alternative messages in the mainstream.

- *Rebel Bookseller: How to Improvise Your Own Indie Store and Beat Back the Chains* (Laties): part memoir, part history of the book industry and part practical advice on getting started in the bookselling industry from Laties' 20 years of bookselling and community organising.
- *Alternative Publishers of Books in North America* (Anderson, ed.): an annotated listing and description of around 160 independent North American publishers, together with the areas they publish in.
- Spin project tutorials on strategic communication, or, how to use the media to articulate your message: http://spinproject.org/article.php?list=type&type =22.
- How to write a protest letter, by Jennifer L. Pozner of Women in the Media: http://www.bitchmagazine.com/archives/04_03slash/protest.shtml.
- Allied Media Conference: an annual, weekend-long gathering of influential, underground media-makers and committed social-justice activists. It has become the primary forum in the US for building a large-scale social movement around media issues that centres on issues of race, class, gender and other systems of oppression. The conference brings together those working at the cutting edge of independent media-making: daring filmmakers, ambitious radio producers, serious publishers, skilled Web designers, and trend-setting artists, musicians and performers.: http://alliedmediaconference.org.

Conclusion

Last, but certainly not least, there are ways to find people and organisations off-line, face to face! The regional Arts or Film Council organisations listed above (p. 265) are good ways of finding out what is happening in your area, and of connecting with local groups who may share your interests. Or watch out for events in your town. The best way of getting involved with alternative media is by getting involved with alternative action.

17 Funding and finance

Introduction

There is a huge range of projects you might be seeking to fund which fall under the rubric of 'alternative media'. From a magazine or e-zine to a news report, from a personal website to transnational portal, from a radio programme to a radio station, from a short documentary to a low-budget feature film. You might be thinking of 'no budget' or hundreds, thousands, even millions of pounds or dollars. In this section we have aimed to address some general principles of how to approach the whole business of funding and, as Mark Dunford and Kate Coyer each emphasise, it is an essential prerequisite to be clear about the definition of your project and its budget and to fully and realistically research potential sources of finance.

If you are considering applying for grant money, it is always a useful exercise to picture your project from the point of view of a potential funder. Every funding organisation has its own policy, objectives, criteria. How does your project enable the funder to fulfil its own goals? Have you really done the appropriate research to answer that question? Most organisations have very full information on their websites and many are prepared to meet to discuss a project before you submit a completed application. It is also well worth talking to colleagues or friends who have knowledge or personal experience with a funder who can offer more detailed advice. This 'mentoring' can be invaluable if you are approaching one of the large and complex funders such as the European Union, a foundation or a television company. Also, it is often highly appropriate to contact the programme officer for a particular grant you are interested in – they can tell you if your project might fit the range of what they are looking to fund.

Funders tend not only to fund very specific types of cultural production but also to be geographically specific. This will range from local or city to regional to national to international remits. For example, a regional fund will look to see a real benefit to its region in your project while the European Union, with some exceptions, will be interested in pan-European projects. Many of the large foundations will only be prepared to fund projects in particular countries and these policies and priorities might change from year to year. It is also important not to let a funder dictate the direction of your project. While you might change your mind along the way, ultimately, it is your vision you are seeking support for and it might be better to consider a funder that is a better fit than embark on a project you are less enthused about.

In 'Successful fundraising in the UK', Mark Dunford gives an overview of the main organisations in the UK most likely to support cultural projects as well as offering essential advice on how to approach raising finance. Then Kate Coyer, in 'A place where money grows on trees?', as well as adding to Mark's advice, looks at several ways you could approach fundraising in addition to approaching funding bodies in a conventional way. This practical thinking 'outside the box' is going to be applicable to many alternative media projects. Her bottom line is to be sure your source of funding matches the values of your project, and to think creatively about building support for your project along horizontal lines, rather than 'just' looking for the big grants – because you never know when that money will dry up. Most major straight funders, after all, are not seeking to fund alternatives!

It is a truism but nevertheless true that networking is one of the most useful attributes of successful fundraisers. Building your network of colleagues, supporters, funders, potential partners and collaborators could be a decisive factor in raising the money for your project. In spite of all the technology, people still like to meet people, put a name to a face, pick up a sense of who you are and your passion for your project. Whether we like it or not meeting the person from the funding agency over a coffee or a drink could make the difference. So take every opportunity to get out there – writing up the project and filling in the application form is only one part of the fundraiser's skills.

Whatever the type and scale of your project, researching every possible funding source or means of income generation is going to be the key to success. Apart from personal advice and your own networking and contacts, the Internet of course offers a brilliant research tool.

Listed below are a selection of organisations, books and sites which offer particularly good information and links.

Global

- **One World:** www.uk.oneworld.net A global site on human rights and sustainable development with many independent sites in many continents and countries (see, for example, http//africa.oneworld.net). Huge amount of information including sources of funding.
- **UNESCO:** http//portal.unesco.org A massive source of global information about many aspects of culture, projects and policy, including UNESCO-supported cultural and media projects in the world.

Europe

- **EUCLID:** www.euclid.info Vast information about cultural funding in Europe. Extensive links to other culture portals, information on funds and funding, individual European countries. Also some very good downloads and fact files on European funding.
- Sharing Knowledge for Culture: http//eufunds.culture.info Excellent on all the European funds – structural funds, transnational funds, third-country funds.
- **CUPID:** http//cupid.culture.info Database of cultural projects that have been funded from European funding programmes.
- **Foundation:** http//foundation.culture.info Another European cultural portal. Excellent and detailed links to UK regional and national cultural funding as well as to all the other EU countries on culture and cultural funding. Also useful resources-for-fundraisers section.
- **KORDA Database:** www.korda.obs.coe.int Superb definitive database for film in Europe with excellent links to funds from every regional agency.

USA

- **Foundation Centre:** http//foundationcenter.org Excellent links to all the foundations in the US plus good information on funding and raising funds.
- **The Funding Exchange:** www.fex.org Very good information and links to numerous community and social funds.
- **The Media Channel:** www.mediachannel.org Part of the One World global network. Comprehensive information on media in the US. Very good links.
- **Independent Television Service:** www.itvs.org Funding for public service television. Good links. See especially producer resources.
- **New York State Council on the Arts:** www.nysca.org Funder and information on the New York area, links to other useful sites.
- **The Screenplayers:** www.screenplayers.net/financing Brilliant links to national and regional, primarily film, funding agencies with some European and global links.
- *Filmmaker Magazine:* www.filmmakermagazine.com Independent film in the USA with useful information on funding and fundraising.
- **Student Filmmakers:** www.studentfilmmakers.com Portal site for student filmmakers. Very good links and information.
- **Alliance for Community Media:** www.alliancecm.org Information, news, issues and links on community media.

Books

There are few if any books which cover the whole area of alternative media funding and most of the guides to funding deal with film, documentary or video financing. The following are useful but see also the section on Training in this book where there is reference to several alternative media books which also touch on funding.

- *UK Film Financing Handbook: How to Fund Your Film* (Davies and Wistreich 2005): www.netribution.co.uk.
- *Shaking the Money Tree: How to Get Grants and Donations for Film and Video* (Warshawski 2003) Michael Wise Productions: www.mwp.com.
- *The Art of Funding Your Film: Alternative Financing Concepts* (Dean 2003), Dean Publishing: www.fromtheheartproductions.com

Business planning

If you are making an application for a medium- to large-sized project funders will often request a business plan. Do not be put off or intimidated by this. Writing a business plan can be very useful – it is a methodical and logical way of thinking through your project from many points of view, not only financial, and can be of positive benefit to you and your project. You will find many online resources and books about writing business plans but most of them do not relate directly to media and culture. The following three sites offer very useful guides:

- **Cultural Enterprise Office:** www.culturalenterpriseoffice.co.uk. Very useful on all aspects of financial planning and writing business plans.
- **Arts Advice:** www.netgain.org.uk/business/planning/business_plan.asp
- **Arts Council of Wales:** www.artswales.org.uk/publications/Business_plan_guidelines_September_2005.

17.1 Successful fundraising in the UK

Mark Dunford

Competition for funds is fierce and only the strongest proposals secure the money needed to transform an idea into a real project. Fundraising can be a thankless task; especially for someone who is just starting out and maybe lacks the track record that many funding agencies like to see. This chapter maps out the range of funds available for community-based media production work, and provides some helpful hints on the best way to approach funders.

The media industry

The most obvious port of call for media production is the media, yet conversely this is probably the hardest place for newcomers to secure support. Most of the major players are in the private sector and are naturally wary of high-risk community projects. They operate in a world where you are only as good as your last project. Supporting productions without a clear commercial pedigree represents an unnecessary risk and is generally seen as something to avoid. In many ways the BBC is similar and, apart from a few very specific strands designed to support newcomers, it is hard for people without a professional reputation to access the corporation's resources.

There are ways round this. Aspirant filmmakers can develop links with a well-established independent production company, and this can help you unlock the doors to broadcast commissions. The price you pay for this is a certain loss of control over the development and financing of a project.

Public-sector funds to support UK media

The leading public-sector funding agency for the media work in the UK is the UK Film Council. Established in 1999 through the merger of a number of funding agencies, the UK Film Council is a single strategic body designed to support the development of film across the UK. It operates a number of different funding programmes for production, ranging from major feature films through to digital films made by young people. It also supports the distribution of independent and non-English-language films.

The various funding programmes overseen by the UK Film Council are all, theoretically, open to newcomers. Indeed, the New Cinema Fund is explicitly charged with supporting new and challenging work. Like all funding programmes it is heavily oversubscribed, but over the past seven years has established an impressive reputation for lively and inventive work.

The UK Film Council also supports the national and regional screen agencies in Scotland, Wales and across the nine English regions. These development agencies are charged with supporting local talent and building the local media economy so that more businesses flourish outside the M25. They are always caught between the ambitions of the UK Film Council and the reality of the limited resources available to develop regional media work. The more successful are those that have combined media funding with finance secured from a range of different public- and private-sector funders, to establish resources of a scale which is large enough to make a significant difference.

The unavoidable conclusion is that the number of projects seeking finance for any media work in the UK vastly exceeds the funding available. Successful fundraising for community-based work requires tenacity and an ability to combine different sources of funding to realise a project, particularly if the project in question could be considered difficult or challenging.

Successful community-media companies have secured public-sector funds from a range of different funding regimes, by thinking beyond the obvious to draw in support from different sources, including:

- DCMS Lottery programmes: big lottery fund which provides funding for projects working with specific target groups. It is best to check the website for details of specific programmes (http://www.biglotteryfund.org).
- National Endowment for Science, Technology and the Arts: supports creativity and innovation. Information is available via the website (http://www.nesta.org).

Business support agencies

Business Link can support the creation of local business with small grants, while sector-specific agencies such as CIDA in East London provide funding for creative businesses in a given geographical area

Regeneration funding

Most regeneration funding is based around specific localities, but savvy media businesses have been able to secure funds as part of a contribution to a wider regeneration strategy. One way of approaching this is to conceive of a programme of work embracing a number of productions rather than a single piece of work. The simplest starting point for national funds is the Government Funding website which provides an overview of national funding available through key departments (http://www.governmentfunding.org.uk).

Trusts and foundations

UK Trusts and Foundations donate some £2 billion a year to charities, roughly the same amount as awarded by the government in grants. Charities like the Media Trust and Hi8us have secured valuable funds from this sector, but it is a notoriously conservative world which tends to favour more established, less commercial artforms. Information on funding from Trusts is available from a range of different sources including the Trustfunding website overseen by the Directory of Social Change (see http://www.trustfunding.org.uk).

Corporate sponsorship

The corporate sector is usually approached with fresh-faced optimism but, despite the widespread growth of corporate social responsibility programmes in the last five years, it is the hardest nut to crack. Most support is offered as 'in-kind' expertise, or as a discount on advertised rates. Funding is hard to secure and usually goes to high-profile, well-known projects.

Approaching funders

It is not unusual to apply for dozens of grants without success. There are literally hundreds of grant-giving bodies scattered across the UK, and although competition is always fierce there are ways to increase your chances of success. Fundraisers need a thick skin.

Define your project

The most obvious starting point for every funding proposal is the project in question. Funders are always more likely to support something which is clear and easy to describe over something which appears complicated or unwieldy. Applicants need to work on simple project descriptions which are not cluttered with jargon. The rule is, keep it simple.

Projects need simple, memorable titles which are used throughout the proposal. There is nothing more mind-numbing for an assessor than reading a document where every second sentence starts, 'The project will . . .'

Be realistic

Fundraising is a pragmatic task. Applicants need to be realistic about what they are likely to get, how they set about getting it and when the work needs to be done. Careful planning is the essence of successful fundraising.

At the most basic level you need to be sure that your project is eligible to apply. If a particular funding scheme is unable to fund individuals, then there is simply no point approaching them unless it is done through a properly established organisation. This may sound obvious but roughly 10% of all applicants fail basic eligibility checks. No matter how strong the proposal is, it remains an aspiration unless it is eligible to be funded.

Fundraising takes time, and you should never underestimate the amount of work needed to compile even the simplest proposals. Always aim to submit a proposal in advance of any advertised deadline. Likewise funders always take time to assess proposals, and usually this is longer than the stated turnaround times. You need to find out how long it will take to review applications and then plan accordingly. It is sensible to add on a few weeks to account for bureaucratic delays outside your control. Projects which are scheduled to start within the advertised assessment period will inevitably raise questions from the assessment team.

Find the right blend of funding

Few, if any funders, will fully finance a project, so most proposals require a financial partnership constructed by the applicant. Applicants need to think very carefully about how this is put together, and work on the assumption that the different funding regimes will talk to each other about each proposal. Each fund operates under different rules, so you need to check to ensure that the funds you approach work together and can do so on your project.

Identifying the right blend takes time and effort. The Internet is an invaluable research tool for funding, and there are various newsletters providing information on different types of funding; some are free but most charge. Specialist trade press also provide information on funding and it is wise to go beyond the media press.

Research funds you are approaching

You need to learn as much as possible about the sources you intend to approach. Find out what has been supported before and see if there is anyone you know who has secured funds from the same source; if so, ask their advice.

It is important to make contact with the staff team working in a funding agency so they know you are about to approach them. Always go to any advice sessions or seminars available for prospective applicants. This is the time to discover whether your project has a realistic chance. If, for example, a particular Trust works with young people but rarely funds media work then you can discover why. It may be that no one has applied, but then again it could be because the trustees believe filmmaking is a crass, commercial activity. Better to learn these things before you apply.

Do not get distracted

Do not be tempted by the sudden availability of funds. Funding given for a specific purpose can only be used for that purpose. If the aims of the funding programme do not fit with your own then move on; you can easily end up doing something that is not part of your intended programme.

Prepare the application

Careful preparation is the basis of a solid application. All the answers need to be drafted carefully within stated word limits. Proposals should be written in clear language, without unnecessary jargon or sector-specific terms which can confuse the reader. The aim is to demonstrate you have the skills, experience and knowledge needed to realise an excellent project.

Additional information can be provided in supporting documents. Many funders will request comparable information. It is sensible to build a fundraising toolkit which includes all the basic supporting documentation together with answers to questions which recur across different schemes, for example information on the members of the organisation's management board. A resource like this will make subsequent bids simpler.

Before you submit a proposal it is good practice to commission a dummy assessment. Get a critical friend with expertise in funding to review your proposal, so revisions can be made before it is submitted. Authors often get too close to their work and extra advice can sharpen a proposal. An experienced freelance consultant will usually do this for a small fee, but if you do not have the resources ask a colleague or friend.

Remember to address the right person in a simple covering letter. Applications starting 'Dear Sirs' show a lack of basic knowledge about the funder that does not bode well for a long-term relationship.

Include the right backing documents

It sounds obvious but you need to make sure everything requested is submitted with the application. Failing to provide the correct information will at best delay a proposal and may even render it ineligible. If something is not available explain why in the covering letter.

Plan your budget and cashflow

Every project requires a budget and a cashflow. This needs to show what is going to be spent, and when funds are likely to be needed. The key is to be realistic by showing why you need the funds you are requesting to make the project happen. Do not look for all funding in advance as it will almost certainly not happen that way. It is also good practice to include a basic risk analysis demonstrating you have identified possible risks within the project, and have plans to address them.

Record how you spend the money

It is essential you keep all the paperwork to demonstrate how you spent the money. Funders often visit projects as part of their regular monitoring work and some may want to work closely with you on the delivery of the project, especially if you are a new client running something which is outside their normal world. In all cases, they will expect you to have strong financial management in place so they can be assured funding is spent wisely.

Conclusion

Funding for community-based media work is limited, and what little there is available is highly competitive. Community media practitioners have been forced to think outside conventional media circles to develop sustainable projects. Many successful organisations have looked to new sources of grant income, without jeopardising their original mission. The consequence has been a blurring of the boundaries between different types of work and the growth of a stronger, more vibrant community media sector. Dogged research and thoughtful forward planning have underpinned this success; these are the fundamental components of successful fundraising.

17.2 A place where money grows on trees?

Self-financing and DIY fundraising

Kate Coyer

There are funding models that run the gamut from maxing out your credit card to obtaining foundation or government grants, as detailed in the first part of this chapter. Chances are, your project will be funded by a variety of sources over time, including grants, subscription, advertising, donations, fundraising events, product sales and associated merchandising. Before panic sets in about how to raise the money, it is best to take stock of the possibilities and needs. Production costs vary. While you do not want to feel limited creatively by the costs, neither do you want to start something you cannot complete. It is one thing to raise start-up funds, but sustainability is that much more difficult.

The first thing to ask is, how much money do you need to get started? Make a wish list of what you need and think through every aspect of your project, relying on your projected timeline. Though your master plan may include distributing DVDs to every community centre in the country, or a monthly full-colour glossy magazine, it might take some time to build up the necessary funds. *Clamor* Magazine opted to produce quarterly issues in order to maintain visual and editorial standards that might have been unobtainable in a monthly publication. So the next step is to get real. What do you *really* need to get started? What can you get away with? Must you purchase a top-of-the-line powerbook G5 Intel Pentium aristocrat or will your three-year-old laptop suffice? Adjust your start-up budget accordingly!

In terms of equipment or skills needed, see what can be acquired at no cost.

Are there free, open-source software programs you could use for editing software or Web design? Can you borrow software from a friend? Can you reuse old
media (i.e., erase digital tapes or re-record over other unwanted tapes)? Can you
build anything you might need yourself? For example, if you are building a radio
station, consider soldering your own transmitter rather than buying one pre-
built. Sometimes the more you start from scratch, the more empowered the work
becomes. Can you use facilities you might have access to – university, community
centre, public library, local radio or TV station, other like-minded groups? You
might also consider involving more people. This might defray the costs, and it
might also turn an individual project into a real collaboration.

The next thing to consider is distribution. How many copies will you produce?
What is the role your website will play in terms of publicity or distribution? Have
you enough server space to handle expected traffic to your site and/or the multimedia capabilities required?

After you have set a project budget everyone is comfortable with, the next step
is of course finding the necessary funds. An important point to be made here is
that if you have not already set a mission statement or vision statement for the
project, now would be the time. How a project is funded can say a lot about the
kind of project it is. Obviously, if your work is about tearing down the walls of
capitalism, you will not be seeking corporate advertising. However, you might
carry advertisements from organisations or alternative products related to your
mission and values. And if your objective is to reach inner-city, low-income youth,
it is unlikely you will raise significant funds from local individual donations. Part
of raising funds in your community is doing outreach – letting people know about
your project and building a support base. Staying true to your principles should
drive your fundraising efforts.

Following is a list of ten ideas for raising money culled from a variety of projects and people. The intention of this list is simply to spur some ideas, as it is by
no means exhaustive.

1 *Individual donations.* If a wealthy heiress has not yet bestowed cash blessings
   on your project, you can raise a fair amount of money from small, individual contributions. Make every ten-pound donation count! To start, you could
   launch a 'capital campaign' or special fundraising incentives for founders, to
   encourage people to give bigger donations at the start than they might be
   able to sustain on a regular basis. For example, a community station whose
   frequency is 106.7 might use this to encourage listeners to donate £106.07
   in exchange for their name on a founders' wall or other lasting tribute. See
   if you know anyone who works for a company that matches the donations
   employees give.
2 *Subscriptions and/or listener contributions.* Charging for a paper copy of your
   zine or paper makes sense, but becomes trickier when talking about online
   content or broadcasting. Almost every public and community-run television
   and radio station in the US holds on-air fund drives, spending one week to

ten days on air, asking (at times begging!) listeners to become members and donate $20–$100 or more for the year. These might be tedious listening, but are very popular in the US. Money raised on-air ranges from millions at the largest public TV stations to a few thousand dollars at low-power, neighbourhood radio stations. Stations typically give contributors 'incentive' gifts that have been donated in return for their donations, and many offer 'member benefits' such as discounts to local shops and restaurants.

3 *Fundraising events, benefit concerts and film screenings* are a lot of fun, just be careful you do not burn out putting on one big party so there is no energy left to make media! You might also consider small events like film screenings or guest speakers who conclude their remarks with a funding pitch for which you have outreached to key potential donors. Or, ask a local performing artist if an upcoming show can be used to fundraise for your project. The filmmakers went deeply into personal debt making their award-winning documentary *Unprecedented: The 2000 Presidential Election*, and one of them gambled the whole of her retirement savings to complete filming – a very risky endeavour. When it came time to edit the film, they received support from a Hollywood producer, and raised money through friends who held viewing parties where the film would be screened, followed by a discussion, and the proverbial hat passed around the room.

4 *Merchandise.* T-shirts, stickers, sports bottles, mugs, you name it – just be sure it is something people will actually want to spend money on. You might be able to get a donation of transistor radios or buy books at a wholesale price to resell. Consider using non-sweatshop T-shirt companies if ethical labour is part of your organisation's values. Many people are willing to spend a few pounds more for an ethical T-shirt manufacturer. Prometheus Radio began offering on-site silk screening of T-shirts so those who cannot afford a new shirt can bring their own and silk screen the design for only a fiver.

5 *Selling DVDs and CDs.* Indymedia London holds DVD burning parties before large events. In making their own copies, production costs are kept down, and the savings passed on to the buyer! If your group does not have a compilation of your own, consider joining forces with a local musician or filmmaker to sell their product at your events and share the revenue.

6 *Finding support from a major donor.* Indymedia UK received a large donation from the band Chumbawamba. The band was paid the sum when one of their songs was used in a car commercial. Instead of fighting the usage, Chumbawamba took the corporate money and wrote a cheque to Indymedia. Ask around, you never know! The broader your outreach, the more likely it is that such a fairy god-band will cross your path.

7 *Advertising and sponsorship.* It is not uncommon to have a strict policy about what kinds of businesses you will accept advertising from. Many groups will favour local businesses and companies promoting products related to their work (i.e. a music zine would likely carry advertisements from a record store or label). Public and community broadcasters in the US cannot take

advertisements (in the UK, community stations can – in the majority of cases – raise up to 50% of their income from adverts), but they can carry 'underwriting', or sponsorship of programmes, which is also allowable in the UK up to a certain percentage (i.e. 'this show is brought to you by . . .').

8 *Local grant money and one-off grants from unexpected places.* In the US, it is difficult to get grants for a media project, especially grassroots media projects. You are more likely to get a grant for social-justice work, under which the media project is a piece of a whole, but media-specific grants remain elusive for most Americans. If you are setting up a collaborative project that involves working with young people in your area, consider looking for local neighbourhood grants, regional funds, community sources, local arts councils, etc. You never know what you might unearth.

9 *In-kind donations.* The gift of products, services, equipment. Some official and some unofficial. It is always nice to have a friend who works in a photocopy shop, especially when time to print fliers. And it is also nice to have supporters who work for companies that might be willing to donate office furniture, computers, legal services, etc.

10 *Be as creative as the work you are making.* In short, have fun, hold a contest, a raffle, an online auction, a bake sale – whatever it takes. Try to enlist supporters to hold a fundraising event for you. Again, think of your fundraising as part of your outreach.

Lastly, it is crucial to keep excellent records of all the donations you have received. Not only for tax records and bookkeeping, but so that you might build a database of funders. Bush Radio in South Africa had a crisis when they were evicted from the building they had called home for over a decade with little advance warning. Because of the respect and admiration they have earned for their work, and the strength of their funders' database, they were able to raise money in a short amount of time to cover the unexpected move. Moreover, it is important to keep those records so that you can properly thank the people who have helped you. It may sound like motherly advice, but a simple, handmade thank-you card makes a much-appreciated follow up. When it comes to both giving and receiving, a little can go a long way!

18 'We are the network . . .'

....

These are edited extracts from a video message by Subcomandante Marcos of the Zapatista movement, to the 'Freeing the Media Teach-In', held in New York City in early 1997:

> We're in the mountains of Southeast Mexico in the Lacandon Jungle of Chiapas and we want to use this medium . . . to send a greeting to the Free the Media Conference in New York.
>
> A global decomposition is taking place, we call it the Fourth World War – neoliberalism: the global economic process to eliminate that multitude of people who are not useful to the powerful – the groups called 'minorities' in the mathematics of power, but who happen to be the majority population in the world. We find ourselves in a world system of globalization willing to sacrifice millions of human beings . . .
>
> The great monsters of the television industry, the communication satellites, magazines, and newspapers seem determined to present a virtual world, created in the image of what the globalization process requires.
>
> We have a choice: we can have a cynical attitude in the face of the media, to say that nothing can be done about the dollar power that creates itself in images, words, digital communication, and computer systems that invade not just with an invasion of power, but with a way of seeing that world, of how they think the world should look. We could say, well, 'that's the way it is' and do nothing. Or we can simply assume incredulity: we can say that any communication by the media monopolies is a total lie. We can ignore it and go about our lives.
>
> But there is a third option that is neither conformity, nor skepticism, nor distrust: that is to construct a different way – to show the world what is really happening – to have a critical world view. By not having to answer to the monster media monopolies, independent media has a life work, a political project and purpose: to let the truth be known. This is more and more important in the globalization process. This truth becomes a knot of resistance against the lie. It is our only possibility to save the truth, to maintain it, and distribute it, little by little . . .

In August 1996, we called for the creation of a network of independent media, a network of information. We mean a network to resist the power of the lie that sells us this war that we call the Fourth World War. We need this network not only as a tool for our social movements, but for our lives: this is a project of life, of humanity, humanity which has a right to critical and truthful information. (Marcos 1997)

'We are the network, all of us who resist.' (Marcos 2001: 117)

Resources

....

As will be obvious from the rest of this book, the Web has become a key resource for finding out about alternative media and acquiring appropriate knowledge and skills. This section is a list of the websites of groups, organisations and campaigns mentioned in the book, in addition to some additional selected sites, listed alphabetically. For a break-down of many of these sites by topic (funding, media activism, etc), please refer to chapter 16 ('DIY media'). All sites have been viewed between March and September 2006.

Adbusters: www.adbusters.org
Alliance for Community Media: www.alliancecm.org
Allied Media Conference: http://alliedmediaconference.org/
Almost Normal Comics: members.tripod.com: almostnormalcomics/id181.htm
Alternative Press Review: www.altpr.org
Alternative and free radios in Germany: www.querfunk.de/radios.html
Alternative Radio: www.alternativeradio.org
Alternet: www.alternet.org
Amber Films: www.amber-online.com
Ambient TV: www.ambienttv.net
Anarchist Book Fair: www.anarchistbookfair.co.uk/
Artella magazine: www.artellawordsandart.com
Article 19: www.article19.org
Arts Advice: www.netgain.org.uk/business/planning/business_plan.asp
Arts Council of England: www.artscouncil.org.uk
Arts Council of Northern Ireland: www.artscouncil-ni.org/
Arts Council of Scotland: www.scottisharts.org.uk
Arts Council of Wales: www.artswales.org
Arts Council of Wales: www.artswales.org.uk/publications/Business_plan_
    guidelines_September_2005.
The Art of Funding Your Film: www.fromtheheartproductions.com
Association for Progressive Communications (APC): www.apc.org
Association of Student Radio Alumni (UK): www.studentradioalumni.com
Audacity (open source audio editing): www.audacity.sourceforge.net
Audio Theatre: www.audiotheater.com/phone/phone.html
Audio Port: www.audioport.org

Banksy: www.banksy.co.uk
Barbieinablender project: www.Barbieinablender.org
BBC Capture Wales: www.bbc.co.uk/Wales/capturewales
BBC Create: www.bbc.co.uk/create
BBC Creative Archive: www.creativearchive.bbc.co.uk
BBC Online Tutorials: www.bbctraining.com/onlineCourses.asp
BBC Style Guide: www.bbctraining.com/journalism.asp
BBC Video Nation: www.bbc.co.uk/videonation
Be the Media Encyclopaedia: www.bethemedia.com
Benton Foundation (media ownership): www.benton.org/?q=initiatives/
    ownership
Bibliotheque: www.lunar-circuitry.net/bibliotheque
Big Lottery Fund: www.biglotteryfund.org
Big Noise Films: www.bignoisefilms.com
bitch magazine: www.bitchmagazine.com/
Blogging 101: www.unc.edu/%7Ezuiker/blogging101/index.html
Boing Boing: http://www.boingboing.net
Broken Pencil: www.brokenpencil.com
Bulb: www.bulbmag.co.uk
Bust magazine: www.bust.com/
Bittorent: http://bittorrent.org
British Film Institute: www.bfi.org.uk
Broadcasting, Entertaintment, Cinematograph and Theatre Union (BECTU):
    www.bectu.org.uk
Broadcasting regulators:
    Australia: www.dcita.gov.au/
    Canada: www.crtc.gc.ca/eng/welcome.htm
    Ireland: www.bci.ie/
    South Africa: www.nab.org.za
    UK: www.ofcom.co.uk
    US: www.fcc.gov
BrokeZinesters mailing list: www.groups.yahoo.com/group/BrokeZinesters
Bush Radio: www.Bushradio.co.za
Camcorder Guerillas: http://camcorderguerillas.net
Campaign for Press and Broadcasting Freedom: www.cpbf.org.uk
Campus Progress: www.campusprogress.org/
Centre for Development Communication: www.uoguelph.ca
Center for International Media Activism: www.cima.org
Champaign-Urbana Wireless Network: http://cuwireless.net
Christian Aid: www.christrianaid.org.uk
Civiblog: www.civiblog.org/blog/BloggingResources
CKUT: www.ckut.ca
Clamor magazine: www.clamormagazine.org/
College Music Journal (CMJ): www.cmj.com

Columbia Journalism Review: www.cjr.org

The Comics Journal: www.tcj.com

Common Frequency (US): www.commonfrequency.org

Communica: www.comunica.org

Communication Initiative: www.comminit.com

Communication Rights in the Information Society Campaign: www.cris.org

Communication for Social Change Consortium: www.communicationforsocial
   change.org

Community Arts course at the University of Strathclyde: www.strath.ac.uk/sca/
   ug-info/communityarts.htm

Community Broadcasting Association of Australia: www.cbaa.org.au

Community Media Association (CMA): www.commedia.org.uk

Community Media Association Resource Handbook: www.commedia.org.uk/
   library.htm

Community Media Network, Ireland: www.cmn.ie/

Community-media.com: www.community-media.com/index.html

Community Radio Manual from the Open Society Foundation for South Africa:
   www.osf.org.za/File_Uploads/pdf/CRM-1-prelims.pdf

Community Radio Toolkit: www.communityradiotoolkit.org

Community Spectrum Taskforce: www.rmit.edu.au/appliedcommunication/cst

Corporation for Public Broadcasting, US: www.cpb.org

Creative Commons: http://creativecommons.org/

Creative Commons licensed sounds to use in creative radio making: http://
   freesound.iua.upf.edu/

Critical Art Ensemble: http://www.critical-art.net

Cross Radio: http://www.crossradio.org/

Cultural Enterprise Office: www.culturalenterpriseoffice.co.uk

Culture Jammers Encyclopaedia: www.sniggle.net/

CUPID: http://cupid.culture.info

Current TV: www.current.tv

Cyber Journalist: www.cyberjournalist.net/

Democracy Now!: www.democracynow.org

Democracy TV: www.getdemocracy.com

Desi Radio: www.desiradio.org

Digital Futures: A Need-to-Know Policy Guide for Independent Filmmakers: www.
   itvs.org/digitalfutures/

DIY media: www.diymedia.net

Electronic Freedom Frontier: www.eff.org

Electronic Freedom Frontier Bloggers: www.eff.org/bloggers/lg/

EUCLID: www.euclid.info

Factsheet 5: www.factsheet5.org

Feminist International Radio Endeavours (FIRE): www. fire.or.cr

Filmmaker magazine: www.filmmakermagazine.com

Flicker: www.hi-beam.net/cgi-bin/flicker.pl

Forest of Dean Radio: www.fodradio.org/

Foundation: http://foundation.culture.info

Foundation Centre : http://foundationcenter.org

Free Press: www.freepress.net

Free Radio Berkeley: www.freeradio.org/

Free Radio Olympia: www.frolympia.org/website/index.php?module=faq&FAQ_
    op=view&FAQ_id=1

Free Reporters Network: http://freereportersnetwork.awardspace.com/

Free Speech Radio News: www.fsrn.org

Free Speech TV: www.freespeech.org

Freevlog: http://freevlog.org/tutorial/

The Funding Exchange: www.fex.org

Funferal (setting up a radio station): http://funferal.org/mt-archive/000192.l#1b

Grrl Zine Resource: www.grrlzines.net

Global Voices: www.globalvoicesonline.org/

Greenpeace: www.greenpeace.org

The Guardian Student Media Awards: http://media.guardian.co.uk/studentmedia
    awards

Guerilla Girls: www.guerillagirls.org

Guerrilla News Network: www.guerrillanews.com

HOPE (Hackers on Planet Earth): www.hopenumbersix.net

De Hoeksteen: www.hoeksteen.dds.nl/main.php3

The Hoot: www.thehoot.org

How to Blog: www.emilyrobbins.com/how-to-blog/

How to Write a Protest Letter: www.bitchmagazine.com/archives/04_03slash/
    protest.shtml

I-Tunes Video: www.apple.com/itunes/videos

Independent Television Service: www.itvs.org

Indymedia: www.indymedia.org

Indymedia Radio: www.radio.indymedia.org

Indymedia UK: www.indymedia.co.uk

Indymedia Video: http://video.indymedia.org/en/

Infoshop: www.infoshop.org/

Insightshare: www.insightshare.org

Institute of Development Studies: www.ids.ac.uk

Institute of Local Television: www.localtvonline.com

Intercollegiate Broadcast System (UK): www.ibsradio.org

International Development Research Centre: www.idrc.ca

Internet Archive: www.archive.org

Izzyvideo: www.izzyvideo.com

J18: http://bak.spc.org/j18/site/

Journal of Aesthetics and Protest: www.journalofaestheticsandprotest.org

Kein portal: www.kein.org & www.kein.tv

Kill Radio: www.killradio.org

KORDA Database: www.korda.obs.coe.int
LabourStart: www.labourstart.org
LabourStart TV: www.labourstart.org/tv
Letter to the Prime Minister: www.alettertotheprimeminister.co.uk
Listen Up!: www.listenup.org/
Livejournal: www.livejournal.com/community/zinereviews
London Musicians' Collective: www.l-m-c.org.uk/
Lux: www.lux.org.uk
Make magazine: www.makezine.com
Malaysiakini: www.malaysiakini.com
Manhattan Neighbourhood Network: www.mnn.ortg and www.youthchannel.org
MediaACT: www.mediact.org
Media Alliance: media-alliance.org
Media Channel: www.themediachannel.org
Media Institute: http://www.mediainstitute.org/
Media Justice Fund: www.fex.org/content/index.php?pid=51
Media geek: www.mediageek.net
MELT: www.lovemelt.com
Minga Informativa: www.movimientos.org
Minidisc.org: www.minidisc.org
Moblog UK: www.moblog.co.uk
MPlayer: www.mplayerhq.hu
MySpace: www.myspace.com
NRG Transmitters: www.nrgkits.com
National Alliance for Media Arts and Culture: www.namac.org
National Campus and Community Radio Association, Canada: www.ncra.ca
National Conference on Media Reform: www.freepress.net/conference/
National Endowment for Science Technology and the Arts: www.nesta.org/
National Federation of Community Broadcasters, US: www.nfcb.org
National Radio Project: www.radioproject.org
National Union of Journalists: www.nuj.org.uk
National Union of Students: www.nusonline.co.uk/
NESTA: www.nesta.org
Nettime Digest: www.nettime.org
NewAssignment.Net: http://newassignment.net/
New Global Vision: www.ngvision.org
New Pages Zine Rack: www.newpages.com/magazinestand/zines/default.htm
New Style Radio: www.newstyleradio.co.uk/
New York State Council on the Arts: www.nysca.org
Next 5 Minutes: http://www.next5minutes.org
Ofcom: www.ofcom.co.uk
OneWorld: www.oneworld.net
OneWorld Radio: www.radio.oneworld.net
OneWorld radio technical manual.ttp//radio.oneworld.net/article/view/66913/1/

OneWorld Radio Training links Training links from One World radio:
    http://radio.oneworld.net/section/training/publications
OneWorldTV: http://tv.oneworld.net
Online Journalism Review: http//www.ojr.org/
Open Democracy: www.opendemocracy.net
Open Knowledge Foundation: http://okfn.org
Our Media: www.ourmedia.org
Our Media/Nuestros Medios: www.ourmedianet.org
Outfoxed: www.outfoxed.org
Outloud Project: www.outloud.tv/
PARK4DTV: www.park.nl/park_cms/public/
Pacifica Radio: www.pacifica.org
Panos Institute: www.panos.org.uk
Paper Tiger: www.papertiger.org
Participatory Culture: www.participatoryculture.org
Peace Institute: http://www.mirovni-institut.si/
Peoples Social Action: www.agp.org
Phlog: www.phlog.net
Podcasting resources:
    www.how-to-podcast-tutorial.com/
    www.voxmedia.org/wiki/How_to_Podcast
    www.podcasting-tools.com
Poynter online: http://www.poynter.org
Poopsheet: www.poopsheetfoundation.com
Prisoners of the Iron Bars: www.prisioneiro.com.br/ingles/index.htm
Prometheus Radio Project: www.prometheusradio.org
Public Radio Exchange: www.prx.org
Punk Planet: www.punkplanet.com
Radical Software: www.radicalsoftware.org
Radio 4 All: www.radio4all.net
Radio: An Illustrated Guide: http://artbabe.com/comicsandart/journalism/radio/
    radiobook.html
Radio Is Our Bomb: www.dojo.ie/active/bomb.htm
Radio La Luna: www.radioluna.com
Radio Populares: Radiopopulares.org
Radio Regen: www.Radioregen.org
Razorcake: www.razorcake.com
Reclaim the Media: www.reclaimthemedia.org
Rec networks: www.recnet.com
Red Pepper: www.redpepper.org.uk
Reporters Without Borders: www.rsf.org
Resonance FM: www.resonancefm.com
Ruckus society: www.ruckus.org
SALTO: www.salto.nl

A Series of Fallopian Tubes: www.seriesoffallopiantubes.com/
SchNEWS: www.schnews.org.uk
Scottish Arts Council:: www.scottisharts.org.uk
Scottish Screen: www.scottishscreen.com
Screenplayers: www.screenplayers.net/financing
Shaking the Money Tree: How to Get Grants and Donations for Film and Video:
    www.mwp.com
Sharing Knowledge for Culture: http://eufunds.culture.info
Skillset the UK sector skills council for the audio visual industries: www.skillset.org
Social Centers UK: www.londonarc.org/social_centre_network.html
Social Science Research Council, Media Research Hub: http://mediaresearchhub.
    ssrc.org/
Soul City: www.soulcity.org.za
South East European Network for Professionalization of Media (SEENPM):
    http://www.seenpm.org
Spin Project: www.spinrpoject.org
Sprouts Radio: www.sprouts.org
Student Filmmakers: www.studentfilmmakers.com
Student Newspaper Survival Guide: http://collegenewspaper.blogspot.com
Student Press Law Center: www.splc.org/
Student Radio Association (UK): www.studentradio.org.uk
Stumptown Printers: www.stumptownprinters.com
Takeover Radio: www.takeoverradio.co.uk/
Tales from the Public Domain: Bound By Law?: www.law.duke.edu/cspd/comics/
Tehelka: www.tchelka.com
Telestreet: www.telestreet.it
Ten Page News: http://members.aol.com/vlorbik
Third Coast Audio International Festival: www.thirdcoastfestival.org/
Third World Majority: www.thirdworldmajority.org
Tranquil Eye Free Media Papers: www.tranquileye.com/free/study
Transom: www.transom.org
Trustfunding: www.trustfunding.org.uk
UK Film Financing Handbook – How to Fund Your Film: www.netribution.co.uk.
UK government funding: www.governmentfunding.org.uk
UK Lottery: www.biglotteryfund.org
Undercurrents: www.undercurrents.org
Undead Art Project: www.UndeadArt.org
UNESCO: http://portal.unesco.org
Unesco Community Radio Handbook: www.unesco.org/webworld/publications/
    community_radio_handbook.pdf
United African Alliance Community Center: www.uaacc.habari.co.tz/
United Graphics: www.unitedgraphicsinc.com
University of California, Berkely School of Journalism 5 Steps to Multimedia
    Reporting from UC Berkeley: http://dev.journalism.berkeley.edu/multimedia/

UnLimited Media: www.unlimitedmedia.co.uk
Urban 75: www.urban75.com
Use It: www.useit.com
Utne Reader Associate: www.utne.com
V2V portal: http://v2v.cc
Videoletters: www.videoletters.net
Video Activism: www.videoactivism.org/resource.html
VLC Player: www.videolan.org/vlc/
Voice of the Listener and Viewer: www.vlv.org.uk
W3 Web Accessibility Initiative (WAI): www.w3.org/WAI
Walmart: the High Price of Low Cost: www.walmartmovie.com
We Are Everywhere: www.weareeverywhere.org
Web statistics: www.w3schools.com/browsers
Welsh Arts Council: www.artswales.org
WeSeize: www.geneva03.org
What the hack: http://whatthehack.org/
Who Makes the News?: www.whomakesthenews.org/
Wiki: wiki.org
Wikipedia: www.wikipedia.org
Witness: www.witness.org
Women in Media and News: www.wimn.org
Women's International News Gathering Service: www.wings.org
Wordpress Blog tool: http://wordpress.org/
World Association of Community Radio Broadcasters (AMARC): www.amarc.org
World Intellectual Property Organization: www.wipo.int
World Social Forum: www.forumsocialmundial.org
World Student Press Agency (APEM): http://www.studentpa.info/
World Wide Web Consortium (W3C): www.w3.org
Worldwide links to 700 community and public access television sites:
     www.communitymedia.se/cat/index.htm
*Xeroxography Deb*t: www.leekinginc.com/xeroxdebt
Yes! magazine: www.yesmagazine.org/
Yes Men: www.yesmen.org
You Are Hear: www.youarehear.co.uk/
YouTube: www.youtube.com
Youth Media Council: www.youthmediacouncil.org/
Youth Media Toolkit: www.ymdi.org/toolkit/
Youth Radio: www.youthradio.org
Zine Book: www.zinebook.com
Zine Scene on Livejournal: www.livejournal.com/community/zine_scene
Zinesters list: http//www.zinesters.net/
Zinestreet: www.zinestreet.com
Zinethug: www.zinethug.com

Bibliography

Aarseth, E. (1997) *Cybertext: Experiments in Ergodic Literature*, Baltimore: Johns Hopkins University Press.

Abel, J. and Glass, I. (1999) *Radio: An Illustrated Guide*, Chicago: Artbabe Army Publishing.

'About Woomera' (2003) *Four Corners*, Australian Broadcasting Corporation, broadcast 19 May, transcript available at http://www.abc.net.au/4corners/content/2003/20030519_woomera/default.htm, accessed 13 February 2006.

Adams, M.H., and Massey, K.K. (1995) *Introduction to Radio: Production and Programming*, Madison, WI: Wm. C. Brown Communications.

Airflash (2004) 'Report from AGM', Sheffield: Community Media Association.

Airflash (2005) '7/7', Sheffield: Community Media Association.

Anderson, C. (2006) *The Long Tail: How Endless Choice Is Creating Unlimited Demand*, London: Random House Business Books.

'Annie and Sam' (2003) 'From Indymedia UK to the United Kollektives,' *Media Development*, 4.27, http://www.indymedia.org.uk/en/2004/12/302894.html, accessed 1 May 2006.

Arnison, M. (2001) Open Publishing Is Free software, http://www.cat.org.au/maffew/cat/open-pub.html, accessed 1 May 2006.

ASCUN (2005) 'Seminario regional sobre medios de comunicación universitarios en América Latina y el Caribe': http://www.ascun.org.co/foro5/medios/medios.htm, accessed 20 May 2006.

Ashley, L. and Olson, B. (1998) 'Constructing Reality: Print Media's Framing of the Women's Movement, 1966–1986', *Journalism and Mass Communication Quarterly*, 75.2 (Summer), pp. 263–77.

Atton, C. (1996) 'Anarchy on the Internet: Obstacles and Opportunities for Alternative Electronic Publishing', *Anarchist Studies*, 4 (October), pp. 115–32.

Atton, C. (2000) 'Are There Alternative Media after CMC?', *M/C Reviews*, 12 April, www.uq.edu.au/mc/reviews/features/politics/altmedia.html, accessed 1 May 2006.

Atton, C. (2002a) *Alternative Media*, London: Sage.

Atton, C. (2002b) 'News Cultures and New Social Movements: Radical Journalism and the Mainstream Media', *Journalism Studies*, 3.4, pp. 491–505.

Atton, C. (2004) *An Alternative Internet: Radical Media, Politics and Creativity*, Edinburgh: Edinburgh University Press.

Balanya, B., Doherty, A., Hoedeman, O., Ma'anit, A. and Wesselius, F. (2000) *Europe Inc.: Regional and Global Restructuring and the Rise of Corporate Power*, London: Pluto Press.

Baldwin, C. (dir.) (1995) *Sonic Outlaws*, documentary film, San Francisco.

Barlow, John Perry (8 February 1996) 'A Declaration of the Independence of Cyberspace' (retrieved 1 August 2006 from http://homes.eff.org/~barlow/Declaration-Final.html).

Barlow, M. and Clarke, T. (2002) *Global Showdown: How the New Activists Are Fighting Global Corporate Rule*, Toronto: Stoddart.

Batty, P. (1993) 'Singing the Electric: Aboriginal Television in Australia', in T. Dowmunt (ed.), *Channels of Resistance*, London: British Film Institute.

BBC (2006) *A World in Your Ear*, broadcast on BBC Radio 4, 23 April.

BBC Press Office (2006) 'Creative Future – detailed press briefing', www.bbc.co.uk/pressoffice/pressreleases/stories/2006/04_april/25/creative_detail.shtml, accessed 2 June 2006.

Behling, M. (2006) Das Wachstum des Indymedia-Netzwerks: Das erste global agierende alternative Mediennetzwerk. Version 15.03.2006, http://www.perspektive89.com/2006/04/11/das_wachstum des_indymedia_netzwerks_das_erste_global_agierende_alternative_mediennetzwerk, accessed 1 May 2006.

Benson, R. (2003) 'Commercialism and Critique: California's Alternative Weeklies', in N. Couldry and J. Curran (eds), *Contesting Media Power: Alternative Media in a Networked World*, Lanham, MD: Rowman and Littlefield, pp. 111–27.

Berman, M. (1982) *All that Is Sold Melts into Air: The Experience of Modernity*, New York: Penguin Books.

Bignell, J. and Orlebar, J. *The Television Handbook*, London: Routledge.

Bookchin, M. (1986) 'A Note on Affinity Groups', in M. Bookchin, *Post-scarcity Anarchism*, 2nd edn, Montreal: Black Rose.

Boorstin, D. (1992 [1961]) *The Image*, New York: Vintage.

Borderhack (2000) 'Countdown to Borderhack': http://mail.v2.nl/v2east/2000/Jul/0089.html, accessed 1 June 2006.

Bouwer, A.R. (2003) 'Freedom of the Student Press in South Africa', academic.sun.ac.za/journalism/news/archive/conference03/papers/bouwer.doc, accessed 30 May 2006, Stellenbosch: Stellenbosch University.

Bowman, S. and Willis, C. (2003) 'We Media: How Audiences are Shaping the Future of News and Information', http://www.hypergene.net/wemedia/weblog.php, accessed 11 November 2006.

Boyle, D. (1997) *Subject to Change: Guerilla Television Revisited*, New York: Oxford University Press.

Braithwaite, J. and Drahos, P. (2000) *Global Business Regulation*, Cambridge: Cambridge University Press.

Branwyn, G. (1997) *Jamming the Media: A Citizen's Guide to Reclaiming the tools of Communication*, San Francisco: Chronicle Books.

Briggs, A. (1995) *The History of Broadcasting in the United Kingdom*, Oxford: Oxford University Press.

British Film Institute Productions (1977) *1951–1976* London: BFI.

British Film Institute Productions (1981) *The New Social Function of Cinema*, London: BFI.

Brown, M. (2005) 'The News from Near You', *Media Guardian*, 12 December 2005.

Burnett, C. (2001) personal interview, Los Angeles.

Burroughs, W. (1982) 'Interview with William S. Burroughs', in J. Calder (ed.), *A William Burroughs Reader*, London: Picador, pp. 262–7.

Camcorder Guerillas (2002) *Urban Guerillas*, http://scotland.ideasfactory.com, accessed 1 June 2006.

Carlsson, U. (2005) 'From NWICO to Global Governance of the Information Society', in H. Oscar and T. Thomas (eds), *Media and Global Change: Rethinking Communication for Development*, Göteborg, Sweden: Nordic Information Centre for Media and Communication Research and Buenos Aires: Conselho Latino-Americano De Ciências Sociais.

Carroll, W.K. and Hackett, R.A. (2006) 'Democratic Media Activism through the Lens of Social Movement Theory,' *Media, Culture and Society*, 28.1, pp. 83–104.

Castells, M. (1997) *The Information Age: Economy, Society and Culture. Volume II: The Power of Identity*, Oxford: Blackwell.

Castells, M. (2001) *The Internet Galaxy*, Oxford: Oxford University Press.

Caton, B. (1979) 'Public Radio in Virginia', Working Paper no. 12, Virginia State Telecommunications Study Commission, Richmond. ERIC, ED 183 209.

Çelen Özer, A. (2006) 'The Program Structures, Types and Contents of Radios Belonging to Universities in Turkey' (*Türkiye'de Üniversitelere Ait Radyoların Program Yapısı, Tür ve İçerikleri*), PhD dissertation, Marmara University, Faculty of Communications, Istanbul.

Chalaby, J.K. (ed.) (2005) *Transnational Television Worldwide*, London: I.B.Taurus.

Circuit (1965) Cambridge: F. and P. Piggott.

Clement, E. and Oppenhiem, C. (2002) 'Anarchism, alternative publishers and copyright', *Anarchist Studies* 10.1 (Spring), pp. 41–69.

Community Media Association (2001) 'CMA manifesto', www.commedia.org.uk/manifesto, accessed 14 February 2005.

Community Media Association (2004) 'Historic Day in the Long Journey of Community Radio': http://www.commedia.org.uk/articles/230704.html, accessed 23 July 2004.

Community Media Association (2005) 'Mission statement', www.commedia.org.uk, accessed 14 February 2005.

Cordeiro, P. (2005) 'Experiências de rádio produzidas para e por jovens: o panorama português das rádios universitárias', paper presented at I Encuentro Iberoamericano de Radios Universitarias, Granada, Spain, 13–16 March 2005.

Couldry, N. (2000) *The Place of Media Power*, London: Routledge.

Couldry, N. (2003a) *Media Rituals: A Critical Approach*, London: Routledge.

Couldry, N. (2003b) 'Beyond the Hall of Mirrors? Some Theoretical Reflections on the Global Contestation of Media Power', in N. Couldry and J. Curran (eds). *Contesting Media Power: Alternative Media in a Networked World*, Lanham, MD: Rowman and Littlefield.

Couldry, N. and Curran., J. (eds) (2003) *Contesting Media Power: Alternative Media in a Networked World*, Lanham, MD: Rowman and Littlefield.

Court, J. (2006) 'People Power II in the Philippines: The First e-Revolution?', World Government Assessment, United Nations University, http://www.unu.edu/p&g/wga/publications/people power_ii.pdf, accessed 24 July 2006.

Coyer, K. (2005) 'If It Leeds It Bleeds', in W. deJong (ed.), *Global Activism, Global Media*, London: Pluto Press.

Coyer, K. (2006) 'Community Radio Licensing and Policy: An Overview', Policy Review, Global Media and Communications, Sage.

Crisell, A. (1997) *An Introductory History of British Broadcasting*, London: Routledge.

Critical Art Ensemble (1999) 'Electronic Civil Disobedience, Simulation and the Public Sphere' posted to <nettime-l@desk.nl> (11 January 1999)

Crook, T. (1998) *International Radio Journalism: History, Theory and Practice*, London: Routledge.

Curran, J. and Seaton, J. (1997) *Power without Responsibility*, London: Routledge.

Curran, J. et al. (eds) (2000) *Media Organisations in Society*, London: Arnold.

D'Arcy, M. (2000) 'Galway's Pirate Women', in C. Mitchell (ed.), *Women and Radio*, London: Routledge.

Dardenne, R. (1996) *A Free and Responsible Student Press*, St Petersburg, FL: Poynter Institute for Media Studies.

Davies, P.A. and Wistreich, N. (2005) 'UK Film Financing Handbook – How to Fund Your Film', www.netribution.co.uk, accessed 1 May 2006.

Dawkins, Richard (1976) *The Selfish Gene*, Oxford: Oxford University Press.

DcTV (2006) http://www.dctv.ie, accessed 28 July 2006.

Deacon (1996) 'The Voluntary Sector in a Changing Communication Environment', *European Journal of Communication*, 11.2, pp. 173–99.

Deacon, D. and Golding, P. (1994) *Taxation and Representation: The Media, Political Communication and the Poll Tax*, London: John Libby.

Deacon, Fenton, N. and Walker, B. (1995) 'Communicating Philanthropy: The Media and the Voluntary Sector in Britain', *Voluntas*, 6.2, pp. 119–39.

Dean, C.L. (2003) *The Art of Funding Your Film: Alternative Financing Concepts*, Dean Publishing, www.fromthehcartproductions.com, accessed 12 September 2006.

Dean, M. (2003) *$30 Film School*, New York: Muska and Lipman/Premier-Trade.

Debord, G. (1987 [1967]) *The Society of the Spectacle*, Exeter: Rebel Press.

Debord, G. (1994) *Society of the Spectacle*, New York: Zone Books.

Debord, G. and Wolman, G. (1981 [1956]) 'Methods of Detournement', in K. Knabb (ed.), *Situationist International Anthology*, Berkeley: Bureau of Public Secrets, pp. 8–14.

De Duve, T. (1996) *Kant after Duchamp*, Cambridge, MA: MIT Press.

Department of Foreign Affairs and Trade (2005) 'Australia Now: Broadcasting and Online Content', www.dfat.gov.au/facts/broadcasting.html, accessed 2 May 2006.

Dery, M. (1993) *Culture Jamming: Hacking, Slashing and Sniping in the Empire of Signs,* Westfield, NJ: Open Magazine Pamphlet Series no. 25.

Dickinson, M. (1999) *Rogue Reels*, London: BFI.

Dovey, J. (1993) 'Old Dogs and New Tricks', in T. Dowmunt (ed.), *Channels of Resistance*, London: BFI, pp. 163–75.

Dovey, J. (1996) 'The Revelation of Unguessed Worlds', in J. Dovey (ed.), *Fractal Dreams: New Media in Social Context*, London: Lawrence and Wishart, pp. 109–35.

Dowmunt, T. (ed.) (1993) *Channels of Resistance*, London: BFI.

Dowmunt, T. (2000) 'Access – Television at the Margins', in P. Holland (ed.), *The Television Handbook*, London: Routledge, pp.188–93.

Downing, J. (1984) *Radical Media: The Political Experience of Alternative Communication*, Boston, MA: South End Press.

Downing, J. (2001) *Radical Media: Rebellious Communication and Social Movements*, Thousand Oaks, CA: Sage.

Downing, J. (2002) 'Independent Media Centres: A Multi-local, Multi-media Challenge to Global Neo-liberalism', in M. Raboy (ed.), *Global Media Policy in the New Millennium*, Luton: Luton University Press, pp. 215–32.

Downing, J. (2003) 'Audiences and readers of alternative media: the absent lure of the virtually unknown' in *Media, Culture and Society*, 25.5, pp. 625–45.

Duncombe, S. (1996) 'Notes from the Underground: Zines and the Politics of Underground Culture', in S. Berman and J.P. Dansky (eds), *Alternative Library of Literature: 1994–1995*, Jefferson, NC: McFarland.

Edinburgh '76 Magazine No 1: *Psycho-Analysis/Cinema/Avant-Garde*.

Elsey, E. and Kelly, A. *In Short: A Guide to Short Film-Making in the Digital Age*, London: BFI Modern Classics.

Elwes, C. (2005) *Video Art: A Guided Tour*, London: I.B. Taurus.

Enrile, T.J. (2005) *A Popular Guide to Building a Community FM Broadcast Station*, Oakland: Free Radio Berkeley.

Evan (2001) email correspondence, 1 November, http://lists.indymedia.org/mailman/listinfo/mediapolitics, accessed 1 May 2006.

Everitt, Anthony (2003a) 'New Voices: An Evaluation of 15 Access Radio Projects', London: Radio Authority.

Everitt, Anthony (2003b) 'New Voices: An Update – October 2003', London: Radio Authority.

Farley, C. (2006) personal communication with the author, 30 May.

Farnsworth, J. (2005) personal communication with the author, 24 May.

Fenton, N., Golding, P. and Radley, A. (1995) 'Charities, Media and Public Opinion', *Research Bulletin* (HMSO), 37.10–15 (Winter), pp. 10–15.

Fleming, C. (2002) *The Radio Handbook*, London: Routledge.

Florida, R. (2003) *The Rise of the Creative Class*, New York: Basic Books.

Ford, T.V. and Gil, G. (2001) 'Radical Internet Use', in J. Downing (ed.), *Radical Media: Rebellious Communication and Social Movements*, Thousand Oaks, CA: Sage, pp. 201–34.

Forde, S., Meadows, M. and and Foxwell, K. (2002) *Culture, Commitment, Community: The Australian Community Radio Sector*, Brisbane: Griffith University.

Fountain, N. (1988) *Underground: The London Alternative Press: 1966–74*, London: Routledge.

France, L. (1999) 'Two Minutes of Fame', *Independent*, 7 March 1999.

Frank, T. (2002) 'Why Johnny Can't Dissent', in S. Duncombe (ed.), *Cultural Resistance Reader*, London: Verso, pp. 316–27.

Frasca, G. (2004) 'Videogames of the Oppressed: Critical Thinking, Education, Tolerance, and Other Trivial Issues', in P. Harrigan and N. Wardrip-Fruin (eds), *First Person: New Media as Story, Performance, and Game*, Cambridge, MA: MIT Press, pp. 85–94.

Fraser, N. (1997) 'Rethinking the Public Sphere: A Contribution to the Critique of Actually Existing Democracy', in C. Calhoun (ed.), *Habermas and the Public Sphere*, London: MIT Press.

Freedman, E. 'Activist Television', the Museum of Broadcasting: http://www.museum.tv/archives/etv/A/htmlA/activisttele/activisttele.htm, accessed 31 May 2006.

Free Press (2006) Press release: CUWiN releases free open source wireless networking software, http://www.freepress.net/press/release.php?id=45&print=t.

Freedman, S. (2006) 'Outside Voices: Samuel Freedman on the Difference between the Amateur and the Pro', http://www.cbsnews.com/blogs/2006/03/30/publiceye/entry1458655.shtml, accessed 6 June 2006.

Freire, P. (1972) *Pedagogy of the Oppressed*, London: Penguin.

Fiske, John (1992) 'The cultural economy of fandom' in Lisa A. Lewis (ed.), *The Adoring Audience: Fan Culture and Popular Media*, London: Routledge, pp. 30–49.

Gaber, I. and Willson, A.W. (2005) 'Dying for Diamonds: The Mainstream Media and NGOs – a Case Study of Action Aid', in W. De Jong, M. Shaw and N. Stammers (eds), *Global Activism, Global Media*, London: Pluto Press, pp. 95–109.

Galloway, A.R. (2004) 'Social Realism in Gaming', *Game Studies*, 4.1: http://www.gamestudies.org/0401/galloway, accessed 13 February 2006.

Garcia, D. (2004) 'A Global Sense of Place: A Report on the Eterea 2 Meeting of Italian Tactical Television Makers', Nettime: http://www.nettime.org/Lists-Archives/nettime-l-0404/msg00016.html, accessed 31 May 2006.

Garcia, D. (2006) 'Learning the Right Lessons', http://www.metamute.org/?q=en/Learning-the-Right-Lessons, accessed 31 May 2006.

Garcia, D. and Lovink, G. (1997) 'The ABC of Tactical Media', Nettime: http://subsol.c3.hu/subsol_2/contributors2/garcia-lovinktext.html, accessed 31 May 2006.

Gauntlett, D. (1996) *Video Critical: Children, the Environment and Media Power*, Luton: John Libbey Media.

G8 Gleneagles website (2006) http://www.g8.gov.uk/servlet/Front?pagename=OpenMarket/Xcelerate/ShowPage&c=Page&cid=1100186246454, accessed 1 May 2006.

G8 Radio homepage (2005) http://g8radio.net, accessed 1 May 2006.

Gellor, L. (2005) personal interview, London.

George, S. (2004) *Another World Is Possible If . . .*, London: Verso Books.

Gibson, O. (2005) 'Young Blog Their Way to a Publishing Revolution', *Guardian*, 7 October, p. 9.

Gidal, P. (ed.) (1976) *Structural Film Anthology*, London: BFI.

Gillmor, D. (2006) *We the Media Grassroots Journalism by the People, for the People*, New York: O'Reilly.

Gimarc, G. (1994) *Punk Diary: 1970 1979*, New York: St Martin's Press.

Ginsburg, F.D. (2002) 'Screen Memories', in F.D. Ginsburg, L. Abu-Lughod and B. Larkin (eds), *Media Worlds: Anthropology on a New Terrain*, Berkeley: University of California Press.

Gitlin, T. (1980) *The Whole World is Watching: The Mass Media in the Making and Unmaking of the New Left*, London: California Press.

Glasgow University Media Group (1976) *Bad News*, London: Routledge.

Glasgow University Media Group (1980) *More Bad News*, London: Routledge.

GNU website (2006) http://www.gnu.org/philosophy/free sw.html, accessed 1 May 2006.

Golding, P. (1992) 'Communicating Capitalism: Resisting and Restructuring State Ideology', *Media, Culture and Society*, 14.4, pp. 503–22.

Goldsmiths (n.d.) MA in Community and Cross-sectoral Arts, www.goldsmiths.ac.uk/study-options/postgraduate/MA-Community-Arts.php, accessed 5 July 2006.

Gómez, G. (n.d.) 'The Cultural Diversity Debate in Current Multilateral Processes', WSISPapers. www.Choike.org, accessed 1 May 2006.

Gordon, J. (2000) *The RSL: Ultra Local Radio*, Luton: University of Luton Press.

Green, J. (1988) *Days in the Life: Voices from the English Underground*, London: Heinemann.

Gregory, S., Caldwell, G., Avni, R. and Harding, T. (2005) *Video for Change: A Guide for Advocacy and Activism*, London: Pluto Press.

Gumucio Dagron, Alfonso (2001) *Making Waves: Participatory Communication For Social Change*, New York: The Rockefeller Foundation (online at: www.comminit.com/strategic thinking/pdsmakingwaves/sld-2593.html – accessed 10 September 2007).

Haasch, H. (2005) 'Testimony of Harry Hap Haasch on Behalf of the Alliance for Community Media on November 3 Staff Draft Bill, the US House of Representatives Committee on Energy and Commerce Subcommittee on Telecommunications and the Internet', Alliance for Community Media, Washington DC, November.

Habermas, J. (1989) 'The Public Sphere', in *Jurgen Habermas on Society and Politics: A Reader*, S. Seidman (ed.), trans. S.W. Nicholson, Boston: Beacon Press.

Hadden, J. and Swann, C. (1982) *Prime Time Preachers*, Reading, MA: Addison-Wesley Publishers.

Hall, S. (1990) 'Cultural Identity and Diaspora', in J. Ruthford (ed.), *Identity, Community, Culture and Distance*, London: Lawrence and Wishart, pp. 222–37.

Halleck, D. (2002) *Hand-Held Visions: The Impossible Possibilities of Community Media*, New York: Fordham University Press.

Hallett, L. (2005) personal interview, London.

Hamilton, J. and Atton, C. (2001) 'Theorizing Anglo-American Alternative Media: Toward a Contextual History and Analysis of US and UK Scholarship', *Media History*, 7.2, pp. 119–35.

Harding, T. (2001) *The Video Activist Handbook*, London: Pluto Press.

Harrigan, P. and Wardrip-Fruin, N. (eds) (2004) *First Person: New Media as Story, Performance, and Game*, Cambridge, MA: MIT Press.

Hartley, J. (2005) *Creative Industries*, Cambridge: Blackwell.

Hebdige, D. (1979) *Subculture: The Meaning of Style*, London: Methuen.

Hencher, G. (1994) http://www.bbc.co.uk/videonation/articles/u/ukmirror.shtml, accessed 28 July 2006.

Hendy, D. (2000) *Radio in the Global Age*, Cambridge: Polity Press in association with Blackwell.

Herman, E. and Chomsky, N. (1988) *Manufacturing Consent: The Political Economy of the Mass Media*, New York: Pantheon Press.

Herz, J.C. (2005) 'Harnessing the Hive', in J. Hartley (ed.), *Creative Industries*, Malden, MA: Blackwell, pp. 327–41.

Hind, J. and Mosco, S. (1985) *Rebel Radio: The Full Story of British Pirate Radio*, London: Pluto Press.

Howe, J. (2005) 'Art Attack', *Wired*, 13 August, pp. 112–17.

Howklins, J. (2002) 'Comments to Mayor's Commission on the Creative Industries', London: London Development Agency, http://www.creativelondon.org.uk/upload/pdf/JohnHowkins talk.pdf, accessed 19 October 2005.

Hughes, D. (2003) 'Australia Funds Asylum Game', *BBC News*, 30 April, (http://news.bbc.co.uk/2/hi/asia-pacific/2987745.stm (accessed 13 February 2006).

Human Rights and Equal Opportunities Commission (2004) 'A Last Resort? The National Inquiry into Children in Immigration Detention', (http://www.hreoc.gov.au/human_rights/children_detention_report), accessed 13 February 2006.

IMC Essay Collection (2006) http://docs.indymedia.org/view/Global/ImcEssayCollection, accessed 1 May 2006.

IMC Feedback Report (2006) http://docs.indymedia.org/view/Global/FieldIMCHowTo, accessed 1 May 2006.

Imcista (2005) 'G8 Day 1: G8 Blockades, Mass Arrests and Fence Breaches', published 7 June: http://www.indymedia.org.uk/en/2005/07/317077.html.

Indymedia Docs (2006) http://docs.indymedia.org/view/Local/ImcUkG8, accessed 1 May 2006.

Indymedia Wiki (2006) http://docs.indymedia.org/view/Local/UkNetworkMajorReports, accessed 1 May 2006.

Indymedia UK (2006) http://www.indymedia.org.uk/en/2005/07/315987.html, accessed 1 May 2006.

Isaacson, J. (2006) *DIY Screenprinting: A Graphic Novel*, Microcosm Publishing, Bloomington, IN.

Jaromil (2000) Dyne:bolic, http://www.dyne.org, accessed 1 June 2006.

Johnson, B. (2006) 'Britain Turns off – and Logs on', *Guardian*, 8 March.

Jenkins, H. (2003) 'Quentin Tarantino's *Star Wars?* Digital Cinema, Media Convergence, and Participatory Culture', in D. Thorburn and H. Jenkins (eds), *Rethinking Media Change*, Cambridge, MA: MIT Press, pp. 281–312.

Jolliffe, G. and Jones, C. (2000) *The Guerilla Film Makers Handbook*, London: Continuum.

Jordon, J. (1998) 'The Art of Necessity', in G. McKay (ed.), *DIY Culture: Party and Protest in Nineties Britain*, London: Verso.

Joyce, D. (2005) 'An Unsuspected Future in Broadcasting: Negativland', in A. Chandler and

N. Neumark (eds), *At a Distance: Precursors to Art and Activism on the Internet*, Cambridge, MA: MIT Press, pp. 176–89.

Juhasz, A. (1994) 'So Many Alternatives', *Cineast Magazine*, XX.4: http://www.actupny.org/diva/cineaste.html#anchor878308, accessed 31 May 2006.

Julien, I. (2006) untitled unpublished conference presentation, London: AVPhD.

Keck, M and Sikkink, C. (1998) *Activists beyond Borders: Advocacy Networks in International Politics*, Ithaca: Cornell University Press.

Keeble, R. (2005) *The Newspapers Handbook*, London: Routledge.

Khera, Ajit (2005) personal interview, London.

Kidd, J. (2005) 'Capture Wales: Digital Storytelling and the BBC', unpublished PhD thesis, Cardiff School of Journalism, Media and Cultural Studies.

King, L. (ed.) (2002) *Game On: The History and Culture of Videogames*, New York: Universe.

Klein, N. (2000) *No Logo*, London: Flamingo.

Knabb, K. (ed.) (1981) *Situationist International Anthology*, Berkeley: Bureau of Public Secrets.

Kovach, B., Rosenstiel, T., and Mitchell, A (2004) "The State of the News Media 2004," journalism.org: http://www.stateofthenewsmedia.org/journalist_survey_commentary.asp

Kronschnabl, Ana and Rawlings, Thomas (2004) *Plug in Turn on: A Guide to Internet Filmmaking*, London: Marion Boyars.

Kurtz, Howard (2003) '"Webloggers," Signing on as War Correspondents,' *Washington Post*, 23 March, p. F04.

Langlois, A. and Dubois, F. (eds) (2005) *Autonomous Media: Activating Resistance and Dissent*, Montréal: Cumulus Press.

Lasn, K. (1999) *Culture Jam: The Uncooling of America™*, New York: Eagle Brook.

León, O. Burch, S. and Tamayo, E. (forthcoming) 'Societies-in-Movement: The Latin American *Minga Informativa*', in S. Stein, C. Rodriguez and D. Kidd (eds), *Making Our Media: Global Initiatives Toward a Democratic Public Sphere. Volume II: National and Global Movements for Democratic Communication*. Cresskill, NJ: Hampton Press.

Lessig, L. (2004) *Free Culture*, New York: Penguin. (Transcript of Lawrence presenting a keynote speech on free culture at the Open Source convention on 24 July 24 2002. The transcript can be found at http://www.oreillynet.com/pub/a/policy/2002/08/15/lessig.html. Page 1 accessed 14 September 2007.)

Lewis, I. (2000) *Guerilla TV– Low Budget Programme Making*, Oxford: Focal Press.

Lewis, P.M. (1994) *Community Radio-Employment Trends and Training Needs. Report for Transnational Survey*, Sheffield: AMARC Europe.

Lewis, P.M. (2002) 'Radio Theory and Community Radio', in N.W. Jankowski and O. Prehn (eds), *Community Media in the Information Age: Perspectives and Prospects*, Cresskill, NJ: Hampton Press.

Lewis, P.M. and Booth, J. (1989) *The Invisible Medium: Public, Commercial and Community Radio*. London: Macmillan.

Liang, L. (2004) *Guide to Open Content Licenses*, Rotterdam: Piet Zwart Institute.

Linke, J. (2005) 'Open Channels for Germany', in D. Rushton (ed.), *Local Television Report: ACTO – Local Television Papers*, Edinburgh: School Press for the Institute of Local Television.

Lovink, G. and Garcia, D. (1999) 'D. DEF of Tactical Media', http://laudanum.net/geert/files/1021/index.shtml?1078909338.

Lunch, N. and Lunch, C. (2006) 'Insights into Participatory Video: A Handbook for the Field', www.insightshare.org/training_book.html, accessed 1 August 2006.

McChesney, R.W. (2000) *Rich Media, Poor Democracy*, New York: The New Press.

McChesney, R.W. (2001) 'Global Media, Neoliberalism and Imperialism', *Monthly Review*, 52.10, pp. 1–19, www.monthlyreview.org, accessed 1 August 2006.

McCluskey, J.J. (2000) *Starting a Student/Non-commercial Radio Station*, Needham Heights, MA: Simon and Schuster.

McDonald (1995) 'Left of the Dial', *U. Magazine*, April 20–1.

McDonough, T. (ed.) (2002) *Guy Debord and the Situationist International: Texts and Documents*, Cambridge, MA: MIT Press.

McGann, N. (2005) *Wired FM*, Limerick: Wired FM.

McGregor, L.W. (2003) 'President's Message', *In Synch*, 14.2, June, Honolulu, Hawaii, www.olelo.org/news/insynch/INSYNCHJUNE.pdf, accessed 1 May 2006.

McKay, G. (ed.) (1998) *DIY Culture: Party and Protest in Nineties Britain*, London: Verso.

Mackenzie, R. (1994) *84 Hours*, broadcast BBC 2, March.

McNair Ingenuity (2004) 'Listener Survey Report Fact Sheets', http://www.cbonline.org.au/index.cfm?pageId=44,133,2,0, accessed 2 May 2006.

Macpherson, D. (ed.) (1980) *British Cinema Traditions of Independence*, London: BFI.

McRobbie, A. (2002) 'Holloway to Hollywood: Pleasure in Work in the New Cultural Economy?' in P. Du Gay and M. Pryke (eds), *Cultural Economy*, London: Sage.

Manovich, L. (2001) *The Language of New Media*, Cambridge, MA: MIT Press.

Marcos, S. (1997) 'Statement of Subcomandante Marcos to the Freeing the Media Teach-In', www.tmcrew.org/chiapas/e_media1.htm, accessed June 29 2006.

Marcos, S. (2001) *Our Word is Our Weapon: Selected Writings*, London: Serpents Tail.

Marcus, G. (1989) *Lipstick Traces: A Secret History of the Twentieth Century*, London: Picador.

Markels, A. (2000) 'Radio Active: Up against the megastations in the battle for the airwaves', Wired Magazine, http://www.wired.com/wired/archive/8.06/radio_pr.html.

Martin, M. (1994) *British*, broadcast BBC 2, March.

Marx, K. and Engels, F. (1968) *Selected Works*, London: Lawrence and Wishart.

Matheson, D. and Allan, S. (2003) 'Weblogs and the War in Iraq: Journalism for the Network Society?' paper presented at the Digital Dynamics conference, Loughborough, UK, 6–9 November.

Meikle, G. (2002) *Future Active: Media Activism and the Internet*, New York: Routledge.

Meikle, G. (2003–4) 'Indymedia and the New Net News', WACC, (http://www.wacc.org.uk/wacc/publications/media_development/archive/2003_4/indymedia_and_the_new_net_news

Melucci, A. (1996) *Challenging Codes: Collective Action in the Information Age*, Cambridge: Cambridge University Press.

Milam, L.W. (1988) *Sex and Broadcasting: A Handbook on Starting a Radio Station for the Community*, San Diego: Mho and Mho Works.

Minority Press Group (1980a) *Here is the Other News: Challenges to the Local Commercial Press*, London: Minority Press Group.

Minority Press Group (1980b) *Where is the Other News: The Newstrade and the Radical Press*, London: Minority Press Group.

Mirapaul, M. (2003) 'Online Games Grab Grim Reality', *New York Times*, 17 September, E1.

Mitchell, C. (2000) 'Sisters Are Doing It . . . From Fem FM to Viva! A History of Contemporary Women's Radio in the UK', in C. Mitchell (ed.), *Women and Radio*, London: Routledge, pp. 189–202.

Mitchell, C. (2000) 'On Air/Off Air: Defining Women's Radio Space in European Women's Community Radio', in C. Mitchell (ed.), *Women and Radio*, London: Routledge, pp. 189–202.

MNN (2005) *What's On Program Guide*, 5.1 (Fall).

'The Modern Age' (2003) *Edge*, 126 (August), pp. 58–67.

Murdoch, G. (1994) 'Corporate Dynamics and Broadcasting Futures', in H. Mackay and T. Sullivan (eds), (1999) *The Media Reader: Continuity and Transformation*, London: Sage.

Murphy, D. (2006) 'Campaign of the Week: Undercurrents – Film-Makers', *Guardian*, 11 April.

Nadir homepage (2005) http://www.nadir.org/nadir/initiativ/agp/resistg8/reflection/g82005disset.htm, accessed 1 December 2005.

Najam, A. (1999) 'Citizen Organisations as Policy Entrepreneurs', in D. Lewis (ed.), *International Perspectives on Voluntary Action: Reshaping the Third Sector*, London: Earthscan Publications.

National Council for Voluntary Organisations (NCVO) (1990) 'Effectiveness and the Voluntary Sector', Report of a Working Party established by NVCO.

National Lawyers Guild (2004) 'Dunifer Brief', www.nlgcdc.org/briefs/dunifer.html, accessed 17 March 2004.

Negativland (1995) *Fair Use: The Story of the Letter U and the Numeral 2*, Concord, CA: Seeland.

Neville, R. (1995) *Hippie, Hippie, Shake: The Sixties*, London: Bloomsbury.

Newman, J. (2004) *Videogames*, London: Routledge.

Newman, J. (2005) 'Playing (with) Videogames', *Convergence*, 11.1, pp. 48–67.

Nicholls, S. (2003) 'Escape Game Wires the Minister', *Sydney Morning Herald*, 30 April, p. 1.

Nigg, H. and Wade, G. (1980) *Community Media*, Zurich: Regenbogen-Verlag.

Nocchi, M. (2005) 'Facoltà di frequenza tra comunicazione partecipativa e sfida culturale. L'evoluzione della radio dell'Università di Siena', MA dissertation in communication sciences, Siena: Università degli Studi di Siena.

Notes from Nowhere (ed.) (2003) *We Are Everywhere: The Irresistible Rise of Global Anticapitalism*, London: Verso.

Nusonline (2006) 'Highs, Lows and Words of Wisdom': http://www.nusonline.co.uk/studentmedia/tips/270921.aspx, accessed 1 June 2006, London: National Union of Students.

Ofcom (2007) 'Community Radio', http://www.ofcom.org.uk/radio/ifi/rbl/commun_radio/.

Olson, B. (2000) 'The History of Public Access': http://us.geocities.com/iconostar/history-public-access-TV.html, accessed 31 May 2006.

O'Pray, M. (1996) *The British Avant-Garde Film 1926–95*, London: Arts Council/John Libby.

Ó Siochrú, S. (2005) 'Global Media Governance as a Potential Site of Civil Society Intervention', in R. Hackett and Y. Zhao (eds), *Democratizing Global Media: One World, Many Struggles*, Lanham, MD: Rowman and Littlefield.

Ó Siochrú, S., Girard, B. and Mahan, A. (eds) (2002) *Global Media Governance: A Beginner's Guide*, Lanham, MD: Rowman and Littlefield.

Otto, L. (2006) 'Community Radio, Radio Community,' *Yes! Magazine*, http://www.yesmagazine.org/article_list.asp?Type=3&ID=Lilja%20Otto, accessed 19 October 2006.

Padovani, C, and Pavan, E. 'The Emerging Global Movement on Communication Rights: A New Stakeholder in Global Communication Governance?' in L. Stein, C. Rodriguez and D. Kidd (forthcoming) *Making Our Media: Global Initiatives Toward a Democratic Public Sphere. Volume II: National and Global Movements for Democratic Communication*. Cresskill, NJ: Hampton Press.

Palumbo, R. (2003) 'Movimenti e radio', in P. Ortoleva and S. Scaramucci (eds), *Enciclopedia della Radio Garzanti*, Milano: Garzanti.

Parklyn, R. (2004) personal interview, London.

Penrose, M. (1924) *The Radio Girls at Forest Lodge*, New York: Cupples and Leon Company.

Perrotta, R. (2005) *Facoltà di frequenza. La prima radio universitaria italiana*, Roma: Carocci editore.

Phillips, A. (2006) *Good Writing for Journalists: Narrative, Structure, Style*, London: Sage.

Pimlott, H. (2000) 'Mainstreaming the Margins', in J. Curran (ed.), *Media Organisations in Society*, London: Arnold.

Plant, S. (1992) *The Most Radical Gesture: The Situationist International in a Postmodern Age*, London: Routledge.

Priestman, C. (2002) *Web Radio: Radio Production for Internet Streaming*, Oxford: Focal Press.

Rabiger, M. (2005) *Directing the Documentary*, Oxford: Focal Press.

Raimakers, B. (1992) *The Zapbook* (a photocopied publication accompanying Next 5 Minutes 1).

Randon, A. and Perri, G. (1994) 'Constraining Campaigning: The Legal Treatment of Nonprofit Policy Advocacy across 24 Countries', *Voluntas*, 5.1, pp. 27–58.

Rawlings, T. and Kronschnabl, A. (2004) *Plug In Turn On: A Guide to Internet Filmmaking*, London: Marion Boyars Publishing.

Rees, A. (1999) *A History of Experimental Film and Video*, London: BFI.

Resonance FM (2006) 'Programme listings': http://www.resonancefm.com/listings/20051206.html, accessed 14 July 2006.

Rodriguez, C. (2001) *Fissures in the Mediascape: An International Study of Citizens' Media*, Cresskill, NJ: Hampton Press.

Rodriguez, O.R. (1997) 'La radio en la Universidad Javeriana': http://www.uady.mx/sitios/radio/ariadna/articulos/javeriana.html, accessed 20 May 2006.

Rowbotham, S. and Benyon, H. (2001) *Looking at Class: Film, Television and the Working Class in Britain*, London: Rivers Oram Press.

Rushton, D. (2005a) *Local Television Renewed: Essays on Local Television 1994–2005*, Edinburgh: School Press and Institute for Local Television.

Rushton, D. (ed.) (2005b) *Local Television Report: ACTO – Local Television Papers*, Edinburgh: School Press for the Institute of Local Television.

Sarnoff, E. (2002) *Alternative Burden: The Importance of Localism and Non-Profit College Radio.*

Sauls, S.J. (1995) 'College Radio', paper presented at the Annual Joint Meetings of the Popular Culture Association/American Culture Association, Philadelphia, PA, 12–15 April.

Sauls, S.J. (1996) 'National College Radio Study: Audience Research and National Programming', paper presented at the 41st Annual Broadcast Education Convention, Las Vegas, NV, 12–15 April.

Sauls, S.J. (1997) 'Who's Running College Radio', paper presented at the Annual Joint Meetings of the Popular Culture Association/American Culture Association, San Antonio, TX, 26–9 March.

Sauls, S.J. (1998) 'The Role of Alternative Programming College Radio', paper presented at the Annual Meeting of the Southwest/Texas Popular Culture Association/American Culture Association, 30 January.

Sauls, S.J. (2000) *The Culture of American College Radio*, Iowa: University of Iowa Press.

Scannell, P. and Cardiff, D. (1991) *A Social History of Broadcasting: 1922–39 – Serving the Nation, Volume 1*, London: Blackwell.

Schlesinger, P. (1990) 'Rethinking the Sociology of Journalism: Source Strategies and the Limits of Media-Centrism', in M. Ferguson (ed.), *Public Communication and the New Imperatives*, London: Sage.

Sénécal, M. and Dubois, F. (2005) 'The Alternative Communication Movement in Quebec's Mediascape', in D. Skinner, J. Compton and M. Gasher (eds), *Converging Media, Diverging Politics: A Political Economy of News Media in the U.S. and Canada*, Lanham, MD: Rowman and Littlefield.

Seymour-Ure, C. (1987) 'Leaders', in B. Pimlott and J. Seaton (eds), *The Mass Media in British Politics*, Aldershot: Dartmouth Publishing Company.

Shamberg, M. and the Raindance Corporation (1971) *Guerrilla Television*, New York: Holt, Rinehart and Winston.

Shaw, J. and Robertson, C. (1997) *Participatory Video: A Practical Approach to Using Video Creatively in Group Development Work*, London: Routledge.

Shumway, C. (2001) 'Participatory Media Networks: A New Model', Reclaim the Media: http://www.reclaimthemedia.org/stroeis.php?story= 02/05/21/6042306, accessed 26 November 2002.

Sklair, L. (1997) 'Social Movements for Global Capitalism: The Transnational Capitalist Class in Action', *Review of International Political Economy*, 4.3, pp. 514–38.

Sklair, L. (2001) *The Transnational Capitalist Class*, Oxford: Blackwell.

Smith, Matthew J. (1999) 'Strands in the Web: Community-Building Strategies in Online Fanzines,' *Journal of Popular Culture*, 33.2, pp. 87–99.

Smiths (2006) *Editor's office*: http://smithsold.gold.ac.uk/editorsoffice/, accessed 15 July 2006, London: Goldsmiths.

Sneyd, A. (2003) 'Globalizing Embedded Liberalism: Some Lessons for the WTO's Development Round', Robarts Centre Research Papers. Toronto: Robarts Centre for Canadian Studies, York University.

Sniggle.net (2007) 'Guerrilla Hacks', http://sniggle.net/guerilla.php.

Sreberny, A. (2005) 'Globalization, Communication, Democratization: Towards Gender Equality', in R. Hackett and Y. Zhao (eds), *Democratizing Global Media: One World, Many Struggles*, Lanham, MD: Rowman and Littlefield.

Starr, A. (2005) *Global Revolt: A Guide to the Movement against Globalization*, London: Zed Books.

Stoneman, R. (1979) *Independent Film Workshops in Britain 1979*, Torquay: Grael Communications.

Stoneman, R. (1992) 'Sins of Commission', *Screen*, 33.2, reprinted in Dickinson, M. (1999: 174–87).

Stoney, G. (2005) personal conversation with Tony Dowmunt, New York.

Sturmer, C. (1993) 'MTV's Europe: An Imaginary Continent' in Dowmunt, T. (ed.) (1993) *Channels of Resistance*, London: BFI, pp. 50–66.

Sussman, E. (ed.) (1989) *On the Passage of a Few People through a Rather Brief Moment in Time: The Situationist International, 1957–1972*, Cambridge, MA: MIT Press.

Tacchi, J. (2000) 'The Need for Radio Theory in the Digital Age', *International Journal of Cultural Studies*, 3.2 (August), pp. 289–98.

Terranova, T. (2001) 'Demonstrating the Globe: Virtual Action in the Network Society', in D. Holmes (ed.), *Virtual Globalization: Virtual Spaces/Tourist Spaces*, London: Routledge, pp. 95–114.

Terry, J. and Calvert, M. (eds) (1997) *Processed Lives: Gender and Technology in Everyday Life*, London: Routledge.

Theobald, J. (2006) 'The Intellectual Tradition of Radical Mass Media Criticism: A Framework', in D. Berry and J. Theobald (eds), *Radical Mass Media Criticism: A Cultural Genealogy*, London: Black Rose Books (also available online at www.fifth-estate-online.co.uk).

Thomas, R. (2005) personal interview, London.

Thompson, M. (2004) 'Building Public Value', London: BBC.

Thornton, P., Phelan, L. and McKeown, B. (1997) *I Protest!*, Sydney: Pluto Press.

Thumin, N. (1999) 'It's about Horizons: Television and Community Space; the Case of Video Nation Shorts', unpublished MSc thesis, London School of Economics.

Tilly, C. (2004) *Social Movements, 1768–2004*. Boulder, CO: Paradigm.

Tower, C. (2006) personal communication with the author, 22 May.

Toynbee, P. (1999) *Radio Times*, 12 March.

Tridish, P. and Coyer, K. (2005) 'A Radio Station in Your Hands Is Worth 500 Channels of Mush! The Role of Community Radio in the Struggle against Corporate Domination of Media', in Elliot D. Cohen (ed.), *News Incorporated: Corporate Media Ownership and Its Threat to Democracy*, Amherst, NY: Prometheus Books.

University of Strathclyde (n.d.) Community Arts Course at the University of Strathclyde, www.strath.ac.uk/sca/ug-info/communityarts.htm, accessed 1 June 2006.

Updike, N. (2005) 'The Nancy Updike Interview', *Transom.org*, http://www.transom.org/guests/specialguests/nancy_updike.html, accessed 19 October 2005.

Uzelman, S. (2005) 'Hard at Work in the Bamboo Garden: Media Activists and Social Movements', in A. Langlois and F. Dubois (eds), *Autonomous Media: Activating Resistance and Dissent*, Montréal: Cumulus Press, pp. 17–28.

V2V (2003) 'Manifesto', http://www.rekombinant.org/old/media-activism/article.html.sid=115, accessed 1 June 2006.

Vaid, I. (1994) 'Why?' http://www.bbc.co.uk/videonation/articles/u/uk_why.shtml, accessed 16 June 2006.

Varsity (2006) *About Varsity*: http://www.varsity.co.uk/index.php?option=com_content&task=view&id=6208&Itemid=57, accessed 2 June 2006, Cambridge: Varsity Ltd.

Paco Velasco: Interview to Modesto Emilio Guerrero from Aporrea in September, 2005. It can be read at www.aporrea.org//n65771.html.

Wade, G. (1980) *Street Video*, Leicester: Blackthorn Press.

Walker, J. (2001) *Rebels on the Air: An Alternative History of Radio in America*, New York: New York University Press.

Waltz, M. (2005) *Alternative and Activist Media*, Edinburgh: Edinburgh University Press.

Warshawski, M. (2003) *Shaking the Money Tree: How to Get Grants and Donations for Film and Video*, Michael Wise Productions, www.mwp.com, accessed 12 September 2006.

Weaver, C. (2005) personal interview, London.

Webster, M. (1997) *Finding Voices, Making Choices: Creativity for Social Change*, Nottingham: Educational Heretics Press.

Whittaker, J. (2004) *The Cyberspace Handbook*, London: Routledge.

Widgery, D. (1971) *OZ* 5th Anniversary issue, Oz Publications Ink Ltd.

Williams, R. (1974) *Television: Technology and Cultural Form*, London: Fontana.

Wolf, M. and Perron, B. (eds) (2003) *The Video Game Theory Reader*, New York: Routledge.

Wollen, P. (1996) 'The Two Avant-Gardes', in M.O'Pray (ed), *The British Avant-Garde Film 1926–1995: An Anthology of Writings*, Luton: University of Luton Press.

Zapatistas (1997) 'Zapatistas' Second Declaration of La Realidad for Humanity against Neoliberalism', http://www.geocities.com/CapitolHill/3849/dec2real.html, accessed 1 May 2006.

Zhao, Y, and Hackett, R. (2005) 'Media Globalization, Media Democratization: Challenges, Issues, and Paradoxes', in R. Hackett and Y. Zhao (eds), *Democratizing Global Media: One World, Many Struggles*, Lanham, MD: Rowman and Littlefield.

Index